Making Borders in Modern East Asia

Until the late nineteenth century the Chinese–Korean Tumen River border was one of the oldest, and perhaps most stable, state boundaries in the world. Spurred by severe food scarcity following a succession of natural disasters, from the 1860s countless Korean refugees crossed the Tumen River border into Qing China's Manchuria, triggering a decades-long territorial dispute between China, Korea, and Japan. This major new study of a multilateral and multiethnic frontier highlights the competing state- and nation-building projects in the fraught period that witnessed the First Sino-Japanese War, the Russo-Japanese War, and the First World War. The power plays over land and people simultaneously promoted China's frontier-building endeavors, motivated Korea's nationalist imagination, and stimulated Japan's colonialist enterprise, setting East Asia on an intricate trajectory from the late imperial to a situation that, Song argues, we call "modern."

Nianshen Song is Assistant Professor of History at the University of Maryland, Baltimore County.

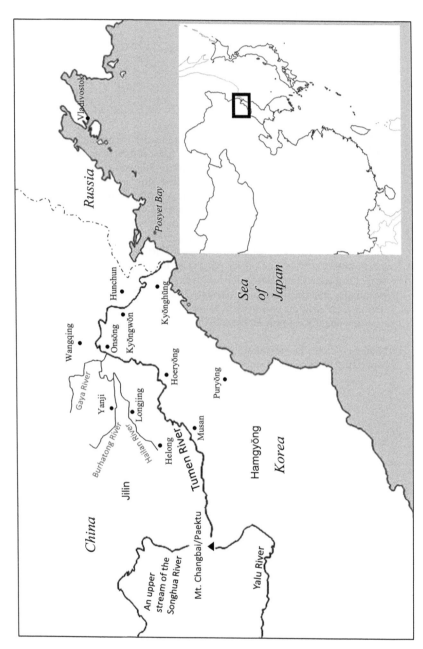

The Tumen River Region

Making Borders in Modern East Asia

The Tumen River Demarcation, 1881–1919

Nianshen Song

University of Maryland, Baltimore County

CAMBRIDGE
UNIVERSITY PRESS

CAMBRIDGE
UNIVERSITY PRESS

University Printing House, Cambridge CB2 8BS, United Kingdom

One Liberty Plaza, 20th Floor, New York, NY 10006, USA

477 Williamstown Road, Port Melbourne, VIC 3207, Australia

314–321, 3rd Floor, Plot 3, Splendor Forum, Jasola District Centre, New Delhi – 110025, India

79 Anson Road, #06-04/06, Singapore 079906

Cambridge University Press is part of the University of Cambridge.

It furthers the University's mission by disseminating knowledge in the pursuit of education, learning and research at the highest international levels of excellence.

www.cambridge.org
Information on this title: www.cambridge.org/9781107173958
DOI: 10.1017/9781316795491

© Nianshen Song 2018

First published 2018

Printed in the United Kingdom by Clays, St Ives plc

A catalogue record for this publication is available from the British Library.

ISBN 978-1-107-17395-8 Hardback

Contents

Figures

Maps

Tables

Acknowledgments

This book would not have become what it is had I not received immeasurable help and encouragement from the University of Chicago, where I learned how to become a historian. The intellectual and spiritual debt I owe to my mentors – Bruce Cumings, Prasenjit Duara, James Hevia, and James Ketelaar – is simply beyond words. Kenneth Pomeranz kindly read the early version of the manuscript and made invaluable comments. Choi Kyeong-Hee took great care of the project and put me in contact with other scholars. Jacob Eyferth generously contributed his knowledge whenever I call on him. The History Department, the Division of the Social Sciences, and the Center for East Asian Studies funded several of my field trips. Curators at the East Asian Library, especially Zhou Yuan, always responded enthusiastically to my requests. It is truly a privilege to have this kind of support at the beginning of a career.

The book was largely revised at Vassar College, where I was a Mellon Postdoctoral Fellow for three years. Friends and colleagues there taught me how to be a good teacher as well as an efficient writer and researcher. I thank, among others, Nancy Bisaha, Robert Brigham, Maria Höhn, Julie Hughes, James Merrell, Quincy Mills, Qiu Peipei, Su Fubing, and Zhou Yu. At the University of Maryland, Baltimore County, where I now serve on the faculty in History and Asian Studies, I received immense encouragement and support from my colleagues and students. With their backing, the completion of this book went surprisingly smoothly. For this, I thank Christy Chapin, Amy Froide, Meredith Oyen, Yang Fan, Constantine Vaporis, and many, many others.

My research was made possible with financial assistance from various institutions: the Social Science Research Council, the Academy of Korean Studies, the Harvard-Yenching Library, the American Geographical Society Library, the Korea Foundation, and the Northeast Asia Council of the Association for Asian Studies. Numerous individuals helped me during my research trips in China, Korea, Japan, and the United States. For my China travels, my gratitude goes to Cui Shunji, Diao Shuren, Jiang Longfan, Jin Chenggao, Jin Chunshan, Li Hongxi, Liu Debin, Sun

Chunri, Wang Qiubin, Yang Zhaoquan, Yi Baozhong, and many more. Doing archival research and interviews on ethnic and border issues in Yanbian (and China in general) can be very tricky. I thank Huang Guangchun, Jin Xianghu, Li Fanjun, Qu Jianjun, and Wei Xiaoli for making the process less so. I would like to express my deepest gratitude to the late Professor Quan Hexiu, whom I could always rely on whenever there was difficulty, and Professor Li Huazi, who took me on the most exciting research trip into the deep forest of Mount Changbai/Paektu. In Korea, staff of the Kyujanggak Library at Seoul National University and the Jangseogak Library at the Academy of Korean Studies (AKS) offered amicable assistance. Li Chengzhu at the AKS shared his abundant knowledge on the history of Korea and the Korean-Chinese. I wish to acknowledge the hospitality and help given by Liu Di and Zhao Hongwei in Japan. My research there also benefited from long conversations, in some noisy restaurants in Ueno, Tokyo, with Professors Jin Guanglin and Bai Rongxun, two outstanding Korean-Chinese historians. I am also grateful to Tobi Mayer-Fong, who kindly invited me to become a visiting scholar at Johns Hopkins University, and to Kang Mikyung at the Harvard-Yenching Library, Zhang Nongji at the Harvard Law School Library, and Jovanka Ristic at the American Geographical Society Library, who guided me to many treasures in their massive collections.

Over the years I have presented different parts of the manuscript at various workshops and conferences. It is impossible to name all those who offered valuable comments, criticism, and suggestions, but I must thank those who helped to create these important intellectual platforms: Eric Vanden Bussche, Nicole Constable, Hang Xing, Nicholas Harkness, Hasegawa Masato, Douglas Howland, Kim Nan, Kim Seon-min, Ronald Knapp, Kwon June Hee, Kirk Larsen, Nicole Levit, Joshua Van Lieu, Ma Jian, James Millward, Scott Relyea, Victor Seow, Shao Dan, Su Xiaobo, David Szanton, Wang Sixiang, Wang Yuanfei, Xie Qiong, Yang Myungji, and Theodore Jun Yoo. Through our discussions at different phases of my research and writing, I learned a lot from Gao Shihua, Ken Kawashima, Lam Tong, Andre Schmid, Sun Ge, Tang Xiaofeng, and Wang Hui.

Academic research, for the most part, is lonely work. But I am lucky to belong to a community of scholars who enthusiastically shared their cross-disciplinary findings and trans-regional concerns on East Asian studies. They kept urging me to think and rethink themes of border and people, nation and society, and time and space: Chae Jun Hyun, Han Ling, Hirata Koji, Hui Kwok-wai, Eleanor Hyun, Ishikawa Tadashi, Stacie Kent, Kim Seong Un, Kim Taeju, Lee Cheng-Pang, Li Yuhang, Lin Le, Liu Xueting, Covell Meyskens, Cameron Panwell, Seng Guo Quan, Seto Tomoko, Teh Limin, Saul Thomas, Tian Geng, Wang Fei

Hsien, Wang Liping, Jake Werner, Xiao Tie, Xu Jin, Xu Peng, Yamaguchi Noriko, Ryan Yokota, Elaine Yuan, Zhang Ling, Zhang Yang, Zhao Hai, and Zhong Yijiang. I want to thank Hsia Kechin for translating some legal texts from the original German and Kim Ji Young for sharing her study on Ch'oe Nam-sŏn. I am grateful to Wang Yuanchong, who not only reviewed the whole manuscript but also constantly offered his ideas on the history and historiography of Sino-Korean-Japanese relations over the past seven years.

My editor at Cambridge University Press, Lucy Rhymer, worked diligently at every stage of the publication process. Two anonymous reviewers provided insightful comments and criticism. I appreciate their time and contribution to this book.

Lastly, support from my parents and family is so crucial to me that I simply cannot deliver my gratitude in words. I dedicate this work to them, especially my wife, Zhao Yanling. And I thank our children, Chuhe and Charles, for bringing so much joy to us.

A Note on Romanization

In general, this study takes a critical stand on various boundaries that came along with the regime of modernity. It seems that nothing illustrates the awkwardness of this kind of modern demarcation more vividly than the different romanizations of Chinese-Han characters in Chinese, Korean, and Japanese (Hanzi, Hanja, and Kanji) texts. For example, one of the key concepts of this study, 間島, must be transliterated as Jiandao (Pinyin system), Kando (McCune–Reischauer system), and Kantō (Hepburn system), respectively, for the Chinese, Korean, and Japanese contexts. I can't just choose one of them and use it consistently in my narrative, simply because the signified is not exactly the same for each, and the term had quite different political connotations in its respective contexts. The romanized forms, on the other hand, tear the natural integrity of the term (written in the same Chinese characters in all three languages) into fragments. As a remedy to the incorrigible, I have given different romanized versions simultaneously whenever necessary. I am sincerely sorry for the possible confusion caused by this strategy. Perhaps it shows the unfortunate fact that, in the end, nobody is able to completely escape the prison made by reconstructing everything in terms of nation states: land, people, language, culture, and history.

Measures

1 *chi* (China) ≈ 0.32 m
1 *chō* (Japan) ≈ 9917 m²
1 *jin* (China) ≈ 0.59 kg
1 *kung* (Korea) ≈ 2.5 m
1 *li* (China) ≈ 576 m
1 *mu* (China) ≈ 667 m²
1 *ri* (Korea) ≈ 420 m
1 *shang* (China) = 15 *mu* ≈ 1 hectare

Abbreviations of Some Sources

GXCZPZZ   *Guangxu chao zhupi zouzhe*
HCFDTYMD   *Hunchun fudutong yamen dang*
JACAR   *Japan Center for Asian Historical Records*
QJZRHGXSL   *Qingji zhongrihan guanxi shiliao*

Introduction
A Lost Stele and a Multivocal River

In July 1931 a historic stele marking the Chinese–Korean border disappeared mysteriously. The last people to see it were a group of fifty-six tourists who were escorted by 100 patrol soldiers from the local Japanese-Korean garrison.[1] They passed the stele at around 9:30 a.m. on the 28th, shortly before the tourists and their escorts separated. The next day, when the tourists returned from their sightseeing at Heaven Lake (C. Tianchi; K. Ch'ŏnji), a splendid crater lake on the peak of Mount Changbai (K. Paektu), they were surprised to find that the stele was no longer there. A wooden marker reading "the trail up Mt. Paektu" had been installed beside the empty base. Apparently, it was a planned theft. No record shows the stele ever being seen again.

Made of normal limestone, the stele was approximately 3 *chi* high and 2 *chi* wide and weighed over 100 *jin* (see Figure 1). It was located approximately 5 kilometers southeast of the summit of Mount Changbai. Japanese and Korean sources call it a "demarcation stele" (J. *teikaihi*; Kr. *chŏnggyebi*), as it marked the origins of the two Sino-Korean boundary rivers: the Yalu (K. Amnok) flows westward and the Tumen (K. Tuman) flows east. It indicated the starting point of one of the oldest, and perhaps most stable, state boundaries in the world. Chinese sources, naming it after the Qing official who erected it in 1712, generally call it the "Mukedeng stele" (*Mukedengbei*).

The story of the stele goes back to 1710, the forty-ninth year in the reign of Qing emperor Kangxi and the thirty-sixth for the Chosŏn king Sukchong. In that year a criminal case was brought to the attention of both courts. Nine Koreans violated the Yalu River border in order to poach ginseng. Running into five Qing, they murdered them and took their belongings. In recent years trespassing incidents like this one had occurred repeatedly. Qing emperor Kangxi decided that the time had

---

[1] The event is recorded in Shinoda Jisaku, *Hakutōsan teikaihi* (Tokyo: Rakurō Shoin, 1938), "Preface," pp. 1–2.

Figure 1 The Mukedeng stele
Source: *Atō Ingashū*, vol. 1, no. 5.

come for a comprehensive and conclusive clarification of the geographic division between his empire and the Chosŏn.

Obsessed with the new surveying and cartographic techniques, Emperor Kangxi was conducting a grand mapping of his entire empire, including not only Inner China, Mongolia, Manchuria, and Tibet but also Korea. In seventeenth-century Europe as well as China, cutting-edge cartography was a critical tool for imperial powers.[2] Introduced by Jesuits, the early modern technologies proved advantageous over indigenous technologies, especially in a military sense. This was well proven in an armed confrontation between Qing and Russia in the Amur River basin (1685–1689). Kangxi's mapping project served two practical purposes: allowing his regime to acquire updated geographical data on Manchuria that would assist in countering Russian expansionism, while also permitting the creation of a highly accurate imperial atlas that incorporated

[2] James R. Akerman, "Introduction," in James R. Akerman, ed., *The Imperial Map: Cartography and the Mastery of Empire* (Chicago: University of Chicago Press, 2009), pp. 1–10.

Chinese as well as Inner Asian territories.[3] Prior to 1710 Kangxi had already sent several survey teams to Manchuria. Through these surveys, Kangxi promoted Mt. Changbai as the royal ancestral mountain, further strengthening the foundation myth of the monarch and the sacredness of Manchuria.[4] Naturally, the project included the border region between the Qing and Chosŏn. Although no one disputed the boundary formed by the Yalu and Tumen Rivers, a small section between the two rivers' respective headwaters had yet to be clearly defined. Surrounding the summit of Mt. Changbai, the area was characterized by an extremely harsh climate and a complicated drainage system. The 1710 homicide case provided Kangxi with a good excuse to demarcate this ambiguous section of the border once and for all.[5]

The emperor entrusted a local Manchu official named Mukedeng with this task. Mukedeng was the superintendent (C. *zong guan*) of Dasheng ("hunting") Ula, a local branch of the Imperial Household Department (*neiwufu*). A former imperial guardsman, his regular duty was to oversee the collection of local wild products and deliver them to Beijing. Perhaps for this reason, the emperor assumed Mukedeng was more familiar with the local terrain than anybody else. In 1711 Kangxi assigned him to supervise the homicide trial in a Korean border town and ordered him to investigate the Qing–Korean boundary after the trial.

But Mukedeng's survey attempt in 1711 failed, because of the lack of cooperation from the weather and Korean officials alike. Aware of the situation, Kangxi, for a second attempt in 1712, asked the Board of Rites to issue a decree to the Korean court, assuring the latter that the purpose of the mission was only to "survey our borderland and will not involve your country." Just in case there were difficulties and dangers along the road, he asked the Chosŏn regime "to lend a bit of assistance."[6]

The Chosŏn received Kangxi's requests with great reluctance and caution. Having suffered two invasions by the Manchu "barbarians" and been forced to submit to the Qing, the Korean kings and literati were hostile towards the Qing regime. Through its intelligence network in China, the Chosŏn court assumed that the Manchu could not successfully

---

[3] Peter Perdue, "Boundaries, Maps, and Movement: Chinese, Russian, and Mongolian Empires in Early Modern Central Eurasia," *International History Review*, vol. 20, no. 2 (1998), pp. 263–286; Laura Hostetler, "Contending Cartographic Claims: The Qing Empire in Manchu, Chinese, and European Maps," in Akerman, *The Imperial Map*, pp. 93–132.

[4] Mark Elliott, "The Limits of Tartary: Manchuria in Imperial and National Geographies," *Journal of Asian Studies*, vol. 59, no. 3 (2000), pp. 603–646.

[5] *Qingshilu*, vol. 246, Kangxi 50-05.

[6] *Chosŏnwangjo sillok*, Sukchong 38-2-24.

control China for an extended period and that it would only be a matter of time before they were expelled. Thus, when Kangxi launched his grand geographic survey in Manchuria and fostered imperial worship of Mt. Changbai, the Koreans speculated that the Qing was just preparing a route to retreat and worried that this would harm Korea once again.[7] Chosŏn's initial response was to cite the difficult terrain or the harsh weather to avoid assisting the survey missions. This strategy worked in 1711. But, when Kangxi urged for a second time, the Koreans felt they had to cooperate, although with the intention of securing more territory to the south of Mt. Changbai.[8]

In May 1712 the Qing and Chosŏn teams met in Huju, a Korean border town on the Yalu River.[9] They traced the river upstream all the way to Mt. Changbai. A Korean interpreter, Kim Chi-nam, informed Mukedeng that both the Yalu and Tumen Rivers originated from the Heaven Lake. Therefore, instead of tracing the other border river, the Tumen, upstream to determine its correct source, Mukedeng decided to search for what he believed to be the shared source of both border rivers at the summit. His team and some of the Korean escorts reached the top on June 14 and started to look for the source. At a site southeast of the summit, they found a ridge that was quite close to the headwater of the Yalu River. Mukedeng decided that this ridge should be regarded as the "drainage divide" (C. *fenshuiling*; K. *punsuryŏng*) of both the Yalu and Tumen Rivers. So the only job that remained was to find the source of the Tumen connecting to this drainage divide. However, this task proved much harder than they had expected: the intricate nature of the river system and the intermittent water flows in this mountain forest made it extremely difficult to define a true source. After four days of arduous exploration and debate, they finally agreed to choose one of the small streams that gushed out dozens of *ri* east of the drainage divide as the true source of the Tumen. Explaining that this stream had emerged after "flowing underground" from the divide, Mukedeng ordered that a stele be erected on the drainage divide as the mark. He also asked the Korean staff to build a row of earthen and wooden barriers in the future to connect the stele with the Tumen headstream.[10]

---

[7] See, for example, *Sŭngjŏngwŏn ilgi*, Sukchong 26-2-26.

[8] *Chosŏnwangjo sillok*, Sukchong 38-2-27, 38-3-8.

[9] For detailed accounts of the 1712 demarcation, see Kim Chi-nam, "Pukjŏngnok"; Pak Kwan, "Pukjŏng ilgi"; and Hong Se-dae, "Paektusangi," all collected in *Paeksan Hakpo*, no. 16 (1974), pp. 195–262, and no. 17 (1974), pp. 225–229. For an account in English, see Andre Schmid, "Tributary Relations and the Qing–Choson Frontier on Mount Paektu," in Diana Lary, ed., *The Chinese State at the Borders* (Vancouver: UBC Press, 2007), pp. 126–150.

[10] *Chosŏnwangjo sillok*, Sukchong 38-5, 6.

On June 18 the stele was engraved and installed. Written in Chinese, the inscription read:

> The Great Qing Superintendent of [Dasheng] Ula, Mukedeng, arrived here when surveying the border on Imperial Order.
> Observing that the Yalu River is in the west and the Tumen is in the east, [the surveyors] engrave this stele on the drainage divide as the mark.
> The fifteenth day of the fifth month, the fifty-first year of Kangxi.

Far from being the end of the problem, this was just the beginning. When the Koreans later returned to build the barriers, they discovered that the stream Mukedeng had chosen was wrong: it somehow turned north and eventually joined the Songhua (Sungari) River, a tributary of the Amur River in the far north. However, after intensive internal debate, the Chosŏn court decided not to bother the Qing with such a "trivial" mistake. Instead, the Korean official who supervised the project arbitrarily built a barrier to connect another stream in the south. As a consequence, in Beijing, the Qing government never became aware of the error. Since border security had been relatively stable, no Qing official after Mukedeng ever surveyed the border again. As the earthen and wooden barriers gradually eroded, so did the memory of the demarcation itself. What was worse, even the Qing documents related to this mission were lost, possibly in a fire.

In Korea, by contrast, the Mukedeng mission of 1712 was extensively recorded and widely remembered. From the mid-eighteenth century, geographers and mapmakers have viewed the Mukedeng stele as a marker of Korean territory rather than an indicator of the source of the Tumen River. However, the Korean knowledge of the boundary was rather incoherent. While the Qing documents referred to the river as 土門 (pronounced "Tumen" in Chinese), the Chosŏn documents used the name 豆滿 (pronounced "Tuman" in Korean) predominantly. Both names, arguably, are transliterated from the Manchu *tumen sekiyen*, which means "the origin of ten thousand rivers."[11] Decades after the 1712 demarcation, some Koreans inherited the traditional view that the Tumen/Tuman, being different names of the same river, was indeed the border. Some other literates, however, generated a new theory that the Tumen and Tuman were two rivers separated from each other. According to this theory, the border river was not the "Tuman" but another river that originated in Mt. Paektu/Changbai and flowed further north. Yet their theory about this "real" border river was even more confusing: some named it the "T'omun" River (土門江) while others called it "the Division River"

---

[11] Yu Fengchun, "Tumen, Tumen yu Douman, Douman zhi ciyuan yu yiyin kao," *Zhongguo bianjiang shidi yanjiu*, vol. 19, no. 2 (2009), pp. 118–126.

(分界江; K. Pungyegang). Some indicated that this river was actually the Hontong River (混同江, Songhua/Sungari River), whereas still others insisted that it was located between the Sungari and the Tuman.[12] This caused great inconsistency regarding the exact location of the boundary during the late Chosŏn period.

The ambiguity eventually turned into an official territorial claim more than 170 years after the installation of the stele, when thousands of poor Korean peasants crossed the Tumen River and cultivated wildlands in southeast Manchuria. Was the Tumen the boundary? Which river was actually the Tuman? Which stream was its headwater? Upon these controversial questions rested a recurring Qing–Chosŏn territorial dispute. The contradictions surrounding a contested and multivalent boundary river developed into a Sino-Japanese political conflict in the early twentieth century when Japan, after gaining control of Korea, proceeded to colonize Manchuria. Closely associated with this problem was the question of which country had the right to rule the Koreans immigrants – thousands in the 1880s, increasing to nearly 300,000 by the end of the 1910s – in the area north of the Tumen, a place called "Kando" in Korea and "Yanbian" in China. The dispute involved not only the three East Asian countries but also Russia, whose colonial expansion triggered and accelerated the long-term demarcations of the land and people. With East Asia being drawn into a global capitalist and imperialist system, the resource-filled Tumen River area, a remote frontier that had been maintained wild and undisturbed for centuries, suddenly became a geopolitical hotspot for a multilateral regional, even global, competition.

Historical Spaces in East Asia

This book tells the story of the disputes and demarcations over this boundary river from 1881 to 1919. Rather than engaging in the debate about "territorial sovereignty," I examine how basic elements of state – land, people, border, and historical memory – presented and evolved in a concrete time and space. Using demarcation as method, I display the transformation of nineteenth-/twentieth-century East Asia in the imperialist, colonialist, and nationalist contexts. At the center of my narrative are the exploration of the borderland, the formation of the immigrant society, and various efforts of state and nonstate forces to competitively penetrate the frontier society. I pay special attention to how indigenous

---

[12] Nianshen Song, "Imagined Territory: Paektusan in Late Chosŏn Maps and Writings," *Studies in the History of Gardens and Designed Landscapes*, vol. 37, no. 2 (2017), pp. 157–173.

and European perceptions of people and land were entangled and implemented in this outlying region through various local practices. Knowledge
and practices employed in the demarcations (e.g., geographical perception, cartographic techniques, and legal codes), I argue, shaped the
modern formation of East Asian nations and states on a local level. As
negotiations both stalled and progressed over the years, the conventional ways of understanding and regulating land, people, border, state,
and historical memory changed dramatically. The simultaneous contests over both the border and the Korean diaspora promoted China's
frontier-building endeavors, motivated Korea's nationalist imagination,
and stimulated Japan's colonialist enterprise. It foreshadowed the rise
of nationalism and imperialism in twentieth-century East Asia. In other
words, through the lens of boundary making this book examines the
unfolding of "modern" in the East Asian context.

A boundary, as Martin Heidegger famously said, "is not that at which
something stops but...is that from which something *begins its presenc-
ing*."[13] This perspective applies to a frontier as well. A frontier is not
merely a periphery but is a place of interactions. Locating the Tumen
River region – a multilateral frontier – at the center, my narrative invites
states to a joint borderland and emphasizes complex intercommunica-
tions between all neighboring polities in this peripheral place. I regard
this region as a loosely "fixed" sociogeographic unit, whereas nations
and states were more or less fluid. It was only through the projects of
demarcation (of both land and people) that states and nations took their
current shapes. In addition, the space of a nation and that of a state
do not overlap precisely. Migration and historical memory may extend
a national space beyond state boundaries. The Korean community in
China's Yanbian region, for example, extends the Korean "national
space" into Chinese territory. Similarly, because ethnic Koreans in
Yanbian were integrated into a new notion of a "Chinese nation," the
Chinese and Korean national spaces overlap there.

What is written in this book is a multilateral and multilayered local
history. Concerning the spatiality of history writing, my narrative departs
from most previous scholarship on the Tumen boundary dispute, which
argued predominately for exclusive sovereignty and nationality. Instead,
my work echoes other emerging trends in East Asian studies and engages
in a broader conversation on the nature of East Asian transitions in late
imperial and modern periods.

---

[13] Heidegger, Martin, "Building Dwelling Thinking," in *Poetry, Language, Thought*, trans.
Albert Hofstadter (New York: Harper & Row, 1971), pp. 141–160, 154, emphasis in
original.

A number of Japanese, Chinese, and Korean scholars have extensively studied the trilateral dispute on the Tumen River boundary, aiming to argue for the national "sovereignty" of the Tumen north bank.[14] The nationalist paradigm reflects the ideology of the nation state system, which, many believe, is a product of the Peace of Westphalia constructed by European states in the late seventeenth century. I use "Westphalian time-space" to refer to the view that sees nations as separate and equal polities regulated by international law, each with its own distinguishable territory and exclusive past. Introduced to East Asia through Euro-American colonization, this temporal-spatial perception was adopted and adapted locally to counter Western (and later Japanese) intrusions. The tension between colonialism and anticolonialism stimulated new scholarships on Manchurian history and geography. Under the Westphalian time-space ideology, East Asian scholars in the early twentieth century created parallel traditions of Manchurian studies. In Japan the school of "Manchurian-Korean history" (*mansenshi*) was a crucial part of Japanese Oriental historiography (*Tōyō shigaku*). Seeing Manchuria as an independent, non-Chinese historical space, the *mansenshi* school made great scholarly achievements with the vigorous support of the South Manchuria Railway Company, a national colonial agency of the Japanese empire.[15] In response, Chinese historians, notably Fu Sinian, Jiang Tingfu, and Jin Yufu, initiated the historical studies of northeast China (*dongbeishi*), vigorously arguing for Chinese sovereignty over Manchuria.[16] Under similar colonial pressure, the Korean nationalist historians, such as Sin Ch'ae-ho, also turned their eyes from the peninsula to the continent, seeking to revive Korean national spirit in Manchuria.[17] All of them justified an exclusive sovereign claim of a territorial space by rewriting history.

---

[14] Representative works include but are not limited to Shinoda Jisaku, *Hakutōsan teikaihi*; Sin Ki-sŏk, *Kando yŏngyukwŏn e kwanhan yŏn'gu* (Seoul: T'amgudang, 1979); Yang T'ae-jin, *Han'guk ŭi kukkyŏng yŏn'gu* (Seoul: Tonghwa Ch'ulp'an Kongsa, 1981); Zhang Cunwu, *Qingdai zhonghan guanxi lunweji* (Taipei: Taiwan shangwu yinshuguan, 1987); Yang Zhaoquan and Sun Yumei, *Zhongchao bianjie shi* (Changchun: Jilin wenshi chubanshe, 1993).

[15] The magnum opus of this school includes the sixteen-volume *Mansen chiri rekishi kenkyū hōkoku* and the two-volume *Manshū rekishi chiri*, both financed by the South Manchuria Railway Company. The authors include Shiratori Kurakichi, Yanai Watari, Inaba Iwakichi, Matsui Hitoshi, and Wata Sei.

[16] See Fu Sinian, ed., *Donbei shigang* (Beiping: Guoli zhongyang yanjiuyuan lishi yuyan yanjiusuo, 1932); Jiang Tingfu, *Zuijin sanbainian dongbei waihuanshi* (Taipei: Zhongyang ribaoshe, 1953); Jin Yufu, *Dongbei tongshi: Shangbian* (Chongqing: Wushi niandai chubanshe, 1943).

[17] See Sin Ch'ae-ho, "Toksa sillon," "Chosŏn Sanggosa," "Chosŏnsa yŏn'guch'o," etc., in *Tanjae Sin Ch'ae-ho chŏnjip* (Seoul: Tanjae Sin Ch'ae-ho Sŏnsaeng Kinyŏm Saŏphoe, 1982).

Within their contexts, the nationalist arguments deserve to be understood with sympathy. Yet today they have become part of the problem, as they deny the possibility of a transnational dialogue regarding the historical inclusiveness of the region.

Younger generations try to break away from the uninational narrative and seek instead to apply a multinational perspective.[18] Their studies emphasize the interactions of Japan, China, and Korea (and to a lesser extent Russia) in the formation of a national space, employing the frameworks of international relations, international law, or nation state construction. But most of them still see nation states – homogeneous, simple, and rigid – as the only actors. Positing the conflict in an inter*national* system, their efforts reveal the indiscriminate approval of Westphalian time-space.

In Western academia, Westphalian time-space has been gradually dissolved along with the criticism of the modernization theory. Scholars in East Asian studies denaturalize the nation state system, exposing the colonialist nature of international law, modern diplomatic protocols, and the international system.[19] At the same time, they thoroughly reject nationalist historiography under the overall rethinking of the Enlightenment and social Darwinism.[20] Echoing this historiographical shift, Andre Schmid, one of the few Western scholars who writes explicitly about the making of the Korean northern boundaries, sees the Tumen demarcation as part of the nation-making process in Korea. Not until the late nineteenth and early twentieth centuries, his work demonstrates, did a newly imagined "Korean nation" emerge and nationalist thinkers start to use romantic nostalgia for the past to support their political appeals in the present.[21]

With this acknowledgment, I propose to use the "local" as an alternative spatial unit to examine the border makings in the Tumen River

---

[18] Yi Sŏng-hwan, *Kindai Higashi Ajia no seiji rikigaku: Kantō o meguru Nichi-Chū-Chō kankei no shiteki tenkai* (Tokyo: Kinseisha, 1991); Jiang Longfan, *Jindai zhongchaori sanguo dui jiandao chaoxianren de zhengce yanjiu* (Mudanjiang: Heilongjiang chaoxianminzu chubanshe, 2000); Bai Rongxun, *Higashi Ajia seiji gaikōshi kenkyū: "Kantō kyōyaku" to saiban kankatsuken* (Osaka: Ōsaka Keizai Hōka Daigaku Shuppanbu, 2005); Yu Fengchun, *Zhongguo guominguojia gouzhu yu guomintonghe zhi licheng: yi 20 shiji shangbanye dongbei bianjiang minzu guomin jiaoyu weizhu* (Harbin: Heilongjiang jiaoyu chubanshe, 2006).

[19] Lydia H. Liu, *The Clash of Empires: The Invention of China in Modern World Making* (Cambridge, MA: Harvard University Press, 2004); James Hevia, *English Lessons: The Pedagogy of Imperialism in Nineteenth-Century China* (Durham, NC: Duke University Press, 2003); Alexis Dudden, *Japan's Colonization of Korea: Discourse and Power* (Honolulu: University of Hawai'i Press, 2005), just to list a few.

[20] Prasenjit Duara, *Rescuing History from the Nation: Questioning Narratives of Modern China* (Chicago: University of Chicago Press, 1995).

[21] Andre Schmid, *Korea between Empires, 1895–1919* (New York: Columbia University Press, 2002).

region. My concept of "local" contains at least three geographical layers: "multilateral local," "regional local," and "global local." Although different, these layers are dynamically interconnected with one another.

Multilateral Local

The Tumen River region is a borderland encompassed by Chinese Manchuria, Korean Hamgyŏng, the Russian Far East, and the Sea of Japan. As an integrated socioecological unit, it is a multilateral local as opposed to a domestic local. It accepts influences from and responds to all state players in Northeast Asia. As early as the 1910s and 1920s Japanese scholars in Oriental historiography, notably Naitō Konan, Shiratori Kurakichi, Yanai Watari, and Wata Sei, already emphasized the relative independence of this historical realm, albeit with obvious colonialist connotations. Contemporary Japanese economic historians, notably Tsurushima Setsurei and Nishi Shigenobu, also underline the unique geographic and economic status of the Tumen River region in Northeast Asia, seeing it as a "Natural Economic Territory."[22]

The sociogeographic focus of this book, the northern bank of the Tumen River, is located in the southeastern part of Jilin Province in northeast China. Unlike other borderlands, this one was not only a model of conventional statecraft on frontier ruling but also an example of competitive yet symbiotic sociopolitical transitions in China, Korea, and Japan. In the hundreds of years before the 1880s, the region remained unexploited because of the Manchu Empire's strict ban on agricultural exploitation. When the Qing finally opened it for development, it was immediately integrated into national, regional, and global competitions. Nation- and state-building projects of the three East Asian countries, bolstered by nationalist, colonialist, capitalist, and imperialist agendas, overlapped and interlaced here. For China, this place was (and is) an ethnic frontier – first a Manchu frontier, then an ethnic Korean frontier. The "interiorization" of frontiers constituted a consistent theme throughout China's nation and state formation. For Korea, the place is a key to a progressive narrative of past and present. Mt. Paektu in particular was regarded as the cradle of both the ancient Korean civilization and the modern Korean state. To Japan, the place connected two of the most important colonies, Korea and Manchuria, and was a testing ground of the Japanese dream for building a pan-Asianist empire. With multiple players competing for

---

[22] Tsurushima Setsurei, *Tomankō chiiki kaihatsu* (Suita: Kansai Daigaku Shuppanbu, 2000); Nishi Shigenobu, "Tomankō (Tomonkō) chiiki kaihatsu niokeru 'NET (Natural Economic Territory)' ron no igi," *Kan Nihonkai kenkyū*, no. 7 (2001), pp. 14–23.

and transforming the space in turns and together, the history of this frontier was synchronous to the winding path of East Asian history as it twisted its way through the twentieth century.

Borders, as "complex social institutions,"[23] mean different things to different actors. Central governments, grassroots officials, local dwellers, and trespassers view the same division line in distinctive ways. Borderland is an organic space combining a geographic realm, its natural ecology, and human activities. It is a relatively independent social unit yet never really independent from the making of state and nation. Studies on nation state building predominately view it as a top-down project, focusing on how states or elite thinkers impose a new "vision" from above. But, seen from the border, nation and state building also work from the bottom up. In his study on the Spanish-French boundary in the Pyrenees, Peter Sahlins argues that "states did not simply impose their values and boundaries on local society. Rather, local society was a motive force in the formation and consolidation of nationhood and the territorial state."[24] Similarly, in the Tumen River region the local was not merely a receiver of multiple state influences. The people in the region were making their own choices to engage with various kinds of government policies. Actors at the local level – officials, community leaders, commoners – proactively provided innovative and flexible solutions to concrete problems.

Pragmatist practices, along with the "vision" of elites, created the identity of a community, which was not necessarily attached to any single state. Local maintained a multifaceted relationship with the states – resistant, cooperative, or mutually exploited, urging states to adjust their policies. Moreover, local itself was multifaceted. The hostility between rival states created tension between antagonistic groups in this multilateral local. Without downplaying the role of central governments and elites, I emphasize the problem-solving efforts of grassroots agencies, highlighting their rationales and how their experiments pushed the overall transformation of East Asia.

Regional Local

A region is not a community of states in a given geographic realm. Rather, it is co-constituted by polities and societies through various

---

[23] Sandro Mezzadra and Brett Neilson, *Border as Method, or, the Multiplication of Labor* (Durham, NC: Duke University Press, 2013), p. 3.
[24] Peter Sahlins, *Boundaries: The Making of France and Spain in the Pyrenees* (Berkeley, CA: University of California Press, 1989), p. 8.

cross-boundary linkages: politics, economy, culture, rite, religion, patterns of living, and memories of the past. A region therefore is a fluid unit, a world instead of an inter*national* system. Here I adopt Peter Perdue's idea that regional units "are defined not by political and administrative structures, but by concentrations of populations, commercial links, and cultural transactions. They do not exclude each other."[25] In imperial East Asia, Confucian ideology and geopolitical structure helped to form a dynamic region, which was composed of a center (oftentimes the regime of the Chinese central plains) and multiple subcenters (such as Japan, Vietnam, Korea, and Siam). In Western academia this region is generally believed to be organized by the "tributary system." I prefer to call this flexible and multivocal regional order the *zongfan* (宗藩) hierarchy, so as to highlight the sociological, philosophical, and cosmological roots of this indigenous term.[26] The Tumen River demarcation occurred in a period during which the conventional *zongfan* hierarchy had been interrupted and transformed by a new order of international law. Not only were different states involved in the process but old and new regional orders collided and collaborated.

Emphasizing the regional element of a local history is to further decentralize any particular state in my narrative. Various polities participated in a regional system for diverse reasons. They interpreted the system in their own ways. A region thus must be understood as jointly comprised and constructed. China, for example, could not unilaterally create the *zongfan* order if other states did not accept, adapt, and implement the arrangement for their own benefits. On the other hand, no matter how different their views were, these polities were bound by certain shared principles. In this way they defined each other. So, from a regional perspective, no country can monopolize its own historical memory. Evelyn Rawski argues not only that Chinese history needs to be examined through its interactions with other Northeast Asian entities, but that "Korea and Japan are better understood by classifying them with the Manchurian states which constituted China's northeast frontier."[27] The

---

[25] Peter Perdue, "Eurasia in World History: Reflections on Time and Space," World History Connected, 2008, http://worldhistoryconnected.press.illinois.edu/5.2/perdue.html, accessed April 13, 2017.

[26] According to *Ci Yuan*, *zongfan* refers to "the imperial clans who were bestowed." Put in a simplified way, *zong* implies a hierarchical arrangement based on family genealogy wherein the ranking of authority is in order of seniority and proximity to the direct descendant. Such a relationship was extended metaphysically to the political realm in which the central regime (*zong*) bestowed subordinate regimes and was, at the same time, supported and protected (*fan*) by them. See the term *zongfan* and the related terms *zong*, *zongshi*, and *fan* in Lu Erkui, ed., *Ci yuan* (Shanghai: Shangwu yinshuguan, 1915).

[27] Evelyn Rawski, *Early Modern China and Northeast Asia: Cross-Border Perspectives* (Cambridge: Cambridge University Press, 2015), p. 4.

Tumen River frontier is a meeting ground of multiple states and societies in Northeast Asia. The entire region is reflected within it.

Introducing a regional lens also helps us understand the transregional nature of the Tumen River dispute. The contest over the Sino-Korean border and the Koreans in Manchuria was not a problem concerning only interstate relationships but one that invited interregional intervention. Owen Lattimore's work on Manchuria in the 1930s addresses this aspect. Instead of seeing the international competition over influence in Manchuria as a conflict between nation states, Lattimore portrays it as a clash of three "civilizations": the "traditional" Chinese, communist Russian, and "modern" Western civilizations.[28] This argument stresses the mutual absorption and repulsion between different cultures and modes of production and suggests a power struggle that transcended international relations. The Tumen River region was at the forefront of Lattimore's cultural conflict in Manchuria.

Global Local

An increasingly salient trend in East Asian studies is to review the regional histories in a global context. There are generally two paradigms. The first one reexamines modern East Asian development within a framework of capitalist expansion. It draws heavily upon the world system theory of Immanuel Wallerstein and is revealed in the works of Mark Selden, Giovanni Arrighi, Hamashita Takeshi, and Timothy Brooks, among others. These scholars are particularly interested in exploring how trade helped to integrate Asia into a dynamic global community and how certain commodities (e.g., silver, tea, or opium) fueled early modern global connections. East Asia, they argue, was always an inseparable part of and an important contributor to the world capitalist nexus. This thesis is clearly pertinent to the current research. In her study of the Manchurian Koreans, Hyun Ok Park shows how a global trend of the commodification of land and labor, through Japanese colonization, shaped Korean nationalism in Manchuria.[29]

While recognizing global capitalism as an important modeling force imposed upon local society, we also need to acknowledge a reciprocal motion. For example, crops produced in Manchuria (e.g., soybeans, millet, and rice) had a remarkable impact on the operation of the East

---

[28] Owen Lattimore, *Inner Asian Frontiers of China* (Boston: Beacon Press, 1962); Owen Lattimore, *Manchuria, Cradle of Conflict* (New York: Macmillan, 1932).

[29] Hyun Ok Park, *Two Dreams in One Bed: Empire, Social Life, and the Origins of the North Korean Revolution in Manchuria* (Durham, NC: Duke University Press, 2005).

Asian capitalist system. During the early exploitation of the Tumen River region, the transboundary circulation of crops, whether in market or nonmarket form, had a significant influence on the financial market in Japan. The history of Manchurian rice began with the Korean rice cultivators who migrated to the north of the Tumen River. Until the 1920s rice production in Manchuria, mainly by Korean emigrants, became indispensable to the overall Japanese colonial and capitalist construction, which in turn aggravated Japan's aggressive land annexations in both Korea and Manchuria. In other words, the local actively intervenes in a global system.

The second paradigm that reexamines East Asia in a global perspective is a scholarly orientation towards "Qing imperialism." This trend – containing works such as comparative studies on the European and Qing empires and that of the "New Qing History" school, which highlights the Inner Asian nature of the regime – reminds us that the Qing was not an outsider in the historical trajectory of territorial expansion in the early modern world. The Qing's frontier conquests and transformations in particular bolster this argument. Combining what he calls the "Eurasian similarity thesis" and "Altaic school," Peter Perdue not only highly values the Qing state builders' capacities to integrate vast ethnic frontiers into the empire but proves that the Qing was not at all a latecomer when compared to its European counterparts in terms of certain scientific and technological progress. Triggered by the Qing's ambitious military needs, "knowledge of technological advances diffused rapidly across Eurasia."[30]

The Tumen River region was not left out in this global circulation of knowledge and ideas, particularly the use of cartography and international law. But I want to emphasize that this spread was not necessarily a linear process towards "advance," nor was it a one-directional diffusion from Europe to Asia. For example, European cartographic methods were applied to survey and map the Qing territory in the early eighteenth century but were not used to map the Tumen River border one and a half centuries later. Despite the progressivist view, cartographers flexibly pick the mapmaking methods that best serve concrete intellectual and political needs. Advancement of technology more often than not was not the top priority. The Tumen River demarcation tested newly adopted legal institutions such as international law and nationality law. Local officials did not just accept these new institutions but creatively refashioned indigenous institutions in accordance with new institutions. By discussing the aspects of technology and jurisprudence, I demonstrate how certain

---

[30] Peter Perdue, *China Marches West: The Qing Conquest of Central Eurasia* (Cambridge, MA: Belknap Press of Harvard University Press, 2005), p. 539.

knowledge, being produced and disseminated globally, manifested itself locally.

Synthesizing the three layers of the local, the Tumen River region revealed itself to be a "transsystematic society," to borrow the concept of Wang Hui. In response to an intensive global dialogue on China's ethnic/frontier issues, Wang attempts to see China, a multiethnic and multicultural complex, as a "transsystematic society" (*kua tixi shehui*). This dynamic concept refers to "an interrelated social and cultural pattern, formed through the interactions, communications and coexistence of different cultures, ethnic groups and regions."[31] He specifically mentions why the concept is useful for historical writings:

> In terms of historiography, a common phenomenon in the nationalist era is that a single ethnic group, religion, or language community is used as the unit of narrative. If, however, these ethnic groups, religions, and languages were interlaced in one region, one village, or one family, this kind of narrative may reduce, exaggerate or twist their complicated relations. For me, "transsystematic society" generalizes this kind of unique historical phenomenon which is usually ignored or simplified by modern knowledge. It therefore provides a possibility to redescribe these phenomena.[32]

The Tumen River region embodies the "transsystematic" nature of China and East Asia. The immigration and exploitation of this region shows how, in a turbulent era, competitive political, economic, social, and cultural forces worked together and transformed a wild frontier into a wellspring of East Asian modernity.

---

[31] Wang Hui, *Dongxi zhijian de "Xizang wenti": wai er pian* (Beijing: Shenghuo, dushu, xinzhi sanlianshudian, 2011), pp. 269–270.

[32] Ibid., p. 271.

1 Crossing the Boundary
The Socioecology of the Tumen River Region

It was 1881, the year of the snake. Li Jinyong, a middle-ranking Qing official on a survey trip to the Hunchun region in Jilin, discovered that Korean peasants were claiming wildland on the northern side of Tumen River. Called *Nanhuang weichang* (Nanhuang Enclosure), this border zone was a royal hunting ground that had recently been opened for cultivation. Li had been sent to investigate potential arable land and recruit Han Chinese peasants in northern China to resettle there. What astonished him was not just the scale of the squatting – thousands of Koreans working on areas no less than 2000 *shang* – but the fact that the peasants held land certificates issued by the Korean officials. Li immediately sent back word of this situation. In his report he described how a Korean military officer named Cho Pyŏng-ji admitted to him that more than half the local Korean population now relied on the harvest from the north bank. "These people knew they had crossed the border to farm, and they begged nothing but exceptional mercy."[1]

Border trespassing was not a new problem, nor was this the first time that it had caught the attention of the Qing government. Similar cases had played out in the previous two centuries. But border trespassing was occurring on an unprecedented scale in 1881. Two sets of circumstances triggered this situation. First, in the 1860s and 1870s, severe natural disasters continuously struck Hamgyŏng-do, a northeast province already infamous for its poverty. Second, in 1860 Russia aggressively extended its territory all the way to the mouth of the Tumen River, where it abutted both the Qing and Korea, and started to recruit Korean peasants to cultivate this newly acquired Far East frontier. The situation Li Jinyong discovered, then, was happening as both the Qing and Chosŏn were suffering the intrusion of imperialism and struggling to survive internal and external crises. A seemingly familiar problem became enmeshed within the overall turbulence that threatened the two countries' control over

---

[1] Zhu Shoupeng, ed., *Donghua xulu* [The Guangxu reign], vol. 44 (Shanghai: Shanghai guji chubanshe, 2002), pp. 14–15.

their borderlands. It stimulated a series of policy reforms to secure the frontier, which led to a decades-long political conflict over the region. This chapter analyzes the policies of the Qing and Chosŏn towards the Korean squatters in the early 1880s. To do so, we must understand the border trespassing problem in light of the long-term socioecological situation in the Tumen River region. In particular, we must look at how both the Qing and Chosŏn viewed and governed this area. We also need to examine the squatter problem within the framework of their bilateral relationship, the contemporary challenges to this relationship, and their reactions to social political crises both internally and externally.

The Tumen River Region: Northeast Qing versus Northeast Korea

The Tumen River is one of the two rivers that separate the Korean Peninsula from northeast China, known as Manchuria in Western languages.[2] Both rivers have their origins in Mount Changbai (K. Paektu), a splendid volcano and the highest mountain in the area. The Yalu (K. Amnok) River flows roughly southwestward into the Bohai Sea and the Tumen (K. Tuman) northeastward into the Sea of Japan (K. Tonghae). This natural carved line, made up of Mt. Changbai and the two rivers, is arguably one of the oldest state boundaries in the world that is still effective today. The Yalu became Korea's northwestern border in the late fourteenth century during the Koryŏ dynasty (918–1392). The northeast border along the mid and lower Tumen River was solidified in the fifteenth century during the early Chosŏn dynasty (1392–1897).[3]

Before the Tumen was made the border, various Jurchen tribes had for generations inhabited the area across the river. In the mid-fourteenth century Möngke Temür, the chief of the Odori tribe, moved his people from the Amur River region to the two sides of the mid and lower Tumen River. Accepting official titles from both Chosŏn Korea and Ming China, Möngke Temür struggled to survive amid the Ming, Chosŏn and rival Jurchen tribes.[4] On the Chosŏn side, before establishing the long-lasting

---

[2] For the name "Manchuria," see Elliott, "The Limits of Tartary"; Owen Lattimore, *Inner Asian Frontiers of China* (Boston: Beacon, 1967), pp. 105–106.

[3] For the historical change in Korea's northern border, see Gari Ledyard, "Cartography in Korea," in J. Brian Harley and David Woodward, eds., *The History of Cartography*, vol. 2, book 2: *Cartography in the Traditional East and Southeast Asian Societies* (Chicago: University of Chicago Press, 1987), pp. 235–345, 288–291.

[4] Diao Shuren, "Lun qian ming shiqi Eduoli nüzhen yu ming chaoxian de guanxi: jianlun nüzhen dui chaoxian xiang tumenjiang liuyu tuozhan jiangyu de dizhi yu douzheng," *Zhongguo bianjiang shidi yanjiu*, vol. 12, no. 1 (2002), pp. 44–54.

dynasty in 1392, Yi Sŏng-gye had accumulated his military and political power in the southern Hamgyŏng area. His success was largely attributed to his amicable relationship with the local Jurchens. In the early Chosŏn period the policy towards the Jurchens was a two-way strategy: recruiting and assimilating those who were submissive while suppressing those who were not.[5] In this way Chosŏn's influence gradually extended in the region. On the Ming side, Zhu Yuanzhang, the founding emperor, was eager to extend his political influence in Manchuria to further expel his Mongol rivals. He established nominal control (*jimi*) over the region by assigning local Jurchen leaders as the commanders of military posts (*wei*).[6] Möngke Temür was appointed as the commander of the Jianzhou Left Commandery (*Jianzhou zuo wei*). In 1433 he was killed in an internal clash, and his tribe had to migrate westward. Taking advantage of the weakness of the Jurchens, King Sejong of Chosŏn (r. 1418–1450) decisively expanded his territory to the southern bank of the Tumen River. Kim Chong-sŏ, a prominent Chosŏn general, explained the purposes of this strategic move: "to recover the territory of the ancestor kings," "to use the long river as a natural barrier," and "to gain the expediency of defense."[7] Six garrisons (K. *yukchin*) – Kyŏngwŏn, Hoeryŏng, Chongsŏng, Kyŏnghŭng, Onsŏng, and Puryŏng – were successively set up near the river. Both Ming and Chosŏn later treated the Tumen and Yalu as their border.

In the late sixteenth century Nurhaci (1559–1626), the direct descendant of Möngke Temür, inherited the leadership of the Jianzhou Left Commandery, which had been relocated to the Liaodong Peninsula. Unifying other Jurchen tribes and allying with some Mongol tribes, he established the Later Jin dynasty (Manchu, *aisin gurun*) in 1616 and announced its independence from the Ming.[8] In 1636 his son Hong Taiji renamed the regime as "the Great Qing" (*daicing gurun*) and the Jurchen people as "Manchu" (*Manju*).[9] Twice invading Chosŏn (in 1627

---

[5] Yu Pŏn-yong, "Wangjosillok e nadanan Yijojŏngi ŭi yain," *Paeksan Hakpo*, vol. 14 (1973), p. 6.

[6] Li Jiancai, *Mingdai Dongbei* (Shenyang: Liaoning renmin chubanshe, 1986).

[7] Chŏng Yun-yong, *Pungno Kiryak* (Seoul: Asea Munhwasa, 1974), p. 304.

[8] About the rise of Nurhaci, see Gertraude Roth Li, "State Building before 1644," in Willard J. Peterson, ed., *Cambridge History of China*, vol. 9, part 1: *The Ch'ing Dynasty to 1800* (Cambridge: Cambridge University Press, 2002), pp. 9–72.

[9] The Manchu was not composed of the Jurchen only, neither all Jurchen tribes turned into Manchu. According to Wang Zhonghan, the main body of the Manchu was composed of the Jianzhou and Haixi tribes. Although some members of the Donghai/Yeren tribes also joined the Manchu, a portion were assimilated to Koreans. The question of whether Manchu is a strict "ethnic" entity and when the Manchu identity was formed has provoked significant debates in recent years. I use the term here to refer to the

and 1636), Hong Taiji forced Korea to renounce its loyalty to Ming China and concede the superior rule of the Qing. In the post-war agreement, the two regimes promised to "keep their own territories" (C. *ge shou feng jiang*).[10] In 1644 the Qing conquered the Ming and became the new rulers of China. Along with this military campaign, the majority of the Qing population at the time (around 140,000 banner soldiers and hundreds of thousands of their family members and servants) were taken out of Manchuria.[11]

In the following two centuries the Qing and Chosŏn forbad illegal crossing of the Yalu and Tumen Rivers. People who violated the border ban were publicly beheaded. The Qing even demolished houses and farms close to the border.[12] Japanese jurist Shinoda Jisaku, an international law expert and colonial official in Korea in the 1930s, characterized the vast area north of the Tumen River as a "buffer zone," a territory abandoned by the Qing. He called it "a naturally formed neutral zone and no-man's-land, belonging to neither China nor Korea."[13] This picture, though accepted by many contemporary scholars,[14] is quite misleading. An inhabited area is by no means tantamount to an ungoverned or "neutral" one. Nor was the lack of settlement in the region solely the result of an adverse natural environment. It was also a political arrangement. The Qing government deliberately maintained the wildness of the region north of the Tumen River. In other words, the state played a critical role in creating the seemingly non-governmental status of the region.

---

people who self-identified as Manchu in the banner system of the Qing. See Wang Zhonghan, *Qingshi manzushi jiangyigao* (Xiamen: Lujiang chubanshe, 2006); Mark Elliott, *The Manchu Way: The Eight Banners and Ethnic Identity in Late Imperial China* (Stanford, CA: Stanford University Press, 2001); Edward J. M. Rhoads, *Manchus and Han: Ethnic Relations and Political Power in Late Qing and Early Republican China, 1861–1928* (Seattle: University of Washington Press, 2000).

[10] *Chosŏnwangjo-sillok, Injo Sillok*, 5-3-3.

[11] According to Wang Zhonghan, during Hong Taiji's reign (1626–1643) the total Manchu population was one million. See Wang Zhonghan, *Qingshi xin kao* (Shenyang: Liaoning daxue chubanshe, 1990), p. 65. Some recent studies believe the number of Manchu moving out of Manchuria was over one million. See Zhang Jie and Zhang Danhui, *Qingdai dongbei bianjiang de manzu, 1644–1840* (Shenyang: Liaoning minzu chubanshe, 2005).

[12] The Chosŏn court, on the other hand, did not prohibit its subjects from living near the border. The Korean local officials realized the imbalance of the policy. See *Chosŏnwangjo-sillok, Sokchong Sillok*, 14-08-15.

[13] Shinoda Jisaku, *Hakutōsan teikaihi* (Tokyo: Rakurō Shoi, 1938), pp. 22–24. Also see the appendix chapter "Kando mundai no kaiko," p. 298.

[14] See, for example, Sin, *Kando yŏngyukwŏn e kwanhan yŏn'gu*. Also see Yi Sŏng-hwan, *Kindai Higashi Ajia no seiji rikigaku: Kantō o meguru Nichi-Chū-Chō kankei no shiteki tenkai* (Tokyo: Kinseisha, 1991).

Qing Rule in Manchuria

Before the 1880s the north bank of the Tumen River was in the scope of Hunchun, a lower-level military garrison governed by Ningguta of Jilin. Jilin, along with Heilongjiang and Shengjing (Ma. Mukden), was one of the three realms comprising Qing's Manchuria.[15] An understanding of the political circumstances surrounding the river region relies in part on recognizing Qing's administration over Manchuria.

Manchuria was a unique domain of the Qing Empire. As many scholars have correctly pointed out, Manchuria, like Mongolia, Xinjiang, Tibet, and the southwestern provinces, was a Qing frontier.[16] Yet if the word "frontier" refers to a marginal zone in political, economic, and social terms, then Manchuria was much more than a frontier. It was the cradle of the ruling people called "Manchu," who saw Mt. Changbai in the upper Tumen region as their sacred birthplace. It was here, according to Manchu myth, that the ancestor of the Aisin Gioro clan began to thrive. Aside from its spiritual meaning, Manchuria was the political foundation of the empire. Nurhaci, the founding father, adopted an extremely effective military/social institution known as the Eight Banners (Ma. *jakūn gūsa*) and won decisive battles against his rivals in the area. Hence it was frequently alluded to in Qing documents as the "place of the rising dragon" (C. *longxing zhidi*). It was regarded as the base of the royal family, the ruling group, and the entire dynasty. In short, the Manchu believed the region preserved the Manchu essence.[17] Precisely because Manchuria, unlike other frontiers, was first and foremost a sacred homeland, it is hard to pinpoint a simple concept to define the Qing emperor's attachment to it. He was the lord of all local tribes, the head of the Manchu, the guard of family/clan property, the patron of local gods, and the protector of the lifestyle of the ruling population.

Qing's Manchuria spanned a far-flung geographic realm that defied a singular categorization. Consisting of multiple ecological and cultural spaces, it included the Liaodong Peninsula, the east end of the Mongolian steppe, the Khingan Ranges, and the southeastern part of Pacific Russia (including Sakhalin Island). The southwest corner, the

---

[15] Neither Manchu nor Chinese documents use the term "Manchuria" to refer to this northeastern domain. In the Qing dynasty, people sometimes used "eastern provinces" or simply "Shengjing/Mukden," although neither was an official name. For the convenience of this narrative, I keep the term "Manchuria" to indicate the Qing's domain of Shengjing, Jilin, and Heilongjiang.

[16] Lattimore, *Inner Asian Frontiers of China*.

[17] Mark Elliott elaborately describes how this land was sacralized in the early Qing. See Elliott, "The Limits of Tartary."

Liaodong Peninsula, was explored as early as the fourth century BC by agricultural immigrants and was one of the food bases of the Qing. The western edge of Manchuria supported the nomadic lifestyle of Mongols. The rest and the majority of this domain consisted of thickly forested mountains and wetlands within which various local tribes (once all included under the umbrella term "Manchu") subsisted on hunting, fishing, and foraging. As Owen Lattimore points out, rather than remaining separate from one another, these various cultural-ecological zones merged and overlapped to a certain degree.[18]

The Qing administration in Manchuria therefore featured both the blend of multiple ways of living and the region's multilayered significance to the empire. During most of the Qing period, Manchuria was generally governed through the Eight Banners system. This distanced it from both the Six Boards system applied in Chinese provinces and the Board for the Administration of Outer Subordinates (C. *Lifanyuan;* Ma. *tulergi golo-be dasara jurgan*) system applied to all other Inner Asian frontiers.[19] But we must emphasize the "generally," because within the banner system there were diverse government institutions that, though not necessarily attached to each other, often overlapped in function. The most important institutions included the three military governors known as "generals" (C. *jiangjun;* Ma. *amban janggin*), the Five Boards of Mukden (C. *Shengjing wubu*), and some civil bureaucracies. Another institution relevant to our discussion was the Imperial Household Department (C. *neiwufu*).

The military governors (or generals) were originally set to supervise military/banner affairs in the three realms of Manchuria: Shengjing in the west,[20] Jilin in the east,[21] and Heilongjiang in the north.[22] Facing Russia's threat, from the mid to late Qing the three generals were established as the top government bodies, with Shengjing General having authority over the other two.[23] In Jilin and Heilongjiang, where civilian populations were few, the generals acted as the superior leader in charge

[18] Lattimore, *Inner Asian Frontiers of China*, p. 105.
[19] Robert H. G. Lee, *The Manchurian Frontier in Ch'ing History* (Cambridge, MA: Harvard University Press, 1970), pp. 24–40, 59.
[20] It was first established as "Liaodong General" in 1662, then "Fengtian General" in 1665. The title "Shengjing General" was finalized in 1747.
[21] It was established first as "Ningguta General" in 1662. In 1677 the institute office was moved from Ningguta to Chuanchang, later called Jilin. In 1757 the name was officially changed to "Jilin General."
[22] Derived from Ningguta General and established in 1683.
[23] For a detailed description of the development of the three generals, see Shao Dan, *Remote Homeland, Recovered Borderland: Manchus, Manchukuo, and Manchuria, 1907–1985* (Honolulu: University of Hawai'i Press, 2011), pp. 25–39.

of both military and civilian businesses. Before 1860 the territory ruled
by the Jilin General was the largest among the three. Its expansive realm
contained the whole Ussuri and Sungari River regions, the lower Amur
River region, and Sakhalin Island.[24] Hunchun, which governed the north
side of the Tumen River, was a banner garrison in the rank of assistant
commandant (C. *xieling*). Hunchun reported to the vice commander-
in-chief (C. *fudutong*) of Ningguta until 1870, when it was supervised
directly by the Jilin General. In 1881 it was officially promoted to the
rank of vice commander-in-chief.[25] Banner soldiers in Hunchun and
Ningguta were mainly "new Manchu" (Ma. *ice Manju*) recruited from
the Warka tribe in the Tumen and Ussuri River regions.[26] Chinese historian Ding Yizhuang suggests that, in the early Qing period, the most
important duty of Ningguta and Jilin was to supply banner troops to
Shengjing and the whole empire.[27]

After conquering Ming China and transferring most of its government institutions to Beijing, the Qing made the old capital, Mukden (C.
Shengjing or Shenyang), the "auxiliary capital." To highlight the city's
superior political status, Five Boards of Mukden were set up to parallel the Six Boards in Beijing. They oversaw affairs of rites (*li*), finance
(*hu*), works (*gong*), punishment (*xing*), and war (*bing*) in Manchuria.[28]
Other local-level civil bureaucracies, notably the Prefect of Fengtian (C.
Fengtian fuyin), also developed to govern the growing population of Han
civilians who had migrated to Manchuria (especially in the Liaodong
region). Although most civil bureaucracies reported to the generals, over
time a banner–civilian dual system gradually emerged in Manchuria. That
said, such a transition was more observable in Shengjing, where most of
the civilian population was concentrated, than in Jilin and Heilongjiang.

A government body that belonged to neither the banner system nor
the civilian system was the Imperial Household Department. Granted
the duty of managing business for the royal family, the department
was not directly involved in local administration. A branch in Jilin, the
Superintendent Yamen of Dasheng Ula (Ma. *butha ula*), was in charge of
collecting wild produce, such as river pearls, mink, honey, pine nuts, etc.,
in reserved mountains and offering these tributes to the emperor.[29] It

[24] See Ma Dazheng, ed., *Zhongguo bianjiang jinglue shi* (Zhengzhou: Zhong zhou gu ji chubanshe, 2000,) pp. 331–333. Also see Tan Qixiang, ed., *Zhongguo lishi ditu ji*, vol. 8
(Beijing: Zhongguo di tu chubanshe, 1982), pp. 5–6.

[25] Li Shutian, ed., *Hunchun shi zhi* (Changchun: Jilin wenshi chubanshe, 1990), p. 45.

[26] Wu Zhenchen, *Ningguta ji lue* (Shanghai: Shanghai gu ji chubanshe, 2002).

[27] Ding Yizhuang, *Qingdai baqi zhufang yanjiu* (Shenyang: Liaoning min zhu chubanshe,
2003), pp. 78–81.

[28] There was no Board of Civil Appointment in the auxiliary capital.

[29] *Dashengwula zhidian quanshu* (Changchun: Jilin wenshi chubanshe, 1988).

sometimes functioned as a secret channel connecting the Forbidden City in Beijing with the forbidden zones on the frontier. As Evelyn Rawski argues, the department "blurred the boundary between the emperor's personal affairs and the affairs of state."[30] This perhaps partially explains why in the 1710s, when Emperor Kangxi wanted to investigate the Qing–Korean border, he ordered neither the Board of Rites (the government body dealing with the Chosŏn affairs) nor local banner troops. Instead, he entrusted the mission to Mukedeng, the superintendent of Dasheng Ula (see the Introduction). For the Qing emperor, the Manchuria–Korean border area concerned the security of both the imperial state and the imperial family.

The diverse modes of subsistence and governance in Manchuria were accompanied by an equally multifaceted approach to land reclamation that accommodated both local preferences and Qing political control. This was particularly the case in Jilin.

In theory, the exploitation of a large part of Manchuria was prohibited. But this policy hardly meant the wilderness was kept pristine. In fact, land usage in Manchuria took several forms, including government manors, banner farms, civilian farms, and hunting enclosures. The income from government manors (*guan zhuang*), usually cultivated by criminals in exile or serfs, went directly to state revenue. Banner farms (*qi di*) served as subsistence farms for stationed banner soldiers and their non-banner tenants, while civilian farms (*min di*) were registered farms reclaimed by non-banner migrants, mostly Han, regardless of whether they had official permission.[31] Hunting enclosures (*wei chang*) belonged to the royal family and were strictly prohibited from any agricultural development. A large section of the Tumen north bank, where the Korean squatters settled, was a hunting enclosure.[32] All four categories were the result of particular political considerations. Official manors and banner farms supported the livelihoods of stationed troops and their families, and strengthened frontier defense against Russian expansion. The hunting enclosures helped preserve the Manchus' lifestyle. The civilian farm, the dominant form of land claim in the late Qing period, was a kind of flexible regulator. By encouraging or limiting the expansion of civilian farms, the government made sure that there was a channel to transfer

[30] Evelyn Rawski, *The Last Emperors: A Social History of Qing Imperial Institutions* (Berkeley, CA: University of California Press, 1998), p. 180.
[31] Wu Tingyu, *Qingdai manzhou tudi zhidu yanjiu* (Changchun: Jilin wenshi chubanshe, 1992).
[32] Tan Qixiang, "Qingdai dongsansheng jiangli zhi," in *Chang Shui Ji* (Beijing: Renmin chubanshe, 1987), pp. 167–168.

population pressure in north China without threatening the Manchu dominion of Manchuria.

Because of political concerns, then, Manchuria during the Qing dynasty was neither entirely closed off nor completely opened up.[33] Land reclamation policy in Manchuria was different in time and shifted in space to meet practical governmental needs. From the mid-seventeenth century to the early eighteenth, for example, the Qing encouraged Han peasants to cultivate land in Shengjing. The policy expanded only to limited areas in Jilin. Yet, from the mid-eighteenth to the mid-nineteenth centuries, the Qing reversed course and banned agricultural migration to Manchuria, especially Jilin.[34] This also explains why the Manchurian Han population were mostly in Shengjing.

The Qing preferred to maintain this contrast in population and political-economic function. Since Jilin served a dual purpose as a Manchu base and a front line against Russia, it had to be carefully exploited and preserved at the same time. To reconcile these two tasks, banner farms and government manors were allowed to expand, whereas civilian migration was carefully restrained. From 1648 to 1681 the Qing government built several willow palisades (C. *liutiao bian*), which served as internal borders separating three ecological zones: the agricultural zone in Liaodong, the nomadic zone in the steppe area, and the forested zone of the rest. No one was allowed to cross the palisades without a government-issued certificate, at least in theory. By the late nineteenth century the population density of Jilin (1.79 per square kilometer in 1870; 1.93 in 1880) was significantly lower than that of Shengjing (21.85 in 1870; 30.42 in 1880).[35] Civil bureaucracy in Jilin was also much less developed, and there was little cultivation.[36]

In practice, the dual policy of preservation and exploitation, much as the central government may have pushed it, was hard to implement. One of the main obstacles was the gradual degradation of "the Manchu way," a consistent theme in Qing history as the social and economic exchanges between interior China and Manchuria blurred distinctions.[37] Living

---

[33] Lin Shixuan, *Qing ji dongbei yimin shibian zhengce zhi yanjiu* (Taipei: Guoli zhengzhi daxue lishixue xi, 2001).

[34] He Fei, "Qingdai dongbei tudi kaifa zhengce de Yanbian ji yingxiang," *Dongbei shidi*, no. 5 (2006), pp. 56–60.

[35] Lin, *Qing ji dongbei yimin shibian zhengce*, p. 380. The figures were quoted from Zhao Wenlin and Xie Shujun, *Zhongguo renkou shi* (Beijing: Renmin chubanshe, 1988), p. 475.

[36] From the Yongzheng reign (1723–1735) to the Daoguang reign (1821–1850) the area of banner farms was increased by merely three times, while that of the government manor did not expand at all. See Zhang and Zhang, *Qingdai dongbei bianjiang de manzu*, p. 175.

[37] Although whether this trend could be seen as "sinicization" or "acculturation" is highly debatable, most scholars do not deny that, from at least the eighteenth century onward,

in interior China (especially Beijing) for generations, most banner soldiers were unwilling to transfer to the bitterly cold and barren frontier.[38] Jilin was especially unwelcoming in natural, social, and culture terms. Even Emperor Kangxi, on his 1682 trip to Shengjing and Ningguta, lamented that the weather was so ferocious and the life of banner soldiers "extremely hard."[39] For quite a long time a major source of new residents had been Han exiles, many of them elites and intellectuals.[40] Local banner men, who inherited their status and titles from their fathers, bore the obligations of both military defense and agricultural production. A long-term peace dating from the late seventeenth century meant banner communities in Jilin were generally agrarianized. Additionally, since the early nineteenth century local banner soldiers openly claimed wildland in prohibited zones or illegally sold their lands on the market, suggesting a significant shift in native economic and social structures.[41] From the mid-Qing onward the Manchu language was less and less used even in this Manchu homeland. Han Chinese gradually replaced Manchu as the dominant written language in official documents, even though high-rank positions were held exclusively by the Manchu and Mongolian banner men. According to a Hunchun gazetteer compiled in the early twentieth century, by the late Qing period local Manchu custom "cannot be distinguished from Han custom."[42]

The decline of the Manchu way was aggravated by the ongoing inflow of Han peasants and refugees, mainly from Shandong and in part due to constant famines in north China. The slow but steady arrival of refugees gradually changed the ethnic composition in the region. As a result, nineteenth-century Jilin witnessed the gradual but unstoppable destruction of the land system. Government manors and banner farms were substantially commercialized and privatized, hunting enclosures were secretly reclaimed, and the number of civilian farms skyrocketed.[43] Attracted by prolific natural resources, Han and Hui Muslim merchants progressively connected Jilin to other parts of the empire. These

---

the characteristics used to mark the Manchu way of life –the Manchu language and mounted archery – had been practiced less and less by the Manchu.

[38] Ding, *Qingdai baqi zhufang yanjiu*, 2003, p. 161.

[39] Zhang and Zhang, *Qing dai dongbei bianjiang de manzu*, pp. 150–152; quoted from *Qing shengzu shilu*.

[40] Feng Erkang, "Qing chu Jilin manzu shehui yu yimin," In *Qing shi lun cong* (Shenyang: Liaoning guji chubanshe, 1995), pp. 117–132; Li Xingsheng, *Dongbei liuren shi* (Harbin: Heilongjiang Renmin chubanshe, 1990).

[41] See Zhongguo bianjiang shidi yanjiu zhongxin; Zhongguo diyi lishi dang'anguan, ed., *Hunchun fudutong yamen dang* (HCFDTYMD) (Guilin: Guangxi shifan daxue chubanshe, 2006); *Ningguta fudutong yamendang*, Chinese First National Historical Archive.

[42] Li, *Hunchun shi zhi*, p. 637.

[43] Zhang and Zhang, *Qingdai dongbei bianjiang de manzu*, p. 107.

migrations stimulated the market economy that was beginning to permeate this forest society. A boom in local trade conducted largely by Hui Muslim merchants converted frontier garrisons, such as Hunchun, into local commercial centers.[44]

Though reluctant, the Qing had to adapt its policy to match the reality in the region. Facing increasing pressures from Russian expansion, Han refugees flooding the area, and consistent lobbying by officials, the Qing court started to lift the settlement ban in parts of Jilin in the 1850s and 1860s.[45] The new policy slowly extended to other realms. In 1881 the Nanhuang Enclosure on the north bank of the Tumen was declared open.[46]

Chosŏn Rule in Hamgyŏng

On the Korean side, the Tuman (C. Tumen) River area was under the jurisdiction of the Hamgyŏng-do, a northeastern frontier of the country.[47] Like Manchuria for the Qing monarch, the Hamgyŏng region was once a home base for the Chosŏn regime. It was in the southern part of Hamgyŏng that the royal Yi family built up its political foundation.[48] But the Chosŏn paid more attention to the south and treated the northern realm as a marginal zone, comparable to Qing's Manchuria. After King Sejong had established the six garrisons in the mid and lower Tuman River in the fifteenth century, another garrison called Musan was set up and moved to the upper river region in 1684 during King Sukchong's reign. Originally a town under the garrison of Puryŏng, the new Musan garrison replaced Puryŏng as one of the Six Garrisons along the Tuman. All these garrisons were later upgraded to the administration of prefecture (*pu*) and supervised by civil bureaucracy. This system of governance did not change much until the very end of the dynasty.

In the early Chosŏn period the northern Hamgyŏng region, known as Kwanbuk, was important mainly for defense purposes. The regime brought in settlers to colonize the newly claimed frontier and recruited local Jurchens to be "civilized/naturalized" (*kwihwa*) as peasants. Koreans

---

[44] The Koreans who traveled to Hunchun recorded it specifically. See *Yŏnggodap pukchŏngji*, Kyujanggak archive # 951.054-Y42.

[45] Lin, *Qing ji dongbei yimin shibian zhengce*, pp. 115–119.

[46] Jiang, *Jindai zhongchaori sanguo dui jiandao chaoxianren de zhengce yanjiu*, p. 146.

[47] The province was first founded as Yŏnggil-do in 1413, then became Hamgil-do and Yŏngan-do in 1416 and 1470, respectively. The current name was determined in 1509.

[48] The great-great-great-grandfather of King Taejo (Yi Sŏng-gye) was invested by the Mongol Yuan China as a *darughachi*, or governor, of the Hamgyŏng area. The title was inherited by the Yi family until Yi Sŏng-gye and his father helped King Kongmin of Koryŏ to expel the Mongols from the region.

in the southern provinces from all classes – *yangban* (gentry or aristocracy), *chungin* (middle classes), *sangmin* (commoners), and *ch'ŏnmin* (vulgar commoners) – were encouraged by the state to migrate north to the six garrisons. As a reward, *sangmin* would get government appointments and *ch'ŏnmin* would be freed as *sangmin*. The consequence of the population influx could be gauged linguistically. According to *Pungno Kiryak*, a gazetteer compiled in the early nineteenth century, the "dialect spoken in the Hamgyŏng province is the most different kind, but it is not heard in the Kwanbuk towns. This is because the residents were originally from the south and their offspring all keep their original (southern) dialect."[49] The northern territory kept absorbing people from the south to ease the growing population pressure countrywide. From 1648 to 1864 the population in Hamgyŏng increased tenfold (from around 69,000, or 4.51 percent of the whole country, to around 696,000, or 10.96 percent of the whole country). Within the province, the population increase in Kwanbuk was more rapid than that in the southern part.[50]

Kwanbuk was designed as an agriculturally based military bastion run roughly like the Qing banner system. Agricultural activities were organized in accordance with the military institution called the Five Guard System (*Owije*), whereby all peasants were registered to a local "guard" and served the military in one way or another.[51] A fatal flaw of the system was that the Kwanbuk region, infamous for its harsh natural conditions, was not really suitable for large-scale farming. Its mountainous location provided poor soil and made irrigation extremely difficult. A famous Korean geographer, Hong Yang-ho (1724–1802), described the region as "a barren land in the very end of the north. Even in the third month of the spring there is still no flower blooming, while in the eighth month, snow already appears."[52] Unlike most parts of the peninsula, arable land in Kwanbuk was mainly dry field as opposed to wet (paddy) field. A large portion of it was what locals called "fire field" (*hwajŏn*), which could be reclaimed only once every several years by burning the vegetation. Even as late as the 1910s arable fields in northern Hamgyŏng comprised just 12 percent of farmland in the whole province.[53] Compared to ample and fertile uncultivated lands on the opposite side of the Tumen River, lands

---

[49] Chŏng Yun-yong, *Pungno Kiryak* (Seoul: Asea Munhwasa, 1974) p. 401.
[50] Li Huazi, *Qingchao yu chaoxian guanxi yanjiu* (Yanji: Yanbian daxue chubanshe, 2006), pp. 168–169.
[51] Chŏng, *Pungno Kiryak*, p. 422. See also Sun Chunri, *Zhongguo chaoxianzu yi min shi* (Beijing: Zhonghua shu ju, 2009), p. 73.
[52] Hong Yang-ho, "Puksae kiryak," in Yuk Nak-hyŏn, ed., *Kando yŏngyukwŏn kwan'gye charyojip* (Seoul: Paeksan Munhwa, 1993), pp. 301–317, 301.
[53] Sun, *Zhongguo chaoxianzu yimin shi*, p. 67; quoted from *Chōsen chishi shiryō*.

on the south bank were overcultivated. *Pukkwan kisa*, a record compiled in 1783, described how "all arable fields are reclaimed, to the extent that there is almost no uncultivated soil even on ridges."[54] On top of that, contrary to the situation on the north bank, local peasants bore heavy taxes and were subject to corvée.

The living standard in Kwanbuk was among the lowest in Chosŏn. Hong Yang-ho reported that "people have to rely on government subsidies, and grain is distributed in accordance with the number in the household. They rarely eat brown rice, only cook millet or barley as gruel."[55] As for clothing, according to the local gazetteer *Pukkwan chi*, "This place doesn't produce cotton, so people grow hemp and weave it all year. But after no more than a few looms of work, they have to turn all the products in as tax. As a result, men wear dog fur whether it is summer or winter, whereas women cover their bodies with cloth patched together from hundreds of pieces of rags in all four seasons."[56]

The poverty was aggravated by social bias and discriminatory policies. The Koreans saw the native Jurchens who once occupied the region as no better than savages. Though Jurchens were assimilated through centuries of co-living and intermarriage, commoners in Kwanbuk were still regarded as racially different, if not inferior. Records written mainly by southern literati were full of exotic ethnographical descriptions. Most claimed that long cohabitation with "the Jurchen barbarian" led local residents to inherit "the vulgar fashion of the north."[57] Even local *yangban* were despised. According to *Pungno Kiryak*, "Local literati read nothing other than *The Great Learning* and use this book as the sole source for exams and lectures. Even so, they hardly understand the meaning of the text."[58] In a society that embraced the neo-Confucian values more than anything else and was rigidly classified according to family genealogy, opportunity was terribly unfavorable to the Kwanbuk people.[59] To make matters worse, after putting down a large-scale rebellion in 1467 led by Yi Si-ae, a local strongman with Jurchen lineage, the Chosŏn government banned Hamgyŏng residents from taking the civil and military service examinations for almost a hundred years. The social ladder for

---

[54] Hong Ŭi-yŏng, *Pukkwan kisa* (Kyujanggak, 1783) pp. 134–135.
[55] Hong, "Puksae kiryak," p. 302.
[56] Chŏng, *Pungno Kiryak*, p. 403.
[57] Hong, "Puksae kiryak," p. 301.
[58] Chŏng, *Pungno Kiryak*, p. 403.
[59] Jang Yoo-seung, "Regional Identities of Northern Literati: A Comparative Study of P'yŏngan and Hamgyŏng Provinces," in Kim Sun Joo, ed., *The Northern Region of Korea: History, Identity, and Culture* (Seattle: University of Washington Press, 2011), pp. 62–92.

local people was so constrained that officials born in the province were rarely promoted to higher ranks. And as the Qing consolidated its power, the defense function of the northern frontier was no longer as critical as before, further marginalizing the region. Despite being the birthplace of the monarchy, it was neglected socially, overexploited agriculturally, and discriminated against politically.

Natural and social conditions severely challenged the state policy of fortifying the frontier by migration. After Sejong's reign (1418–1450) increasing numbers of locals fled southward. In response, harsh laws were issued to prohibit population flows from the frontier to the hinterland. As convicted criminals in other provinces were exiled to Hamgyŏng, local criminals were merely exiled to other regions within the province. Until the early nineteenth century money was not allowed to circulate in Kwanbuk.[60] Commerce was restrained, and local business was mostly done through barter trade. Even land was sold and purchased in cattle or clothes, as opposed to the use of silver or copper in other provinces. All measures, it seems, were designed to seal off the region from the rest of the country.

The semi-isolationist policy, however, could not prevent the people from moving. When the Kwanbuk Koreans were deprived of access to the south, they turned north.

Trans-Border Exchanges: Markets, Smuggling, Logging, and Poaching

"[B]orders always have two sides," as Sandro Mezzadra and Brett Neilson argue; "they connect as well as divide."[61] Previous studies on the Qing–Chosŏn boundary dispute, focusing almost exclusively on the prohibition against border trespassing before the mid-nineteenth century, tend to underestimate mutual interactions across the border. Recent scholars have reminded us of the enormous dynamic of transregional connections in early modern maritime East Asia.[62] The same perspective can be applied in a reexamination of the nature of the cross-Tumen activities between the people of the Qing and Chosŏn. Border trade, smuggling, logging, and poaching were common forms of cross-river interaction. After legal communication paved the way for illegal border crossing, the ban on the border, though strict, was hardly efficiently enforced. The

---

[60] Chŏng, *Pungno Kiryak*, p. 411.
[61] Mezzadra and Neilson, *Border as Method*, p. 4.
[62] See, for example, Hamashita Takeshi, *Higashi Ajia sekai no chiiki nettowāku* (Tokyo: Kokusai Bunka Kōryū Suishin Kyōkai, 1999).

permeable border then contributed to the making of a regional economy and social relations.

Official border markets were the routine channel connecting residents on the two sides. Among the three border markets between Qing and Chosŏn, two of them (Hoeryŏng and Kyŏngwŏn) were located in the Kwanbuk region. Supervised by local officials in the two countries, border markets played a crucial role in the local economy. During the 230-odd-year history of the Hoeryŏng and Kyŏngwŏn markets, the duration of each trade season extended from 20 days to sometimes 90 days, and the items in exchange expanded far beyond governmental limits.[63] Korean cattle, plows, and salt were exported to Jilin in exchange for horses, clothes, and a whole range of daily appliances. *Puksae Kiryak* records that people in Hunchun flooded into the markets in Kwanbuk: "Several decades ago, fewer than 1,000 sleds or 400 to 500 riders came to do business. In recent years the number of sleds has expanded to 4,000 to 5,000, and riders have also expanded a lot."[64] According to Chinese historian Zhang Cunwu, border markets helped to guarantee agricultural development in Jilin and also increased the revenue of the Chosŏn government. The exchanges through these markets even stimulated early capitalist accumulation in Korea.[65]

The official border markets composed only a small part of the total cross-river trade. There was also a booming smuggling trade triggered by the Qing's enormous demand for Korean products, especially ginseng and sea cucumber. Trade in these products was, in theory, monopolized by the government, but the underground trade was enormously profitable and it could easily evade the law (and even receive secret assistance from corrupt officials).[66]

Compared to smuggling, poaching and logging were more commonly practiced by local residents, especially the Koreans. Unlike smuggling, which aimed at profit, poaching and logging were subsistence efforts. More often than not, those Korean refugees who crossed to the resource-rich north got help rather than caught. The reason, according to the *Pungno Kiryak,* was the long-time interaction between peoples on both banks through official border markets: "People in Hunchun had traveled back and forth to the Kyŏngwŏn market for hundreds of years. [The two sides] could roughly understand the languages and are gradually

[63] Zhang Cunwu, *Qinghan zongfan maoyi 1637–1894* (Taipei: Zhongyang yanjiuyuan jindaishi yanjiusuo, 1978), p. 216.
[64] Hong, "Puksae kiryak," p. 308.
[65] Zhang, *Qing han zongfan maoyi,* pp. 224–227.
[66] Seonmin Kim, "Ginseng and Border Trespassing between Qing China and Choson Korea," *Late Imperial China,* vol. 28, no. 1 (2007), pp. 33–61.

familiar with each other. Therefore, during years of hunger, residents in Kyŏngwŏn often cross the river... When they encountered hunters on the other side, they were comforted by kind words and provided [food] to save them from hunger."[67]

The lack of records makes it difficult to measure the scale of illegal border crossing, but there are indications that it was commonplace and even encouraged by untenable governmental prohibitions and contrasting policies. From 1644 to 1711 dozens of cases led to bilateral negotiations, while from 1729 to 1764 registered cases were as few as twelve.[68] Those numbers have to be considered within the context of the Qing's increasing tolerance towards the Korean stowaways from the eighteenth century onward.[69] Many of these cases were recorded only because they involved felonies such as murder and robbery. As long as the trespassers did not commit violent crimes, the Qing usually let the Chosŏn interrogate them alone, requesting the latter only to report the suggested sentences. In some cases when the Chosŏn court sentenced poachers to immediate capital punishment, the Qing government commuted the sentences to reprieve or exile so as to demonstrate the mercy of the superior state. By the same token, the punishment of local Korean officials for their dereliction of duty was gradually extenuated.[70] These lenient punishments made the prohibition on the border almost impossible to enforce seriously. By the late eighteenth century, border trespassing had become such a daily practice of the Kwanbuk Koreans that local officials did not even bother to report it. The ban, noted the *Pungno Kiryak*, thus "exists only in principle."[71]

Illegal river crossing became so prevalent that eventually even the local Qing government acquiesced to the phenomenon. The office of the vice commander-in-chief of Hunchun in 1881 ordered that Korean refugees be treated in a friendly manner: "[We recently found Korean people who had] sneaked across the border river and went to our villages to exchange goods privately. Though going against the law, those foolish vagrants were forced by poverty... When encountering Korean crossers, you should politely persuade them to return and not bully them."[72]

---

[67] Chŏng, *Pungno Kiryak*, p. 446.
[68] The first number is from Zhang, *Qinghan zongfan maoyi*, p. 252. The second number is from Li Huazi, "17, 18 shiji zhongchao weirao chaoxianren yuejing wenti de jiaoshe," *Hanguoxue lunwenji*, 2004, vol. 13.
[69] This was due largely to the Qing's successful suppression of the "revolt of the three feudatories" in southern China, which made it more confident of its surroundings.
[70] Li, "17, 18 shiji zhongchao weirao chaoxianren yuejing wenti de jiaoshe."
[71] Chŏng, *Pungno Kiryak*, p. 447.
[72] HCFDTYMD, vol. 108.

Border crossing on such a regular basis effectively connected the two sides of the Tumen River and revealed the integrity of the region as an ecological, geographical, and social whole.

Early Negotiations between Qing and Chosŏn

Before the 1860s recorded border trespassing cases were mostly about poaching or logging, but there were occasional reports of Korean squatters cultivating the wildlands of the north. This was the case in both the Yalu and Tumen River regions.[73] Usually caught, squatters were escorted back to Korea and their possessions destroyed. Early squatters took precautions, such as making day trips or working seasonally. In the Tumen area, pioneer squatters were dispersed and farmed on scattered, small, and inconspicuous plots. To avoid being repatriated, some even disguised themselves as Qing by shaving the hair on the front of their heads and changing their dress.[74]

In 1860 a devastating flood engulfed the Kwanbuk region, taking numerous lives and property.[75] The following year saw another flood; two years later the area flooded yet again. In fact, during the 1860s and 1870s the region was battered by natural disasters so persistently that Korean peasants lost not only their homes but their base for survival: land. Thousands of hopeless Koreans crossed the Tumen River, fleeing north to either Manchuria or Russia.[76] Refugees' lives were miserable: in Hunchun desperate Korean peasants would trade their children for only a few dozen liters of rice.[77] During this phase, however, most refugees only begged for food rather than trying to resettle. The majority of them returned home after a while, either voluntarily or forced by the two governments.[78]

---

[73] A detailed record about Korean squatters on the Yalu north bank is *Kangbuk Ilgi*, written by Ch'oe Chong-bŏm. See Kwangmin Kim, "Korean Migration in Nineteenth-Century Manchuria: A Global Theme in Modern Asian History," in Yeh Wen-Hsin, ed., *Mobile Subjects: Boundaries and Identities in the Modern Korean Diaspora* (Berkeley, CA: University of California Press, 2013), pp. 17–37.

[74] Guo Tingyi and Li Yushu, eds., *Qingji zhongrihan guanxi shiliao* (QJZRHGXSL), vol. 2 (Taipei: Zhongyang yanjiuyuan jindaishi yanjiusuo, 1978), pp. 143–148, "The Case of Li Dongji."

[75] *Ilsŏnlok*, Ch'ŏlchong 11-07-24.

[76] A large number of Korean also crossed the other border river – the Yalu – and went to Fengtian.

[77] Wu Luzhen, *Yanji bianwu baogao*, in Li Shutian, ed., *Guangxu dingwei Yanji bianwu baogao; Yanjiting lingtu wenti zhi jiejue* (Changchun: Jilin wenshi chubanshe, 1986), pp. 9–165, 60.

[78] Ibid.

The trend ultimately led to peasants openly squatting on wildlands on the north bank around the same time the Qing opened Jilin for agricultural migration. Local Koreans explained the reason for their squatting in the early 1880s: "In recent years [Qing] hunters and peasants who moved to this place have significantly increased. In our humble opinion, since the area…is unoccupied, it seemed not inappropriate for us in the inferior country to follow them and live here."[79] Illegal cultivation was permitted, even encouraged, by Korean local officials. In 1880, with the endorsement of the commissioner of Hoeryŏng Prefecture, local peasants reclaimed a hundred *shang* of land on the north bank. This project was joined by peasants in the surrounding prefectures in the next spring. Soon a piece of land 500 *li* long and 40–50 *li* wide was broken up for farming.[80]

Hence came the scenario that begins this chapter: Qing official Li Jinyong, who was assigned to survey the wildland in Hunchun, was surprised to find out that the Hamgyŏng government had issued land certificates to the Korean squatters. Receiving Li's report, Ming'an, the Jilin general, and Wu Dacheng, the grand minister supervising the defense affairs of Ningguta, realized that this was a crisis as well as an opportunity. Russia's threat was close and pressing. But, despite substantial efforts to encourage Han Chinese peasants to resettle in Jilin, the area was still too remote and harsh. Since it was hard to repatriate the squatters in such great numbers, Ming'an and Wu Dacheng suggested that, rather than expel them, the Jilin government could put them under Qing jurisdiction. Contradicting the centuries-old border prohibition law, their proposal marked a turning point not only for Qing frontier policy but also for the cross-border relationship.

To justify this policy, the two frontier ministers employed traditional *zongfan* rhetoric and argued that the Koreans were essentially subjects of the Qing. In their joint memorial to Emperor Guangxu (r. 1875– 1908) in late 1881, Ming'an and Wu expressed sympathy for Korean peasants: "[T]hough living on the periphery, they are all like newborn babies to the Celestial Empire. If we followed previous cases to deport them vigorously, we are afraid that thousands of poor people will lose their homes simultaneously, which is truly pitiful." They suggested the emperor allow the Koreans working on reclaimed land to stay and pay taxes and rents to the Jilin government.[81] In March 1882 Ming'an and Wu submitted another memorial asking the emperor "to extend imperial

---

[79] *Kantō ni kansuru Shōjō-gun kyōchō komonjo* (Hansŏng: T'onggambu, 1907).
[80] Sun, *Zhongguo chaoxianzu yimin shi*, p. 125.
[81] Zhu, *Dong hua xu lu*, vol. 44, pp. 14–15.

benevolence (*huang ren*)" to the squatters. The memorial even excused Korean officials for their misbehavior: they did not do it intentionally but simply confused the border river with one of its tributaries, since the local topography was extremely complex and had changed after recent floods. This was followed by their path-breaking policy suggestion:

> As we discussed, those who cultivate the land of the Central Plains (*zhongyuan*) should be regarded as the people of the Central Plains. Other than applying for a land certificate, they have to join our household registration (*bantu*) and enshrine our culture (*zhengjiao*). In addition, they have to switch their style of hat and cloth (*guanfu*) to ours before a set time. But we could follow the [example of] Miao people in Yunnan and Guizhou, and let them keep their customs for now (*zan cong ge bian*)...[82]

Special attention needs to be paid to several key phrases in this short paragraph, so as to understand this memorial's extraordinary political implication. First, the term *zhongyuan* (中原) dilutes Jilin's marginality. Literally meaning "the Central Plains," *zhongyuan* ordinarily functions as a blanket term referring to the mid and lower Yellow River region, which exists in Chinese mythology as the core area of politics and civilization. The imprecise geopolitical and geocultural term contrasts with *bianjiang*: frontier or margin. Only in limited contexts could *zhongyuan* also signify the general realm of *zhongguo* (the Middle Kingdom, or China), as opposed to *waiguo* (foreign or outer states).[83] Manchuria was certainly never recognized as *zhongyuan* by either the Han or the Manchu. However, by employing this rather ambiguous term, these two frontier ministers (Ming'an was a Manchu and Wu a Han) deliberately blurred the nature of the border being crossed, weakening the division between the Middle Kingdom (Qing) and its tributary state (Korea). Shying away from boundary law that emphasizes the segregation of the two countries, the memorial implied that the problem should be resolved through a transcendental political spirit unifying the two peoples of Qing and Korea. As suggested in the first memorial with the phrasing that the Koreans "are all like newborn babies to the Celestial Empire," the two ministers embraced a cosmopolitan value in line with the logic of "all under heaven" (*tianxia*), which sees the Chinese emperor as a superior lord not only to China but also its tributary states.

---

[82] Zhongguo diyi lishi dang'anguan, ed., *Guangxu chao zhupi zouzhe* (GXCZPZZ), vol. 112 (Beijing: Zhonghua shuju, 1996), pp. 242–243.

[83] For more on how the word *zhongguo* was used by Qing rulers, see Zhao Gang, "Reinventing China: Imperial Qing Ideology and the Rise of Modern Chinese National Identity in the Early Twentieth Century," *Modern China*, vol. 32, no. 1 (2006), pp. 3–30.

The second term, *bantu* ("household registration"), represents a conceptual structure that highlights the unity of two basic elements of state: territory and population. The term is hard to render precisely in English. In modern Chinese it simply means "territory," yet in classical Chinese the term is a compound word composed of two characters. *Ban* (版) refers to the household register and *tu* (圖) to the map of farmland. In an agrarian society, the state relied on the household and farmland registration system to assign tax and labor duties, so as to enforce its authority. In late imperial China, the word *bantu* signified the fulfillment of state domination. As described in *The Draft History of Qing*, "[A] state's domain is called '*bantu*': '*ban*' indicates it has people, while '*tu*' indicates it has land."[84] For Ming'an and Wu Dacheng, expelling the squatters would waste the land and thus amount to inefficient rule. By incorporating them into Qing registers, the frontier wildland would be consolidated as a source of state power. Given that Qing's Jilin was by no means a typical agrarian society, the *bantu* as Ming'an and Wu used it expressed more than just a rhetorical stance but perhaps a new vision of the frontier that departed from the conventional view of Jilin as merely "a land of archery and riding."

The term *zhengjiao*, a combination of "politics" (*zheng*, 政) and "education" (*jiao*, 教), raised questions of cultural affiliation as a badge of imperial identity. To frontier ministers, geographic borders cannot distinguish "us" from "them." Instead, a more substantial boundary should be drawn by "culture." Cultural affiliation defines who "we" are. The question is, what did "culture" indicate here? Didn't Chosŏn, a country strictly ruled by neo-Confucian doctrines, always "enshrine our *zhengjiao*," to the extent that Korean culture was more similar to that of China than many of the frontiers under the Qing's rule (such as Tibet, Mongolia, Xinjiang, and the southwest)? The Korean literati certainly regarded themselves as culturally more "Chinese" than the Chinese who submitted to the Manchu rule.

The answer could be found in the next line, containing the term "style of hat and cloth," or *guanfu* (冠服). In this context, it was an indirect reference to the rule that males shave the front of their heads, braid their hair in a queue, and wear Manchu-style clothes. Compulsory hair shaving was a power play targeting mainly ethnic Han during the entire Qing period. Refusal to adopt such a hairdo suggested revolt. Yet the "hair or head" policy was never intended to reach to other ethnic frontier regions or subordinate states such as Chosŏn or Annam (Vietnam). In Chosŏn,

---

[84] Zhao Erxun, *Qing shi gao*, vol. 283 (Beijing: Zhonghua shu ju, 1977), p. 10186.

though maintaining the apparel of the Chinese Ming dynasty symbolized ongoing Korean loyalty to the Middle Kingdom, hair shaving, no matter the circumstances, was seen as barbarization. Documents show that some Korean poachers, despite having their sentences commuted by the Qing, were still beheaded by their own government precisely because they disguised their identity by shaving their hair.[85] For both the Qing and Chosŏn, hair and dress style was more than just a cultural symbol. It represented a distinct political message of control.

However, Ming'an and Wu did not expect to apply the hair-shaving policy immediately. Instead, they proposed to follow "the example of the Miao people (*Miao ren*) in Yunnan and Guizhou." But the difference between ruling Koreans in Jilin and extending imperial control into the Miao realm in southwest China is quite obvious. The latter combined military conquest, cultural assimilation, and, most important, the abolishment of the native chieftain institution (called *tusi*) and reestablishment of civil bureaucracy (*gaitu guiliu*).[86] Besides, the Miao people, who had lived in their realm for centuries but never formed their own state, were by no means comparable to the Koreans, who had only recently traveled from their home state into unsettled land. So what on earth did it mean to "comply with" the Miao case?

The next clause, *zan cong ge bian*, "let them keep their customs for now" (or literally "let them do whatever is convenient"), reveals the answer. The wording is closely associated with one of the Qing's most critical pieces of statecraft when interiorizing its ethnic frontiers, namely "ruling with local customs" (*yin su er zhi*, 因俗而治). As many historians point out, "ruling with local customs" has two mutually dependent aspects in the local practices in Qing's Miao realm. On the one hand, the state allowed local legal and social norms to be used in carrying out local affairs. On the other, the state, by emphasizing the superior authority of state law, indicated that this practice was merely an expedient way, or a transitive stage, towards ultimate political integration.[87] By raising *zan cong ge bian* and the Miao case, the Qing officials were insinuating a

---

[85] Li, "17, 18 shiji zhongchao weirao chaoxianren yuejing wenti de jiaoshe."

[86] Studies on the southwest frontier are many. For example, see Donald S. Sutton, "Violence and Ethnicity on a Qing Colonial Frontier: Customary and Statutory Law in the Eighteenth-Century Miao Pale," *Modern Asian Studies*, vol. 37, no. 1 (2003), pp. 41–80; "Ethnic Revolt in the Qing Empire: The 'Miao Uprising' of 1795–1797 Reexamined," *Asia Major 3rd Series*, vol. 16, no. 2 (2003), pp. 105–152; John Herman, *Amid the Clouds and Mist: China's Colonization of Guizhou, 1200–1700* (Cambridge, MA: Harvard University Press, 2007); Laura Hostetler, *Qing Colonial Enterprise: Ethnography and Cartography in Early Modern China* (Chicago: University of Chicago Press, 2001).

[87] Huang Guoxin, "'Miaoli': Qing wangchao Hunan xinkai miaojiang diqu de falu zhidu anpai yu yunzuo shijian," *Qingshi yanjiu*, vol. 8, no. 3 (2011), pp. 37–47.

model for the future reformation of Jilin, or perhaps even Manchuria in general. Despite the dramatic distinctions between the southwest and the northeast, the ministers clearly had a frontier-building agenda that went far beyond Jilin: the development of Jilin would be part of an empire-wide enterprise of borderland integration.

Beijing approved their suggestion with positive expectations. The eleven-year-old Emperor Guangxu, under the instruction of assisting ministers, wrote an encouraging comment on their memorial. In childish handwriting, it reads:

> The Korean poor occupied and cultivated wildlands in Jilin. Seen from the perspective of frontier officials, there of course is a division between "us" and "them" (*bi ci zhi fen*). But seen from the perspective of the imperial court, there is no difference between China and foreign (*zhong wai zhi bie*)... No need to set excessive regulations.

Coming from the emperor's mouth, the expression "no difference between China and foreign" was even more radical than the ministers' vision that "those who cultivate the land of *zhongyuan* should be regarded as the people of *zhongyuan*." Although he endorsed the strategy of removing the geographical boundary between peoples, the emperor simultaneously stressed the security of territory. "[We can] forgive innocent civilians who cultivate land and behave themselves," he said, "but we must also expel those who take advantage [of our tolerance] and usurp our frontier. Let [the officials] do it prudently."[88] The court then ordered the frontier ministers to census the Korean population and to register them under the jurisdiction of Hunchun and the newly founded Dunhua County. At the same time it notified the Chosŏn government of the decision and reiterated the ban on the border.

Yet the Chosŏn court objected. The State Council (Ŭijŏngbu) reported to King Kojong that "China does not expel our people due to its policy of mollification (*hoeyu*)...yet how can the principle of law be violated?"[89] In his memorial to the Qing's Board of Rites, Kojong employed the same *zongfan* rhetoric, only to emphasize the hierarchical order between his country and the Qing: "The relation of my inferior state to your Celestial Kingdom is like a family consisting of the center and the outer. In essence [the Chosŏn is] almost like a domestic subordinate [to the Qing]. The border of the superior and the inferior is the natural defense of the Tumen River." He blamed those "foolish people in my inferior state" for "violating the border ban," but, since the two countries had

---

[88] GXCZPZZ, vol. 112, p. 243.
[89] *Chosŏnwangjo sillok. Kojong sillok*, 19-08-11.

different customs, "it will be really problematic if they cause troubles." The king insisted the border ban be rigorously implemented so that "the borderland residents in my inferior state will never cross the boundary."[90] Upon his request, the Qing revised the previous decision and ordered the local officials to repatriate all the Korean squatters in one year.

In 1883, as the deadline approached, both governments made arrangements in accordance. The Qing Magistrate of Dunhua County issued a note in spring to the Chosŏn prefects in Hoeryŏng and Kyŏngsŏng, asking them to recruit all the Koreans back in autumn. Around the same time the Chosŏn court appointed Ŏ Yun-jung, a grant minister who at the time was negotiating trade treaties with the Qing, as the commissioner who would supervise repatriation.

However, when Ŏ arrived, local Koreans approached him, begging to stay. They submitted to Ŏ a number of written complaints, demonstrating historical, geographic, and political justifications for their border trespassing. The geographic descriptions in these complaints were not consistent,[91] yet they generally argued three main points. First, located further north was a "division river" (K. Pungyegang, 分界江) that was determined by the demarcation stele erected by the Qing official Mukedeng in 1712. Second, the wilderness between this "division river" and the Tumen (K. Tuman, 豆滿) River was a forbidden zone where neither the Qing nor the Chosŏn people were allowed to enter. Third, in recent years more and more Qing people had penetrated the forbidden zone to hunt or cultivate; the hungry Koreans were lured to the area to do the same. In this way local Koreans challenged the Tuman's status as the border and insisted that the real border was further north. On top of that, they also employed the *zongfan* framework and Confucian rhetoric, arguing that, since they were also subjects of the (Qing) emperor, it would be a great virtue if the Qing government permitted them to stay: "*The Book of Poetry* says: '*Under the wide heaven, all is the king's land; within the sea-bounds of the land, all are the king's servants.*' [...] Our country enshrines the imperial calendar and titles, and embraces the imperial authority. In that sense we are the emperor's servants and our lives depend on his land."[92]

---

[90] QJZRHGXSL, p. 973.

[91] For example, some argue that the "division river" was the T'omun (土門) River, which was a northern tributary of the Tuman River. Some argue it was actually the Hontong (混同) River (an upper tributary of the Sungari River), with T'omun and Tuman just different names for the same river. See *Kantō ni kansuru Shōjō-gun kyōchō komonjo*. The texts were compiled by the Japanese Resident-General of Korea in 1907.

[92] QJZRHGXSL. The sentence from *The Book of Poetry* is quoted from J. Legge's translation.

Ŏ Yun-jung was surprised to learn that there was a "division river" other than the Tuman. Under local Koreans' guidance, he dispatched an assistant to investigate the demarcation stele and bring back the rubbing. Convinced by both the complaints and the rubbing, Ŏ asked the officials of Hoeryŏng and Chongsŏng to reply to their Qing counterpart, explaining that the whole "squatting" issue was due to Qing officials' confusion of the two rivers, one called T'omun (C. Tŭmen, 土門), the other Tuman (C. Túmen, 圖們 in China and 豆滿 in Korea). The T'omun/Tŭmen was the real boundary river, whereas the Tuman/Túmen, which the Koreans had crossed, was but a Korean domestic river. The land between these two rivers was Korean territory previously set up by the Chosŏn government as a forbidden zone: "[Our two countries] are always divided by the T'omun River. My country knows that other than the Tuman River, there is a tributary called T'omun."[93] From their description, it seemed that what they called the T'omun River was what the Chinese called the Hailan River (海蘭河), a smaller river flowing into one of the northern tributaries of the Tumen/Tuman, the Burhatong (Ma. *Burhatu*) River, which joins the main stream in the lower course near Onsŏng.[94]

In the next two years more Koreans were encouraged to move to the north side of the Tuman River, which caused a series of conflicts over land reclamation between the Han and Korean settlers.[95] Local officials on both sides urged their governments to clarify the boundary. Back in Hansŏng (Seoul), King Kojong changed his previous stance. In June 1885 he submitted a note to the Qing suggesting a joint demarcation, observing "that land indeed belongs to my inferior state; the people in my inferior country live on the land of my inferior country; nothing seems wrong."[96] In response, Qing's Zongli yamen, an institution in charge of foreign affairs, entrusted the Jilin general with solving the issue. At this juncture, a problem with people – how to settle the Korean refugees – turned into a dispute over territory.

East Asia in Crisis, Tumen in a Nexus

The Sino-Korean border dispute has never just been about the border per se, nor merely a bilateral conflict or any other dyadic tension. Rather, it was a local manifestation of the overall sociopolitical transitions in the

---

[93] Ibid., pp. 1910–1913.
[94] Again, their view represented just one of several versions of the "T'omun River" that emerged in the late Chosŏn era. For detailed discussion, see Chapter 2.
[95] QJZRHGXSL, pp. 1913–1918.
[96] Ibid., pp. 1898–1899.

Northeast part of the Eurasian Continent. Being a gateway of human interactions in East Asia for a long time, Northeast Eurasia (the Tumen River region included) was one of the most dynamic sources of regional competition, particularly in the late nineteenth century.[97] The following section thus places the Qing–Korean border dispute within a structure of multilateral and multilayered local history. It argues that what happened in the border region proceeded under the joint influence of each variant in historical logic that prevails in the surrounding entities, while at the same time leveraging its own effect on the whole network of interactions. The local is organically woven into a multileveled power nexus composed of multiple cores and peripheries of politics, economy, and culture. Thus, to understand the history of a particular locale we need to consider its position in this complex nexus, which links various agencies with their own motives and actions.

Internal Crises: Border Problem, People Problem

To illustrate this view of the dynamics of the local, let us first look at the example of the Qing–Chosŏn ginseng trade and examine how such a small commodity contributed to the bilateral boundary making. Ginseng was the most critical and profitable commodity within Qing–Chosŏn trade. It was also a major cause of illegal border crossing. As early as the eighteenth century the price of ginseng in the Qing market had already reached ten times that of gold and 156 that of silver.[98] In the nineteenth century the demand for Korean ginseng (specifically a steamed and dried form called red ginseng) continued to grow, partly because people believed it was a cure for opium addiction. As demand increased, ginseng poaching and smuggling became rampant, and Beijing and Hansŏng rigorously enforced the border prohibition as a way to enhance the state monopoly. For Chosŏn, taxes on ginseng production and trade were an important state revenue in addition to agriculture. Income from ginseng funded new governmental projects, such as building a Western-style army, and paying for diplomatic expenditures.[99]

---

[97] Nianshen Song, "Centralising the 'Far East': Historical Dynamic of Northeast Eurasia," in Jing Huang and Alexander Korolev, eds., *The Political Economy of Pacific Russia: Regional Developments in East Asia* (London: Palgrave Macmillan, 2016), pp. 53–76.

[98] Zhang, *Qinghan zongfan maoyi*, p. 224. He also provides a hypothesis of a Korean interpreter in the mission to the Qing who sold ginseng in Beijing, bringing back white silk to sell in Seoul. According to his calculation, such a business trip could earn him a profit as high as 75 percent.

[99] Ibid., pp. 231–232.

As I will address in detail later in this chapter, a certain capitalist impulse mingled with an imperialist impulse to "open" Korea led the Qing and Chosŏn to soften previous regulations in their bilateral trade relationship, which eventually led the two governments to transform the regulated border market into comprehensive "free" trade. The boundary was redefined accordingly: instead of strictly regulating the flows of people and money, the governments allowed merchants to go back and forth at any time while still prohibiting permanent resettlement. Serving as the background of the bilateral demarcation, ginseng smuggling was never an isolated phenomenon in the two countries' borderlands. Rather, it concerned a new form of linkage between frontiers and hinterlands, and past and present.

By the same token, the issue of "vagrants" (C. *liumin*) in Jilin should also be put into the larger context of social transition. The vagrant problem was closely associated with a dual trend observed in both the Qing and Chosŏn. On the one hand, there was the accelerated pressure of domestic overpopulation; on the other, the decline of government capacity to oversee the mobility of the population. In China, this dual trend threatened Qing's control over the Jilin frontier in at least three ways. First, large numbers of peasants in overpopulated north China migrated to less populated Jilin, breaking down the prohibition policy. Second, as part of the empire-wide corruption of the banner system, government manors and banner farms in Jilin were privatized and commercialized. Many wildlands were illegally cultivated even by banner men themselves. Third, rebellions occurred one after another. Local banner troops in Jilin were often transferred to other places to suppress or prevent rebellions, making the defense system in Jilin vulnerable. For example, during the Taiping Rebellion (1851–1864), the government transferred 400 out of 500-odd banner soldiers from Hunchun, but only about 40 of them eventually returned.[100] Some remnants of the rebellion, after being suppressed, fled to Jilin and became bandits. All these troubles, to say nothing of the consistent external threat of Russian expansion, forced the Qing to alter the policy against immigration in Jilin to one of "consolidating frontiers by migration" (C. *yi min shi bian*). Around the same time the new policy was pursued not just in Manchuria but in almost all Qing's borderlands, including Mongolia, Xinjiang, and the southwest provinces.

In Korea, the reform launched by the regent, the Taewŏn'gun, aggravated notoriously factious politics, which severely undermined the state's ability to counter external threats. When it came to exploiting the

---

[100] Yanbian chaoxianzu zizhizhou dang'anguan, ed., *Hunchun fudutong yanjiting gaikuang* (1983), p. 97.

peasants, however, the Taewŏn'gun and his political opponents were on the same page. As James Palais argues, with their high concentration of arable land, Korean peasants were severely deprived by "a regressive land tax, administrative corruption, and usury."[101] In the Kwanbuk region, although land tax was somewhat lower than elsewhere, the burden of the grain loan (a usury in the form of the government reserve) was much heavier than that in more developed regions in the south. Extreme poverty pushed the Koreans to cross the Tumen River, with two temptations beyond the boundary. First, in order to solidify its control over the newly established Primorskaya Oblast (Maritime Region), Russia started to recruit Korean settlers to come to the area. Second, in response to that, the Qing gradually opened Jilin for cultivation. The flood of "vagrants" (both Han Chinese and Koreans) in Jilin, then, was the result of a chain reaction to a series of internal and external pressures that linked up at least three capitals and three frontiers: Beijing–Hansŏng–St. Petersburg and Jilin–Kwanbuk–Primorsky.

External Crisis: Russia and Japan

Internal crises often entangled with external menaces; they worked together and interacted as both cause and effect. One of the most notable themes of mid-nineteenth-century East Asia was the intensive conflicts between expansionary capitalist/imperialist powers and recessive states. Those conflicts marked the gradual marginalization of East Asia in the long development of the capitalist system. The coming of imperialist gunboats profoundly affected almost every aspect of the political, social, and economic ecologies at the eastern end of the Eurasian continent. Among all the external threats, Russia and Japan were perhaps the most salient.

Tsarist Russia had challenged the Qing Empire by expanding into Siberia and Outer Manchuria as early as the mid-seventeenth century. But it was not until the mid-nineteenth century that Russia extended its influence to the Tumen River region. Having been defeated in the Crimean War (1853–1856), Russia had to turn east to expand its gain in the "Great Game" with Britain. In 1858 Russia successfully forced the Qing to sign the Treaty of Aihui by threatening a war against the latter, who had already been badly battered by both the Taiping Rebellion and the Second Opium War. In 1860 Russia, along with the British Empire and France, compelled the Qing to concede to the Convention

---

[101] James B. Palais, *Politics and Policy in Traditional Korea* (Cambridge, MA: Harvard University Press, 1975), p. 67.

of Beijing. According to these two treaties, the traditional Russo-Qing boundary defined by the Treaty of Nerchinsk in 1689 was abolished. The new Russian border extended all the way to the Ussuri River and the outlet of the Tumen River. The vast territory of Outer Manchuria, a million square kilometers of land ranging from present-day south Khabarovsk Krai, the Jewish Autonomous Oblast, the Amur Oblast, to the Primorsky Krai, now officially belonged to Russia.[102] For the first time in history, Russia became neighbor to both China and Korea. Occupying just 15 kilometers from the very end of the Tumen River, Russia emerged as a new player in the Tumen region. It blocked Manchuria's channel to the Sea of Japan, turning Jilin into an inner land frontier. From the perspective of geopolitics, the Tumen, which connects the interior of the Manchuria–Korean region with the Pacific Ocean, became a strategic intersection of East and West, a linchpin of the global imperialist/colonist competition.[103]

To cement its control over Primorskaya Oblast, Russia encouraged domestic and foreign immigration, providing new settlers with material support.[104] Starting in 1863, the Hamgyŏng Koreans were repeatedly found relocating to Primorsky, with the number ranging from dozens to over a thousand. Since the two countries were connected only by a short section of the Tumen outlet, most Korean immigrants found it more convenient to enter Russia through Jilin.[105] The situation alarmed the Qing and Chosŏn for several reasons. For one, many Koreans on their way to Russia ended up resettling in Jilin. By occupying wild land or wandering in villages as beggars, these Koreans posed a threat to the government's control over local societies. Then, too, so many Koreans went across the boundaries so often that they caused multilateral diplomatic problems. In the 1860s and 1870s Chosŏn repeatedly requested the Qing to communicate with Russia, urging Russia to repatriate the refugees to Korea. Russia refused, on the grounds that it did not have a diplomatic relationship with Chosŏn, neither should an issue related to Chosŏn be handled by the Qing.[106] Along with this came the problem of local bandits, who crossed borders to rob new settlements. Suspects

---

[102] The Qing also lost its claimed sovereignty of Sakhalin Island.

[103] John J. Stephan, *The Russian Far East: A History* (Stanford, CA: Stanford University Press, 1994).

[104] Alexander Lukin, "Russian Views of Korea, China, and the Regional Order in Northeast Asia," in Charles K. Armstrong, Gilbert Rozman, Samuel S. Kim, and Stephen Kotkin, eds., *Korea at the Center: Dynamics of Regionalism in Northeast Asia* (New York: M. E. Sharpe, 2006), pp. 15–34.

[105] QJZRHGXSL, vol. 2, p. 9.

[106] Ibid., pp. 251–252, 256–257.

(mainly Chinese or Korean vagrants) disguised their identities or naturalized as Russian citizens in order to seek extraterritorial protection.[107] Finally, there was a larger geostrategic concern. Along the Qing–Russian boundary in Central Asia, Russia kept penetrating into the Qing's northwest borderland, especially in the Muslim frontier of Xinjiang.[108] In the view of the Qing, by recruiting and granting protection to Korean settlers, Russia not only further sabotaged the Qing's frontier security (as it had done in Xinjiang) but also shook Qing authority over its most loyal subordinate by extending its influence into the peninsula.

Faced with the Russian threat, the Qing ordered Hunchun officials to rigorously monitor the Qing–Korean border and stop Koreans from going to Russia through Qing territory. At the same time, it asked the Chosŏn to recall those who had resettled in Primorskaya. If Korean vagrants were found in Jilin, Qing officials would contact their Chosŏn counterparts to extradite them, sometimes even loaning them travel expenses.[109] In 1881 the Qing court appointed Wu Dacheng, a competent Han literati, as a high-ranking minister in charge of frontier affairs in the Ningguta region. The position was temporarily established to assist the Jilin general to consolidate defense in the Jilin–Russian borderland. One of Wu's most important policies was to recruit Han peasants to cultivate the Jilin wildland in the border region. The Qing court ultimately took the advice of Wu and other officials to open the Jilin borderland for reclamation. Only in this context can we comprehend Ming'an and Wu's proposal to register Korean squatters as Qing subjects. Behind the frontier ministers' carefully crafted *zongfan* rhetoric, Qing's first and foremost concern was Russian incursions, not Korean trespassers.

Pressure from St. Petersburg alarmed not only the Qing and Chosŏn but also Japan. As early as the late eighteenth century Russian explorers in the Far East had made their first contact with the Japanese via the Matsumae clan. Control over Sakhalin Island (C. Kuye; J. Karafuto) served as a longstanding point of controversy. In May 1875 the two states signed the Treaty of St. Petersburg, in which Japan gave up its territorial claim to Sakhalin. In exchange, Russia recognized Japan's ownership over

---

[107] Detailed discussion on the Russo-Korean boundary and identity issues can be found in Alyssa Park, "Borderland Beyond: Korean Migrants and the Creation of a Modern State Boundary between Korea and Russia, 1860–1937," Ph.D. dissertation, Columbia University, 2009.

[108] David Schimmelpenninck van der Oye, "Russian Foreign Policy: 1815–1917," in Dominic Lieven, ed., *Cambridge History of Russia*, vol. 2: *Imperial Russia, 1689–1917* (Cambridge: Cambridge University Press, 2006), pp. 554–574; David Brophy, *Uyghur Nation: Reform and Revolution on the Russia–China Frontier* (Cambridge, MA: Harvard University Press, 2016).

[109] QJZRHGXSL, p. 173.

all the Kuril Islands up to the Kamchatka Peninsula. This also marked the initiation of the yet unsolved Russo-Japanese territorial dispute over the Kuril Islands.

In 1876, less than a year after signing the Treaty of St. Petersburg, Japan forced Chosŏn to sign its first unequal treaty: the Treaty of Kanghwa. Opening its ports and yielding its extraterritoriality, the treaty dragged Chosŏn into a global capitalist/imperialist system. It marked Japan's further expansion in East Asia, following the announced annexation of the Ryukyu Kingdom and the invasion of Taiwan in previous years. The first article of the treaty defines Chosŏn as an "independent state that enjoys the same sovereign rights as does Japan."[110] For Japan, the article denied hundreds of years of Qing–Chosŏn *zongfan* connection, replacing this hierarchical order with new interstate principles of "independence" and "sovereign rights." In other words, Japan denied Chosŏn as a subordinate state of the Qing.

Controlling the Korean Peninsula had been a long-held ambition for some nineteenth-century Japanese elites. In 1873 a famous debate occurred in Tokyo about whether to invade Korea. Saigō Takamori, a leading figure of the Meiji Restoration, advocated the invasion in order to transfer the problem of unemployed ex-samurai and force Korea to "open" to Japan. His opponents, however, believed Japan was still too weak to sustain the potential Western interventions invited by the invasion.[111] The "debate over conquering Korea (*seikanron*)" was, in a way, reconciled with the Treaty of Kanghwa three years later. This exposed the fact that there had been no dispute among the Meiji politicians on whether to expand Japanese power to the continent, just disagreements on when to do it and how.

Japan's penetration into Korea further aggravated the factious politics of the Chosŏn court and trapped the weak government in consistent turmoil. There were successive *coups d'état* in 1882 (the Imo munity) and 1884 (the Kapsin coup). Both revealed the increasing and irreconcilable conflict between the factions supported by Japan and those who tried to resist. The 1882 Imo munity led to the Japan–Korea Treaty of Chemulpo, in which Chosŏn agreed to pay a large sum of compensation and granted Japan the right to station troops in Hansŏng. The 1884 Kapsin coup, in which Japanese soldiers directly confronted the Qing-stationed troops led by Yuan Shikai, had a more critical outcome: the Qing–Japanese Convention of Tianjin. Although the convention required both countries

---

[110] Henry Chung, ed., *Korean Treaties* (New York: H. S. Nichols, 1919), p. 205.
[111] Herbert E. Norman, *Japan's Emergence as a Modern State: Political and Economic Problems of the Meiji Period*, 60th anniversary edn. (Vancouver: UBC Press, 2000).

to withdraw troops from the peninsula, it acknowledged that Japan henceforth had the same right as the Qing to intervene in Korea militarily. Perhaps it is not an exaggeration to say that the Convention of Tianjin made Chosŏn a de facto dual subordinate of both the Qing and Japan.

By the time the Qing–Chosŏn frontier dispute appeared on the horizon, the Tumen River region (or overall Manchuria) had already become an arena for several powers old and new. Local competition was profoundly impacted by contests in other parts of the countries as well as other parts of the globe. That the Qing–Chosŏn border dispute occurred in this place and at this moment was not so much a coincidence as a result of the reciprocity of all the internal and external crises.

Challenges to Qing–Korean Relations: Bilateral and Multilateral

Finally, let us examine the Tumen boundary dispute through the lens of the Qing–Chosŏn bilateral relationship and its evolution in the 1880s. The traditional Qing–Chosŏn *zongfan* hierarchy was conducted with a pair of dualist principles: for the Chosŏn, "serving the great" (K. *sadae*); and, for the Qing, "cherishing the inferior" (C. *zixiao*). The two, in an ideal model, construct a dynamic balance that regulates the mutual rights and obligations in a patriarchal system. Many current scholars, adopting international law as the universal norm of state-to-state relations, tend to denounce the *zongfan* structure as an "abnormal" international relationship. Some deny it existed on any substantial level, insisting the *zongfan* principles were merely ritualistic and symbolic gestures generated by China's centralist delusion. Others reduce it to a coercive power relation that China forced upon its surrounding countries.[112] Yet modernist international theory itself, as James Hevia argues, is a hegemonic discourse rooted in a specific historical context.[113] It creates an artificial boundary in dividing the Oriental past from the "universal modern" and ignores the complexity and flexibility of the *zongfan* hierarchy. It also neglects the fact that such a structure, like other state-to-state orders, was mutually constructed rather than unilaterally imposed.[114]

With the global expansion of the imperialist international system, the Qing–Chosŏn *zongfan* hierarchy faced unprecedented challenges. That Chosŏn claimed itself to be both autonomous and a subordinate regime

---

[112] Scholars of Korean history, for example, often emphasize the *sadea* aspect in the Sino-Korean relationship, while leaving out the corresponding aspect of *zixiao*.

[113] James Hevia, *Cherishing Men from Afar: Qing Guest Ritual and the Macartney Embassy of 1793* (Durham, NC: Duke University Press, 1995), p. 27.

[114] Nianshen Song, "'Tributary' from a Multilateral and Multi-Layered Perspective," *Chinese Journal of International Politics*, vol. 5, no. 2 (2012), pp. 155–182.

to the Qing – yet neither a dependent of nor an equal partner with the latter – presented a dilemma that bitterly puzzled Euro-American powers that were eager to exploit the Korean market. Chosŏn leaders consistently rejected requests for diplomacy and trade by redirecting those requests to the Qing. But both Qing and Chosŏn gradually realized that the *zongfan* hierarchy could no longer remain indifferent to the wave of imperialist intrusion. It needed to change, either to be reformed by the Qing and Chosŏn themselves or to be twisted by external forces (as Japan did in 1876). The enormous gap between Chosŏn's deep-seated distrust of the capitalist powers and those powers' untamable desire to "open" Korea provided the Qing an opportunity to intervene in Chosŏn's foreign and domestic politics. The Imo mutiny and Kapsin coup required just such an intervention to suppress unrest. Soon the Qing tightened its control by appointing a young officer, Yuan Shikai, as the Qing imperial resident of Hansŏng, taking charge of customs and army training, and granting extraterritoriality to Qing subjects in Korea. If at any moment in history China acted, in Western words, as a "suzerain" to Korea, the stretch of several years after the two coups was probably that moment.

Qing's reactions to the Korean coups, some scholars would argue, indicated China's imperialist aggression and a huge rupture in the history of the bilateral relationship.[115] But, from another perspective, they could also be seen as the continuation of the conventional relationship. After all, the Chosŏn government twice sought help from the Qing and requested military intervention. The alteration of Qing's Chosŏn policy, from non-intervention to direct intervention, marked not so much a change to the *zongfan* principle as its adaptation. Sending troops to Chosŏn in the name of "protecting the subordinate" (*baohu shuguo*) might be seen as the fulfillment of the superior lord's historical obligation. Although Qing troops had not set foot in Korea since 1638, the action was reminiscent of the precedent set in the 1590s, when Ming China helped Chosŏn defend against the Japanese invasion launched by Toyotomi Hideyoshi.

Yet significant changes did happen within the hierarchy. The most remarkable was that both countries added multilateral diplomatic principles to their bilateral *zongfan* framework. From the 1870s onward the Qing and Chosŏn initiated some unprecedented institutional changes in the face of Western and Japanese pressures on Korea. On the Qing

---

[115] See Kirk W. Larsen, *Tradition, Treaties, and Trade: Qing Imperialism and Chosŏn Korea, 1850–1910* (Cambridge, MA: Harvard University Press, 2008). Also see Okamoto Takashi, *Zokkoku to jishu no aida: Kindai Shin-Kan kankei to Higashi Ajia no meiun* (Nagoya: Nagoya Daigaku Shuppankai, 2004).

side, the duty of bilateral affairs, once monopolized by the Board of Rites, was substantially reassigned to the newly established "diplomatic" institutions. While the ceremonial exchanges, such as paying tribute and bestowing titles, remained under the supervision of the board, the agency responsible for other affairs – trade and boundary issues included – switched to the Zongli yamen, a government body equivalent to the Office of Foreign Affairs. In this way, the Qing–Chosŏn relationship was partially included in the Qing's overall "diplomatic" terrain.[116]

On the Chosŏn side, the Office of State Affairs (T'ongni kimu amun) was set up in 1880, which was revised to the Foreign Office (T'ongni kyosop t'ongsang amun) in 1883. Within the amun, "Serving the Great" (Sadae) and "Neighborly Relations" (Kyorin) were two departments (sa) dealing with China and Japan, respectively. Out of all twelve departments of the amun, only these two were set up for specific states. In other words, both the Qing and Chosŏn made efforts to relocate the bilateral zongfan hierarchy in a general multilateral network, while cautiously maintaining its distinctiveness within such a network. Some scholars have described the phenomenon as "one diplomacy, two systems."[117] As Key-Hium Kim puts it: "The 'long twilight' of the Chinese tribute system gave the existing world order in East Asia a dualistic character that was partly Eastern and partly Western, partly traditional and partly modern."[118]

Just as Japan had debated about conquering Korea, a few Qing officials in the 1870s and 1880s deliberated the "Chosŏn strategy."[119] Although the debates differed in many ways, both shared the anxiety of losing Korea. In the Qing's case, officials agreed that it was in the best interest of the Qing to strengthen the geopolitical alliance with Chosŏn so as to protect the barrier of China's eastern frontier. Li Hongzhang, the most powerful figure in Qing diplomacy, advocated a relationship with Chosŏn that would build diplomatic ties with Western countries in order to counter the colonial ambitions of both Russia and Japan. Through Li's mediation and even direct intervention, Chosŏn negotiated its diplomatic relations with the United States in 1882. Before the two countries signed the United States–Korea Treaty as equal partners, the

---

[116] Wang Yuanchong, *Remaking the Chinese Empire: Manchu–Korean Relations, 1616–1911* (Ithaca, NY: Cornell University Press, forthcoming).

[117] Quan Hexiu, "Wanqing duiwai guanxi zhong de 'yige waijiao liangzhong tizhi' xianxiang chuyi," *Zhongguo bianjiang shidi yanjiu*, vol. 19, no. 4 (2009), pp. 70–83.

[118] Key-Hium Kim, *The Last Phase of the East Asian World Order: Korea, Japan, and the Chinese Empire, 1860–1882* (Berkeley, CA: University of California Press, 1980), pp. 328–329.

[119] These officials, including Huang Zunxian, He Ruzhang, and Zhang Jian, among others, proposed various policies towards Korea, the most radical one (by Zhang Jian) suggesting turning Korea into a Chinese province.

Chosŏn was instructed to issue a note to the United States, saying: "The Chosŏn has long been a *shubang* (country subordinate) to China, yet both her internal government and her foreign intercourse have always been autonomous... With regard to all the duties which must be performed by Chosŏn because the latter is subordinate to China, the United States shall have absolutely no concern with any part [of such duties]."[120]

As an evidence of the Qing's superior authority, Chosŏn had to use the Qing calendar (using the reign year of the Qing emperor) in all its official correspondence with the United States. This was a key form of *sadae* called "enshrining the orthodox calendar" (C. *feng zheng shuo*). Taking the United States–Chosŏn relationship as the model, the Qing went on to move Chosŏn into diplomatic relationships with Britain and Germany in 1883, with Italy and Russia in 1884, and with France in 1886. The core question for the Qing was how to refashion the Qing–Chosŏn hierarchy in accordance with Western diplomatic discourse, so as to protect it from being completely destroyed by the latter. The solution was to make the Chosŏn–Western "equal" relations parallel to the Chosŏn–Qing hierarchical relations, and to confirm this parallel by international treaties and diplomatic documents. The hybrid nature of the bilateral connection was vividly expressed by a letter that Yuan Shikai submitted to King Kojong in 1886: "The Chosŏn rules the country and takes care of the people by itself. She establishes treaties and diplomatic relations with other countries. In so doing she is indeed autonomous – only under the supervision [*shou xia*, 受轄] of China."[121]

The Chosŏn was by no means a passive recipient of this transformation. In 1882 King Kojong proposed enlarging trade relations with the Qing by modifying existing regulations on bilateral trade and lifting the prohibitions on maritime traffic. Included in his proposal was a request to set up a residential envoy to Beijing. Skillfully employing *zongfan* rhetoric, his request nevertheless exposed Chosŏn's attempt to reconstruct the hierarchy along the lines of Western-style diplomacy. Kojong explained that he specifically made these proposals because "nowadays many changes occur in the world and the situation alters daily... We should not constrain ourselves with old regulations."[122] The Qing did not miss the subtle implication embedded in the submissive wording. For the Qing, expanding bilateral trade might well arrest Russian and Japanese aggression, but exchanging residential envoys suggested some

---

[120] The translation is quoted, with a little revision, from M. Frederick Nelson, *Korea and the Old Orders in Eastern Asia* (New York: Russell & Russell, 1967), pp. 147–149.
[121] *Chosŏnwangjosillok, Kojong sillok*, 23-07-29.
[122] QJZRHGXSL, vol. 2, p. 596.

sort of "diplomatic equality." Beijing thus approved Kojong's request to open trade but firmly rejected that of residential envoys. The king soon submitted an apologetic memorial to withdraw the suggestion of envoys. But the decision to replenish commercial relations still marked a historic evolution in the conventional *zongfan* interaction. It was an important adjustment initiated by Chosŏn and the Qing to reassure themselves, in such a turbulent situation, of their best interests within the existing framework.

In October 1882, two months after the Qing sent troops to suppress the Imo munity in Korea, the two countries signed the Regulations for Maritime and Overland Trade between Chinese and Korean Merchants (C. *zhongchao shangmin shuilu maoyi zhangcheng*), the first of three bilateral trade agreements in the 1880s. The preface to the Regulations clearly emphasized that Chosŏn was a *shubang* (subordinate state) so that the regulations were applied exclusively between a "suzerain" and a "vassal": "The new regulations now decided upon are understood as a preferential treatment applying to China's vassal only, and other nations are not to participate therein."[123] Analyzing the eight articles of the Regulations in detail, Hamashita Takeshi believes they showed that the Qing attempted "to make the existing tribute trade consistent with the forms of treaty port trade."[124] It is possible to see this attempt from two perspectives. On the discursive level, the two countries reassured each other that the bilateral hierarchy was the absolute precondition of the trade relation, whereas, on the practical level, they made treaty port trade independent of the existing tribute trade. This also revealed the self-adjustment of the hierarchy: the Qing–Chosŏn relationship acquired an organic equilibrium between the principle of bilateral connection (*zongfan*) and the principle of multilateral interactions (treaty system).

The new institution soon had its local echoes. In the next year two additional local treaties were negotiated and signed by Ŏ Yun-jung (the Korean minister also assigned to cope with the squatter issue) and his Qing counterparts. These two treaties regulated Korean trade with Shengjing and Jilin and replaced the 230-year-old official border market

---

[123] The translation of the text is revised from *Treaties, Conventions, etc. between China and Foreign States* (Shanghai: Statistical Department of the Inspectorate General of Customs, 1917). The title of the treaty is originally translated as "Regulations for Maritime and Overland Trade between Chinese and Korean Subjects."

[124] Hamashita Takeshi, "Tribute and Treaties: Maritime Asia and Treaty Port Networks in the Era of Negotiation, 1800–1900," in Giovanni Arrighi, Hamashita Takeshi, and Mark Selden, eds., *The Resurgence of East Asia: 500, 150 and 50 Year Perspectives* (London: Routledge Curzon, 2003), pp. 17–50.

with "free trade."[125] Both treaties, following the Regulations for Maritime and Overland Trade, emphasized the exclusiveness of such a commercial privilege: the Qing–Chosŏn hierarchical rites had to be strictly obeyed. The general norms of the bilateral trade defined in the 1882 Regulations were refined and applied to local conditions. Some elements of the previous border markets remained and were reframed. For example, new customs houses were set up near the old border markets to supervise the trade. In Jilin a Commercial Bureau (*shangwu zongju*), with a branch and a checkpoint, were set up in Helongyu, Xibujiang, and Guangjiyu, which were on the opposite bank of Hoeryŏng, Kyŏngwŏn, and Chongsŏn. In certain areas locally produced cloth was permitted to remain as the currency, since silver and copper money had not begun circulating. And, in all three treaties, the critical role of a certain commodity was highlighted: while other goods were taxed at 5 percent, red ginseng alone was taxed at 15 percent.[126]

The free cross-border trade brought two outcomes. The first was the accelerated economic integration of the Northeast Asian region, a process that Hamashita believes was triggered by neither a "tribute principle" nor a "treaty principle," but by a "regional principle" that "sought to encompass core–periphery trading activities."[127] It is possible to perceive the Tumen River as more of an "internal" channel connecting the Manchurian–Korean markets than an absolute division of the two societies. On the other hand, by emphasizing the exclusiveness of the trade reciprocity, the Qing and Chosŏn also drew a new boundary between "us" and "them," so as to reject outside forces encroaching on their economic and political affairs.

The second outcome, closely related to the first, was the intensive concern over the Tumen and Yalu boundaries. In all three trade regulations, both countries reconfirmed that the Yalu and the Tumen Rivers made up the Sino-Korean border, and they reiterated the persistence of a border ban. Yet some Qing officials still worried that the free flow of population would have negative consequence. During the negotiations, the Shengjing general, Chongyi, and the Fengtian prefect, Songlin, co-submitted a memorial expressing their concerns about border security. They warned that Russia and Japan might take advantage of Chosŏn's

---

[125] The two treaties are the Regulations for Border Trade between Fengtian and Korean People (*Fengtian Chaoxian bianmin jiaoyi zhangcheng*) and the Local Regulations for Free Trade between Jilin and Korean Merchants (*Jilin Chaoxian shangmin suishi maoyi difang zhangcheng*).

[126] The texts of all three treaties can be found in many anthologies. I use Quan Hexiu, ed., *Jindai zhonghan guanxi shiliao xuanbian* (Beijing: Shijie zhishi chubanshe, 2008).

[127] Hamashita, "Tribute and Treaties," p. 42.

trade privilege and intrude into Manchuria through the peninsula. "Mt. Changbai is vital to the fate of our state... We have to prepare in advance."[128] Emperor Guangxu agreed: Chosŏn, he said, was more critical than other subordinate states, such as Ryukyu and Vietnam, and the border should be cautiously monitored to prevent "evil-doers" (*jian ren*) from sneaking in.[129]

At the very moment when the Korean squatters became a source of political dispute between the Qing and Chosŏn, then, the frontier space was experiencing a tremendous conceptual and practical reconstruction. The impulse of this reconstruction loomed in the background of both the interior evolution of and exterior menaces to East Asian society. The Tumen River served not merely as a state border for the Qing Empire but as a dual symbol of imperial inclusiveness (in allowing the Korean squatters to stay and encouraging bilateral trade) and exclusiveness (in fending off Russia and Japan). To understand the further complications of the Qing's strategic consideration on the Manchurian borderland, we may turn to another imperial comment responding to Wu Dacheng's proposal to opening Jilin. Written in June 1882, three months after the approval to recruit Korean squatters for farming, the emperor reminded the frontier minister:

Jilin is a land of military importance. The top priority [on that land] is hunting, the second is grazing, whereas agriculture should be the last. There are two shortcomings for cultivation: first, it would make a great number of vagrants congregate here and [turn Jilin into] a hotbed for fugitives; second, if all efforts contributed to agriculture, I am afraid [the local Manchus] will lose their tradition of riding and archery. These two things should be considered profoundly.[130]

Blending as it does Manchu ideology with the concerns of realpolitik, this comment, along with others above, manifested the multilayered political-ritual significance of the Manchurian frontier. The governance and vision of this borderland were consistently reconstructed by various pressures, and by transborder agencies involving at least three interacting spatial layers: domestic, bilateral, and multilateral. On the domestic level, population pressure in Korea and China escalated the competition for resources. It stimulated the exploration of frontiers, challenging internal geographic, social, ethnic, and political boundaries imposed by the states. On the bilateral level, the Qing and Chosŏn were struggling to maintain and reform the *zongfan* hierarchy that had existed for several centuries. The attempt to include the Korean squatters in Qing's administration

---

[128] GXCZPZZ, vol. 112, p. 249.
[129] Ibid., p. 250.
[130] Ibid., vol. 92, p. 555.

demonstrated such an effort. However, on the multilateral/global level, the coming of gunboat diplomacy questioned and undermined the *zongfan* order, urging Qing and Chosŏn to refashion the traditional connection with new institutions. This was the time that, in East Asia and on a global scale, frontiers and boundaries were being defined and redefined by colonial expansion and capitalist intrusion. A new diplomatic and trade system required states to clarify and reinforce the distinctiveness of their realms and populations. In 1881, the year of the snake, the Tumen River region was about to become a knot within a sophisticated nexus composed of multilateral and multilayered power interactions. It transcended the division of cores from peripheries and of one country from another. At that moment no one would have expected the squatter problem to eventually push China and Korea to revisit their overall understanding of people and land in the following decades.

2 Dynastic Geography
Demarcation as Rhetoric

In September 1885 Yi Chung-ha, the prefect of Ambŏng in Hamgyŏng, received an edict from Hansŏng. He was appointed as Chosŏn's leading delegate on a boundary survey. Together with the Qing delegates, he would have to investigate the border region to figure out where the "T'omun border" was. Upon his departure, the middle-aged official wrote a poem to record his complicated feelings:

> From five-colored clouds descended the king's noble decree,
> In the ninth month of the year I will go to the northern frontier.
> For three centuries, the border has been difficult to discern,
> Two thousand *ri* afar the custom is hardly the same.
> So anxious I am for I lack the talent for this negotiation, yet
> So enormous is the king's grace that he entrusts me with the mission.
> With this task in mind, all night I could not sleep,
> Till dawn's horn came from east, urging me to leave.[1]

Yi had every reason to feel anxious. For one, he was not a native and had assumed his job in Hamgyŏng only recently. He had never been to this northeast province before this job, much less to the Tuman borderland, a remote frontier where, as he said, "the custom is hardly the same." But a lack of familiarity with the local situation was not the hardest part. What was more daunting was the task of settling a territorial dispute with the Qing, a superior state to Chosŏn. "Finding out the old boundary," as the job described, was essentially a demarcation. But, although doing so depended on a solid understanding of local geography and history, it was not a geographical or historical issue but first and foremost a political one.

From 1885 to 1887 Yi and his Qing counterparts conducted two rounds of demarcations on the Tumen/Tuman River boundary. Eventually, despite two years of careful investigations and intensive debates, they failed

---

[1] Yi Chung-ha, "Ŭlyu kuwŏl pungmyŏng pal t'omun kamgyejihaeng," in Yi Chung-ha, *Iadang chip* (Seoul: Yi Hŭng-jong, 1975).

to reach a final agreement. Further attempts were first postponed, then suspended, until Japan reignited the controversy in the 1900s. This chapter examines the Qing–Chosŏn negotiation through the lens of the history of ideas. It explores how geographic knowledge and power structures (both domestic and inter-state) shaped each other in the Tumen region in the 1880s. Borrowing a Foucauldian perspective, I analyze the representations of the region in conventional geographical works in China and Korea, a tradition I call "dynastic geography." I pay more attention to the rhetoric, rather than textual evidences, the two contested parties employed. Such rhetoric involved not only language but also technology. Specifically, I ask what cartographic method was used – or not used – to make the demarcation map, and what its political indication was. To further understand the intellectual significance of the Qing–Chosŏn demarcation, I contextualize it in a broader geopolitical backdrop and compare it with two other demarcations: that of the Qing–Russian border and the Qing–Vietnamese border, conducted around the same time. In so doing I show how diverse ideas of "boundary" were produced out of these boundary-making practices in imperial East Asia. Finally, I introduce the careers of two local officials: Yi Chung-ha of Chosŏn and Wu Dacheng of the Qing. How did they understand boundaries, frontiers, and states? How can we interpret their frontier-building efforts in the long trajectories of the national and state transitions in late imperial Korea and China?

Geographic Knowledge before the Demarcations

Studies of terrain and rivers – and the human activities associated with them – have a long tradition in both China and Korea. Compiled in 111 AD, the *Hanshu* (*History of the Former Han Dynasty*) for the first time categorized *dili*, what would be called "geography" in modern English, as one of the treatises (*zhi*) in official Chinese history. Following the Chinese example, the first official history of Korea, the *Samguk sagi* (*History of the Three Kingdoms*, compiled in 1145), also listed *chiri* (C. *dili*) as one of its treatises. However, unlike the contemporary discipline of geography, which emphasizes space rather than time, traditional geographical studies in China, known as *yu di xue* (studies about earth), focus predominantly on the development and evolution of the natural and human conditions in a given space. Therefore, *yu di xue* was categorized as a subfield of history in the traditional "Four Categories of Literature" (*si bu*, i.e., Confucian classics, histories, philosophies, and anthologies of poetry and other belles-lettres). Historical records rather than field research played a critical role in producing the *yu di xue* knowledge.[2] For that reason, Gu Jiegang, one of the most prominent Chinese historians of the twentieth century, interpreted *yu di xue* as "evolutional geography" (*yange dili*).[3] The term is widely accepted and seen as the predecessor of the contemporary discipline of historical geography in China.[4]

However, intimacy with history was just one feature of conventional geography in East Asia. In both China and Korea, geographic studies had a distinctive function: to collect information for administrative purpose. Such information included the evolution of government, local terrain, history, products, customs, architecture, celebrities, statistics regarding arable land and population, and ancient relics. Producing historical knowledge of a geographic space, whether in official histories or local gazetteers, was above all a way to regulate contemporary political recognition. Moreover, such knowledge, sometimes mixed with astronomy and geomancy (*fengshui*) and woven into a sophisticated nexus of imperial cosmology, presented spatial evidence for the legitimacy of the regime.

Here I adopt the term "dynastic geography" to refer to the traditional geographical studies in Confucian East Asia.[5] Although it emphasizes the political significance of spatial recognition, the term is nevertheless different from "political geography" as used by Western geographers, notably Friedrich Ratzel and Halford Mackinder. Political geography studies how a certain political outcome is determined by its spatial environment. Dynastic geography, by contrast, is closer to what Foucault describes as "an administration of knowledge, a politics of knowledge, relations of power," presenting itself as "forms of domination designated by such notions as field, region and territory."[6] That said, while Foucault uses geographic conceptions to indicate the form and strategy of what he calls "governmentality," dynastic geography itself is the product of Confucian

---

[2] Tan Qixiang, *Chang shui cui bian* (Shijiazhuang: Hebei jiaoyu chubanshe, 2000), "Preface," pp. 2–3. Also see Gu Jiegang, *Dangdai zhongguo shixue* (Shanghai: Shanghai guji chubanshe, 2006), p. 18. The geographic knowledge produced in imperial China included maps. Richard Smith mentions: "'History' was an especially prominent value in Chinese maps…time and space remained closely connected." See Richard J. Smith, *Mapping China and Managing the World: Culture, Cartography and Cosmology in Late Imperial Times* (New York: Routledge, 2013), p. 52.

[3] In 1934 Gu Jiegang and Tan Qixiang founded *Yu Gong*, the first journal devoted to classic geographic studies. The English title of the journal was first "The Evolution of Chinese Historical Geography," then changed to "The Chinese Historical Geography."

[4] Hou Renzhi, *Lishi dili xue si lun* (Beijing: Zhongguo keji chubanshe, 1991), pp. 126–140.

[5] Tang Xiaofeng, *From Dynastic Geography to Historical Geography: A Change in Perspective towards the Geographical Past of China* (Beijing: Commercial Press International, 2000).

[6] Michel Foucault, "Questions on Geography," trans. Colin Gordon, in Jeremy W. Crampton and Stuart Elden, eds., *Space, Knowledge and Power: Foucault and Geography* (Aldershot, UK: Ashgate, 2007), pp. 173–182, 177.

political ideals and practices. It in turn strengthened political recognition and led to political actions.

Dynastic geography, like any geographic knowledge, intertwines spatial discourse, imagination, and reality. It goes without saying that the reality of a space and the interpretation of it never match precisely. Yet they are mutually constructed. For example, according to *Yu Gong*, China's earliest and arguably most important geographic canon, a prehistorical sage king, Yu the Great, divided his domain into nine administrative regions (*zhou*) during his legendary flood-taming trips. Hence, the Nine Zhou notion bears a strong implication of legitimate rulership over the Middle Kingdom. Gu Jiegang argues that the Nine Zhou concept, which emerged no earlier than the Warring State period (475–221 BC), reflected an idealized geo-administrative arrangement of a unified state. Although based on "real terrain," the Nine Zhou remained as an imagined political blueprint for centuries. It had never been institutionalized until as late as 213 AD.[7] After that, most of the names of these nine regions persisted to the present day.[8] Praising *Yu Gong* as "the most scientific record" of ancient Chinese geography,[9] Gu nevertheless remarks that the Nine Zhou concept "seemed real but was actually fictitious, [yet later] turned from fiction to reality."[10]

With its indication of political legitimacy, the Nine Zhou notion spread beyond ancient China. When Silla terminated the Three Kingdoms period and unified the Korean Peninsula (668 AD), it borrowed the Nine Zhou institution from China and established nine *ju* – exactly three *ju* in each of the former three kingdoms. Once again, a fiction turned itself into reality.

The interactions of imagination and reality create serious challenges in studying historical geography in East Asia. The main reason, as Tan Qixiang and Gu Jiegang put it in 1934, is that, "as natural terrain changed, so did administrative divisions… In many instances one name referred to different things; in many other cases different names referred to one thing."[11] In other words, both text and nature could be the source of problems.

The Tumen River region was an apparent example of such interaction and slippage between text, imagination, and natural contour. Unlike the hinterlands, which attracted the most scholarly attention,

---

[7] Gu Jiegang, "Yu Gong," in Hou Renzhi, eds., *Zhongguo gudai dili mingzhu xuandu*, vol. 1 (Beijing: Xueyuan chubanshe, 2005), p. 3.
[8] Tang, *From Dynastic Geography to Historical Geography*, p. 25.
[9] Gu, "Yu Gong," p. 1.
[10] Ibid., p. 3.
[11] Tan Qixiang and Gu Jiegang, "Fa kan ci," *Yu Gong*, vol. 1 (1934), p. 2.

the northeastern borderlands of the two countries were marginalized economically and intellectually. Rarely was detailed geographical study generated about this wild frontier. Since historical text, poor in quality though it often was, was a more accessible and legitimate source of knowledge than field surveys, most records about this region ended up as mixtures of half-myth and hearsay. To add to the problem, any inconsistent or mistaken records or transcriptions, or a trivial misreading of an unfamiliar text, would cause great confusion. This was in part because the writing system was shared by the Korean and Chinese. The Korean name of a subject, all written in Chinese characters, could be different from the Chinese name of the same subject. The dispute over whether the Tuman (written as 豆満 in the Korean records) and the Tumen (圖們 or 土門 in the Chinese records) were the same river illustrates this problem. Sometimes a name written in the same characters meant different things. For example, the name 長白山, which literally means "Mt. Long White," was frequently seen in both Qing and Chosŏn gazetteers. In Chinese records (pronounced as *Changbai shan*) it refers to the highest mountain in the Manchuria/Korea area, the one the Koreans call *Paektu san* (Mt. White Head.) However, in Chosŏn gazetteers "Mt. Long White" (pronounced as *Changbaek san*) refers to another mountain, south of the *Paektu san*. Only occasionally did the Korean documents also use 長白 山 to refer to Mt. Paektu. Inconsistency of this kind had caused serious troubles for ages.[12]

The dynamics and volatility of the border region also made earlier geographic records hardly comprehensive, let alone entirely reliable. Over time tribes migrated, topographical marks changed, and towns and garrisons relocated. For instance, between the early and late fifteenth century the locations of the Jurchen tribe led by Möngke Temür and the border garrisons of Hoeryŏng were recorded quite inconsistently in the *Annals of the Chosŏn Dynasty* due to the gradual northward extension of the Chosŏn territory and the retreat of the Jurchen.[13] Nokt'undo, a small island of approximately 32 square kilometers originally located at the estuary of the Tumen River, exemplifies the challenge of topographic changes. It had been Korean territory since the late fifteenth century. But, with constant changes in the canal and sand sediment, the island gradually adjoined the north shore and eventually became part of the

---

[12] An example is the dispute between the Ming and Koryŏ about 鐵嶺 (C. Tieling; K. Ch'ŏllyŏng). See Li Huazi, "Mingchu yu chaoxian zhijian tieling shewei zhizheng," *Hanguoxue lunwenji*, vol. 16 (Shenyang: Liaoning minzu chubanshe, 2007).

[13] Wang Dongfang, "Guanyu Mingdai zhongchao bianjie xingcheng de yanjiu," *Zhongguo bianjiang shidi yanjiu*, no. 3 (1997), pp. 54–62.

Qing side of the riverbank. When Russia forced the Qing to yield the territory of Outer Manchuria, including 15 kilometers of the Tumen River estuary, in 1860, former Nokt'undo Island was transferred to Russia altogether. Yet Korean settlers kept living on it until the 1930s.[14] Today, activists in South Korea still claim that Russia had no right to take over this part of the territory.

The Korean squatter problem alerted Qing officials to the sophisticated local topography. In Wu Dacheng and Ming'an's 1881 memorial, the frontier ministers even attributed the problem partially to the evolution of local terrain:

[Along the Tumen River] are mountains and bifurcated roads. There are also clusters of rivers and waters, most of which do not have names. Some of them bear similarities with the main stream of the Tumen River... To the north of the land where the Koreans are now farming is a tributary river [of the Tumen]. The bank of this river has been washed wider and wider in recent years. Since the land on its south bank was largely washed away while new land emerged on its north bank, the Korean poor thus confused this tributary river with the main stream...[15]

Geographic awareness of the Tumen River region, especially upstream, where Mt. Changbai/Paektu is located, was associated with dynastic legitimacy in both the Qing and Chosŏn. During the boundary negotiations in the 1880s delegates from both countries frequently alluded to this place as "the land of the rising dragon" to justify their territorial claims. Precisely because it was so prominent in historical-geographic consciousness, it is useful to trace such rhetoric back to when each of the two regimes first produced it and examine how it evolved over time.

Mt. Changbai and the Tumen River of the Qing

Historical memories created by the Manchus, such as those recorded in the *Annals of Manchu* (C. *Manzhou shilu*; Ma. *Manju i yargiyan kooli*), the *Researches on Manchu Origins* (C. *Manzhou yuanliu kao*), imperial documents, and privately composed family genealogies, claimed almost unanimously that the Manchu originated at Mt. Changbai. This claim attempted to cement the Manchu founding myth and to promote Manchu identity. According to the myth, the first ancestor

---

[14] See Kim Kyŏng-ch'un, "Tumangang Hanyuŭi KOREA IRREDENTA e tae ilgo," *Paeksan Hakpo*, nos. 30/31 (1985), pp. 167–214. For media reports, see *Dong-A Ilbo*, "Urittang Urihun yŏngt'obunjaeng hyŏnjangŭl kada (10) Ichhyŏjin sŏm Nokt'undo," June 10, 2004, http://news.donga.com/3//20040610/8070989/1.

[15] GXCZPZZ, vol. 112, p. 242.

of the Aisin Gioro clan, Bukūri Yongšon, was born to a fairy who conceived him by swallowing a red fruit brought to her by a divine magpie as she was bathing in the Bulhuri Lake beside the Bukuri Mountain, east of "Mt. Changbai."[16] The precise locations of the Bulhuri and the Bukuri, however, were not clear in early Qing (and remain controversial).[17] Since the majority of the Manchu moved to interior China after the conquest, knowledge of the Manchu birthplace became increasingly vague. In 1677, only 33 years after his father had taken over Beijing, Emperor Kangxi (r. 1661–1722) issued an edict lamenting that "Mt. Changbai is the place where Our ancestors were originally from, yet now no one has reliable knowledge about it."[18] Therefore, he assigned a team of Manchu officials led by Gioro Umuna to survey Manchuria and identify Mt. Changbai. Upon receiving Umuna's impressive report, Kangxi was convinced that the sublime volcano in Jilin was indeed Changbai the sacred ancestral mountain. He ordered an imperial worship ceremony, following the same protocol applied to the Five Sacred Mountains (C. *wuyue*) in interior China. But whether this Changbai was the one referred in Manchu myth is, according to some scholars, debatable.[19]

The 1677 survey marked the beginning of a series of geographic surveys on the Manchurian frontier during Kangxi's reign. As Mark Elliott points out, these missions later led to a great volume of imperial literature that "testifies to the enduring place of the mountains and the importance of the Manchurian landscape in the collective imagination." Through these efforts, Manchuria in general, and Mt. Changbai in particular, "gradually came to be a symbol of Manchu identity."[20]

Aside from creating the dynastic identity, these missions were directly connected to two other imperial enterprises. The first was the Qing's military strategy in response to the Russian expansion in the northern Manchurian frontier. The second was Emperor Kangxi's ambition to use

---

[16] *Manzhou shilu* (Liaohai shuju, 1934), vol. 1, p. 2; *Qin ding manzhou yuanliu kao*, vol. 1, "Manchu." See also Elliott, *The Manchu Way: The Eight Banners and Ethnic Identity in Late Imperial China* (Stanford, CA: Stanford University Press, 2001), pp. 45–46.

[17] While some scholars, notably Liu Jianfeng, insist the lake was Yuanchi near Mt. Changbai, some others believe it was in today's Xinbin county, Heilongjiang province. See Liu Jianfeng, "Changbaishan ji," in Li Tingyu, ed., *Changbai si zhong* (Taipei: Tailian guofeng chubanshe, 1969), p. 7; Wada Sei, *Tōa shi kenkyū: Manshū hen* (Tokyo: Tōyō Bunko, 1955), p. 380.

[18] *Qing shi lu, shengzu shilu*, Kangxi 16-09.

[19] See Ding Yizhuang and Hu Hongbao, "Cong zupu bianzuan kan manzu de minzu rentong," *Minzu yanjiu*, no. 6 (2001), pp. 58–65.

[20] Elliott, "The Limits of Tartary," p. 614.

longitude/latitude cartography to map the whole empire.[21] Mukedeng's survey of the Qing–Korean borderland was part of this mapping enterprise.[22] During this mission (as mentioned in the Introduction), a stele was erected on the south side of Mt. Changbai to mark, erroneously, the "origin" of the two rivers.

Through several survey missions and worship ceremonies, Mt. Changbai gained a supreme position in the Qing's geographic rhetoric. Kangxi himself was the main creator of the new discourse. Not only did he go on tour to Shengjing and Ningguta several times and make sacrifices at ancestral tombs and mountain, he also produced quite a few writings to promulgate the centrality and gravity of Mt. Changbai in the whole imperial landscape.[23] A particularly interesting episode was a discussion on geography between the emperor and his most competent Han minister, Li Guangdi, in 1709. Kangxi asked the minister whether he knew the topographical origin of the mountains in Shandong province. Li answered, "Probably from Shaanxi or Henan," the hinterland of the Central Plains. Kangxi rejected his answer and said the mountains in Shandong, especially Mt. Tai, actually originated from Mt. Changbai.[24] To elaborate his point, the emperor even issued an essay on geography/geomancy, his main argument straightforwardly expressed by its title: *Mt. Tai Originates from Mt. Changbai.* The political implications of this argument were only too obvious: Mt. Tai, the top of the Five Sacred Mountains in dynastic geography in China, was the symbol of imperial authority. Ever since the Qin dynasty (221–207 BC) the state ceremony of worshiping Mt. Tai had become an indispensable ritual to demonstrate the legitimacy of the regime. In Kangxi's eyes, however, Mt. Tai and Mt. Changbai, located on the Shandong Peninsula and in southern Manchuria, respectively, were connected to each other through the mountain ranges and the Bohai Sea in between. They make up the body of a dragon lying across land and ocean, with Mt. Changbai as the dragon's head and Mt. Tai

---

[21] Perdue, "Boundaries, Maps, and Movement."

[22] Kangxi said that he had assigned capable individuals to measure distances on earth in accordance with "the degree of the sky," so that all mountains and rivers in the northeast were clearly indicated on the map. The Yalu and Tumen Rivers comprised the border with Chosŏn, yet only the spot between these two rivers was unclear. So he dispatched Mukedeng to secretly investigate the border. See *Qing shi lu, shengzu shilu,* Kangxi 50-04.

[23] Stephen Whiteman, "Kangxi's Auspicious Empire: Rhetorics of Geographic Integration in the Early Qing," in Jeff Kyong-McClain and Yongtao Du, eds., *Chinese History in Geographical Perspective* (Lanham, MD: Lexington Books, 2013), pp. 33–54.

[24] *Qing shi lu, shengzu shilu,* 48-11.

the tail.[25] The political connotation was only too clear: the Manchu, like any other "Sons of Heaven," were legitimate rulers of China.

The official Qing documents regarded the Tumen River as one of the three major rivers that originated from Mt. Changbai (with the Yalu and the Huntong/Sungari Rivers being the other two). But the Tumen was written inconsistently as either "Túmen" (圖們) or "Tǔmen" (土門). *The Veritable Records of Kangxi* (*Kangxi shi lu*, compiled in 1731), the *Comprehensive Examination of Literature of the Qing* (*Huangchao wenxian tongkao*, 1787), *The Collected Institutes of the Qing* (*Qinding Da Qing hui dian*, 1787), and the *Comprehensive Institutions of the Royal Dynasty* (*Huangchao tong dian*, 1787) adopted the name "Tǔmen" (土門), whereas *Researches on Manchu Origins* (*Manzhou yuanliu kao*, 1777), the *Comprehensive Record of Shengjing* (*Qinding Shengjing tong zhi*, 1779), and the *Unified Atlas of the Great Qing* (*Qinding Da Qing yi tong zhi*, finalized in 1842) mentioned that the river was once written as "Tongmen" (統門) but was now regulated as "Túmen" (圖們). Almost all documents treated the different terms as multiple transliterations of a single pronunciation. A minor confusion is found in the 1842 edition of the *Unified Atlas of the Great Qing*: aside from an entry for "the Túmen River" in the volume on Jilin, there was a separate entry for "the Tǔmen River" in the volume on Chosŏn.[26] Nevertheless, judging from the context, the two entries are indeed talking about the same border river. This error might have come from the fact that the compilers of this 560–volume dynastic geographic magnum opus, which had been constantly revised in a span of 156 years, failed to thoroughly cross-examine diverse sources (including perhaps the Korean sources) collected in different times.

In most of the Qing geographical documents, the entries for the Tumen River were short and simple. They described the river as flowing northeastward from Mt. Changbai and serving as the northern border of Chosŏn. One exception was *Shui dao ti gang*, a comprehensive study on the Qing's major river systems compiled by Qi Zhaonan in 1761. The entry for the "Tǔmen River" (土門江) not only elaborates painstaking details of the stream's turns, the tributaries, and the towns on the two shores but also provides the longitude and latitude degrees of its

---

[25] Whiteman, "Kangxi's Auspicious Empire"; Jiang Tiesheng and Lü Jixiang, "Kangxi 'Taishan shanmai zi Changbaishan lai' yiwen de lishixue jiedu," *Shehui kexue zhanxian*, no. 6 (2008), pp. 140–146.

[26] See *Qinding Da Qing yi tong zhi*, 1842, "Jilin," vol. 45, pp. 18–19, and "Chosŏn," vol. 421, p. 28. All the literatures mentioned here were from Qinding siku quanshu (Wenyuange).

estuary.[27] Obviously, Qi consulted the *Kangxi Atlas* made by the Jesuits in the early eighteenth century.

Mt. Paektu and the Tuman River of the Chosŏn

In the early Chosŏn period, when the Yi regime had not yet gained solid control over the land south of the Tumen River, Mt. Paektu (i.e., Mt. Changbai) was not regarded as a Korean mountain by dynastic geographers. In the "Treaties of Geography" of the *Annals of Sejong (Sejong Sillok)*, the earliest geographical document of the Chosŏn dynasty, there was very little record of Mt. Paektu, only mention of mountain ridges that originated from it.[28] During Munjong's reign (1450–1452) an official named Chŏng An-jong lectured the king about the geomancy of Korea: "All the mountains and rivers in our country originate from Mt. Paektu, [like] a main vein and its dispersed capillaries."[29] In 1667 King Hyŏnjong (r. 1659–1675) asked a minister whether Mt. Paektu was "our place." The official, Min Chŏng-jung, insisted that "the place is a barbarian land" (*hoji*, 胡地). Yet the chief state councilor, Hong Myŏng-ha, added: "Mt. Paektu is indeed in the barbarian place, yet it is the progenitor of the mountains and rivers of our country."[30] The dialogue reflected a nuanced understanding of Mt. Paektu: it was not considered a Chosŏn mountain, yet from the perspective of geography and geomancy it was regarded as an essential figure of Korean topography.

Kangxi's geographic surveys, especially Mukedeng's demarcation mission in 1712, spurred Chosŏn to redefine the position of Mt. Paektu and the northern frontier in its dynastic landscape and ideology.[31] Chosŏn officials who escorted Mukedeng made him believe that both the Yalu and Tuman originated in the summit. As a result, Mukedeng erected a demarcation stele to the south of Paektu's peak. In this way the Chosŏn successfully expanded its border to the Mt. Paektu region, a realm it had previously never governed.[32] But decades later the Korean literati

---

[27] Qi Zhaonan, *Shui dao ti gang*, vol. 26, pp. 3–6, Qinding siku quanshu (Wenyuange), 1761.

[28] "Chiri chi, Hamgil-do," in *Chosŏnwangjo sillok, Sejong Sillok*, vol. 155.

[29] *Munjong sillok*, vol. 7, Munjong 01-04-14.

[30] *Sŭngjŏngwŏn ilgi*, vol. 204, Hyŏnjong 8-10-03.

[31] Song, "Imagined Territory"; Kang Sŏk-hwa, "Chosŏn hugi Paektusan e taehan insig ŭi pyŏnhwa," *Chosŏn sidae sa hakpo*, vol. 56 (2011), pp. 195–224; Li Huazi, "Chaoxian wangchao de Changbaishan renshi," *Zhongguo bianjiang shidi yanjiu*, vol. 17, no. 2 (2007), pp. 126–135.

[32] See Park Sung-soon, "Hanch'ŏngan kando yŏngyukwŏn punjaenŭi yŏksajŏk chŏngaewa chŏnmang," *Tongyanghak*, vol. 56 (2014), 73–101; Yang and Sun, *Zhongchao bianjie shi*, pp. 184–197; Chen Hui, *Mukedeng bei wenti yanjiu* (Beijing: Zhongyang bianyi chubanshe, 2011), pp. 97–141.

criticized this mission. In the wake of a new Korean identity nourished by long-time cultural hostility towards the Manchu, nostalgia for the Manchurian land (once occupied by the ancient kingdoms of Koguryŏ and Parhae) started to emerge. Scholars such as Sin Kyŏng-jun and Yi Jung-hwi condemned the Chosŏn escort-commissioners for not climbing to the summit together with Mukedeng. The demarcation stele, they said, made Korea lose its "old territory" even as it actually extended Chosŏn's border. Still, other scholars, Yi Ik and Chŏng Yag-yong, saw the demarcation as a final move marking the eventual integration of a Korean world, which was now "as perfect as a golden cup."[33] In any case, the 1712 mission aroused a new wave of dynastic geographical study in Korea, leading to vibrant debates, interpretations, and visions of Korea's place in the world, past and present.

Following the Chinese ritual, the Chosŏn court conducted sacrifice ceremonies to worship the Four Sacred Mountains (*saak*) in its realm. But, for more than 370 years after the founding of the dynasty, Mt. Paektu had been excluded from this strictly regulated ritual.[34] During King Yŏngjo's reign (1724–1776) there was an initiative to include Mt. Paektu in the ceremonies, which led to intensive debates that lasted over six years from 1761 to 1767. Many ministers were hesitant to change the state ritual code. Some opponents argued that Mt. Paektu was beyond the Chosŏn realm, so worshipping it was against the Confucian doctrine that "a prince can (only) worship mountains and rivers within his estate." Supporters, notably King Yŏngjo himself and the grand minister, Han Ing mo, came up with a new theory. They insisted that the northern territory was "the foundation of royal ancestry," and Mt. Paektu was "the birthplace of our dynasty." During the last debate, in 1767, the king urged his opponents to read *Yongbi ŏch'ŏn ga* (*Songs of the Dragons Flying to Heaven*), a dynastic foundation epic and the first poetry written in the Korean alphabet compiled in Sejong's period. A line in the epic says that Mokcho Yi An-sa, the great-great-grandfather of the founding king Yi Sŏng-gye, had lived in Kyŏnghŭng. This, according to Yŏngjo, "proves clearly that Mt. Paektu is a mountain of our country." He continued: "Even if

---

[33] The "golden cup," in classical Chinese, is a metaphor for an integrated territory. See Yi Ik, *Sŏngho sasŏl* (Seoul: Kyŏnghŭi Ch'ulp'ansa, 1967), p. 57; Chŏng Yag-yong, "Kangyŏkko," in *Chŏng Tasan chŏnsŏ* (Seoul: Munhŏn P'yŏnch'an Wiwŏnhoe, 1960), p. 927; Moon Soon-sil, "Hakutōsan teikaihi to juhasseiki Chōsen no Kyōikikan," in Chōsenshi Kenkyūkai, ed., *Chōsen Shi Kenkyūkai ronbunshū*, vol. 40 (Tokyo: Rykuin Shobō, 2002), pp. 39–66.

[34] Kwon Nae-hyun, "Changes in the Perception of Baekdusan during the Late Period of Joseon," *Review of Korean Studies*, vol. 13, no. 4 (2010), pp. 73–103.

[Mt. Paektu] is not in the realm of our country, since worshipping it meets the [Confucian] doctrine of 'requiting and following one's ancestors,' we should still conduct a ceremony from afar. Let alone, it is in our country."[35]

Eventually Yŏngjo, eager to win the argument to strengthen his monarchical power against the fractional politics of the ministers, prevailed. The mountain was identified as the new Northern Sacred Mountain (*pukak*), replacing the former *pukak*, Mt. Pibaek (鼻白山), a mountain north to the birthplace of Yi Sŏng-gye. Starting in 1768, ninety-one years after Emperor Kangxi added the same mountain to the Qing's imperial rite, the Chosŏn state also worshipped it. Thus, Mt. Changbai/Paektu became a sacred mountain of, and enjoyed sacrifices from, both the Qing empire and its subordinate kingdom. More importantly for Chosŏn, it showed that Mt. Paektu, in political terms, was now officially a "Korean mountain." It was now ranked as a significant coordinate in the Korean landscape.

With the new passion for rediscovering Korean geography in the eighteenth century, the 1712 Mukedeng mission was noted down in numerous official documents and gazetteers. Yet, even as geographic theses became increasingly popular among the literati, few authors actually went to the sites to study the local topography. Most of them relied solely on historical records or hearsay, passing on second-hand knowledge. As a result, some basic facts about the Mukedeng demarcation were overlooked, such as the precise locations of the Tumen headwater and the direction of the mound and wooden barriers. Korean authors had long known that the barriers were there, yet few knew where exactly they were. This same confusion surrounded the Tumen/Tuman River: some documents explained that Tumen/T'omun and Tuman were different transliterations of the same name; others began to regard them as two different rivers.

Chosŏn maps in the eighteenth and nineteenth centuries clearly marked the Mukedeng stele and depicted the barrier connecting the stele and the upper stream of the boundary river. In those maps the stele, the barrier, and the river combined to form a crucial part of the visual representation of Korean space. In countrywide, provincial, and local maps, the boundary river system was presented controversially: some marked the Tuman River as the northern border; some drew an additional river in the north, labeling it as either the T'omun River or the Division River (*Pungyegang*). Some marked "the origin of the T'omun River" – i.e., the origin

[35] See *Sŭngjŏngwŏn ilgi*, vol. 1189, Yŏngjo 37-01-13; vol. 1194, Yŏngjo 37-06-02; vol. 1270, Yŏngjo 43-L7-09; vol. 1271, Yŏngjo 43-L7-10.

of the Tuman River; some did not. Most of the maps called the Mukedeng stele the "demarcation stele" and marked the barrier connecting it to the Tuman, but quite a few others indicated that the barrier was actually connected to the T'omun, or Division, River (see Maps 1, 2, and 3).

No doubt the Chosŏn cartographers in the late eighteenth century were not in consensus on the local hydrology and topography. That said, compared to the maps produced beforehand, these post-Mukedeng maps revealed a new vision of territory: a Korean space must have a clear-cut boundary, which could be visualized by Mt. Paektu, the stele, the barriers, and the border rivers.

This, however, is not to suggest that a relatively coherent account of the upper Tuman River region did not exist at all. It did: mainly in local gazetteers. The area was in the jurisdiction of Musan Prefecture, a prefecture set up in the southeast of Mt. Paektu in 1684. Multiple editions of Musan gazetteers were compiled over time. One of the earliest versions is the *Musan pu* section of *Pukkwan chi* (*Records on Northern Hamgyŏngdo*), finalized in 1724.[36] The "miscellanies" section includes the text of a 1672 memorial submitted by Nam Ku-man, a famous member of the literati who later became the chief state councilor (*yŏng'ŭijŏng*). The memorial proposed moving Musan garrison northward to occupy the empty lands left by the Manchus. The idea behind such a policy was to acknowledge the reality that many Korean peasants had reclaimed wildland there, and, more importantly, to strategically expand Chosŏn's territory to the upper Tumen River region. Nam was aware of the risk that the Manchu "barbarians" would discover the expansion and request the return of their land. His suggested response was that "land within the Tuman River is our land," and if the "barbarians" ask for it one day "our country should point at the [Tuman] river to make our argument." Nam's memorial explained that, in the late seventeenth century, the Tuman was indeed regarded as the northernmost limit to which a Chosŏn sphere could reach. Unlike later editions, the 1724 gazetteer did not mention Mt. Paektu at all. The situation changed only in the late Yŏngjo period, when the mountain worship debate was concluded. For example, in *Yŏji tosŏ*, a collection of countrywide gazetteers compiled in the 1760s, Mt. Paektu was recorded in the section of local terrain in the Musan gazetteer.[37]

[36] In Yi T'ae-jin and Yi Sang-t'ae, eds., *Chosŏn sidae sach'an ŭpchi*, vol. 44 (Seoul: Han'guk Inmun Kwahgwŏn, 1989), pp. 391–401.
[37] Kuksa P'yŏnch'an Wiwŏnhoe, ed., *Yŏji tosŏ* (Seoul: Taehan Min'guk Mun'gyobu Kuksa P'yŏnch'an Wiwŏnhoe: pŏngak panp'och'ŏ T'amgudang, 1973), p. 297.

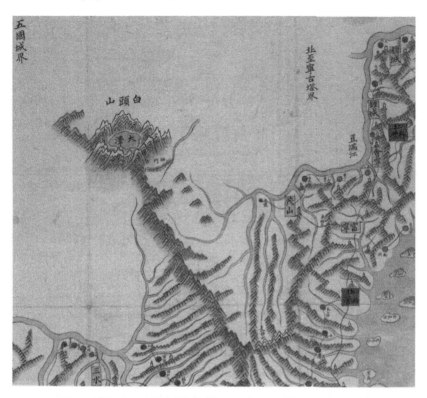

Map 1 Topographical map of Hamgyŏng province (Yŏjido/Hamgyŏng-
do); detail

Note: The map depicts a wooden barrier (柵門) connecting to an
unnamed river, which flows up north towards Qing's Ningguta (寧古
塔). The author of the map seems to suggest that this unnamed river
eventually joins the Tuman River (豆滿江) near Onsŏng (穩城), but the
middle part of the river is entirely missing on the map. This implies
an ambiguous (or complicated) perception of the northern border of
Korea: the map portrays the Tuman as the limit of Korean governance
yet suggests that the demarcation stele determined another border
further north.

Source: Quoted from Yi Sŏ-haeng and Chŏng Ch'i-yŏng, eds., *Ko
chido wa sajin ŭro pon Paektusan* (Sŏngnam: Han'gukhak Chungang
Yŏn'guwŏn Ch'ulp'anbu, 2011), p. 111. Possessed by Kyujanggak
Institute of Korean Studies.

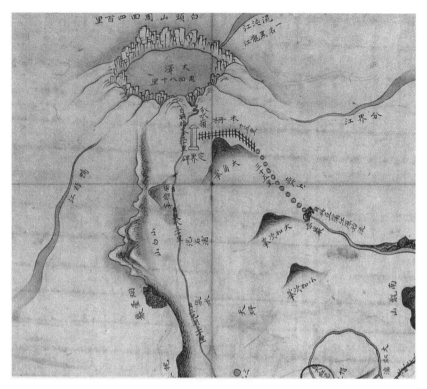

Map 2 The Changp'a area of northern Hamgyŏng province (Pukkwan Changp'a chido Hamgyŏng-do); detail

Note: The map shows four rivers flowing from the Great Lake (大澤) on Paektusan (clockwise: the Hundun River, the Division River, the Tuman River, and the Yalu River). This local map illustrates that "the Hundun River (混沌江) is also called the Heilong River (黑龍江)," indicating the cartographer's accurate knowledge that the Songhua River (Hundun in this case) is a tributary of the Heilong (Amur) River. The demarcation stele connects the Tuman River through, first, a line of wooden barriers (木柵), then a line of earth mounds (土墩). If so, the Tuman should be regarded as the border. But why is there another "Division River" (分界江)? The map doesn't provide an explanation.

Source: Quoted from Yi and Chŏng, *Ko chido wa sajin ŭro pon Paektusan*, p. 189. Possessed by National Library of Korea.

Map 3 General map of the land east to the sea, Hamgyŏng province (Haedong ch'ongdo/Hamgyŏng-do); detail
Note: The map draws the T'omun/Tumen River (土門江) and the Tuman River (豆滿江) as two separate rivers. A wooden barrier (木柵) links the two rivers, yet doesn't connect with the "demarcation stele" (定界碑). Another big river on the upper left, the Hŏntŏng River (Ch. Huntong, 混同江), is usually referred to as the upper stream of the Songhua River. The cartographer of this map thought the T'omun/Tumen River was not the Songhua; and it is not clear which river, the T'omun or Tuman, is the border, despite the fact that all garrisons were within the Tuman.
Source: Quoted from Yi and Chŏng, *Ko chido wa sajin ŭro pon Paektusan*, p. 99. Possessed by National Library of Korea.

In the mid-nineteenth century the Chosŏn government made systematic efforts to produce gazetteers of the whole country. Several editions of Musan gazetteers could be found in *Kwanbuk chi* (1859), *Kwanbuk ŭpchi* (1868), and *Pukkwan ŭpchi* (1872), all geographical records of northern Hamgyŏng.[38] Though censuses on population, fields, and taxes

---

[38] The first two editions are collected in Yi and Yi, *Chosŏn sidae sach'an ŭpchi*, vol. 41. The third edition is collected in Kim Yong-jik, ed., *Ŭpchi, Hamgyŏng-do* (Seoul: Asea Munhwasa, 1986).

were kept updated, most content on local history and terrain was identical in these three gazetteers. In the section on "evolution of government," all three editions noted that the Musan area "was once occupied by the barbarians" and "had long been wasted after the Qing people left." But in 1650 a local official, Chŏng Se-gyu, "thought that the land inside *the Tuman River* was within our border and not a single inch of land must be abandoned." So he submitted an application to allow people to reclaim the land "*till the limit of* the Tuman River." In the section introducing local mountains and rivers, Mt. Paektu was the first entry on the list, showing it was solidly established as a Korean mountain at the time. Describing the mountain as a border separating "us" from "them" (*P'iag yŏnggye*), the entry briefly recorded the 1712 Mukedeng mission, the content of the stele, and the barrier. It also notes that "T'omun" (土門), the place engraved on the Mukedeng stele, located 30 *ri* from the stele, marking the point "where the *Tuman River* surges out." In the entry for the "Tuman River," the gazetteers repeated that the river "originated *from T'omun under* Mt. Paektu." Although both "Tuman" and "T'omun" were mentioned in these documents, judging by the context the T'omun here was not the name of a separate river, but of a place.

The narrative changed after the Qing–Chosŏn territorial dispute occurred in the 1880s. In the 1899 edition of the Musan gazetteer, *Hamgyŏng pukto Musangun ŭpchi*, the description was modified – only slightly in the text but significantly in meaning. Chŏng Se-gyu's story was revised to "the land inside *the Division River* [as opposed to "the Tuman River"] was within our border...so Chŏng submitted an application to allow people to reclaim it..., which *was connected by* [not "till the limit of"] the Tuman River." In the "Mt. Paektu" entry, the original text saying T'omun was "where the Tuman River surges out" was modified to "where *the T'omun River* surged out." A similar revision appeared in the "Tuman River" entry: the original account that the river "originated from T'omun under Mt. Paektu" was altered to "originated from *the southwest* of Mt. Paektu."[39] The new version refutes the previous notion that the Tuman was the border; "T'omun" was now redefined as another river altogether.

The multiple uncertainties stemming from both changes to text and changes in nature were intertwined with the multilayered truths in dynastic geography in East Asia. When a line has to be drawn to distinguish

[39] *Hamgyŏng pukto Musangun ŭpchi*, Kyujanggak, 10999, italics mine. The same narrative could be found in another Musan gazetteer: *Hamgyŏng-pukto Musan-bu ŭpchi*. The year of this gazetteer is unclear, but the collector, the Imanishi collection at Tenri Central Library, identifies it as the twentieth century. Harvard-Yenching Microfilm FK400.

"subjective" realities from "objective" realities, and political notions from geographical conditions, such a task is extremely difficult.

The Demarcations: Ritual Competition

In October 1885 Yi Chung-ha, who had become the "commissioner to investigate the T'omun border" (*T'omun kamgyesa*), arrived at Hoeryŏng. There he met the Qing delegates from Jilin. Like the Chosŏn, the Qing entrusted the investigation to local officials. The chief negotiators were selected from both civilian and military institutions: Qin Ying was a supervising commissary of the Jilin–Chosŏn trade; De Yu, an assistant commandant of the Hunchun vice commander-in-chief; and Jia Yuangui, an assistant commissary of the recruitment and reclamation affairs in Jilin frontier. Jia was later replaced by Fang Lang in the second survey in 1887. Aside from De Yu, who was a banner man in Hunchun, Qin, Jia, and Fang were all Han officials recently assigned to Jilin to look over trade or reclamation affairs.

One thing should be clear: for both the Qing and Chosŏn, the purpose of this joint investigation was not to redraw the boundary. The boundary had *already* been there for ages. It had never changed since it was first established, however vaguely. The job was simply to find out *where on earth* the border was, no more and no less. In other words, the aim of the geographic survey was to seek topographical evidence and match it to historical records. It was not supposed to establish a new border but to "reiterate the old territory." Space had to be identified in accordance with history.

The 1880s demarcation and negotiation, in that sense, was a contest of dynastic geography. Even though they assiduously investigated local terrain, both the Qing and Chosŏn employed various historical records to support their arguments, making sure that spatial reality fit precisely into these records. Insisting that the Tumen River was doubtless the boundary, the Qing delegates quoted laws and governmental instructions to pinpoint, in their view, mistakes made by the Koreans. By the same token, the Chosŏn delegates made most out of the evidence of the 1712 Mukedeng mission, a mission, they argued, that defined the boundary river as the "T'omun." In their arguments, geographic theses mingled with *zongfan* political rhetoric. Each side constantly reminded its counterpart to obey the political obligations of being either a superior or subordinate. When the Qing delegates urged their Chosŏn colleagues to acknowledge the supreme authority of the Qing's geographical documents, the latter checked the former with the very fact that the Mukedeng stele itself was erected "at the (Qing) emperor's order," skillfully implying that nothing could be more authoritative than the emperor himself.

The first round of demarcation lasted two months, from November 6, 1885, to January 4, 1886.[40] The two teams met in Hoeryŏng and went upstream along the Tumen River. Although in agreement with their common target – to identify the old border – the two parties nevertheless diverged on almost every aspect of the mission: what to investigate, how to investigate, and how to interpret specific historical and geographical evidence. Quoting imperial codes and historical records, the Qing insisted that the names "Tumen" and "Tuman" were different transliterations of the same Manchu term. Therefore, the demarcation should focus first and foremost on the river, including all its upper branches. The Koreans rejected it by claiming that the term "Tŭmen/T'omun" (meaning "earth gate") simply described the local terrain. Hence, the most important task was to check the Mukedeng stele as well as the barrier connecting the stele to the Tŭmen/T'omun, where the source of the boundary was located. It was unnecessary, the Korean insisted, to survey all the upper branches of the Tuman. Finding no record of the 1712 Mukedeng mission in their archives, the Qing officials questioned the location of the stele, speculating that the stele had either been erected in the wrong place at the beginning or been deliberately moved to its current location later. This astonished their Chosŏn counterparts, who firmly defended the authenticity of the stele as well as its unquestionable political authority.

During the process the Qing and Chosŏn negotiators communicated with each other through "brush talking" (writing on paper). Yi Chung-ha recorded their negotiations in detail. The exchange quoted below reveals how intensive the debate was. It also illustrates how both sides wittily employed political resources to support their geographical arguments.

The other side [i.e., Qing] said: We are assigned to this job and should follow the memorial of the (Qing's) Zongli yamen. The memorial asked us to "investigate the Tumen River boundary," therefore investigating the lower and upper reaches of the river is the main content of this project whereas checking the stele is just a supplement, like textual research to the main content. Your Excellency got your prominent position by passing the civil service exam in literature. Have

---

[40] Detailed firsthand records of the first joint survey can be found in, but are not limited to, these documents. On the Chosŏn side, Yi Chung-ha, "T'omun kamgye" (Kyujanggak, 21036); "Kamgyesa mundap" (Kyujanggak, 20138); "Mundapki" (Kyujanggak, 21041); "Paektusan ilgi," in "Kamgyesa tŭngnok," in Yuk Nak-hyŏn, ed., *Kando yŏngyukwŏn kwan'gye charyojip*, vol. 2 (Seoul: Paeksan Munhwa, 1993). On the Qing side, QJZRHGXSL, vol. 3, and *Qing waiwubu shoufawen yilei cungao* (Beijing: quanguo tushuguan wenxian suowei fuzhi zhongxin, 2003), pp. 38–52; Yang Zhaoquan and Sun Yumei, eds., *Zhongchao bianjie yange ji jiewu jiaoshe shiliao huibian* (Changchun: Jilin wenshi chubanshe, 1994).

you ever seen a writer who put the main content aside but rushed to write the supplement first? [...]

I [i.e., Yi Chung-ha] said: In the past, Emperor Kangxi erected this stone to mark the border, therefore the stele is the root of the demarcation. To use a metaphor of classic books: the stele is the main text whereas the river is its footnote. How can the stele be called a supplement? Your Excellency is proficient at classical studies and it is impossible that you do not know the distinction between text and footnote. Where did your argument come from? Besides, the stele was engraved "on imperial order," which meant it was at Emperor Kangxi's order. Such a shining stele could last forever. Your argument about "supplement" today is not appropriate. [...]

The other side said: I dare not say I am proficient in classical studies. But I do not think it is proper to say the stele is text and the river the footnote... Your Excellency, please think about it: the river and the stele, which existed first? It is obvious that the river came first. [...] It is clear that the stele is the footnote of the river, yet Your Excellency regards the river as the footnote. You did not think it through.

I said: Your Excellency is skillful at playing on words, so you have this sense of humor. However, when the imperial enterprise rose, all rivers, mountains, and lands were accommodated into the institution. The notion of "from where to where," which was clearly recorded in the emperor's order, is like the canon marking the sun and stars. The specific mountain and water, recorded in accordance with it, fall into the realm of either your big state or my small state. In that case, is the river subordinated to the stele, or the other way around?[41]

The conflict over the metaphor of "text" versus "footnote" may seem verbose today. But it vividly demonstrates how a spatial world was perceived in totally different ways then. For the Qing, the fact that the Tumen River was the border preceded the 1712 demarcation, which, if indeed it happened the way the Korean delegate said it did, was but an attempt to reaffirm the border. Yet the Chosŏn seemed to argue that the history of the border started with the 1712 demarcation. Yi's argument, that the stele determined the river and not the other way around, took advantage of nineteenth-century *zongfan* cosmology, which located everything in reference to the Qing empire at the center. It sounded absurd to make the emperor's words precede the formation of natural terrain, yet this rhetoric put the Qing delegates in an awkward position: they could neither endorse nor argue against it. The geographical perception of time was eloquently woven into the discourse of the political hierarchy by which the Korea official, acting as an extremely reverent subject of Emperor Kangxi, tactfully alerted his rivals of their obligation and urged them to accept his agenda.

[41] Yi, "Mundapki."

Compromised, they divided the group into three teams. Two of them departed to trace two major upper branches of the Tumen, and the remaining one climbed Mt. Changbai to observe the Mukedeng stele. Yi Chung-ha joined the last group, together with Qin Ying and Jia Yuangui. Taking about twelve days, from November 21 to December 3, the trip involved some of the hardest challenges of the mission: extremely harsh weather, dangerous paths, and difficult logistics, to name just a few. Yi was constantly stunned by the sublime scenery – understandable, considering this was the first official joint exploration of Mt. Changbai in 173 years.[42] The team eventually reached the Mukedeng stele on November 25. They made rubbings and scouted the local terrain before returning.

Seeing the Mukedeng stele itself, however, did nothing to narrow the chasm. True, the stele, which indicated that "the Yalu is in the west and the Tumen in the east," was located on a drainage divide. True, a dry ditch west of the stele connected to one of the upper streams of the Yalu River. Also true, another dry ditch east of the stele connected to some stone and earth barriers, which further extended 90 *ri* from the stele. From that point, which the Koreans called "earth gate," the ditch went dozens of *ri* northward until it finally reached a small stream. The problem was that this water had nothing to do with the Tumen/Tuman. Instead, it was one of the headwaters of the Songhua (Sungari), a large river that flowed first north, then east all the way until it joined the Amur (Heilong) River. It was impossible that the Songhua/Amur was the boundary, otherwise the eastern half of the whole of Manchuria, a vast area even larger than the Korean Peninsula itself, would be cut off from the Qing. In fact, the surveyors realized that none of the headwaters of the Tumen or its tributary rivers connected to the stele, with the closest upstream, Hongt'osan Water, still 50 *ri* away from the barrier. The Qing official now confidently claimed that the stele "was either a fake made by people in a later period or a mistake made at the time it was erected." Insisting the Koreans were not cheating, Yi Chung-ha could suggest only that "this is something in the past which we indeed could not understand."[43] After all three teams returned to Musan, the two sides further discussed what they had found. Still unable to reach a consensus, they exchanged official notes before departing, leaving the problem unsolved.

Although the first round of demarcation ended with no agreement, the joint survey did significantly improve the empirical understanding of the Tumen region for both the Qing and Chosŏn. To different extents, both sides altered their original positions. This was especially the case for the

[42] Yi, "Paektusan ilgi," in "Kamgyesa tŭngnok."
[43] Yi, "Mundapki."

Korean representative. After the 1885 survey Yi Chung-ha realized that the "two rivers theory" was untenable and should not be pursued. Along with his formal report to the court, Yi submitted two supplemental reports to explain his personal views on the border issue. In the first supplement (*pyŏltan*) he expressed his worry about the accelerated trespassing and lamented that border towns "would be empty in years": "Even if we acquired land, we would lose people. To empty one place to fill another, this is not beneficial for our state."[44] So he strongly suggested the border prohibition along the Tuman River be strictly reinforced. In the second supplement (*ch'uhu pyŏltan*), Yi traced the evolution of the Tuman border and pointed out that the Tumen and Tuman were in fact the same water, and the Chosŏn had always treated the Tuman as the border: "Documents of the Border Defense Bureau (*Pipyŏnsa*) had said: 'the Tumen River is the Chinese pronunciation of the Tuman River. Let it be known.' From this sentence alone [we could know that] the Tuman River is clearly the boundary river." As for the mystery that the stele did not connect to the source of the river, he believed that it was Mukedeng who had (mistakenly) identified the ditch in the east as the source of the Tuman. The Koreans just followed this mistaken precedent. Seeing the remaining relics (while concealing this discovery from his Qing counterparts), he had to report the situation as he observed it:

After Mukedeng left, our country spent years setting stone barriers from the east of the stele to the source of the Tuman. Since the source of the Tuman did not connect to the ditch, wooden barriers were set to make the connection. We then called the ditch the origin of the Tumen River. Hundreds of years have passed; today those wood barriers are decayed; old markers are buried in a thick copse. Because neither we nor the other side had concrete knowledge about it, the current debate occurred. This time I went into the mountain, secretly looked over the relics, and discovered that there were indeed old markers hidden in the forest. *Fortunately, those markers did not catch the eyes of the other side. But the situation is quite breathtaking and I dare not to hide it in my report.*[45]

Yi's understanding influenced many other Korean officials. Kim Yun-sik, the top official of diplomatic affairs, once discussed the boundary dispute with Yuan Shikai. Kim explicitly said that it was difficult to prove Korea's argument on the basis of the Mukedeng stele. "If we use it to define the border, then all the land of Jilin is included [in Korean territory]. This is definitely unreasonable."[46] Yuan reported to Beijing that "the Korean court knows they made a mistake."

[44] Yi, "Pyŏltan," in "T'omun kamgye."
[45] Yi, "Ch'uhu pyŏltan," in "T'omun kamgye," italics mine.
[46] Kim Hyŏng-jong, ed., *1880-yŏndae Chosŏn-Ch'ŏng kukkyŏng hoedam kwallyŏn charyo sŏnyŏk* (Seoul: Seoul Taehakkyo Ch'ulp'an Munhwawŏn, 2014), p. 635.

On the Qing side, the Zongli yamen carefully studied dynastic geographic documents, including those compiled by the Qing court and the materials regarding the Mukedeng mission delivered by the Chosŏn court. Realizing that many details were incoherent, the yamen decided that "the borderline dispute between the two sides has to be settled by compromise." In a long memorial suggesting a new round of demarcation, the yamen listed several key issues to be clarified and further investigated. Without yielding the bottom line that the Tumen River was the boundary, the yamen's instruction expressed some new opinions. It requested the investigators to carefully examine the meaning of the Mukedeng stele: the inscription did record what Mukedeng "observed" at the time, but said nothing about "demarcation." The implication was that, although the Qing still questioned the function of the stele, it no longer challenged its authenticity. Another issue that concerned the central government was technology. Downplaying the topographical measurement used in the 1885 demarcation as "relying solely on words of the locals" and therefore "not trustworthy," the yamen urged that "only by measuring the latitude (*wei du*) could we be sure [about local terrain]." The preference for European surveying techniques over indigenous ones should be understood in its historical context, a point I elaborate on later in this chapter.

The yamen made it clear that the problem at hand was the same one Emperor Kangxi had tried to settle in 1712: the undefined space between the sources of the Yalu and those of the Tumen. It decided that what needed to be investigated was the section from Musan to the Mukedeng stele. Approaching the end of the memorial, the yamen pointed out an overall principle for future demarcation: "[Our side] should pinpoint the Tumen River conclusively, so that the border identifies itself. The central state [*zhongguo*] always treats its tributaries [*fengfan*] with benevolence. However, we will never tolerate even a slight provocation to our frontier and our principles."[47]

At the same time, Li Hongzhang, the policy maker of Qing foreign affairs, twice asked King Kojong to survey the border again. But the Chosŏn thought it was unnecessary. In October 1886 Kim Yun-sik sent a diplomatic note to Yuan Shikai, suggesting a new resolution. Acknowledging that the Tuman and the Tumen were one river, the note argued that the Hongt'osan (Ch. Hongtushan), the northernmost stream, should be regarded as the source of the river. Moreover, considering the difficulty of forcefully repatriating all the Korean squatters, it sought permission to "borrow land to settle people." These people, proposed the Chosŏn, should be governed by

Chosŏn officials, who would collect land tax and submit it to Qing's Jilin. In that way, "the imperial dynasty will not lose land tax, my humble state will not lose population; the two principles of 'serving the great' and 'cherishing the inferior' will be conveniently implemented. We don't have to send staff to survey again."[48] The Qing rejected the idea.

Another round of surveys and negotiations was conducted that lasted more than two months, from April 29 to July 10 in 1887.[49] This time the geographical dispute was rather trivial. Since both sides now agreed that the Tumen/Tuman was the border, they had only to identify the very top part of its upper stream to finalize the demarcation. Once again, they went to the mountains. In contrast to the bitter conditions they endured in the previous survey, the mission enjoyed perhaps the best season on Mt. Changbai. Yi Chung-ha wrote a rather pleasant poem en route:

> O thou red azaleas in Mt. Changbaek,
> only ready to blossom as late as the fifth month
> No one ever paid thee attention since Mukedeng left, until
> I pass thee by again two hundred year later.[50]

But the topographical problem remained thorny. None of the source streams fit the physical evidence or textual records. While the Chosŏn insisted on designating the Hongt'osan as the Tumen's point of origin, the Qing objected, as it neither matched the description in the documents nor connected to the stele or the barriers. In fact, nobody had acknowledged the existence of the Hongt'osan before. This small stream had been found and named only in the last survey. Yi Chung-ha's justification for how this water connected to the barrier – by flowing 40 *ri* "underground" – was absurd to the Qing officials. The Qing instead proposed the Hongdan River as the source of the Tumen. This Hongdan was a larger stream that flowed from the south, absorbed the Hongt'osan at a lower section, and became the Tumen stem after incorporating an even larger branch, the Sŏdu River, from further south. Yi Chung-ha rejected this notion, because the Hongdan was too far from the Mukedeng stele. More importantly, some hundred-odd Korean households were living in

[48] Kim, *1880-yŏndae Chosŏn-Ch'ŏng kukkyŏng hoedam kwallyŏn charyo sŏnyŏk*, p. 623.
[49] Detailed firsthand accounts of the second joint survey can be found in, but are not limited to, these documents: on the Chosŏn side, Yi Chung-ha, "Pokkam T'omun tamnok" (Kyujanggak, 21035-v.1–3); "Chohoe tamch'o" (Kyujanggak, 21039); "Kamgyesa kyosŏp pogosŏ" (Kyujanggak, 26302); "T'omun kamgye" (Kyujanggak, 21036); on the Qing side, QJZRHGXSL, vol. 4; Jilinsheng dang'anguan et al., eds., *Hunchun fudutong yamen dang'an xuan bian*, vol. 2 (Changchun: Jilin wenshi chubanshe, 1991); Zongli geguo shiwu yamen, ed., *Jichao Fenjie an*; Yang and Sun, *Zhongchao bianjie yange ji jiewu jiaoshe shiliao huibian*.
[50] Yi Chung-ha, "Changbaeksan tojung," in Yi, *Iadang chip*.

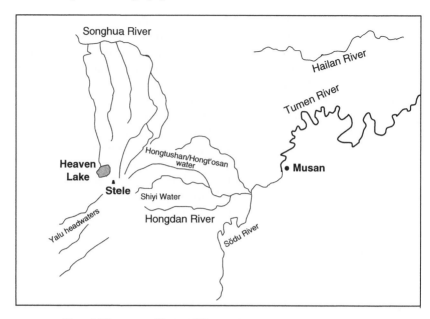

Map 4 The upper Tumen River system

the area between the Hongdan and Hongt'osan. Setting the boundary along this river meant abandoning those populations. Yi tried his best to argue that the Hongt'osan coincided with all the textual evidence and was indeed the "old border" (see Map 4).

The negotiation was trapped in stalemate at this point. But the Qing negotiators were eager to end the debate and willing to make some concessions. One day a Qing representative, Fang Lang, approached Yi and suggested both sides step back a little and agree upon another stream southwest of the Hongt'osan as the real source of the Tumen. In that way, he promised, not only would Korean villagers remain in Chosŏn's realm but the emperor would approve the plan. Yi refused to determine the boundary in such an arbitrary manner.[51]

Approaching the end of the survey, the investigators found another small branch of the Hongt'osan between the Hongt'osan and the Hongdan. The Qing officials urged Yi to recognize this stream, newly named the Shiyi (K. Sŏgŭl),[52] as the source so as to close the boundary

[51] Yi Chung-ha, "Chohoe tamch'o."
[52] The nameless stream in native Korean was called *tolsu* (돌수), meaning "water from stones." A Hanja (Korean Chinese character), 乭, was made to correspond to the term 돌 with a semantic element of "stone" (石) on top and the phonetic element *l* (乙)

case, with both sides making a small concession. Again, Yi firmly rejected the proposal, saying that the stream did not follow the drainage divide where the stele was located.

The divide between two sides had narrowed: both sides agreed that the only undefined area was a small region between the Mukedeng stele and the point where the Shiyi joined the Hongt'osan. Nevertheless, the 1887 demarcation, the last Qing–Chosŏn joint survey, again ended in vain. In later years there were several proposals for completing the project, but first Korea then China rebuffed those plans. The dispute was thus suspended without a final solution.

The Nexus of Qing's Border Makings

Chinese frontiers in the late nineteenth century were suffering comprehensive crises; the state borders were under serious challenges in almost all directions. The territorial dispute with Chosŏn was just one of many similar disputes. In this section I compare the Qing–Chosŏn demarcation with two other boundary-making projects around the same time: the Qing–Russian demarcation in Jilin and the Qing–French demarcation at the Yunnan–Vietnamese border. A look at these other conflicts will help us understand how dynastic geographic principles came into play in different geopolitical contexts. Qing's perception of boundary, it shows, was much more diverse and unstable than we usually believe.

Qing–Russian Boundary Making

Between the two rounds of Qing–Chosŏn border negotiations, in 1886, the Qing conducted another demarcation over the Tumen border, with Russia. The context for the Qing–Russian negotiation dates back to the late seventeenth century, when the Russians invaded the Amur River region and Qing troops besieged Fort Yaksa (R. Albazin) and forced Russia to negotiate. Representatives from both sides met at Nerchinsk (C. Nibuchu) in the autumn of 1689. After furious debates and struggles, the two sides reached an agreement defining the eastern section of the border. The Sino-Russian Nerchinsk Treaty, mediated through Jesuit missionaries and Mongol interpreters, and codified in Latin, Russian, and Manchu, settled the boundary and established the rules for bilateral

---

beneath. Since this was not a standard Chinese character, in official documents it was written as two separate characters, 石乙 (pronounced "shiyi" in Chinese), which then became the official name of the stream.

commerce, personnel exchange, and criminal extradition.[53] Taking the form of a quasi-modern international law, the 1689 Sino-Russian treaty, most scholars agree, revealed the independent and equal status between the two empires.[54] Arguably one of the earliest diplomatic protocols in the modern world, the treaty implied that the practice of sovereign rights was not necessarily foreign to the Chinese imperial order.[55] Despite the fact that the Qing managed their Russian affairs with the Board for the Administration of Outer Subordinates (Lifanyuan), the Qing did not apply the hierarchical *zongfan* principles to the demarcation. This flexible attitude was surely a pragmatic choice, contingent upon historical context.[56] But it also showed that the Middle Kingdom was adaptable enough to treat another great Eurasian power, a power certainly beyond its cosmological realm, according to tenets not that different from modern international law. Nicola Di Cosmo even suggests that the treaty "introduced China to a broader international society; the formation of a new frontier thus became central not only to the development of China's national identity but also to the modern diplomatic history of China."[57]

The bilateral territorial status changed significantly with the 1856 Treaty of Aigun and the 1860 Treaty of Beijing. Russia now expanded all the way to the Tumen River mouth. According to the Treaty of Beijing, the two states should clarify their new eastern border in 1861 by jointly establishing several markers. But, because Qing officials failed to co-supervise the project diligently, Russia either wrongly erected some of the markers or did not erect some at all, and in so doing occupied more Qing land. The problem was not discovered until 1883 by Wu Dacheng. Wu was especially worried about the outlet of the Tumen River where the Qing, Chosŏn, and Russian borders joined together. He observed that Russia had illegally extended its territory to about 50 kilometers east of the Tumen estuary, rather than the 15 kilometers written into the treaty. More importantly, the Russians had set checkpoints in Heidingzi (an

---

[53] Peter Perdue, "Boundaries and Trade in the Early Modern World: Negotiations at Nerchinsk and Beijing," *Eighteenth-Century Studies*, vol. 43, no. 3 (2010), pp. 341–356; Liu Minsheng, Meng Xianzhang, and Bu Ping, eds., *Shiqi shiji sha'e qinlue Heilongjiang liuyu shi ziliao* (Harbin: Heilongjiang Jiaoyu chubanshe, 1992), pp. 256–552; Liu Yuantu, *Zaoqi zhong'e dongduan bianjie yanjiu* (Beijing: Zhongguo shehui kexue chubanshe, 1993), pp. 321–325.

[54] Jiang Changbin, *Zhong'e guojie dongduan de yanbian* (Beijing: Zhongyang wenxian chubanshe, 2007), pp. 106–110.

[55] Wang Hui, *Xiandai zhongguo sixiang de xingqi* (Beijing: Shenghuo, dushu, xinzhi sanlian shudian, 2005), p. 684.

[56] Perdue, *China Marches West*, p. 172.

[57] Nicola Di Cosmo: "Qing Colonial Administration in Inner Asia," *International History Review*, vol. 20, no. 2 (1998), pp. 287–309.

area belonging to the Qing's Hunchun) and recruited Koreans to settle in their new territory. The Jilin borders were in jeopardy.[58]

At Wu's urging, the Qing and Russia launched a demarcation to correct the Jilin–Russian boundary in the Tumen River region in 1886. Wu himself led the Qing delegation. After a careful survey and fierce debates in which almost every *li* of the land was thoroughly calculated and argued over, Wu successfully recaptured the Heidingzi area and made the Russians withdraw to a point 15 kilometers east of the mouth of the Tumen. A stele engraved with a Russian " T " and a Chinese "tu" (±) was erected at the point. Other boundary steles were also reengraved or added. Furthermore, Wu acquired for China the right to navigate to the Sea of Japan via the Tumen River, opening an outward channel for the inland frontier of Jilin.[59] The Qing victory over this demarcation was to a large extent attributed to Wu Dacheng's persistent adherence to the text of the Treaty of Beijing, a treaty that itself was regarded as "unequal."

The Sino-Russian case showed a particular approach to the Qing conceptualization and construct of its geographic limits. The border with Russia was seen as a clear-and-hard line marking the absolute end of the imperial realm. Although in rhetoric the Qing categorized Russia as a part of "all under heaven," in geopolitical practice China never attempted to include Russia in its realm of "imperial benevolence." Behind the Sino-Russian negotiations of both 1689 and 1886 was the spirit of contract, which shared a good deal of common ground with the evolving principles of international law.

Qing–Vietnamese Boundary Making

A few years before returning to Jilin to negotiate borders with Russia, Wu Dacheng had been transferred to the Ministry of Beiyang to assist Li Hongzhang in the Qing–French conflict over Vietnam. This conflict, which later developed into the Sino-French War (1883–1885), eventually led to the redemarcation of the Qing–Vietnamese border, also in 1886. A particularly interesting section was the border in Yunnan province. Unlike the Russian and Korean cases, to which the Qing applied either *zongfan* principles or quasi-international law, the Yunnan–Vietnamese demarcation revealed how the Qing empire adjusted its

---

[58] Wang Yanwei, ed., *Qingji waijiao shiliao*, vol. 57 (Beijing: Shumu wenxian chubanshe, 1987), p. 7.

[59] Wu Dacheng, "Jilin kanjie ji," in *Jinxiandai zhongguo bianjiang jiewu ziliao*, vol. 8 (Hong Kong: Fuchi shuyuan chuban youxian gongsi, 2007), pp. 4087–4090.

spatial conceptualization in accordance with geopolitical changes. Again, the conflict had its origins in the early eighteenth century.

In the 1720s Qing state power infiltrated to the Yunnan frontier, an area that used to be governed by local chiefs (*tusi*).[60] Partially driven by the need to explore copper mines to solve the shortage of copper currency, the Qing officials discovered that two famous mining areas, Dulong and Nandan in the realm of Qing's Kaihua (now Wenshan) Prefecture, had been occupied by the Lê dynasty of Annam for decades. According to historical records, China and Vietnam were divided at this spot by a river called the Duzhou, which included Dulong and Nandan on the Qing side. When the territorial dispute appeared on the horizon, the Lê dynasty employed a strategy similar to the one Korea used: the Vietnamese appointed a smaller stream located north of Dulong and Nandan as the "real" Duzhou River. The dispute was thus focused on which river, the Big (*Da*) or Small (*Xiao*) Duzhou, was the true boundary.[61] Despite constant pressure by local officials to recover lost territory, even by force if necessary, Qing Emperor Yongzheng (r. 1722–1735) refused to fight with a loyal tribute state over a "trivial" piece of land. Remarking upon the memorial submitted by Gao Qizhuo, then the viceroy of Yunnan and Guizhou in 1724, Emperor Yongzheng said:

Talking about the art of governing, if we compare [the policies of] distinguishing territory [*fenjiang*] with cherishing the afar [*huaiyuan*], the latter is more important. While talking about cherishing the afar, if we compare [the policies of] letting them be in awe of our force [*weiwei*] with gratifying them with our virtue [*huaide*], the latter is more important.

Applying this rhetoric, since the Lê "had been submissive for generations," it deserved to be rewarded. Besides, said Yongzheng, "if this land bears profit, how could we, a Celestial Dynasty, contest a small country for profit? If it bears no profit, why bother to contest it at all?"[62] After the Annam king repeatedly expressed his sincerity in "serving the great," the conflict ended with Emperor Yongzheng's bestowing the disputed land to Vietnam and retreating more than 120 *li* from this section of border.

The same spot, however, became a source of conflict again in 1886 after the Sino-French War. Fearing it would face both pressure from the

---

[60] See Charles Patterson Giersch, *Asian Borderlands: The Transformation of Qing China's Yunnan Frontier* (Cambridge, MA: Harvard University Press, 2006).

[61] See You Zhong, *Zhongguo xinan bianjiang bianqian shi* (Kunming: Yunnan jiaoyu chubanshe, 1987), pp. 176–182; Sun Hongnian, *Qingdai zhongyue zongfan guanxi yanjiu* (Harbin: Heilongjiang jiaoyu chubanshe, 2006), pp. 198–217; Peng Qiaohong, "Zhongyue lidai jiangyu bianqian yu zhongfa yuenan kanjie yanjiu," Ph.D. dissertation, Xiamen University, 2006, pp. 107–120.

[62] Sun, *Qingdai zhongyue zongfan guanxi yanjiu*, p. 204.

French in Vietnam and from the Japanese in Chosŏn at the same time, the Qing, which generally fought well on the battlefield, made peace with France and admitted the latter's suzerainty over Tonkin (northern Vietnam). Following the Sino-French Treaty of Tianjin, the two states dispatched teams to redefine the border between China and Tonkin. When negotiating section 2 of the Yunnan–Tonkin boundary, the Qing delegates made it clear that the Vietnamese territory between the Big and Small Duzhou Rivers had been bestowed by China in 1726 in reward for its submission. Since Vietnam was no longer a subordinate state of China, China had to take the land back. A memorial submitted in February 1886 by the Qing viceroy of Yunnan and Guizhou, Cen Yuying, revealed the rationale:

Territories of China and Vietnam adjoin, and most of the advantageous areas are in Vietnam's realm. Vietnam was a former subordinate state [*shuguo*]. We saw it as our barrier and granted it strategic passes. This was in line with the principle "to Make Barbarians in Borderlands as a Guard Fence" [*shou zai si yi*]. But now Vietnam fell to French dominion. If we still kept the old way we will put ourselves in danger.[63]

The French delegates, led by Charles Dillon, denied this kind of *zongfan* logic. They regarded the request solely as a "territory transfer" rather than a boundary change. It was hence beyond their authority to consider such a request.[64] However, facing the difficulties that they did not yet fully control Tonkin and their survey team was constantly ambushed by local militias, the French eventually agreed to compromise.[65] In the final treaty on the Yunnan–Vietnamese border, a larger portion of land between the Big and Small Duzhou Rivers, including Dulong and Nandan, was redistributed to the Qing. From the Qing's perspective, this was simply the "restoration" of the old domain, though it had not substantially controlled the area for more than 160 years.

Not entirely disconnected from each other, the historical trajectory of each bilateral border – the Sino-Russian, Sino-Korean, and Sino-Vietnamese – revealed a unique pattern of boundary making. This analysis of the three demarcations demonstrates that the Qing management of its boundary was not only diverse in perception but flexible in practice. Two different principles of relation building – one based on the *zongfan*

---

[63] Sun Xuelei and Liu Jiaping, eds., *Guojia tushuguan qingdai guben waijiao dang'an*, vol. 21 (Beijing: Quanguo tushuguan wenxian suowei fuzhi zhongxin, 2003), p. 8613.

[64] Xiao Dehao and Huang Zheng, eds., *Zhongyue bianjie lishi ziliao xuanbian*, vol. 2 (Beijing: Shehui kexue wenxian chubanshe, 1993), p. 927.

[65] About the French experience during the demarcation, see the English translation of an 1887 report: Dr. P. Neis, *The Sino-Vietnamese Border Demarcation, 1885–1887*, trans. Walter E. J. Tips (Bangkok: White Lotus Press, 1998).

hierarchy and one based on international treaty – were used simultaneously and pragmatically. Which principle to employ was primarily decided by the status of bilateral relations: whether the other side was recognized as part of the hierarchical world order and, if so, how it posited itself in such an order. The case of the Qing–Vietnamese demarcations in particular illustrated that a fundamental change in bilateral relationships would alter the Qing's recognition of territory. "The national boundaries of these states," as Peter Perdue points out, "were not laid down in the deep mists of history by timeless cultural forces; they were, rather, constructed during their interaction with each other."[66] The creation of border did not fit into the teleological view that sees the difference between the *zongfan* hierarchy and the treaty system as the demarcation between the "traditional" and the "modern."

The Sino-Korean dispute in the 1880s was not resolved through a treaty. But that did not necessarily signal a political failure. Rather, it simply revealed that the mutual political recognition between the Qing and Chosŏn remained relatively untainted. That said, under the same *zongfan* framework the dynastic geography of boundary and territory was about to experience a profound transformation.

Cartography in the Borderland

The Qing–Chosŏn boundary negotiations, according to Andre Schmid, were "a fascinating example of how spatial issues could be contested within the tributary relationship, without explicit reference to Western discourses on space."[67] That said, a specific detail regarding cartographical technology showed an impulse on the Qing part to view the boundary through an unconventional – though not necessarily foreign – lens. As mentioned above, in 1886 the Qing Zongli yamen gave explicit instructions that surveyors should measure the border by latitude. However, in their 1887 demarcation, although both Qing and Chosŏn strictly implemented the Zongli yamen's orders, they ignored the specific technological instruction. When the two sides could not agree on the last section of the border, for example, Yi Chung-ha suggested that they "co-survey and measure the number of *ri* and make the map" as a reference for a future decision. His Qing counterparts responded in full agreement.[68] Traditional cartography was used for the final map as well. The Sino-Korean Demarcation Map (C. Zhonghan kanjie ditu; K. Chunghan kamgye chido), co-signed by the

---

[66] Perdue, "Boundaries and Trade in the Early Modern World."
[67] Schmid, *Korea between Empires*, pp. 209–210.
[68] Wang, *Qingji zhong ri han waijiao shiliao*, p. 2409.

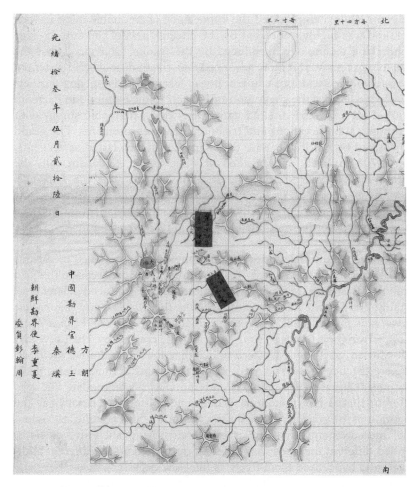

Map 5 The Sino-Korean Demarcation Map (1887); detail
Source: Diplomatic Archive of the Foreign Ministry of Japan.

delegates, employs only a standard "grid system" (see Map 5). That is, the map drawer applied standard square grids to indicate the scale. The map illustrated that every *cun* (3.33 cm) on the map indicates 2 *li*, and each square represents 40 (square) *li*.

The longitude/latitude method was by no means unfamiliar to Chinese and Koreans. In the early eighteenth century the Qing government had already mastered longitude/latitude surveys, triangulation measurement, and projection cartography. During the Qing–Russian confrontation

Emperor Kangxi emphasized the importance of creditable maps in warfare, and was highly impressed by the effectiveness of the cutting-edge mapmaking technology introduced by the Jesuits. Convinced that the graticule system was far more advanced than the traditional grid system (*ji li hua fang*), the assiduous emperor began learning and applying this new knowledge. Under the suggestion of French Jesuit Dominique Parrenin (1665–1741), Kangxi ordered an empire-wide geographic survey with astronomical observations and trigonometric measurements. The grand project, led by ten Jesuits with their Qing assistants, lasted seven years, from 1708 to 1715, and resulted in what Joseph Needham calls the world's most advanced and scientific atlas at the time: the *Imperially Commissioned Maps of All Surveyed* (*huang yu quan lan tu*), known as the *Kangxi Atlas*.[69] The perpetual missions to survey Manchuria and the Qing–Chosŏn borderland, including the 1712 Mukedeng mission, were part of this project.

Although longitude/latitude cartography has been applied in various official and non-official atlases for a century, it did not replace the grid structure. Based on the *Kangxi Atlas*, many atlases produced in later eras, notably *The Unified Landscape Maps of the Imperial Dynasty* (*huangchao yitong yudi quantu*, 1832), made by Li Zhaoluo, and *The Unified Maps of the Great Qing* (*daqing yitong yutu*, 1863), created by Hu Linyi and Yan Shusen, used both Western and indigenous quantitative methods. The coexistence of the two mathematic structures in those atlases demonstrates Chinese cartographers' attempts to accommodate the two different spatial interpretations. While scholars today generally see the adoption of the geodetic graticule as a turn from "unscientific" to "scientific" measurements, the Qing cartographers saw no such division. They applied different methods with different purposes and for different audiences, and hybridized them freely as they saw necessary.[70]

Kangxi's grand project had a great impact on the Qing's East Asian neighbors, such as Japan,[71] but perhaps no one was influenced by the project more directly than Korea, which was included in Kangxi's survey. Because no Jesuits were allowed to enter the country, Kangxi once again sent Mukedeng on an embassy trip to Hansŏng in 1713 with orders to collect geographic data en route. The Koreans absorbed as much new cartographical technique as possible, especially from the Chinese

---

[69] Hostetler, *Qing Colonial Enterprise*.

[70] See Cordell D. K. Yee, "Cartography in China," in Harley and Woodward, *Cartography in the Traditional East and Southeast Asian Societies* (Chicago: University of Chicago Press, 1994), pp. 33–231.

[71] See Funakoshi Akio, *Sakoku Nihon ni kita "Kōki-zu" no chirigakushiteki kenkyū* (Tokyo: Hōsei Daigaku Shuppankyoku, 1986).

technician He Guozhu.[72] Trigonometric measurement, for example, was imported and applied later to many maps. Western geographic knowledge had spread to the peninsula as early as the late Ming era. The Korean literati, like their Chinese peers, were quite interested in the new spatial notions brought by the Europeans. Before the rite controversy in Rome eventually led to the ban on Catholicism in China, Koreans had access to a wide range of materials on European astronomy, calendric systems, and mathematics through the Chosŏn embassies to Beijing.[73] The import of new knowledge stimulated the rise of the *silhak* (practical learning) school, which emphasized realistic and pragmatic approaches to solve sociopolitical problems, and promoted learning from "outsiders," including both Manchu "barbarians" and Europeans.

The *silhak* school encouraged dynastic geographic studies and more accurate mapmaking in Chosŏn.[74] Scholars such as Yi Ik, Hong Da-yong, and Hong Yang-ho, among others, devoted themselves to Korean geography as a way to construct a new recognition of the world as well as the Korean state.[75] The great *silhak* thinker Chŏng Yag-yong (1762–1836) wrote *Kangyŏkko* (*An Investigation of Our Territory*, 1811), a cornerstone of dynastic geography in the late Chosŏn period. The lengthy monograph traces the evolution of Korean territory and insists that the establishment of the Six Garrisons along the Tuman River was great progress towards "recovering the lost land." Criticizing the expansionist argument, which wrongly counted part of Manchuria as Korea's "old territory," Chŏng's study instead sets forth a realist view. This work significantly influenced the formation of territorial consciousness in early twentieth-century Korea.[76]

Maps composed by Chŏng Sang-gi (1678–1752) and Kim Chŏng-ho (1804–1866) represented the heyday of Korean cartography in the eighteenth and nineteenth centuries. The *Taedong yŏjido* (*Atlas of the*

[72] Ledyard, "Cartography in Korea," pp. 299–306.

[73] Zhang, *Qingdai zhonghan guanxi lunwenji*, pp. 326–341.

[74] Survey methods and instruments were particularly improved by the imported knowledge. See Norman J. W. Thrower and Kim Young Il, "Dong-Kook-Yu-Ji-Do: A Recently Discovered Manuscript of a Map of Korea," *Imago Mundi*, vol. 21, no. 1 (1967), pp. 31–49. Some scholars even argue that Western geographic knowledge, though it spread to Korea through Chinese translations, was more positively received in eighteenth-century Korea than in China. See Zou Zhenhuan, "Xifang dilixue de xueshu tiaozhan ji zhonghan xueren de yingzhan," *Fudan xuekan (shehui kexue)*, no. 3 (1999), pp. 72–80.

[75] See Yang Bo-Gyŏng, "Chōsen jidai no chilisho ni kansuru knkyū josetsu," trans. Ryozo Tsuji, *Chōsen Gakubō*, no. 116 (1985), pp. 1–18. About the *silhak* school and the new understanding of state, see Son Sŭng-ch'ŏl, "Chōsen kōki jitsugaku shisō no taigai ninshiki," *Chōsen Gakubō*, no. 122 (1987), pp. 115–144.

[76] Schmid, *Korea between Empires*, pp. 202–205.

Great East), published in 1861 by Kim Chŏng-ho, is arguably the pinnacle of traditional Korean cartography, designed to definitively represent "the final shape of Korea."[77] Comprising 22 volumes and a total of 127 sequences, the atlas revolutionized Korean cartography; Kim used Hansŏng (whose latitude was measured by Chinese technician He Guozhu in 1793) as the fundamental coordinate, and calculated the shape of Korea by measuring relative distances between Hansŏng and other places. The *Taedong yŏjido* reveals the new territorial consciousness of Kim Chŏng-ho and the *silhak* scholars in his generation, which was particularly evident in its representation of the northern border. Mt. Paektu, though still a crucial landmark, was no longer viewed as the starting point in depicting the Korean landscape. In the overall map made up of the 127 individual maps, Mt. Paektu occupies just a tiny spot in northeast Korea, and, as Map 6 shows, its summit was beyond the physical border of the country.[78]

Kim's atlas also confirmed the Tumen/Tuman River as the border and showed the Mukedeng stele as connecting to the headwaters of the Tuman rather than other rivers. Yet, even in this most "scientific" and realistic late-Chosŏn atlas, the Mukedeng stele was still given exaggerated, almost surrealistic proportions: it is one-sixth the size of the Heaven Lake. The emphasis on the origin of the northern border suggests that, no matter how the Korean space was perceived, there was a consistent effort to make history – the 1712 demarcation mission – visible in its construction.[79]

What was the major difference between the European and indigenous quantitative cartographies? Put simply, the graticule (longitude/latitude) system views the globe as a three-dimensional space and so projects a three-dimensional space onto a two-dimensional paper. The grid system, by contrast, sees the earth as a two-dimensional space and emphasizes mainly direct distances between locations. But this difference is not merely technological but, first and foremost, epistemological. The longitude/latitude cartography is best for calculating the absolute location of an abstract point on the globe, whereas the grid cartography helps to visualize the relative relations between one place and another. Dynastic geographic works in East Asia, almost exclusively, measured distances empirically, which was recorded either by length (X number of *li/ri*)

---

[77] Ledyard, "Cartography in Korea," pp. 305–329.
[78] Harvard-Yenching Library, "Kim Chŏng-ho, fl. 1834–1864. Taedong yŏjido / Kosanja [chŭk Kim Chŏng-ho] kyogan, 1864. Harvard-Yenching Library. v. 2," Harvard University, http://nrs.harvard.edu/urn-3:FHCL:3716645?n=14, accessed May 25, 2012.
[79] Song, "Imagined Territory."

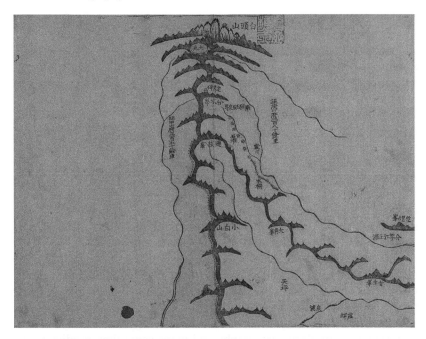

Map 6 Kim Chŏng-ho's *Atlas of the Great East* (*Taedong yŏjido*); the section showing Mt. Paektu
Source: Harvard-Yenching Library of Harvard Library, Harvard University.

or by duration (X days of travel). In modern geography and cartography, the graticule system is dominantly viewed as more objective, advanced, and "scientific."

Why were more objective, advanced, and "scientific" cartographic techniques applied in the early 1700s, but not in the Qing–Korean demarcation in the late 1800s, despite the clear charge from the central government? This question has rarely been touched upon.[80] A lack of skilled technicians, especially in the frontier region, was perhaps an

---

[80] Andre Schmid is an exception. He calls for attention to the same phenomenon – though not specifically on cartography: "Most studies of the spread of Western geographic knowledge to Asia have tended to emphasize its disruptive nature... In such accounts, indigenous geographical knowledge is supplanted by Western cartographic and surveying knowledge. The boundary controversy over the area east of Mount Paeku...reveals a more complicated process of appropriation in Korea, one that does not so neatly match a transition from tradition to modernity as marked by the replacement of a nonterritorial understanding of space by a territorial nation." Schmid, *Korea between Empires*, p. 200.

important reason. The development and learning of European techniques was interrupted in early eighteenth-century China as a result of the rite controversy between Qing Jesuits and the pope in Rome. True, in the mid-nineteenth century politicians and officials in China once again called for the study and practice of graticule cartography.[81] Cutting-edge techniques were introduced during the Self-Strengthening Movement. However, it was one thing for Beijing to suggest that a certain technique be employed, and quite another for Jilin to actually find someone to implement it. The problem also revealed itself in a later episode. In 1889 Beijing ordered all provincial-level governments to submit detailed cartographic surveys for the purpose of compiling the new edition of *Da Qing hui dian*. The Jilin general at the time addressed the difficulty of the task: "Located in the margin, Jilin has always been short on geographical studies. It is not easy to find staff who pay attention to geography."[82]

But, aside from this obvious explanation, we need to consider again the political implications of cartography. Recent scholars have turned their attention to the connection between making maps and making "early modern" states. Thongchai Winichakul, for example, demonstrates that the belief that the state has to be a "geo-body" and confined by a closed boundary line was a myth of nation state ideology.[83] In Siam, the case he researched, modern cartography and maps came first, predicting the construction of a national boundary: "[S]uch technologies create the knowledge of it, create a fact of it, and the entity comes into existence."[84] The Qing case both supports and complicates this view. Laura Hostetler argues that graticule cartography, along with the new conceptualization of space behind it, was "an international enterprise" that was simultaneously employed by all expanding empires on the Eurasian continent, not just those in Europe.[85] Such an epistemological shift, she emphasizes, did not mean departing from tradition.

Different technologies and map styles coexisted in Qing China to suit "different audiences and purposes."[86] For example, with his domain significantly expanded, Emperor Kangxi needed the geographic information

[81] Iwo Amelung, "New Maps for the Modernizing State: Western Cartographical Knowledge and Its Application in 19th and 20th Century China," in Francesca Bray, Vera Dorofeeva-Lichtmann, and Georges Métailie, eds., *Graphics and Text in the Production of Technical Knowledge in China: The Warp and the Weft* (Leiden: Brill, 2007), pp. 685–726.

[82] HCFDTYMD, vol. 137, p. 79.

[83] Thongchai Winichakul, *Siam Mapped: A History of the Geo-Body of a Nation* (Honolulu: University of Hawai'i Press, 1994).

[84] Ibid., p. 15.

[85] Hostetler, *Qing Colonial Enterprise*.

[86] Ibid., p. 10.

of his newly acquired frontiers as well as a panoramic visual representation of the whole empire. The indigenous geography, based on the spatial knowledge of the Central Plains region, was not sufficient to explain the structure of a vast empire containing both the Central Plains and the Inner Asian frontiers. The longitude/latitude cartography served his needs best. However, the foundation of imperial cosmology, far from being entirely altered by new techniques, continued to dominate political practices. "No maps are completely objective representations, independent of the circumstances of their production," says Peter Perdue. The *Kangxi Atlas* and several official atlases that followed it, according to Perdue, "tried to combine new and old techniques, but these remained within the context of the tributary system view of the world."[87]

Graticule cartography, which demonstrated perspective from the center of the governing power, was used by empires in both Europe and Asia to formulate the visual representation of their grand territorial spaces. But the abstract and absolute map was hardly the best choice to illustrate a local space between the Qing and Chosŏn in the 1880s. This was the case for two reasons. First, in a local context, it makes more sense to view a position in a relative, as opposed to absolute, manner. That is, a certain place would get its spatial meaning only from its empirical connections to other places. For practical reasons, in both the Qing and Chosŏn areas, local gazetteers always located a point by referring to its directions and distances from other points. Maps were illustrated with similar information. As Cordell Yee describes it: "[O]ne purpose of the grid was to help a map reader calculate distance and area. This contrasts with the function of the graticule, which has been used primarily as a means of locating position and relating the area mapped to the globe of which it is a part."[88] Since the purpose of the Qing–Chosŏn demarcation was to "reiterate the old territory," which could be traced only through historical connections, the longitude/latitude scale was hardly relevant. In other words, the boundary was determined not by its abstract location on the globe but by its engagement within the surrounding environment.

Second, and more important, since knowledge and technique were themselves the products of a certain political ideology, the cartographic method employed (or not employed) in the Qing–Chosŏn demarcation might have a more nuanced implication. The traditional grid cartography indicated that the map maker and viewers perceived the boundary as a kind of "relation" residing in a complex geographic

---

[87] Perdue, *China Marches West*, pp. 452–456.
[88] Yee, "Cartography in China," p. 124.

and social context. The river line dividing the two countries was not purely imaginary and artificial, nor was it isolated. Rather, it was a physical landmark indicating both division and connection. Here the grid system demonstrated itself as a metaphor of the *zongfan* political order. Within this structure, no polity was self-defined; each entity was defined in relation to and at a distance from other entities. A boundary confirmed by longitude and latitude would imply that the division was equal, absolute, and definitive. By contrast, a boundary expressed by the grid system implied that such a line was meaningful only when reading it with a concrete, materialist geographic nexus. Maps visualize the spatial forms of state. If the *Sino-Korean Demarcation Map* conceptualized part of the "geo-body" of Korea or China, it did not present them as two isolated territorial units adjoined to each other but as two "bodies" organically linked.

The Zongli yamen's technological suggestion, in this sense, exposed Beijing's anxiety to reinterpret the border in a way that departed from the past. That is: it tried to objectify the Qing–Chosŏn division. For the central government, the Qing–Chosŏn boundary was secondary to a concern for the external menace that threatened the empire as a whole. Thus, every inch of land needed to be clearly distinguished in an absolute way so the territorial integrity could be protected. The difference between Beijing and Jilin is quite revealing here. The diverse visions of a space were created under different sociopolitical concerns, exhibiting a perspective gap between the capital and the frontier.

Dynastic Frontier Geography: Yi Chung-ha and Wu Dacheng

Through the 1880s demarcations, the Tumen frontiers in late nineteenth-century China and Korea were inevitably "territorialized." But such a "territorialization" did not necessarily mean a transition from imperial or dynastic state to nation state – at least, not yet. The changes were more complex and subtle, and far from linear. Local bureaucrats who participated in various demarcations were among the first to reconceptualize this borderland. The last section of this chapter introduces the new frontier perceptions of two local officials: Yi Chung-ha of the Chosŏn, a key figure in the Qing–Korean demarcations, and Wu Dacheng of the Qing, who not only promoted the new policy to welcome Korean cultivators but also hosted Qing's demarcation with Russia. Putting their careers in a broader intellectual background helps us to historicize the epistemological turns in Chosŏn and Qing that were embedded in boundary making in the Tumen River region.

Yi Chung-ha: A "Nationalist" Hero?

Two sets of primary sources are most critical to study the 1885–1887 Qing–Chosŏn demarcation. One is governmental documents, including diplomatic exchanges, memorials, and official reports. The other, much more detailed and thorough, is Yi Chung-ha's personal accounts of the negotiation process, including his secret reports, analyses, policy suggestions, diary, and poems. Compared to the former source, the latter, often written in the first person, is considerably more forthright and individualistic. Some of Yi's narratives are quite vivid and colorful, and different genres were intended for different audiences. For example, during the joint survey Yi engaged in poetry exchanges (C. *chang he*; K. *ch'ang hwa*) with the Chinese officials. This was a popular entertainment among Confucian literati to nourish their friendships and, in a tacit way, to test their literary prowess. In his poems Yi did not grudge praise of his Qing counterparts, as in a poem responding to the Chinese delegate Qin Ying:

> We bustle about in this low land,
> For the same task of administering the frontier.
> Introduced from afar, you and I are so congenial,
> Even more than hometown friends of ten years.[89]

In his reports to the king, in contrast, Yi often portrayed the Qing negotiators as rude, coercive, inconsistent, intimidating, and irrational. Facing Yi's impeccable and just argument, he said, they felt ashamed and then turned their shame into anger. One of the most dramatic scenes in his narratives occurred in the second round of demarcation, when Yi Chung-ha had a serious confrontation with his Qing counterparts: "I said in a stern tone: 'My head could be cut off, but state territory could not be carved away. The old documents of the two states record as such. Why do you force me in this way?' "[90]

Since the early twentieth century the phrase "My head could be cut off, but state territory could not be carved away" has become the highlight of the demarcation story and appears frequently in Korean media and historical works. It was almost the brightest spot of Yi's entire life and certainly was the source of his greatest fame after his death. In a biography written by his son, this staunchly righteous sentence was underlined to represent Yi's devotion to his mother country. The Qing official, according to the biography, "was downcast and dared not to respond" (although no such record is found in Yi's original account).[91]

---

[89] Yi Chung-ha, "Hwa Killim p'awŏn Qin Zigao Ying," in Yi, *Iadang chip.*
[90] Yi Chung-ha, "Chohoe tamch'o."
[91] Yi Pŏm-se, "Sŏn kobi haengsang," in Yi, *Iadang chip.*

From the mid-twentieth century onward Korean irredentists, who denied the Tuman River was the border and claimed that the Korean nation (*minjok*) possessed sovereignty over Manchuria, have portrayed Yi Chung-ha as a nationalist idol. One of the most radical irredentist organizations, the Paeksan Society (Paeksan Hakhoe, established in 1966), once used this phrase on its website as a slogan.[92] The emotional scene has been repeatedly reproduced by contemporary Korean (and, to a lesser extent, Japanese) scholars. Understandably, the story of the joint demarcation, based on Yi's account, was often interpreted as a story of heroic resistance: a Korean literati, frail but fearless, bravely stood up to confront an imperialist country's bullying and colonial ambition.

This narrative, of course, anachronistically projects Korea's victimization in the colonization period (1910–1945) onto a *yangban* official back in the late nineteenth century. It isolates Yi's words from their original context, distorting their meaning. Yi made the decapitation statement in conversations in the last phase of the negotiation, when the two sides could not agree on which stream, the Hongt'osan or the Shiyi, should be named as the utmost headwater of the Tumen border. As we now know, the dispute was actually very minor. At the time Yi himself firmly believed that the Tuman River stem was the border and urged King Kojong to strengthen the border prohibition and prevent Korean peasants from trespassing. Although the negotiations sometimes fell into intensive verbal confrontation, Yi's acknowledgment that the Tuman was the border was not an unwilling "concession" to Qing political pressure, as some studies argue.[93] Instead, several secret reports irrefutably and coherently reveal that he came to this conclusion from what he saw in the field as well as official documents. Moreover, when addressing the cause of the dispute in another secret report in 1887, he blamed Ŏ Yun-jung, the official in charge of handling the squatter issue in 1884, for recklessly taking the false geographic theory and instigating the dispute:

The dispute was all because Commissioner Ŏ Yun-jung, who then went to the north, heard rumors from one or two dwellers. After sending people to [investigate and] bring back the rubbings of the stele, he then claimed that the lands north of the Tuman River belong to us, without carefully checking the literature or observing the surrounding terrain. He even made the civil plaint himself and instigated people in Chongsŏng to submit it to the Chongsŏng official. Based on

[92] "Paeksan Hakhoe," www.paeksan.com/frame.htm, accessed March 30, 2012.
[93] See Sin Ki-sŏk, "Kando kwisok munje," in *Kando yŏngyukwŏn e kwanhan yŏn'gu*, pp. 59–61; Yi Sŏng-hwan, *Kindai Higashi Ajia no seiji rikigaku*, p. 24; Akizuki Nozomi, "Chōchū kankai kōshō no hottan to tenkai," *Chōsen Gakubō*, no. 132 (1989), pp. 79–108.

this plaint, the official issued the note to the Dunhua County [of Jilin]. Thus the two sides contested with each other.[94]

He even suggested that King Kojong let Ŏ openly debate with him so that the fact could be clarified and policy made properly.[95] Yi's son, when introducing his father's heroic deed of demarcation, attributed the territorial dispute to two reasons: the wrongly erected Mukedeng stele and dialectic differences in naming the same river.[96] In a word, rather than refuting the Tumen River border, Yi Chung-ha was a crucial figure who upheld it.

It is more appropriate to see Yi as a patriotic *yangban* official-scholar than a nationalist fighter. According to his biography, Yi was the direct descendant of Kwangp'yŏngdaegun, the fifth son of Sejong the Great (r. 1418–1450). Born to a *yangban* family in straitened circumstances, he was talented and diligent in his literary studies. He passed the civil service examination in 1882 and soon joined the bureaucratic system. Demarcating the Tumen border was the first remarkable achievement of his career. His writings during and after the demarcation clearly revealed his attitude towards the border, the people, the state, and Korea's relationship with the Qing. Like Wu Dacheng on the Qing side, Yi also saw the state as the integration of land and people. For this reason, he strongly opposed Ŏ Yun-jung's strategy of encouraging Korean peasants to cross the boundary, and he disagreed with the Qing's attempt to accommodate Korean squatters on the north bank. What worried him most was losing substantial control of the people:

For Jilin, such a harmless policy is but recruiting people to cultivate their wild-land. But for us, it is a policy of losing people, [as a body] losing the acupoint of *miryŏ* [尾閭]. It is our last resort and could only be treated as an expedient measure. We must not see it as a blessing. [...] Because when those refugees migrated dozens, even hundreds of *ri* into the other's realm, their emotion and life departed from us and we could impose neither benevolence nor sanction on them.[97]

Here Yi compared the state to the human body and metaphorically illustrated an organic view of statecraft. Located at the mean point of a body, the acupoint of *miryŏ* (at roughly the tailbone) was believed in traditional medicine to be the aggregation point of energy (K. *ki*; C. *qi*). Taking this sort of "biopolitical" view, the job of demarcation, the dilemma of segregating people from land, would be like depriving the body of energy.

[94] Yi Chung-ha, "Pyŏltanch'o," in "T'omun kamgye."
[95] Ibid.
[96] Yi, "Sŏn kobi haengsang."
[97] Yi, "Pyŏltanch'o," in "T'omun kamgye."

It was impossible for him to accomplish. Before the second demarcation of 1887 he tried (but failed) to reject the assignment of leading the mission again. In his resignation, he explained that the demarcation was not merely about geographic recognition but more of a political decision, a decision too important to be made by him alone.[98]

During the joint demarcation Yi did skillfully and courageously resist pressure from a superior state. Yet his performance was more of maximizing the interest of the Chosŏn within the *zongfan* framework than protesting the framework itself. Precisely because he insisted on the unshakable orthodoxy of the Sino-Korean hierarchical structure, his attitude towards China, like that of many *yangban* literati, was quite sophisticated and controversial. The complexity can be generalized as follows: geostrategically, the Chosŏn needed the security promised by the Qing, but was always on guard to the Qing's potential expansion. In terms of political authority, the Chosŏn admitted the superiority of the Qing while consistently seeking equal, if not more, initiative in the bilateral relationship. Culturally, the Chosŏn literati never completely set aside their hostility towards the Manchus, but their faith in Confucian civilization was deep-seated. Yi Chung-ha was no exception. His writings expressed contempt for the Qing regime but also revealed his self-identification with Chinese culture and history. One of his poems on Mt. Changbai, which he composed during (or immediately after) the demarcation, rather boldly expressed his geopolitical views. After describing the magnificence of the mountain, the poem ends with praise of its supreme political symbolism:

> This place is the imperial homeland [*che hyang*, 帝鄉] of both states,
> The dragon flies and the phoenix dances, and
> It will be worshipped for ten thousand years.[99]

Presuming the poem was not a later revision, the inclusion of a flying dragon and dancing phoenix, with subtle metonymy in the context of Mt. Paektu/Changbai as the "imperial homeland," may have implied a truly daring message. The flying dragon suggests the dynastic founding epic *Yongbi ŏch'ŏn ga* (*Songs of the Dragons Flying to Heaven*) and hints at the origin of the Chosŏn monarch. The dancing phoenix, a euphemistic suggestion of the divine magpie in the foundation myth of the Manchus, may indicate the origin of the Qing. It is perhaps not entirely an overinterpretation to say that Yi, by paralleling the two regimes in terms of their

---

[98] Yi Chung-ha, "Tŏkwŏn Pusa Yi Chung-ha so," in Kim, ed., *1880-yŏndae Chosŏn-Ch'ŏng kukkyŏng hoedam kwallyŏn charyo sŏnyŏk*, pp. 696–698.
[99] Yi Chung-ha, "Tŭng Changbaeksan," in Yi, *Iadang chip.*

shared ancestral birthplace, delicately announced that the Chosŏn was historically and geographically no inferior to the Qing, to the extent that both regimes could be seen as "empire."

Still, equating the two countries did not contradict his wholehearted advocacy of Confucian civilization. When visited the Kija tomb, Yi wrote a poem to express his great respect for Kija (C. Jizi), a legendary sage king who came to Korea from China. According to the Korean Confucian historiography, Kija, a royal member of the Shang dynasty, emigrated from the Central Plains after the Shang was overthrown by the Zhou. He then founded Kojosŏn, the first state in the ancient Korean Peninsula. During the Koryŏ and Chosŏn dynasties, the Korean courts and literati made tremendous efforts to promote Kija's image as Korea's cultural progenitor. The Kija tomb near Pyongyang was such a space to represent this symbolic association.[100] Yi praised Kija for bringing moral teachings to the Koreans: "[M]y fellow people fortunately escaped from becoming barbarians."[101] At this point Yi clearly differentiated himself from modern nationalists. Korean nationalists in the early twentieth century, notably Sin Ch'ae-ho, generally denounced the Confucian historical genealogy starting with Kija, which they believed essentially saw Korea as a derivative of Chinese civilization. Instead, they pursued a more national (*minjok*) lineage and embraced a progenitor distinctively "Korean": the *Tan'gun*. This new historiography will be discussed in Chapter 5.

Wu Dacheng: A Transitional Figure in Manchurian Governmentality

Wu Dacheng (1835–1902), grand minister in charge of frontier affairs in Jilin, was the first Qing official who promoted the policy of accommodating the Korean squatters, so as to defend and develop Jilin (see Chapter 1). In 1886 he was the leading delegate to negotiate with Russia on the Tumen border. Because he successfully regained the territory, Wu is often portrayed as a "nationalist" hero who, like Yi Chung-ha for Korea, staunchly protected national interests. But such an image, too, is quite anachronistic.

Wu's understanding of the frontier and border was not that different from Yi's: he, too, viewed China and Korea within the structure of

---

[100] Sixiang Wang, "Co-constructing Empire in Early Chosŏn Korea: Knowledge Production and the Culture of Diplomacy, 1392–1592," Ph.D. dissertation, Columbia University, 2015.

[101] Yi Chung-ha, "Pae Kija myo," in Yi, *Iadang chip*.

zongfan, rather than *international* relations. He saw the Russians as hostile neighbors (*qiang lin*), referring to them as *yi* (foreigners, or barbarians). In contrast, he considered Korea an outlying barrier (*wai fan*) of China and the Koreans as *min* (people) like Chinese civilians. Korea, he believed, needed to be protected by the imperial dynasty. He expressed this geopolitical view in a poem in *Huang hua ji cheng* (*A Journey of an Imperial Emissary*), a diary-style record of his demarcation trip in 1886:

> Better to prevent the danger before the danger appears,
> The powerful neighbor is gradually connecting with the outlying
>   barrier.
> I wanted to preserve a middle path in between their borders,
> In so doing to protect Korea for ten thousand years.[102]

In the history of modern China, Wu Dacheng is known not only as a competent official but also as an extraordinary scholar on ancient inscriptions and an artist of calligraphy.[103] It is not clear, from his personal account about the demarcation with Russia, whether he regarded himself as first a Confucian scholar or a bureaucrat. Aside from only a few entries, when he negotiated with the Russians face to face, the diary suggests that his main attention was on collecting local inscriptions, practicing calligraphy, and writing poems. He met with Qin Ying and Jia Yuangui, the Chinese delegates who participated in the first round of Qing–Korean demarcation, but mentioned nothing about the event.[104]

Wu was no doubt a transitional figure in terms of Qing's governance in Manchuria. Serving as an aid to Li Hongzhang in his early career, Wu belonged to the group of prominent Han scholar-officials who immersed themselves in the Self-Strengthening Movement. He gained a reputation for openly criticizing government extravagance, including the restoration of the Summer Palace (Yiheyuan), a project later widely blamed as a cause of China's fiasco in the Sino-Japanese War (1894–1895). In 1880, in order to assist the Jilin general on "all things" (*yiqie shiyi*), he was granted a third-ranking position and transferred from northern China to Manchuria. His main job was to rectify the military and political institutions of the frontier region.[105]

---

[102] Wu Dacheng, "Huang hua ji cheng," in Li Shutian, ed., *Songmo ji wen; Hucong dong xun rilu; Qidong lu; Huanghua jicheng; Bianjiang pan ji* (Changchun: Jilin wenshi chubanshe, 1986), p. 296.

[103] Bai Qianshen, "Composite Rubbings in Nineteenth-Century China: The Case of Wu Dacheng (1835–1902) and His Friends," in Hung Wu, ed., *Reinventing the Past: Archaism and Antiquarianism in Chinese Art and Visual Culture* (Chicago: Paragon Books, 2010), pp. 291–319.

[104] Wu, "Huang hua ji cheng," p. 319.

[105] Zhao Erxun, ed., *Qing shigao*, book 41, vol. 450 (Beijing: Zhonghua shuju, 1977), p. 12551.

Wu implemented reforms and policies that resembled what was done in interior China. Facing the devastation of the banner system in Manchuria, he replaced the banner troops with newly established provincial standing armies (*lianjun*), imitating the institutions of the Xiang Army (of Zeng Guofan) and the Huai Army (of Li Hongzhang). To strengthen the defense on the Tumen and Songhua River borders, he founded the Tumen and the Songhua River Navies. He also incorporated the local militia run by Han Xiaozhong, a leader of private gold miners who occupied the mountain area of Jiapigou. In so doing he expanded state influence into the forest region. During his stay in Jilin he added several forts along the Sino-Russian border and established the Bureau of Machine Manufacture in Jilin (Jilin jiqi zhizaoju), the first modern arsenal in Manchuria.[106] He also strongly advocated a policy of recruiting peasants in north China to cultivate newly released wildlands in Jilin. The policies and infrastructure he put into place attracted emigrants and commerce to the area. For example, he exempted new settlers from a reclamation fee and tax and sent staff to purchase cattle in Korea to deliver to farmers in installments.[107] Under his supervision, several civil institutions were created to manage the recruiting issue and civilian affairs.

Although Wu was transferred to Tianjin in 1883 to assist Li Hongzhang with defense during the Sino-French War, the connection between his political career and Manchurian-Korean affairs was far from over. Two years before he returned to Jilin to demarcate the border with Russia, Wu was dispatched to Hansŏng to manage the aftermath of the Kapsin coup. He went to Korea in early 1885 in the name of "investigating the rebels," but his real task was to stop Japan from signing a bilateral treaty with the Chosŏn, bypassing the Qing. Confronting Japanese diplomats, Wu made clear that the Qing would not abandon its engagement in Chosŏn affairs. During his stay in Hansŏng Wu submitted a series of articles to King Kojong urging a reformation of domestic politics.[108] He also sent the king two pieces of his calligraphy, one that read "To Constrain Expenditures; To Love Humanity," the other "People Are the Foundation of State." These concisely captured Wu's own philosophy on statecraft.[109]

In 1888 Wu was appointed the director-general of the Yellow River Administration to tame flooding in Zhengzhou. He commissioned a

---

[106] Gu Tinglong, ed., *Wukezhai xiansheng nianpu* (Peiping: Hafo yanjing she, 1935), pp. 82–102.

[107] *Ningguta fudutong yamendang*, Chinese First National Historical Archive, vol. 851, microfilm no. 135.

[108] About the content of these articles, see Quan Hexiu, "Jindai zhonghan guanxi shi de yiduan neimu," *Wenxian jikan*, no. 1 (2003), pp. 178–196.

[109] Gu, *Wukezhai xiansheng nianpu*, pp. 113–123.

comprehensive geographic survey of the mid and lower Yellow River, employing the graticule method. The result of this survey was *The Map of the Yellow River in the Three Provinces* (Sansheng Huanghe quantu), which, according to Iwo Amelung, was "the first map covering a large area done by Chinese using Western methods."[110] It marked a high point in the modern development of Chinese cartography. Using Beijing as the prime meridian, the map illustrated 2,412 *li* of the watercourse and was regarded as the most accurate map of the mid and lower Yellow River in late nineteenth- and early twentieth-century China. Wu's experience in Jilin might have had an indirect influence on the project. In the map's preface, Wu justified the project by linking it with frontier defense: "The defense of the coastal area, the Yangzi River and the Yellow River would be impossible without maps. Inaccurate maps would be enough to endanger the defense projects."[111]

Wu's last official position was as provincial governor of Hunan. However, his political career ended not in Hunan but in Manchuria. In 1894 both Qing and Japanese troops were sent to Korea to help suppress the Tonghak Rebellion. The incident soon turned into a military confrontation between the Qing and Japan over control of Korea. When the Sino-Japanese War broke out, Wu Dacheng volunteered to lead the Xiang Army from Hunan to resist the Japanese invasion in the Liaodong Peninsula. Amateur military commander as he was, he suffered a crushing defeat, with the Xiang Army being wiped out almost completely. He was permanently removed from office after the war.

With both his successes and failures in Manchuria, Wu Dacheng symbolized the grand transition of local governance and to a large extent foreshadowed the political trajectory of this vast frontier region in twentieth-century China. Manchuria had long been a geographic and political frontier distinct from other parts of the Qing empire. The cradle of the Manchus, especially Jilin, had cautiously distanced itself from Han influence in interior China. For that reason only banner men could hold top civil and military posts in Manchuria. Although the Manchu politician Chongshi, when serving as the Shengjing general (1875–1876), allowed the Han to take charge of some county-level governments, his administrative reforms were limited to the Shengjing area, and Han were assigned only to lower-ranking positions.[112] It was not until Wu assumed his office in Jilin that for the first time a Han was promoted as a high-ranking official in charge of frontier affairs in Manchuria. When sponsoring local

[110] Amelung, "New Maps for the Modernizing State," p. 697.
[111] Gu, *Wukezhai xiansheng nianpu*, p. 194.
[112] Ma, *Zhongguo bianjiang jinglue shi*, pp. 428–429.

reform, Wu not only encouraged Han immigrants but even let many Han become officeholders. Some of them (e.g., Li Jinyong, who discovered the Korean squatter problem) became a new generation of state agents in the late Qing and early Republican era in Jilin. Starting with Wu, Jilin administration was no longer monopolized by the banner troops or the Imperial Household Department. Wu's reforms established a new civil administrative system that gradually replaced the banner system over the next two decades. The rather smooth transition promised the continued presence of state power in the region, however different it might be.

Defeat in the war with Japan led to the general fading of the generation of the Self-Strengthening Movement from the Qing political arena. Like Wu, Li Hongzhang was never able to recover from this major blow. During the confrontation a new political force, the Beiyang clique led by Yuan Shikai, replaced the old generation of elites and emerged as the most powerful military and political force in late nineteenth- and early twentieth-century China. Wu Dacheng's eventual failure represented this shift. Though he himself was not a member of the Beiyang, many important figures of the clique – including Yuan Shikai – were his former colleagues and close friends, and they shared with him similar political ideas. As the Xiang Army was reshaped into the New Army, Wu's frontier policies were reincarnated and continued by the Beiyang officials. Although the clique was composed predominantly of Han born in interior China, many prominent members had first-hand experience in dealing with Manchurian or Korean affairs, as did Wu himself. Some of them, notably Xu Shichang, Tang Shaoyi, Zhu Jiabao, and Duan Zhigui, later not only assumed top positions in the politics of the northeast but also played decisive roles in the central government during the early Republican era. Thanks to this continuity, the frontier-building enterprise initiated by Wu Dacheng and others in the late nineteenth century was not interrupted by the Xinhai Revolution but continued into the Republican era. The process strengthened the political, economic, and military engagement between Manchuria and interior China. The constant practice of territorialization and interiorization, pursued by generations of Han and Manchu politicians, foreshadowed the path by which the Manchu homeland was integrated into a new concept of "China."

3 Making "Kando"
The Mobility of a Cross-Border Society

A few months before the joint demarcation started, the Qing authority in Hunchun received two petitions from a Korean squatter named Yu Un-gŭn. Co-signed by 146 Korean squatters, the petitions expressed their desperation and begged the Qing government to allow them to stay. Their extreme poverty, Yu wrote, had driven these households from "a thousand *ri* afar" to Qing to seek food. North of the Tumen River, on the opposite side of Chosŏn's Chongsŏng Prefecture, they built shelters to farm the wilderness. The region was Qing territory, yet the residents of Chongsŏng did not allow them to settle there because the land was under dispute. Finding themselves trapped in a dilemma, Yu and his fellow squatters begged the Qing local government to grant them land. "We could farm the land," he said, and even "shave our hair to be [Qing] civilians." The Hunchun official forwarded the petitions to Xiyuan, then the Jilin general, who in turn sent them to Beijing, along with a policy suggestion. Xiyuan shifted the tone of the petitions to emphasize that these Koreans were willing to naturalize themselves as Qing subjects. He warned that it would be miserable and dangerous if the Qing forced them to return. "People of Korea are also people of China," Xiyuan explained. "We should settle them down and comfort them, so that they will not go to the enemy."[1] By "enemy," of course, he meant Russia.

There is little record of the voice of early Korean immigrants. When it appears in official documents, it is mainly because their survival strategy matched the Qing local government's security needs. Together, they created the necessary conditions for the emergence of a migrant society on the north side of the Tumen River. "State boundaries are less porous for people and for labor than they are for capital," David Harvey points out, "but they are still porous enough."[2] This chapter unfolds the early societal formation in this region, employing a micro-level lens. My observation turns from space to people and highlights the vibrant human and

[1] QJZRHGXSL, pp. 1765–1768.
[2] David Harvey, *Spaces of Hope* (Berkeley, CA: University of California Press, 2008), p. 46.

social interactions that make up a dynamic border-crossing community. It covers a period starting roughly in the 1880s, when the first agricultural settlement came into being in this area, to 1907, when Japan was fully involved in disputes over the border.

Although this chapter introduces mainly local stories, we should bear in mind that during this period several historic events in Northeast Asia had direct or indirect impacts on this borderland society. The Sino-Japanese War of 1895 upended the Qing's political and military influence in the Korean Peninsula. The "independence" of Chosŏn Korea, however, did not grant Japan exclusive privilege to the peninsula. In early 1896, fearing Japan and the pro-Japanese faction that controlled the court, King Kojong took refuge at the Russian legation in Hansŏng. During his yearlong asylum there the Korean king sought Russian and American involvement in Korean politics to balance Japanese oppression. The following year witnessed the establishment of the Korean Empire and a series of "modernization" reforms. The notion of independence prevailed on the peninsula, along with the spread of anti-Japanese sentiment.

Japan's military triumph brought the country to the forefront of capitalist and imperialist contention over East Asia. When the Treaty of Shimonoseki forced China to cede the Liaodong Peninsula to Japan, three European powers – Russia, France, and Germany – moved to safeguard their colonial privileges in China and urged Japan to return the territory. Japan resented the incident, known as the Triple Intervention, regarding it as a diplomatic humiliation. It triggered gradually increasing tension between Japan and Russia over the Korean Peninsula and Manchuria. In 1900, in the name of suppressing the Boxer Rebellion, Russia invaded and occupied Manchuria, further expanding its influence in Korea. Taking advantage of the Qing's weakness, Korea tried to ally with Russia to challenge Qing control over the Tumen River region. Hansŏng appointed a military officer, Yi Pŏm-yun, to supervise the Korean community in the region. However, with Russia's defeat in the Russo-Japanese War in 1905, Korea fell into Japan's protectorate. The war completely changed the geopolitical map of the eastern end of the Eurasian continent. After getting US support (partly by acknowledging the American Philippines), Japan officially announced its suzerainty over Korea and took over most of the Russian privilege in southern Manchuria. With Port Arthur (Lüshun) in hand, Japan now controlled the east entrance to inner Manchuria. It soon found the need to control the more convenient western entrance: the Tumen River region, where Russian, Chinese, Korean, and Japanese influences overlapped. In 1907, after several secret investigations, Japan decided to officially intervene in the Tumen frontier dispute. In August it established the Temporary

Kantō Branch of the Japanese Resident-General of Korea (Tōkanfu rinji kantō hashutsujo) and marched to the north bank of the Tumen.

The Formation of "Kando"

The area to the north of the Tumen River was, as I have mentioned, originally part of a hunting enclosure reserved for royalty. It was renamed during the gradual process of reclamation. Pioneer Korean squatters called a small piece of farm land "Kando" (間島, C. *Jiandao*; J. *Kantō*) – literally "island (*to*) in between (*kan*)" – and the "Kando" territory kept expanding in the following years. There are different theories as to how this term was created. All of them suggest a close connection with the agricultural activity of the early immigrants. The first person who recorded "Kando" in an official document seems to have been Yi Chung-ha. In one of his reports after the first round of demarcation, he explained:

The so-called Kando was referring to this: in between Chongsŏng and Onsŏng, there is this place where a branch of the Tuman River bifurcates. The land was merely several *kung*... It was from the year of Chŏngch'ok (1877)...that people began to cultivate the land and call it "Kando," thus the origin of the term. After that, the residents in Chongsŏng, Hoeryŏng, Musan and Onsŏng gradually expanded their reclamation area beyond Kando, to the extent that all lands along the river were cultivated. The general name of Kando, therefore, came from the first piece of land being reclaimed. It was not an island in the river.[3]

Some other theories also suggest that the term originated from a small piece of land surrounded by waters.[4]

During the first half of the twentieth century the name "Kando" was repeatedly transformed and reconfigured by Koreans and Japanese alike to refer to a Korean space in southern Manchuria. The scale of Kando varied, depending on how the space was imagined and classified. In a loose sense, "Kando" usually refers to a plain area on the northern (and at some points western) banks of the Tumen River where the first group of trespassers settled. In modern administrative contexts, it roughly overlaps with China's Yanbian Korean Autonomous Prefecture in Jilin Province. The total size of "Kantō," according to some Japanese texts in the early twentieth century, was between the third and fourth largest Japanese islands: smaller than Kyūshū but larger than Shikoku.[5] A few

---

[3] Yi, "T'omun kamgye, Pyŏltan."
[4] Among the popular theories are that "Kando" originally referred to a shoal encircled by the Tumen River and an artificial conduit; that it was a sandbank in the Tumen River; or that the term was transferred from the Korean word 간도 (Hanja, 墾島), "island being reclaimed."
[5] Song Jiaoren, "Jiandao wenti," p. 280.

sources expanded the area to include the north side of the Yalu River, calling it "Western Kantō." In extreme cases, radical irredentist groups in present South Korea imagine "Kando" as a territory so vast that it contains the whole Liaodong Peninsula and extends all the way to Russia's Primorsky Krai, more than 3.5 times the size of the Korean Peninsula.[6] In any case, the name "Kando" was not widely adopted in government documents until the 1900s. Furthermore, except for a ten-year period during the Manchukuo era (1932–1945), when it became the name of a province, "Kando/Jiandao/Kantō" never materialized as either a geographic or an administrative entity. In other words, "Kando/Jiandao/Kantō" was more of a conceptual space that bore connotations of territorial dispute and colonialist design. For this reason, Chinese authorities (from the Qing to the Republic of China to the People's Republic of China: PRC) never recognized the legitimacy of the term. Instead, the Chinese used "Hunchun" and later "Yanji" for this multiethnic area. For the sake of convenience, however, I will still use "Kando"/"Jiandao"/ "Kantō" in certain contexts to refer to the geographic, social, and political space constructed through the early exploitation of the Tumen northern bank.

From the 1880s to 1910 the Qing, Korean, and Japanese authorities gathered statistics and conducted quite a number of governmental surveys to register the land and population of the region. These are the primary sources I have relied on in this chapter. But it was impossible to generate comprehensive and accurate data regarding the local socioeconomic situation. For one, the agencies of different states in the region had competitive governmental agendas. Not only did administrative divisions in those surveys vary but the subject classifications were also remarkably distinct. For example, "Kantō" for the Japanese was not the same administrative area as "Yanji" or "Hunchun" in Chinese, and it was also much larger than the "Kando" to which the Koreans at the time referred. The lower-level administrative units were also assigned quite differently, making it extremely difficult to cross-check the three governments' censuses. Rival state agendas represented diverse ideological perspectives not only about land but also about people. The statistics compiled by different agencies are hardly comparable. When registering the population, for instance, China sometimes categorized residents as "banner men," "civilians," "naturalized cultivators," and "un-naturalized cultivators," the latter two referring to the Koreans. The Japanese divided

---

[6] See Cho Byung-Hyun, "Kangdo yŏngyukwŏn chujang ŭi chijŏkhakjŏk pŏmwi punsŏk," in *Paeksan Hakpo*, no. 90 (2011), pp. 185–211. Also see "Kando toech'at undong punbu," www.gando.or.kr, accessed December 6, 2016.

the population into "Qing people" (*Sin jin*) and "Koreans" (*Kan jin*). It is uncertain how the Japanese investigators fit "naturalized cultivators" into their dualist classification.

Another complication arose from the mobility and instability of the local dwellers. The northern bank region was a newly opened space to which different groups – Manchu settlers, Han immigrants, and Korean refugees – were attracted, each with their own opportunistic expectations. Some settled down, but many others kept moving, searching for better opportunities in places such as the Russian Far East, inner Jilin, Heilongjiang, and Shengjing. Some Koreans returned to their home country or simply moved back and forth periodically. The mobility of early immigrants made accurate statistics on population and demography impossible. To make matters worse, local "banditry" was so rampant that it severely arrested the stability of this social space.

To construct a narrative of the local situation, I combined and synthesized different archives and records from the Qing, Korea, and Japan. I relied rather more on four sources than others. The first source was the *Investigation on Industries in Kantō* (*Kantō sangyō chōsa*) by the Temporary Kantō Branch of the Japanese Resident-General of Korea (Tōkanfu rinji kantō hashutsujo, abbreviated as the Kantō Branch hereafter) in 1907 and 1908. The study, from the Japanese perspective, provided what was probably the most elaborate and updated description of production and relations of production in the society.[7] My second source was the archive of the vice commander-in-chief of Hunchun (Hunchun fudutong yamen), especially from the 1880s to 1910. Unlike the Japanese source, which portrays a rather static picture of the specific moment, the Hunchun archive demonstrates the historical trajectory of the exploitation of the northern bank from the perspective of the Qing local government. Moreover, it also contains a significant number of judicial cases on

---

[7] I will focus more on the area known as "East Kantō." What the Japanese called "East Kantō," or in some contexts "the east part of East Kantō," was the realm opposite Musan, Hoeryŏng, Chongsŏn, and Onsŏng in Korea. It extended north- and eastward to the Ridge of Laoyeling and westward to the Ridge of Mt. Changbai. The area was roughly the combination of modern-day Helong, Longjing, Yanji, Tumen Cities, and Wangqing County of Yanbian prefecture. The acreage was roughly 107 km (east–west) by 120 km (north–south), or 12,840 square km. "East Kantō" contrasted with "West Kantō," which was confined by the First Songhua River, the Ridge of Mudanling, and the Ridge of Mt. Changbai, covering roughly modern-day Antu County and southern Dunhua City of Yanbian Prefecture, the east part of Baishan City, and the southeast part of Jilin City. The area of modern Hunchun City, located on the lower Tumen River region, was not included in "Kantō" in the Japanese context. See Tōkanfu Rinji Kantō Hashutsujo Zanmu Seirijo, ed., *Kantō sangyō chōsasho* (Tokyo: Takashima Kappanjo, 1910). See also Shinoda Jisaku, ed., *Tōkanfu rinji kantō hashutsujo kiyō* (Sōru: Ajia Bunkasha, 1984), pp. 57–60.

cross-border crimes, which lend us an important lens to observe transboundary livelihood and activities at the time.[8]

My third source was the *Socio-historical Survey of Ethnic Koreans in Jilin Province (Jilinsheng Chaoxianzu shehui lishi diaocha)* conducted by the Institute of Ethnography, Chinese Academy of Sciences, from 1958 to 1960. The institute investigated six ethnic Korean villages in Jilin. Among them, five are located in the Yanbian Prefecture and were inhabited before 1900.[9] Interviews from these five villages (Mingdong, Yingcheng, Chongshan, Taixing, and Taipinggou) provide us with precious micro-level information on the early formation of society on the northern bank. Finally, I used a series of Korean censuses done by Yi Pŏm-yun and his staff. They recorded the Korean population and arable lands in the region in 1901 and registered Korean victims of local banditry in 1904.[10] These censuses contain valuable information on local conditions from the Korean perspective.

Population and Land

During the second half of the nineteenth century immigrants from both interior China and surrounding countries rapidly exploited Jilin. Some of them worked as hunters, gold miners, and loggers, but the overwhelming majority of the newcomers were engaged in agriculture. By 1880 the newly reclaimed wildland in Jilin reached 570,000 *shang*, and more than 300,000 *shang* of it were taxed.[11] That did not include unregistered reclamation. In 1894 the Jilin general included Korean households and

---

[8] Chinese First Historical Archive, *Hunchun fudutong yamen dang'an*. There are also two edited and published anthologies. See Zhongguo bian jiang shi di yan jiu zhong xin and Zhongguo diyi lishi dang'anguan, eds., *Hunchun fudutong yamen dang* (Guilin: Guangxi shifan daxue chubanshe, 2006); Jilin sheng dang'anguan and Jilin shifan xueyuan guji yanjiusuo, eds., *Hunchun fudutong yamen dang'an xuanbian* (Changchun: Jilin wenshi chubanshe, 1991).

[9] The sixth village, Shuanghezhen, was in Yongji County, Jilin City. Located relatively far from the Tumen and Yalu Rivers, it was inhabited by the Koreans no earlier than 1909. Among the other five villages, Mingdong, Yingcheng (formerly Kaoshantun) and Taixing (formerly Taiyangcun) were in Yanji County (modern Longjing City); Chongshan was in Helong County; and Taipinggou was in Wangqing County. See Jilinsheng min zu yan jiu sou, ed., *Jilinsheng Chaoxian zu shehui lishi diaocha* (Beijing: Minzu chubanshe, 2009).

[10] These surveys and censuses include: "Kando kŏmin hosu kant'o sŏngch'aek," Kyujanggak, 17191; "Ko-Kando chŏn'gyol sŏngch'aek," Kyujanggak, 17192; "Ko-Kando chŏnmin sŏngch'aek," Kyujanggak, 17193; "Kando kŏmin kanbyŏk sŏnch'aek," Kyujanggak, 17194; "Kyŏngwŏn-gun Wŏlbyŏn hanmin-ho ch'ong chŏn'gyŏl sŏngch'aek," Kyujanggak, 17195; "Hambuk pyŏn'gye sŏngch'aek," Kyujanggak, 17994-v.1–2, microfilm no. M/F75-103-30-G, M/F82-35-56-A.

[11] Zhongguo bianjiang shidi yanjiu zhongxin, ed., *Dongbei bianjiang dang'an xuanji*, vol. 118 (Guilin: Guangxi shifan daxue chubanshe, 2007), p. 166.

Table 1 *Korean population in "Kando" (1901)*

	Musan Kando	Hoeryŏng Kando	Chongsŏng Kando	Onsŏng Kando	Kyŏngwŏn Kando
Household	1,162		386	350	280
Land (*sok*)	267,390	110,811	53,652		127,100

Notes: The Koreans didn't give names to the places on the other side of the river, so they used instead terms such as "Musan Kando" to refer to the place that was opposite Musan across the river. 1 *sok* is about 15 square meters.

land along the Tumen River in governmental registration and established primary administrative institutions. For the first time, 4,308 households and 15,443 *shang* of taxable lands were registered. Koreans living in these near-river communes had a population of 20,899.[12] In 1901 Korean officials for the first time registered Korean households and reclamations near the river. Table 1 was generated from these incomplete statistics.[13]

The number of immigrants had skyrocketed thereafter. Before 1907 the Helongyu region (in the mid-stream) alone accommodated 5,990 Korean and 264 Chinese households, and arable land reached 23,972 *shang*.[14] Note that these figures covered only a portion of the whole cultivator society. According to Chinese archives, by 1907 the entire administration of "Yanji Ting" (sub-prefecture) had 8,925 households (origin unidentified) which were farming 56,968 *shang* of land.[15]

The Japanese investigation of "East Kantō" gave a much larger number of households and overall population, even though the Japanese realm of "(East) Kantō" excluded Hunchun County from the Chinese "Yanji *Ting*." Table 2 is adapted from the *Industries Investigation* done by the Kantō Branch in 1907.[16]

It was obvious that, due to geographic affinity, Korean immigrants – especially those from northern Hamgyŏng – far outnumbered the Han migrants, who came mainly from Shandong province. The same survey estimated that the total arable land, in both plains and hills, was 54,122

[12] QJZRHGXSL, vol. 9, p. 5722.
[13] Summarized from Kyujanggak 17191, 17192, 17193, 17194, and 17195. The numbers are quite small, probably due to the limitation of the surveys.
[14] Wu, "Yanji bianwu baogao," pp. 66–68. The number of total arable land is my calculation. The original number in the text was 25,501 *shang*. But I found it was wrongly calculated.
[15] Ibid., p. 57.
[16] Tōkanfu Rinji Kantō Hashutsujo Zanmu Seirijo, ed., *Kantō sangyō chōsasho*, Nōgyō, p. 58.

Table 2 *Household and population in "Kantō" (1907)*

Koreans		Qing people		Total	
Household	Population	Household	Population	Household	Population
16,101	82,999	3,900	27,371	20,001	110,370
	75.1%		24.9%		Percentage

chō, which is around 53,673 hectares.[17] This number, unlike that of the population, is quite close to the Chinese statistics.

Villages and Settlements

The early explorers, mostly poor peasants, were scattered in plains or gentle hillsides, living only in shacks or huts. Eventually they built houses out of straw, sorghum stalks, earth bricks, and wood. Korean houses were usually separated from each other, thus forming early hamlets and villages. Since land was plentiful and inhabitants were relatively scattered, these settlements were quite small. In the Mingdong area, hamlets were spaced about 2 to 3 *li* from each other and contained different numbers of households, ranging from one to several dozens.[18] In Taipinggou the hamlets were not centralized as a village until 1935. Within the village there were six hamlets, each containing four to eighteen households, scattered in three areas (River West, River East, and Ridge East) 3 to 5 *li* away from each other (see Map 7).[19]

The hamlet or village – called *cun*, *tun*, or *tong* – was the basic unit of the local community. The Jilin government organized the early villages into middle-level units called *she*, or communes. The scale of the communes varied. In a statistic from 1893 on the communes in the Hunchun, Nangang, and Donggou areas, there were fifteen communes composed of 99 villages. The number of households in these communes ranged from as few as 11 to as many as 132.[20]

Most communes concentrated in the middle Tumen section, around a fan-shaped alluvial plain constructed by the Tumen and its three main northern tributaries: the Hailan, the Burhatong, and the Gaya Rivers.

---

[17] Ibid., pp. 22–23.
[18] *Jilinsheng Chaoxianzu diaocha*, "Mingdong village," p. 41.
[19] Ibid., "Taipinggou," p. 312.
[20] Yang and Sun, *Zhongchao bianjie shi*, pp. 380–381.

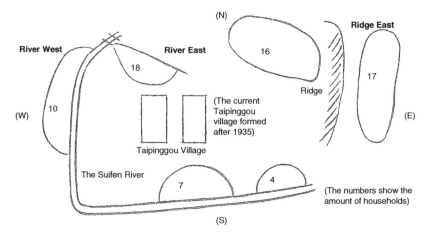

Map 7 Taipinggou village
Source: Revised by author from a map in Jilinsheng minzu yanjiu suo, eds., *Jilinsheng Chaoxianzu shehui lishi diaocha*, p. 312.

Further from this area were fewer communes and less cultivated land. In comparison, communes close to the alluvial plain (small in acreage) generally had greater household density and more arable land. For example, in 1907 the Commune of Guangzong, which covered quite a tiny area opposite from Chongsŏng, had 251 households with nearly 1,014 *shang* of land. In contrast, the Commune of Chungeng, the most northeast commune in Kantō, whose domain extended probably more than 100 times larger than Guangzong, had only 61 households and 1,331 *shang* of cultivated land.[21]

Mobility of the Immigrants

Early immigrants were extremely mobile. This crucial element determined many features of the society. A significant portion of the cultivators, both Han and Korean, had no intention of staying there permanently. Many of them left after accumulating some wealth, either returning home or going further to seek more opportunities. Take the example of Chongshan village, located opposite Musan. Although Korean cultivators came here

---

[21] A Japanese map illustrates the pattern well. See "Kantō Sina si Chōsenjin koshō shamei ryakuzu," in Tōyō Takushoku Kabushiki Kaisha, ed. *Kantō jijō* (Keijō: Tōyō Takushoku Kabushiki Kaisha, 1918), appendix. The data are from Wu, *Yanji bianwu baogao*, pp. 56, 66. The comparison of the size of the two communes is my calculation.

as early as 1870, rarely did they settle down until the early twentieth century.[22] In Mingdong village, the first group of cultivators came mainly from the Six Garrisons, whereas the first settlers were from the regions south of the Six Garrisons, such as Kyŏngsŏng, Myŏngch'ŏn, Kilju, and Puryŏng.[23]

A simple statistic also exposes this migratory aspect. I cross-referenced a household registration in 1901 with a 1904 survey of households that had been victimized by banditry (both were registered by the same Korean authority). Comparing the parts of "Musan Kando" (the area across from Musan), which both surveys record in detail, the result shows that only about 15 percent of the households (63 out of 432) listed in 1904 could be found in the 1901 survey. Of course, the scopes of the two sets of statistics were not exactly consistent: the village boundary changed remarkably, and it is possible that not every household in the victimized villages was looted. But, even if we focus on just one small neighborhood (called "Taeyŏngdong") in the 1904 census, which has the greatest concentration of names from the earlier record, the ratio is merely 20 percent (27 out of 138). By the same token, if we go in the reverse direction, focusing on a small neighborhood (called "Sinhŭngdong samp'o") in the 1901 record whose names appear most often in the 1904 record, the outcome is similar: only 24 percent (12 out of 51) of households in this community remained. This rather rough calculation reveals that, in the area covered by the 1904 survey, the majority of local residents had changed in the last three years.[24]

Social Structure

Most of the Koreans in the 1870s and 1880s who chose to settle down rather than return to their homeland belonged to the subaltern class of slaves and servants.[25] Partially because of that, compared to regular rural societies in Korea, traditional forms of power were not as dominant in social relations. Instead, economic, cultural, religious, and political nexuses formed almost simultaneously in this newly developed social space. Aside from the city of Hunchun, an administrative and economic center of the region established long before Jilin was opened up, several major

---

[22] *Jilinsheng Chaoxianzu diaocha*, "Chongshan village," p. 158.
[23] Ibid., "Mingdong village," p. 5.
[24] The data for my statistics are collected from two sources: "Hambuk pyŏn'gye sŏngch'aek" and "Kando kŏmin hosu kant'o sŏngch'aek."
[25] Wu, "Yanji bianwu baogao," p. 60.

social spheres gradually appeared. The most prominent was Longjing (K. Yongjŏng).

Formerly known as Liudaogou ("the Sixth Ditch"), Longjing is located on the southern bank of the Hailan River. It was first inhabited in 1877 by fourteen Korean households. In 1886 an ancient well dug by the Jurchens was rediscovered there, which attracted more Korean and Han cultivators to gather in the surrounding area. To show the importance of this water source, the village was renamed Longjing, meaning "Dragon Well." Thanks to its excellent soil quality and suitability for irrigation, Longjing became one of the most developed villages in the area. Around 1900 rice was successfully cultivated in a paddy field in Longjing, a first for the whole Kando region. By 1907 101 households (96 Korean, five Chinese) were living in the village. Among the 400 villagers, one-fourth of them were tenants and the rest were owner-peasants. The nearby residents gathered at the rural market of Longjing six times a month to purchase cloth and groceries.[26]

Religious influences – especially the newly imported Western religions, which had stronger mobilization capacities – soon penetrated this nascent and thriving community. In 1897 a Catholic missionary was sent to Longjing by the Wŏnsan Archdiocese of the Paris Foreign Missions Society and converted hundreds of Koreans in the whole Kando area. The first Catholic church was built in Longjing five years later.[27] In 1906 the British Canadian Presbyterian Church, also coming from Wŏnsan, established a branch in Longjing and began to preach Protestantism in the farming community.[28]

The religious nexus contributed to the emergence of the schooling network. This was especially the case for Presbyterian Protestantism. In August 1906 a former high-ranking official and anti-Japanese activist, Yi Sang-sŏl, was exiled to Longjing from Hansŏng after his release from prison. With the help of local Korean Christians, he bought a house from a villager and founded the Sŏjŏn Academy (K. Sŏjŏn sŏsuk; C. Ruidian shushu), the first Western-style school in the immigrant society. More than eighty students were recruited. Many of the teachers and students

[26] Tōkanfu Rinji Kantō Hashutsujo Zanmu Seirijo, ed., *Kantō sangyō chōsasho*, Shōgyō, pp. 1–2. See also Han Shengzhe and Jin Shi, "Longjing kaifa shilue," in Zhengxie Longjing Xian weiyuanhui, Wenshi ziliao yanjiu weiyuanhui, ed., *Longjing wenshi ziliao*, vol. 1 (Longjing: Longjing wenshi ziliao weiyuanhui, 1986), pp. 3–7.

[27] Jin Guangxi, "Yanbian tianzhujiao de yange yu xianzhuang," in Yanbian Chaoxianzu zizhizhou zhengxie, Wenshi ziliao weiyuanhui, ed., *Yanbian wenshi ziliao*, vol. 8 (Yanji: Yanbian wenshi ziliao weiyuanhui, 1997), pp. 1–24.

[28] Han Shengzhe, "'Yingguogang': Longjing jidujiao zhanglaopai jiaohui shimo," in ibid., pp. 93–113.

were both Christian and anti-Japanese. They went on to set up a number of primary and middle schools in the Kando region after Sŏjŏn was shut down by the Japanese in 1907. Despite existing for only eight months, Sŏjŏn is regarded today as both the birthplace of modern education for the Korean-Chinese and the cradle of the Korean nationalist movement in the Yanbian area.[29] From a sociological perspective, Sŏjŏn manifested the organic link and the close affinity of religious, cultural, and political influences in this new nexus. Schools in Kando were initially funded collectively – not that different from most rural schools in China or Korea. A Chinese local report in 1907 showed that every commune had some public lands to fund schools (*yi xue tian*), although some communes had more than others. Students studied Confucian classics but read them in Korean pronunciation. Literacy was high: "[F]our out of ten people can read," according to the 1907 report, even though few of them spoke Chinese.[30]

It was because Longjing was an intersection of all these societal forces that the Japanese chose to build their colonial institution there. The Japanese came to realize the importance of Longjing during a clandestine intelligence-gathering trip to Kantō as they planned for future intervention. The team tried to visit a school (Sŏjŏn) and a Christian church in Longjing but was snubbed by the hosts and treated "rudely" by the principal (Yi Sang-sŏl himself). Nevertheless, after several days of investigating, the team concluded that "Longjing is the topographic center of the Kantō area. In the future when we officially come here, it will be the proper place to set up the institution." It should be noted that the local centers had not yet grown into towns at the time. Only after multiple states competitively set up government institutions there did important villages such as Longjing develop into townships.

Landownership, Production, Ethnic Relations, and Trade

Relations of Land

Land distribution was not an issue for the pioneers. The Jilin Korean Ethnographic Investigation commented that, in the early exploitation of

---

[29] Ibid., pp. 100–101. *Kantō zaijū Kanjin no shinzoku kanshū sonota*, Jangseogak Archive (霞城古書10492-2 B6B-55), Academy of Korean Studies. Li Fengqiu, "Yanbian diyisuo xiandai xuetang: Ruidian Shushu," in Yanbian Chaoxianzu zizhizhou zhengxie, Wenshi ziliao weiyuanhui, ed., *Yanbian wenshi ziliao*, vol. 5 (Yanji: Yanbian wenshi ziliao weiyuanhui, 1988), pp. 1–4.

[30] Yanbian chaoxianzu zizhizhou dang'anguan, ed., *Yanbian qingdai dang'an shiliao huibian* (2004).

Yingcheng, "the one who reclaimed the land could farm on this land, it does not matter who owns it."[31] Similarly, in Taipinggou "the land belonged to the cultivators themselves, and there was no limit on how much one could occupy."[32] When the Qing government started to register the wildland on the Tumen northern bank, it encouraged legal migrants to purchase land titles for a modest sum. The policy to legalize privately cultivated lands triggered the emergence of the first groups of local landlords, mostly Han people with some financial resources. Since there was no restriction on how much land they could contract, they tended to used natural boundaries, such as hills or waters, to mark their properties. For this reason they were called *zhanshanhu*, "the households who occupy the mountains." In Chongshan, one Chinese landlord named Wu contracted more than 100 *shang* of land alone.[33] To farm on such a huge scale of privatized wildland was certainly beyond the ability of a few "mountain occupiers," so they hired Han Chinese and Korean refugees to help. The Koreans living along the southern bank of the river were the main source of labor.

During the initial development of the region the overwhelming majority of Korean cultivators worked as tenants or short-term farmers. In Mingdong, most lands were owned by a Han Chinese landlord, one Dong Han. An older villager later recalled: "At the time when we first came here, Dong Han rented his lands to Korean tenants. He himself also farmed tobacco on a large piece of land. During the busy farming seasons he would hire 100-odd Korean temporary workers from Hoeryŏng. In normal seasons the same lands were farmed by Han Chinese long-term laborers."[34]

The golden period of the "mountain occupiers" ended when all the cultivable wildlands were contracted. From then on, people got land either from market or by inheritance. In this phase a number of Korean landlords emerged. Some of them were foster sons of the Han landlords; some were industrious tenants; some were naturalized Koreans who had settled there for a longer time. The Japanese study in 1907–1908 took eight of the Korean landlords as examples to show that most of them had resettled in the Kantō area for thirty to forty years and identified themselves as Qing in all respects.[35]

---

[31] *Jilin Chaoxianzu diaocha*, "Yingcheng, zuoyequ," p. 46.
[32] Ibid., "Taipinggou," p. 313.
[33] Ibid., "Chongshan village," p. 158.
[34] Ibid., "Mingdong village," p. 4.
[35] *Kantō sangyō chōsasho*, Nōgyō, pp. 29–30.

A notable phenomenon was the emergence of the Korean "nominal landlords." It was partially a strategy in response to the Qing policy that Koreans could own land only if they were registered/naturalized as Qing subjects. In Mingdong, for example, Dong Han died in 1899, and his relatives decided to return to Shandong. The titles to his lands were transferred to three naturalized Koreans, An Sŏng-ju, Kim Pyŏng-ho, and Pak Yun-sŏp. An was Dong's accountant, Kim was the brother-in-law of a powerful local Han Chinese, and Pak's family was also influential in the local community. These three then secretly sold Dong's lands to the un-naturalized Koreans in the nearby villages and deducted a 10 percent commission from each transaction. The strategy benefited both parties: the nominal landlords earned a commission and a portion of the harvest (10 to 20 percent); the Korean peasants who were not willing to be registered/naturalized could become de facto landowners and work as owner-peasants, though in theory they were only the tenants of the nominal landlords.[36] In many other cases, the Korean peasants in a village raised funds together and selected one member, usually a senior family head or a Chinese speaker, to register/naturalize himself. He used the collective funds to purchase land in his name and so became a nominal landlord.

Relations of Production

Although class relations started to take shape in the early phase of settlement, many sources note that class stratification was not salient before 1907. One reason for this was the high mobility of the population. Most of the early Koreans who crossed the river started out as tenants but then either left or became landowners. Another reason was that land distribution had been so favorable to the early settlers that some decided to stay because they could own land by any number of means. The Japanese study in 1907, despite criticizing that the Qing people occupied more land than the Koreans, still counted 80 percent of Qing households and 60 percent of Korean households as "landlords." Altogether it counted 3,120 Qing landlord households occupying 34,320 *chō* of land, and 9,660 Korean landlord households holding 17,870 *chō* of land.[37]

According to Qing policy, no tax was collected on newly reclaimed wildland for the first three to five years. Landlords also exempted rent during the period, and even lent their tenants seeds, tools, cattle, and

---

[36] *Jilin Chaoxianzu diaocha*, "Mingdong village," p. 5.
[37] *Kantō sangyō chōsasho*, Nōgyō, p. 61. One *chō* is roughly 9,917 square meters.

food. After that, of course, tenants were expected to pay rent. Depending on the location and quality of the soil, the rent varied from 20 to 50 percent of the harvest. Later, as the cost of land accelerated, in some fertile areas the rent was as high as two-thirds of the harvest.[38] After a few years of accumulation some Korean tenants were able to purchase land, provided they decided to stay and naturalized themselves as Qing subjects.

Ethnic Relations

Within the society, ethnic relations were largely shaped by cross-boundary employment, trade, adoption, inter-ethnic marriage, and, of course, conflicts. Although no statistics show the scale of these activities, numerous lawsuits in the Hunchun Archive reflect the close economic and social bonds connecting the Han and the Koreans. (Since these civil and criminal disputes involved another important topic of cross-border jurisdiction, I will discuss them in detail in the next chapter.)

As the surrounding states began to intrude on the frontier society, each bringing its own political agenda, they took note of the existing ethnic relations. The Japanese study insisted that Koreans were constantly bullied by Qing officials and "bandits," whereas the *Jilin Ethnographic Investigation* stressed the cooperation and integrity between the two ethnicities. Modern Korean and Korean-Chinese scholars criticize the Qing's naturalization policy and local bandits' harassment yet generally target the Japanese as the oppressors of both the Han and the Koreans. Despite the distinct strategic and ideological motivations, no source denies the simple fact that, although Koreans comprised the majority of the population, from the very beginning the northern bank society was a hybrid immigrant space with extremely vibrant cross-ethnic interactions.

A common misunderstanding is that Korean and Han peasants were the only two groups in the region. They were not. In the Hunchun area, for example, the indigenous Manchu composed a significant portion of the population. Moreover, along with the development of Jilin came many Hui Muslim merchants. Their trade connected the local community with the outside world. As did transport hubs such as Hunchun and Dunhua, and Longjing, too, which became home to Hui merchants after 1900.[39] Added to these groups were Russian and Japanese merchants, who from the 1890s onward increasingly based their cross-border businesses on this multicultural borderland, particularly in Hunchun.

[38] *Jilin Chaoxianzu diaocha*, pp. 5, 46, 159; *Kantō sangyō chōsasho*, Nōgyō, pp. 47–50.
[39] Nan Mingzhe, "Yanbian yisilanjiao jinyuxi," in Yanbian Chaoxianzu zizhizhou zheng xie, Wenshi ziliao weiyuanhui, ed., *Yanbian wenshi ziliao*, vol. 8, pp. 70–77.

Market and Non-Market Trade

With the opening of the Tumen River region, the borderland soon grew to be a center of the regional trading network. The core of this network was the city of Hunchun, a port town located in the lower Tumen River where the vice commander-in-chief of Hunchun was stationed. Merchants from China, Japan, and Russia flooded in, along with agricultural immigrants. Until 1909 Hunchun was home to more than 7,000 people and 500 firms. It was the second largest city in Jilin, next only to the provincial capital at the time, Jilin City.[40] Adjoined by the Russian port of Posyet Bay, Hunchun was an important intersection of several land and maritime routes in Northeast Asia, proudly claiming itself the center of the Hunchun–Vladivostok commercial circle. The business area of the circle covered Jilin and Heilongjiang in Manchuria, the southern part of the Primorskaya, and northern Korea.[41]

The Hunchun–Vladivostok circle then connected with the business circles in Shandong, Shanghai, and Japan. Many Hunchun merchants built their commercial networks by setting up headquarters in Shanghai, their general branches in Hunchun and Vladivostok, and their retail shops in towns and villages in eastern Jilin.[42] Thus, the world capitalist market successfully linked to the multilateral frontier of Jilin–Hamgyŏng–Primorskaya. On the Hunchun market, local agricultural products (soybean bricks, soybean oil, vegetables, livestock, and timber) were exported for exchange with industrial products from interior China and foreign countries, such as fine cloth (made in Japan, Shanghai, the United States, and Britain), oil products (mainly Mei Foo, a local brand of Standard Oil from the United States), matches (Japan), gauze and woolens (Russia), sea food (Russia and Japan), cigarettes (Russia and Britain), and cotton (Japan and Jilin).[43]

In 1903 the Chinese Eastern Railway of Russia (CER) was completed. The CER connected Siberia and Vladivostok through the Manchurian hinterland, so cargo imported to Vladivostok and Posyet Bay could be delivered to inner Manchuria and Russia without passing Hunchun.

---

[40] See Ge Xiufeng, "Hunchun zaoqi duiwai maoyi," in Yanbian chaoxianzu zizhizhou zheng xie, Wenshi ziliao weiyuanhui, ed., *Xiri Yanbian jingji*, vol. 7 (Yanji: Yanbian renmin chubanshe, 1995), pp. 207–214; Huang Jinfu, "Chuyi jindai maoyi zhongzhen, Hunchun," in Yanbian lishi yanjiusuo, ed., *Yanbian lishi yanjiu*, vol. 3 (Yanji: Yanbian lishi yanjiusuo, 1988), pp. 21–31.

[41] Adapted from Huang, "Chuyi jindai maoyi zhongzhen, Hunchun," p. 22.

[42] Ibid., pp. 22–23.

[43] Ge, "Hunchun zaoqi duiwai maoyi," p. 212. Also see *Kantō sangyō chōsasho*, Shōgyō, pp. 112–114, 23–26.

Nevertheless, Hunchun remained a strategic hub of local trade. When the tax in Vladivostok increased or border-crossing was restricted, Hunchun was an ideal alternative. For that reason, smuggling was rampant in this border town.

Another form of trans-border exchange was equally, if not more, significant: the trade of grain across the Tumen River. It was estimated that in the first decade of the twentieth century the majority of the grain harvested in the northern bank were millet and barley. Other crops and hemp took about 10 to 20 percent.[44] A significant portion of them were transferred to the south by both local merchants and the Korean cultivators themselves. Hence, grains were circulated in both market and non-market forms. Compared to the international trade in Hunchun, the grain trade seemed less dazzling, but it was more critical. The cross-river transportation was so easy that grains harvested on the Tumen northern bank had always been delivered in large quantities to the south to support the livelihood of northern Hamgyŏng.[45] With the opening of Jilin, the border restriction was relaxed. Importing grains from Jilin became more and more crucial, to the point that the Yanji/Kando area provided almost the entire food base of Hamgyŏng. In a secret report submitted to the Japanese Foreign Minister in April 1907, the Japanese consulate in Jilin said: "The millet produced in Kantō was mainly exported to northern Korea. People in northern Korea relied on it as their food. In exchange, cattle in northern Korea were imported...so that the status quo of northern Korea is able to be maintained."[46]

Crops harvested on the northern bank, mainly grains but also soybeans and hemp, had such an enormous effect on Hamgyŏng that any disturbance in the north caused chain reactions in the south. More importantly, since grains were such strategic commodities in East Asia, grain production in the Yanji area in certain circumstances could generate a butterfly effect throughout the whole Korean Peninsula, affecting even Japan.

Jilin started to officially recruit Korean cultivators in 1885, the year the Qing and Chosŏn conducted their first joint demarcation. The newly reclaimed wildland had been exempted from taxation in the first three years. Beginning in the latter half of the 1880s, the tax-free Eden on the northern bank gradually vanished, and a large portion of the harvest was handed over to Jilin authorities. In 1888 a severe flood devastated

---

[44] Yanbian chaoxianzu zizhizhou dang'anguan, *Yanbian qingdai dang'an shiliao huibian*.
[45] Fengtian gongshu dang, JC10-1-20585, Liaoning Provincial Archive, Shenyang, Liaoning Province.
[46] JACAR, "Kantō no iōkyō hōkoku," in "Kantō no Hanto Nikanshi Seihan Ryōgoku Fungi Ikken," vol. 1, ref. B03041192100, no. 1-0350.

Jilin, including Hunchun and Dunhua Counties, where a large number of Koreans lived. According to local surveys, the harvest in Hunchun was hardly 40 percent of normal years; Dunhua was even worse, merely 10 to 30 percent.[47] The disaster was so grave that the Jilin general asked Beijing's permission to postpone (but not exempt) that year's agricultural tax in those regions for one to three years. At the same time, to eliminate smuggling and grain outflow, the Jilin general ordered all ferries and bridges illegally constructed by Korean cultivators to be destroyed. The effect of these policies in Hamgyŏng was not recorded in Chinese documents. But, in Korean documents, the Chosŏn repeatedly complained to China regarding both tax and transportation issues.[48]

It was hardly a coincidence that in 1889 the Hamgyŏng authority became the first to announce the suspension of grain exports to Japan. Other provinces, such as rice producers Ch'ungch'ŏng and Chŏlla, followed with similar prohibitions due to recent crop failure there. For Japan, the imported rice and grain from Korea played a critical role in stabilizing domestic crop prices, which were a prominent index of its market system and industrial development.[49] Certainly, Japan could not tolerate the skyrocketing price of rice caused by the Korean embargo. As a response, Japan threatened the Chosŏn government with a military invasion should the latter sustain the ban. The bilateral tension was resolved through the mediation of the Qing minister in Chosŏn, Yuan Shikai, in 1893. The Chosŏn withdrew the embargo and compensated Japan with ￥110,000. Yet, the resolution was a bitter fruit for Chosŏn. The forced compromise exacerbated the food shortage and class tensions. The rest of the story is well known: peasants in Chŏlla, cornered by hunger and the unbearable tax increase, ignited a large-scale peasant rebellion under the religious banner of "Tonghak" (East Learning), which led to the Sino-Japanese War in 1894, the "independence" of Korea, and the end of the Qing *zongfan* world order.

The transport of grains, a life-and-death matter for the societies across the Tumen River, demonstrated the critical geopolitical and geo-economic affinity between northern Hamgyŏng and the Yanji/Kando

---

[47] Jilin sheng dang'anguan and Jilin shifan xueyuan guji yanjiusuo, eds., *Hunchun fudutong yamen dang'an xuan bian*, vol. 2, pp. 507–509.

[48] T'ongni Kyosŏp T'ongsang Samu Amun, ed., *Ch'ŏngsang saan*, Kyujanggak 19571, M/F65-41-1. See also Sŭngmunwŏn, ed., *Kongmun tŭngnok*, 1894; Kyujanggak, 5710-10, M/F67-12-1-E, pp. 1–17.

[49] Yoshino Makoto, "Chōsen Kaikoku-go no Kokumotsu yushutsu ni tsuite," in Chōsenshi Kenkyūkai, ed., *Kindai Chōsen to Nihon teikoku shugi* (Tokyo: Ryūkei Shosha, 1975), pp. 33–60; Yoshino Makoto, "Richō makki ni okeru beikoku yushutsu no tenkai to bōkokurei," in Chōsenshi Kenkyūkai, ed., *Chōsensi Ninshiki no Tenkai* (Tokyo: Ryūkei Shosha, 1978), pp. 101–131.

regions, to the extent that Yanji's economic affiliation with Kwanbuk was much tighter than its affiliation with inner Jilin. This was certainly not an outcome the Qing officials were pleased to see. Recorded in the Hunchun Archive, from 1897 onward the local government frequently issued orders to restrict grain exports. Officials at the grassroots level vigorously enforced the restrictions and punished merchants who dared to challenge it.[50] In the 1899 Sino-Korean Commercial Treaty, signed by the Qing and Korean Empires for the first time as equal partners, the two sides addressed the grain issue with a separate article. They emphasized that China had always prohibited grain exportation and expected Korea to enforce the same prohibition in given circumstances.[51] The geoeconomic affinity between the two frontiers, later, also determined Japan's policy when it officially involved the Sino-Korean territorial dispute and further expanded its interests in Manchuria. In response, the Chinese government once again used the grain embargo as leverage to counter the Japanese penetration.

"Bandits": Between Society and State

In spring 1893 the Chosŏn court, via Yuan Shikai, reported to Qing's Zongli yamen on several cross-border crimes committed by Qing. Some Chinese from Jilin had looted and killed Korean residents in Musan and Chongsŏng. The Korean government hoped that Beijing could urge the Jilin authority to "find methods" to prevent such things from happening again. The Qing government fully approved this petition. In his comments Yuan Shikai lamented that banditry in Jilin "had always been rampant." Murdering for money was quite common. If local governments failed to arrest those bandits, he said, merchants and civilians in the Jilin–Korean borderland would suffer endlessly.[52]

During the formation of the Kando society, a particular challenge to local lives was the constant raids and loots by bandits. Banditry was a major coercive power in this emerging social space, to the extent that it drew tremendous attention from all involved states – the Qing, Korea, Russia, and Japan alike. The situation was especially notorious in the Tumen River region. Shinoda Jisaku wrote that, when the Japanese spy team was on its secret trip to Kantō, they were fully armed to protect themselves not from the Qing army but from bandits: "During our trip...

---

[50] HCFDTYMD, vol. 200, p. 488; vol. 203, pp. 36, 61–62.
[51] See article VI of the Sino-Korean Commercial Treaty signed in 1899, in Chung, *Korean Treaties*, p. 51.
[52] QJZRHGXSL, pp. 3184–3185.

we often heard gunshots when sleeping at night. This was because the local residents thought we were horse bandits. To show that we were also prepared with guns, we, too, shot, to bluff."[53] Banditry provided a good excuse for states to interfere with the society. When Korea and Japan tried to justify their involvement on the northern bank, both claimed that their aim was to "protect the Korean civilians from the Qing officials and bandits." Since banditry was such an influential element in local living, and since it even triggered state competition in the region, the phenomenon deserves to be examined thoroughly.

The current section tries to provide a brief sociological study of the banditry phenomenon, focusing on the origin of banditry in Jilin, the multiple forms, natures, and characteristics of so-called bandits, and their sophisticated relations with the state. Not all of those tagged as "bandits" were actual bandits, so I would suggest another term: "nongovernmental armed force" (NGAF).

What was known as the "banditry problem" in the Tumen River region must be viewed within the background of the rise of the NGAF in Manchuria, which can be traced to local rebellions in the 1860s.[54] The rebels, who grew to prominence in roughly the same period as the Taiping (1851–1864) and Nian rebellions (1851–1868) in interior China, became a source of early bandits and militias in Jilin. Not only that, but local rebellions compelled the Qing to lift the frontier prohibition and encourage immigration as a way to eliminate the internal threat. But the policy was not successful in this regard. The opening of Jilin instead provided a breeding ground for the rise of the NGAF, as it triggered the influx of a large number of unmarried and unemployed young men who found no hope in their home of rural Shandong. During the early exploitation the leaders in some industries (e.g., gold mining and logging) organized collective forces to monopolize their resources and benefits. Some villages organized or hired local militias to protect their harvests. But other NGAF could be more aggressive. Composed mainly of unemployed "wandering people" (*you min*), they were professional bandit militias who looted for a living. In any case the NGAF became a crucial force, sometimes even more important than the state, in creating social order in local societies.

---

[53] Shinoda Jisaku, "Kantō mondai no kaiko," in Koryŏ Sŏrim, ed., *Chedŭng Sil munsŏ: Chosŏn Ch'ongdok sidae kwan'gye charyo*, vol. 9 (Seoul: Koryŏ Sŏrim, 1999), pp. 469–531, 478–479.

[54] Tian Zhihe and Gao Lecai, *Guandong mazei* (Changchun: Jilin wenshi chubanshe, 1992), pp. 56–72.

The capitalist and imperialist struggle over Manchuria aggravated the NGAF problem. According to Shibutani Yuri, the Western and Japanese intrusions since 1840 had severely shaken the Qing's original financial-military system. Local stability had to be maintained by newly mobilized militias-turned-standing-armies, which were neither funded nor controlled by the central court. In Manchuria, where local governments were impaired both administratively and financially, a large portion of the local army had to be recruited from the NGAF, especially bandits, so that banditry could be reduced while governmental power was being enforced.[55] One consequence of this policy, however, was that the boundary between governmental troops, civilians, and bandits tended to be very vague. A man could play all three roles, switching among them periodically or under different circumstances. Tian Zhihe and Gao Lecai point out that, when Russia invaded Manchuria, many government armies scattered and turned into bandits.[56] Indeed, constant warfare in the region not only repeatedly destroyed the Qing's state construction but also forced a large number of former soldiers to seek refuge in (or return to) banditry.

Given the ambiguity of their identity and the scarcity of reliable historical records, solid descriptions of the early NGAF – their number, scale, and geographic distribution – are rare. Government sources show that members of an organized bandit troop could range from dozens to several thousands. In a memorial submitted in 1901, the Jilin general reported that bandits ranged widely after the Russian invasion. Although his government had suppressed or "accepted the submission of" many of them, a remnant bandit troop numbering 500 to 600 was still attacking a town. Two other bandit groups, one numbering over 1,000 and the other 2,000 to 3,000, were infiltrating Jilin from Heilongjiang and Fengtian. Moreover, a group of over 100 bandits fled to Nangang (an area in the mid-Tumen River) after being defeated by the Russians.[57]

In his research in the 1930s, Nagano Akira concluded that Jilin was the "birthplace of Manchurian horse bandits." Most of the larger groups gathered around the railway regions and transportation hubs.[58] Tian and Gao's study reveals that, while the majority of bandits were ethnic Han from Shangdong, in the areas adjacent to Inner Mongolia Mongols composed half of the bandit population. But it was very rare that Manchu

[55] Shibutani Yuri, *Bazoku de miru "Manshū": Chō Sakurin no ayunda michi* (Tokyo: Kōdansha, 2004), pp. 30–46.

[56] Tian and Gao, *Guandong Mazei*, p. 7.

[57] See Zhongguo bianjiang shidi yanjiu zhongxin, *Dongbei bianjiang dang'an xuanji*, vol. 2, pp. 45–51.

[58] Nagano Akira, *Shinahei dohi Kōsōkai* (Tokyo: Sakagami shoin, 1938), pp. 286–287.

banner men turned to banditry.[59] Nor is there evidence of the existence of Korean bandit groups in Manchuria, although many Korean anti-Japanese militias were categorized as such by the Japanese authorities.

In her path-breaking study on peasant insurrections in north China, Elizabeth Perry emphasizes the close association between rural rebels and the local environment (both natural and social).[60] Her framework is valid for analyzing the NGAF phenomenon in Jilin as well. Local NGAF varied in form and nature, and their survival strategies developed in accordance with multiple local ecologies. This makes it impossible to define or categorize them under a single rubric. Perry divides rural rebels in north China into two groups: predatory and protective. Following her model, the NGAF in Jilin could be roughly categorized into three inter-related patterns: predatory, protective, and mixed.

The predatory groups were often called *mazei* (J. *bazoku*). Unlike the term used in the Japanese context, which covered almost all forms of the NGAF in Manchuria, *mazei* or "horse bandit" in the Chinese context referred mainly to those who engaged in collective robbing, looting, kidnapping, or other violent crimes. Their distinctive tactic was horse riding. A more popular term among the locals was *huzi* or *hufei* ("bear" or "bear bandit"), which may have originated from an early custom of wearing masks while robbing. These two terms illustrated the main feature of these bandits: they emphasized mobility while trying to cover their tracks. Horse riding was not an ordinary feature in a farming society, but in Manchuria it ensured that an armed force could easily move between different ecological zones: from forest to farm, hill to plain, and village to town. In some areas, big landlords and famous bandit groups constructed a patron–client relationship. In these cases, local villages and horse bandits composed a community of interests.

The protective groups were distinct from the *mazei* bandits. They were militias built by the leaders of certain communities, and they were called "bandits" simply because they attempted to be free from government control. The most famous NGAF of this kind in Jilin was an organization of gold miners (gold "bandits" or *jinfei*) led by a powerful family named Han who occupied the Jiapigou region near Mt. Changbai. This rather vast realm (the eastern part of which overlapped with the western part of "Kando") was generally known as the Han bianwai, meaning "Mr. Han's domain, beyond the willow palisade."[61] The term reflected the fact

---

[59] Tian and Gao, *Guandong mazei*, p. 7.

[60] Elizabeth Perry, *Rebels and Revolutionaries in North China, 1845–1945* (Stanford, CA: Stanford University Press, 1980).

[61] Li Shutian, ed., *Han bianwai* (Changchun: Jilin wenshi chubanshe, 1987).

that the Han family was the absolute ruler in this peripheral realm. The first generation of the Han bianwai, Han Xiancong, took leadership of local gold miners and monopolized gold production, farming, and logging businesses in the area. He ruled with an iron hand, establishing not only a private militia but also independent financial, administrative, and "judicial" systems. It was said that local people "knew only the Han bianwai, not the emperor." To win Han's support for the government, Wu Dacheng granted him an official title in the fifth rank and renamed him Xiaozhong (meaning "allegiance"). However, state influence remained dispensable in his territory.

In essence an autonomous feudal society, the Han bianwai reached its heyday during the rule of Han Dengju (1869–1919), the grandson of Xiaozhong and the third generation of the Han bianwai. According to Yahagi Fukitsu, the Han bianwai in the early 1900s maintained an army of 600 soldiers and two arsenals. His subjects numbered 5,000 households with a total population of 25,000. He also established ten private schools in his domain.[62] Militias of this kind generally protected local society from the intrusion of outsiders and were rarely involved in looting or robbing. They provided order wherever the state was weak, but they were not in direct opposition to the state.

A third typical form of the NGAF mixed the predatory with the protective. The *paoshou*, or "gunners," were self-organized, or hired, village forces usually found in communities where households were spatially concentrated. In many villages, big landlords fortified their high-walled courtyards with mercenary *paoshou*. During the long winters in Jilin no food could be produced from farming, so collective looting among villages was once a normal pattern of survival. The gunners' responsibility was twofold: to protect their own village from outside banditry but to loot other villages. Like the horse bandits, gunners rode horses to attack communities remote from their own.[63] Long-distance harassment guaranteed that they would not be recognized and avenged by gunners in neighboring villages. A gunner was in a gray zone between civilian and bandit. He represented a distinctive feature of the early agricultural ecology in Manchuria.

As the preceding discussion should make clear, banditry was a prevalent survival strategy in Jilin and throughout the whole of Manchuria, so the Tumen north bank was hardly immune to the problem. In a victim survey done by the Korean authority in 1904, items looted from this area ranged from grain, livestock, and household goods to fine cloth, wigs,

---

[62] Yahagi Fukitsu, *Kōbō 3000nen Shina Bazoku Rimenshi* (Tokyo: Nihon Shoin, 1925).
[63] Watanabe Ryūsaku, *Bazoku shakaishi* (Tokyo: Shūei Shobō, 1981), pp. 26–29.

and jewelry.[64] Early cultivator communities along the Tumen River were indeed more vulnerable than other rural communities. But, in contrast to many popular explanations on the issue, ethnic difference was not the main, nor the only, reason for the vulnerability of this region. Instead, we need to understand the phenomenon from geographical and sociological perspectives. As a newly thriving agricultural society located at the center of the regional trade network, the local community easily fell victim to banditry. To make things worse, hamlets and households were relatively scattered, making them difficult to be effectively defended. Because most Korean residents were tenants, owner-peasants, or small landlords, they had neither the capacity to arm themselves nor the financial means to hire gunners. In 1899 a Qing local magistrate-in-waiting submitted a report to the vice commander-in-chief of Hunchun, petitioning the latter not to withdraw his army from the region. His report described the situation well:

The lands cultivated by the Korean border crossers…extend 600-odd *li* along the river. […] The distances between them vary from 3~ 5 *li* to 10~20 *li*. More than 4,000 households are scattered like stars in the sky or pieces on a chessboard. Roads are bifurcated. It is quite difficult to suppress, pacify, pursue and capture evildoers. The locals rely on a branch of troops for protection. The Koreans live a hard life. They do not have the capacity to establish a local militia and to raise funds and depend on the might of this militia. Therefore, the (temporary) stationed troops, I am afraid, could not be withdrawn in a hurry.[65]

The NGAF in Jilin were no more socially marginal than the competing states were. Any state that wanted to successfully establish authority there had to maintain a subtle relationship with the local NGAF powers. The Qing policy towards "bandits" in Manchuria and throughout the country was a Janus-faced strategy combining suppression and recruitment. If it failed to suppress the insurgency, there was always an alternative: to offer the rebels amnesty and enlist their services. The strategy granted the NGAF a considerably large space to roam between state and society. For ambitious young men in Manchuria, choosing to be bandits was not merely a survival strategy but also a way to gain upward mobility. Ironically, then, it was not uncommon for people to rebel in order to be recruited by the very government they were rebelling against. The most famous example was Zhang Zuolin, a bandit-turned-Beiyang-warlord who ruled Manchuria and north China in the 1910s and 1920s. The sophisticated tension/alliance between state and nonstate forces was

---

[64] Oebu, ed., *Hambuk pyŏn'gye sŏngch'aek* (Kyujanggak 17994-v.1–2), microfilm no. M/F75-103-30-G, M/F82-35-56-A.
[65] HCFDTYMD, vol. 213, pp. 495–497.

sustained for decades, until the late 1940s. Competition between multiple states in Manchuria provided even more room for the NGAF to work with and against contending powers. The situation was not unlike that of the early Communist forces led by Mao Zedong and Zhu De in the intersecting territories of multiple warlords in southern China in the late 1920s and early 1930s. Manchuria was unique in the sense that it was a newly developed agricultural/capitalist society that never ceased being torn by the competing states.

All political forces – state and nonstate alike – were eager to win the NGAF to their side, though most of the NGAF did not have their own political agenda. During the Russian invasion, for example, the Russian army forced the Han bianwai to cooperate in the gold-mining business. In the Russo-Japanese War, both Russia and Japan recruited local bandits to spy or fight on the battlefields. Compared to its enemy, Japan apparently invested more – and was more successful – in organizing a pro-Japanese militia called the East Asian Volunteer Army. Moreover, the image of the "horse bandit in Manchuria" (*Manshū bazoku*) had a significant part in the Japanese colonial scheme in the early twentieth century. Thanks to energetic propaganda by pan-Asian activists, the image was romanticized in the popular media. Much as the image of the cowboy did for the American West, the *Manshū bazoku* became as a cultural icon for imperialist Japan's new wild frontier.

To recruit local NGAF to their anti-Qing campaign, early Chinese revolutionaries, notably Song Jiaoren, paid close attention to this strategic frontier land (see Chapter 5). It was also in these socioecological circumstances that the Korean independent activists in the 1920s and 1930s organized numerous resistant militias, making Manchuria not only the birthplace of anti-Japanese guerrilla warfare but also the cradle of the modern (North) Korean state.

4   Taming the Frontier
Statecraft and International Law

In January 1889 Changshun, then the Jilin general of the Qing, submitted a memorial regarding the financial challenges facing the Bureau of Jilin–Chosŏn Commerce. Established three years earlier, the bureau was responsible for collecting tax on the cross-border trade. But its expenses and receipts were highly imbalanced. As Changshun found out, the tax the bureau collected in a whole year "could not compensate [for] the salaries paid in just one month." Initially, Changshun considered the institution "nothing but pure waste." Upon checking the report of his predecessor, he realized that the bureau had been set up "not merely for the sake of taxation, but for protecting Korea from Russia's rapaciousness." He then petitioned to extend the bureau's operation for three more years.[1]

In the next three years the bureau's financial balance remained poor, despite having its budgets cut twice. In early 1892 Changshun and Li Hongzhang cosubmitted a report on the issue. Six years and nine months after the founding of the bureau, they said, the total tax money it had collected was merely 5,050 taels of silver, whereas the government's investment had exceeded 70,000 taels. "How can we tolerate wasting a huge sum of money on this vainly established bureau?" Yet again, they pointed out that the goal "was to supervise (*jimi*) the subordinate state and suppress banditry, not just to collect tax money." Ever since 1889 the bureau had conducted trials in all suits involving the Korean settlers, making it a de facto local administration. Therefore, the two ministers suggested transforming this tax office into a local bureaucracy. The new institution would be responsible for Jilin's negotiations and communications with the Chosŏn and "mollifying the Korean squatters." They proposed naming the new institution the Bureau of Mollifying Cultivators (*Fu ken ju*), so that "the name and the reality are congruent."[2] Approved

---

[1] GXCZPZZ, vol. 93, p. 103.
[2] Ibid., vol. 112, pp. 323–324.

and implemented, this transition marked one of the early state-building projects in the newly formed immigration society.

The Qing was not alone in attempting to penetrate the local society by installing state bureaucracy. In the first decade of the twentieth century, in the milieu of the Russian occupation of Manchuria (1900–1904), the Russo-Japanese War (1904–1905), and the Japanese "protectorate" of Korea (1905–1910), Russia, Korea, and Japan all tried to introduce state machinery over the north side of the Tumen River. The current chapter examines the state-building strategies for local domination among these four rival powers. In this multilateral frontier, state-building efforts presented a trend I call "competing ascendance." The term refers to the fact that, although the contest between individual regimes was hostile and exclusive, state power overall was profoundly rooted and established in this once wild borderland. Precisely because of the increasingly intensified sovereign competition, each state assured its rule through strengthening a range of "modern" state apparatuses: from militarization to bureaucratization, census to policing, and infrastructure building to knowledge (re)production. These apparatuses, practiced by different countries in different times, intertwined together and rapidly accelerated state capacity in this borderland. As a result, the frontier as a sociopolitical space was comprehensively reshaped in accordance with different agendas and along multiple lines. State building in this space was simultaneously defensive, developmental, colonialist, and imperialist. Not entirely unlike "the birth of the Leviathan" in early modern Europe, the joint efforts to tame the Tumen River region in turn stimulated the formation of a different kind of state in East Asia. In the "de-frontierization" process, new understandings of land, people, border, territory, and state emerged. Their sophisticated relationships were redefined, redesignated, and recategorized. To borrow from Gilles Deleuze and Félix Guattari, the borderland experienced two synchronous dynamics of "de-territorialization and re-territorialization," which fundamentally changed the way the space was perceived.

Different states penetrated the Tumen River region with different strategic concerns. Generally speaking, the Qing, as it began losing Korea from its imperial orbit, tried to interiorize the Manchurian borderland by highlighting divisions among frontier subjects. It no longer took for granted Korean squatters as "newborn babies to the Celestial Empire." For their part, Russia, Korea, and Japan took advantage of Korea's nominal independence and focused on ethnic and social integration across the Tumen River. They all emphasized, albeit with distinct political connotations, that the north bank society was a "Korean" space separated from China. In their struggle a new discursive regime in the form of international law gradually overcame, if not completely replaced, the *zongfan* ideology. Along with this change, the geographical and political meanings of this multilateral frontier were significantly transformed.

Qing: Interiorization and Naturalization

The Qing's state building on the northern bank of the Tumen was an integrated part of its administrative reform in Manchuria, a process that could be called "interiorization." A highly developed civil administration gradually became the dominant form of government. The banner system, though not completely abandoned, was more and more marginalized in local governance. A milestone of this development was that in 1907 the Qing abolished the Shengjing, Jilin, and Heilongjiang generals and turned the three domains into "provinces." Although the term "Northeast Three Provinces" (or simply "East Three Provinces") had informally existed for years, it now became the official name of Manchuria. The former Shengjing general was turned into the viceroy of the East Three Provinces, remaining the top official overseeing all military and civilian affairs in Manchuria. In addition, each of the top officials in the three provinces was *xunfu*, a civilian governor, just as in all other provinces in interior China. The first viceroy (Xu Shichang) and all three governors of the East Three Provinces (Tang Shaoyi, Zhu Jiabao, and Cheng Dequan) were Han, as opposed to Manchu.

The transition did not happen abruptly. Before 1907 a series of reforms had occurred at the local level. The Qing's institutional settings in the immigrant society of the Tumen northern bank demonstrated the enhanced state presence. The civil and military reforms in this place included stationing more troops to defend the Hunchun area and promoting Hunchun to the rank of vice commander-in-chief within the banner system (1881); establishing the Bureau of Jilin–Chosŏn Commerce (1885), which was later transformed into the Bureau of Mollifying Cultivators (1894); and founding the Yanji subprefecture (*ting*) (1902), a civilian administration that replaced the Bureau of Mollifying Cultivators, marking the first appearance of the name "Yanji" applied to an administrative space. Moreover, in the early twentieth century the Tumen River Navy was reestablished (1903); four battalions of the newly organized Jilin local army (called Jiqiangjun) were stationed in Yanji (1903);[3] and the Supervising Commission of Frontier Affairs (Bianwu duban gongshu),

---

[3] According to *Yanbian Chaoxianzu shi*, however, the Jiqiang Army had five battalions and 2,500 soldiers in Yanji. "Yanbian Chaoxian zu shi" bianxiezu, ed., *Yanbian Chaoxianzu shi* (Yanji: Yanbian renmin chubanshe, 2010), p. 63.

a contemporary government branch dealing specifically with the border issue, was set up in Juzijie (modern-day Yanji city) (1907).[4] In 1909 the last banner institution in the region, Hunchun vice commander-in-chief, was dissolved and replaced by the Southeast Circuit of Military Defense (Dongnan lu bing bei dao). This completed the bureaucratic transformation of all ruling institutions on the Tumen north bank.

The process of interiorization outlined above was not a planned series of steps. Rather, many of these institutions were created in response to specific challenges. On the one hand, land exploration continued, bringing social and economic developments such as population growth, the natural increase of villages, and the expansion of agriculture and industry. On the other hand, rival countries' similar efforts also spurred the Qing to speed up state building in the area. The establishment of the Yanji subprefecture, for example, aimed to repair the government system destroyed by the Russian invasion. The founding of the Commission of Frontier Affairs, by the same token, was diametrically opposed to Japan's installation of the Kantō Branch of the Resident-General. In a word, Qing government construction was both a part of the grand transition of the Manchurian governance and a local outcome of regional and national competitions.

In some industries the state established direct domination. The Tianbaoshan silver mine, located near Longjing, for instance, was first discovered by a group of Shandong immigrants in 1884 but soon taken over by the local authority. It drew political support from the central government and financial investment from Jilin general. After importing advanced smelting equipment from Tianjin and getting the energy it needed from nearby coal mines, Tianbaoshan soon became the largest silver and copper producer in Manchuria. From 1890 to 1898 it supplied approximately 3 million taels of silver, with the highest daily output nearly 1,000 taels.[5] The mine employed around 500 Han and Korean workers before it was temporarily shut down in 1899 because of a strike. In this kind of industry, the state had direct and solid control.

The situation in rural areas was different. As the immigrant population rapidly grew and reclaimed land stretched further and further, the Qing state had to rely on grassroots agencies to carry out its powers. In

---

[4] Generated from Yanbian chaoxianzu dang'anguan, *Hunchun fudutong yanjiting gaikuang* (1983); *Yanbian diqu zuzhi jigou yange (1714–1945 nian)* (1986); *Yanjiting zhengzhi dili zhizhang* (1983); *Yanji bianwu gongshu youguan bianwu wenti de gezhong shiliao* (1984).

[5] "Chishitsu Kōsan chōsasho," in Tōkanfu Rinji Kantō Hashutsujo Zanmu Seirijo, ed., *Kantō sangyō chōsasho* (Tokyo: Takashima Kappanjo, 1910), p. 67. See also Li Fengchun and Xu Baojun, "Tianbaoshan kuang shihua," in Zhengxie Yanbian chaoxianzu zizhizhou, Wenshi ziliao weiyuanhui, eds., *Xiri Yanbian jingji* (Yanji: Yanbian renmin chubanshe, 1995), pp. 3–17.

1894, the year the Bureau of Mollifying Cultivators was inaugurated, the Qing divided the bureau's jurisdiction into four administrative zones (*bu*), each containing several communes (*she*) for a total of thirty-nine communes. Following the *baojia* registration system of interior China, the local government organized village households into *pai* (each composed of ten households) and *jia* (each composed of ten *pai*). In practice, the state's power was not able to reach down to the village level. It penetrated instead only to the level of commune (*she*). The local government appointed communal leaders called *xiangyue* (K. *hyangyak*) in accordance with residential recommendations. The *xiangyue* had to be registered Qing subjects, either Han or naturalized Koreans. Although not formal officials, they accepted payment from taxation, typically the harvest of 10 hectares of land and 200 taels of Korean currency.[6] Most local administration, such as household registration, land measurement, tax collection, and community policing, had to be executed through the *xiangyue*. This left the *xiangyue*, most of them big landlords, loopholes to maximize their benefits. In Taipinggou, for example, old villagers recalled that the bureau would remeasure and register arable land every three years. In villages the bureau staff members were received by wealthy locals and landlords, relying on them for information. Taking advantage of this, some unethical landlords fabricated the reclamation data, even transferring other people's land under their own names.[7] Since the overwhelming majority of cultivators were nonnaturalized Koreans who had no legal status, they were particularly vulnerable in the system.

Redefining Subjects: The Policy of "Shaving Hair and Changing Apparel" (Tifa Yifu)

At the time, the Qing's priority was not yet social justice but the problem that a vast area of Qing soil was occupied and claimed by Korean refugees. Wu Luzhen, Qing's chief negotiator in the later Sino-Japanese border conflict, described the situation:

The Korean squatters in Yanji subprefecture worked first as servants, then as tenants, then they got landownership. The realm of their cultivation expanded from the northern bank opposite Musan to the northern bank of the entire Tumen River, and further to the whole realm of Yanji subprefecture. By this point they have almost turned themselves from guests into hosts. [...] The birthplace of our dynasty for several hundred years is now nearly a Korean colony.[8]

---

[6] Jilinsheng minzu yanjiusou, ed. *Jilinsheng Chaoxianzu shehui lishi diaocha* (Beijing: Minzu chubanshe, 2009), p. 6.
[7] Ibid., pp. 314–315.
[8] Wu, "Yanji bianwu baogao," p. 65.

The Qing responded to the challenge with a controversial policy called *tifa yifu,* meaning "shaving hair and changing apparel." In 1890 the Jilin general Changshun got the Zongli yamen's permission to announce a regulation on land certificates: "The Koreans who want to leave are permitted to leave; those who wish to stay must shave hair and change apparel and be registered as subjects along with the Qing civilians (*hua min*). Their lands should be taxed in accordance with the number of years since they reclaimed it."[9]

Recall that, almost a decade earlier, the Jilin officials Ming'an and Wu Dacheng had suggested a similar policy, which was not implemented because of the opposition of the Korean court (see Chapter 1). The two policies, one in 1882 and the other in 1890, sound identical but were actually quite different when placed in their respective contexts. The 1882 proposal, that the Koreans "have to switch their apparel to ours before a set time," was conditioned by the expedient of "let them do what they want for now." The real purpose was to encourage Korean labor to develop Jilin and to populate the frontier. There was a long-term goal of cultural assimilation to be realized only at some stage in the future. In 1890, with the border essentially wide open and Koreans moving back and forth across the Tumen River freely, the main problem was to have an efficient way to constrain the fluidity of population and wealth. The Qing's urgent task was to keep the privilege of landownership in the hands of people who chose to resettle permanently and submit to Qing jurisdiction. The hair-shaving policy, then, was fundamentally a politico-economic measure to ensure Qing control of its land and people. Such a policy did not request all Koreans living on the northern bank to be naturalized compulsorily, only those who desired a land title. Separating the right of residence and the right of landownership also avoided an abrupt labor shortage.

Many scholars see the hair requirement as ethnic persecution or cultural assimilation.[10] Indeed, the 1890 hair-shaving requirement recalls the brutal "hair or head" policy after Qing's conquest of interior China in the seventeenth century (when all Han males were forced to shave their foreheads and adopt a Manchu-style queue). However, in 1890 neither ethnic nor cultural assimilation was the intention. The request was no doubt unpopular: despite the fact that some pioneer immigrants and big landlords volunteered to be naturalized, the majority of Korean cultivators – small landlords, owner-peasants, and tenants – refused to

---

[9] Ibid.
[10] See, for example, Jin Chunshan, *Yanbian diqu chaoxianzu shehui de xingcheng yanjiu* (Changchun: Jinlin renmin chubanshe, 2001), p. 97.

change their appearance. Korean official Cho Chon-u, after investigating the "Kando" area in 1897, reported that the Koreans "who shaved hair and changed apparel are not even one in a hundred."[11] After the Russian invasion in 1900, many naturalized Koreans fled south and shifted back to Korean apparel. When they returned once again to the northern bank, many retained Korean hairstyles and dress, leaving the Qing officials in great confusion.[12] A 1907 report by the Helongyu official even said that "not a single Korean is now dressing Chinese cloth."[13] The pragmatic form of landownership also encouraged choice. As mentioned before, the Koreans in practice could acquire land without shaving and changing. As long as they trusted their nominal landlords who registered the land for them, they could have their land in substance without owning it on paper. The strategy was widely adopted and even acquiesced to by the Qing officials. As a result, the hair order was never vigorously imposed in the Korean community. If assimilation was the goal, how could both the controversial policy and the contradictory reality coexist?

To answer this question, we need first to understand why hairstyle and dress were such an important issue to the Koreans. Ethnic/national identity might be one explanation, but certainly not the only one. Hairstyle and apparel in Chosŏn, like that in Tokugawa Japan, marked first and foremost a person's social identity. As codified in one's apparel, one's social status came before ethnic/national status. Within the Korean community, both men and women had to strictly follow a certain hair and dress code in order to distinguish their caste and marriage status. Switching to the Manchu queue and dress meant not just turning oneself into a "barbarian" but also detaching from one's entire social network and becoming an outcast in the community. A large portion of the early Korean cultivators did not want to permanently relocate to the north side. Many constantly traveled back and forth. Eliminating their marks of social identity meant burning their bridges, hence, it was the last thing they would accept. As shown in a petition submitted to the Korean Kyosŏp t'ongsang amun (Department of Foreign Affairs) by some cultivators, the major concern for ordinary Koreans was the social rather than political or ethnic meanings attached to hairstyle:

We believe that people live in peace by following ordinary custom. Once [the custom] is changed, self-suspicion and fear will be aroused, and they will feel abashed in front of others. Therefore they are ashamed to meet people in their

---

[11] Kim No-gyu, "Pugyŏ yosŏn," in Yuk Nak-hyŏn, ed., *Kando yŏngyukwŏn kwan'gye charyo-jip*, vol. 2 (Seoul: Paeksan Munhwa, 1993), pp. 332–370, p. 352.
[12] "Hamgyŏng nampukto naekŏan," Kyujanggak 17983, no. 1-242-244.
[13] Yanbian chaoxianzu zizhizhou dang'anguan, *Yanbian qingdai dang'an shiliao huibian*.

native land and dare not return. Those pitiful victims! Their ancestors' tombs and their affinities and families are all on the other side of the river. But they could not conduct ancestor worship nor meet kin during the ritual ceremony.[14]

The shaving-and-changing therefore presented itself as a parallax policy. At a time when there was as yet no nationality law, it was difficult for the Qing to effectively protect state property from being peopled by nonsubjects, especially in a highly mobile frontier society. Hoping to constrain the mobility of wealth, the state decided to associate exclusive economic privilege with symbolic apparel. The main concern was local economy and security. For this reason, the state tolerated the lack of compliance by the majority of the Korean population, who did not change their apparel, provided that lands were controlled by those who did. But, seen from Korean eyes, the policy was one of ethnic assimilation and humiliation. After all, being able to return was the precondition for which many poor peasants endured leaving home in the first place. Consequently, many of them left Yanji and others resisted with their "hidden transcript": nominal landownership. Such an equilibrium was sustained for years until a more serious and complex challenge – not just who owned the land but who belonged to the "nation" – urged the Qing to create its first nationality law, in 1909 (see Chapter 6).

Cross-Border Crime

The problem of redefining people extended beyond the realm of land-ownership. A major problem in the north bank society involved cross-border crime and legal jurisdiction. Before the opening of Manchuria, when border trespassing was a severe crime, the Qing handled this malfeasance through the *zongfan* institution. If the criminal was a Qing subject, the Qing arrested him – even chased him into Korea's realm, if necessary – and brought him to a Qing trial. If the criminal was a Korean, the Qing sent him to Chosŏn and let the Chosŏn authority conduct a trial and execute punishment according to Korean laws. Only when the crime involved serious violence, such as murder, did the Qing make a joint hearing with the Korean court.[15] The nonnaturalized Korean cultivators, however, were in a jurisdictional gray zone: they were not Qing subjects, yet they lived on Qing land. To further complicate the situation, after 1895 even Korea became a gray area: it was no longer a subordinate state of the Qing, yet the legal code had not yet been revised to redefine

---

[14] "Ch'ŏngsang saan," Kyujanggak 19571, M/F65-41-1.
[15] Li, *Qingchao yu chaoxian guanxi shi yanjiu*, pp. 189–191.

the judicial principles of cross-border crimes. Local authorities thus had to create their own mode of resolution.

Two homicide cases on trial between 1895 and 1899 illustrate one mode. The first case was the murder of Liu Fucheng. In 1894 Musan peasant Yi Hoe-yŏng crossed the Tumen River and served as a tenant working on 5 *shang* of land owned by Han Chinese landlord Liu Fucheng. Regarding the land as a good place for a grave, Yi secretly buried his grandfather's corpse there. Upon discovering the grave, Liu asked Yi to remove it. Their conflict was mediated by local gentry, and Liu finally agreed to sell Yi the land encircling the gravesite. But, without a guarantor, Yi had to leave his nephew, Yi Ch'ŏng-song, as a hostage before returning to Musan to raise funds. Days later, on a rainy morning, Yi Hoe-yŏng came to visit his nephew. Having failed to gather enough money, Yi was upset and drunk. On the way back, he fell from a cliff and died. Venting his anger on Liu Fucheng, the nephew, Yi Ch'ŏng-song, summoned his relatives across the river, and together they beat Liu to death.[16] The second case was the robbing and murder of Su Haoqing in 1895. Su, a Han Chinese peddler, attended the wedding of a Korean friend. Three Korean cultivators who were also guests at the wedding robbed and killed him on his way home.[17]

In both cases the Qing local government arrested and detained the suspects, investigated the crime sites, gathered evidence, and adjudicated in accordance with Qing codes. Yet, after years of processing each case, the Qing did not carry out the punishments. At the end of both verdicts local officials explained that the criminals "are Koreans who temporarily crossed the river and tenanted. They came in the spring and returned in the fall, without shaving hair and changing apparel. They are not registered in our jurisdiction [*bantu*]." The verdicts declared that the criminals should be escorted to Korea and their cases turned over to the local Korean officials "as an example, a warning." The basis of these decisions was not any codified law but precedent. Local judicial practice hence separated the trial, which emphasized Qing jurisdictional authority, from the actual punishment, which was cautiously constrained and often passed on to Korea. Superficially, the practice did not entirely overthrow the conventional jurisdictional custom, as if the *zongfan* structure remained effective.

In September 1899 the Qing and Korean Empires signed the first "equal" treaty between the two countries, the Qing–Korean Commercial Treaty. Two articles in this treaty dealt specifically with the issue of

---

[16] HCFDTYMD, vol. 182, pp. 64–67; vol. 198, pp. 215–235.
[17] Ibid., vol. 185, pp. 366–367; vol. 198, pp. 237–248.

interstate jurisdiction. Article V indicated that a Chinese or Korean criminal would be adjudicated according to the laws of his native country, regardless of the nationality of the victim or whether the crime occurred in China or Korea. If the criminal committed a crime in the other country, consular authorities would be responsible for enacting punishment:

A Chinese subject who commits any offense in Korea shall be tried and punished by the Chinese consular authorities according to the laws of China.

A Korean subject who commits any offense in China shall be tried and punished by the Korean consular authorities according to the laws of Korea.

A Chinese subject who commits any offense against the life or property of a Korean in China shall be tried and punished by the Chinese authorities according to the laws of China.

A Korean subject who commits any offense against the life or property of a Chinese in Korea shall be tried and punished by the Korean authorities according to the laws of Korea.

Regarding people who had already resettled in the other country, article XII both enacted cross-border amnesty and prohibited any further cross-border migration in either direction:

All persons who have already crossed the frontier and reclaimed ground shall be allowed to pursue their avocations in peace and enjoy protection for their lives and property. From this time forward migration across the frontier shall be prohibited on both sides in order to avoid complications.[18]

These two articles reflected, in fact, two distinct principles of interstate jurisdiction. Article V clearly demonstrated the idea of extraterritoriality, whereas article XII still continued the *zongfan* practice – at least from the Qing's viewpoint. As Shengjing general Zengqi once wrote to his Korean counterpart in 1901, article XII "would definitely not have been created were there not several hundred years of Sino-Korean friendship."[19] In this remark he alluded to a criminal case in which a Chinese bandit asserted that he was appointed by the Qing government to rule the Korean cultivators (in the Yalu River region). In response to the Korean side's request, Zengqi promised he would investigate the case yet also explained that articles V and XII, which the Koreans cited as grounds for the request, should not be employed indiscriminately. Article V, said Zengqi, applied only to the trade ports (where there were consular authorities), while article XII meant that the cultivators in Manchuria must rely on the protection of (Qing) local officials.[20] Zengqi made his

---

[18] Chung, *Korean Treaties*, pp. 50, 53–54.
[19] Zhongguo bianjiang shidi yanjiu zhongxin, *Dongbei bianjiang dang'an xuanji*, vol. 36, p. 3.
[20] Ibid., pp. 2–7.

implication clear: the Korean government had no authority to protect the Korean cultivators living in Qing border regions.

Russia: Railway Colonialism and Coadministrative Prefecture

The Qing's interiorization of its northeast frontier was suspended in 1900 when Russia invaded and occupied Manchuria. Unlike Japan, Russia never cultivated a strong developmental and colonial interest in this newly reclaimed frontier.[21] Instead, from the late nineteenth century to the early twentieth century Russia had just two straightforward strategic visions for its Far East territory: to connect this remote region with its European heartland and to acquire ice-free ports in the eastern end of Eurasia. The plan was part of Russia's overall strategy to win the global competition against its European rivals in the western end of the Eurasian continent. The most important part of the Far East enterprise was to construct the Trans-Siberian Railway (TSR). Russian foreign minister Aleksei Lobanov-Rostovsky expressed it clearly: "Our goals may be seen as two-fold: securing an ice-free port on the Pacific Ocean and the annexation of a number of areas in Manchuria, which would be essential in making the construction of the Trans-Siberian Railway easier."[22]

In 1891 construction of the eastern part of the TSR began at the urging of the future Tsar Nicholas II after he returned from a journey around the world, including a visit to Japan. The original plan was to connect Vladivostok and Chelyabinsk through Khabarovsk, Chita, and Irkutsk, bypassing Manchuria. But the harsh weather and frozen soil made the project extremely difficult. A more convenient and feasible alternative, suggested by minister of finance Sergey Witte, was to connect Vladivostok and Chita through Manchuria. Taking credit for the mediation that forced Japan to return the Liaodong Peninsula, Lobanov-Rostovsky lured Li Hongzhang into signing the Sino-Russian Secret Treaty (Li–Lobanov Treaty) in 1896, which granted Russia the right to build and control the trans-Manchurian railroad, known as the China Eastern Railway (CER).[23] The project began in 1897. The next year Russia started to pave a southward branch of the CER, connecting

---

[21] That said, many Russian intellectuals did see the Siberian expansion as the hope of building a new and strong state, and they regarded the Amur River as Russia's Mississippi. See Mark Bassin, *Imperial Visions* (Cambridge: Cambridge University Press, 1999).

[22] Felix Patrikeeff and Harold Shukman, *Railways and the Russo-Japanese War: Transporting War* (London: Routledge, 2007), p. 17.

[23] Victor Zatsepine, *Beyond the Amur: Frontier Encounters between China and Russia, 1850–1930* (Vancouver: UBC Press, 2017), pp. 100–103.

Harbin in Heilongjiang and Port Arthur (Lüshun), an ice-free navy port at the tip of the Liaodong Peninsula. Part of this branch was known later as the South Manchurian Railway. The building of the CER and supporting institutions increased Russian investment in Manchuria. From 1896 to 1904 the total Russian investment reached 563.5 million rubles. Russian engineers, technicians, and managers came to work for the CER along with more than 100,000 Chinese laborers and merchants.[24]

In 1900 the Boxer Rebellion in north China spread to Manchuria. Fearing that Chinese mobs would destroy the CER, Russia launched an invasion at the end of July. Encountering limited resistance from the Qing, the Russians soon occupied most of Manchuria, including the Hunchun area. But, under pressure from Britain, the United States, and Japan, in April 1902 Russia agreed to withdraw its troops in eighteen months. In spite of this agreement, however, Russia did not move its army out of Hunchun until March 1905. Russia's presence severely damaged Qing authority in the region, granting Korea an opportunity to expand to the northern bank of the Tumen. At the same time, Russia also found it advantageous to enlarge its influence in Korea, well aware of Korea's intentions in the Tumen region.

In light of this recognition, Russia sent the former consul general and a personal friend of Kojong (now emperor of Korea), Karl Ivanovich Weber, as a special envoy to Hansŏng. He offered the Korean foreign minister, Yi To-jae, a resolution on the "Kando issue": setting up a coadministrative prefecture.[25] The governor of this prefecture would be voted into office by local Koreans and Russians, and the local authority would be protected by both Russian and Korean armies. In exchange, Russia required to rent Masanp'o, a warm-water port in the south of the peninsula.[26] But Korea was reluctant. According to Shinoda Jisaku, Russia further suggested establishing an administrative committee composed of Russia, Qing, and Korea to deal with the disputed region.[27] Again, nothing materialized. Russia's overwhelming influence in Manchuria and Korea worried its Euro-American rivals, especially Britain and the United States. With their encouragement and financial support, Japan,

---

[24] Ibid., p. 107. Wang Xiaoju, *E'guo dongbu yimin kaifa wenti yanjiu* (Beijing: Zhongguo shehui kexue chubanshe, 2003), p. 254.

[25] Kotō Bunjirō, "Kan-Man Kyōkai Rekishi," *Rekishi Chiri*, vol. 6, no. 12 (1904), pp. 1–16, 14–15. The Russian resolution was also recorded in Song, "Jiandao wenti," which is the source of all Chinese scholarship on the incident. But Song made a mistake in his narrative: he regarded Weber as the Russian Consul General at the time. Weber's term in fact ended in 1897.

[26] Yi Sŏng-hwan, *Kindai Higashi Ajia no seiji rikigaku: Kantō o meguru Nichi-Chū-Chō kankei no shiteki tenkai* (Tokyo: Kinseisha, 1991), pp. 35–36.

[27] Shinoda Jisaku, *Hakutōsan teikaihi* (Tokyo: Rakurō Shoin, 1938), p. 234.

which was deeply concerned about the Russian expansion in Asia, provoked a war and forced Russia to retreat to northern Manchuria. With the Russian defeat, so went Korea's hope to leverage Russia to win over Kando.

Korea: Militarization and Territorialization

The Korean government's attitude towards "Kando" was not always consistent. Ever since the Chosŏn dynasty was restyled as the Korean Empire (1897), local officials and elites in Hamgyŏng province had submitted several survey reports urging Hansŏng to negotiate with Beijing about administrative rights in the northern bank region.[28] They reignited the old theory that the Tuman and the Tumen were not the same and argued that Korean peasants, who comprised the majority of the local population, should be ruled by the Korean Empire. In 1898 former low-rank officer O Sam-gap, along with others, submitted such a petition. However, the Korean Foreign Ministry firmly rejected his petition, saying it "repeated previous people's mistake and was not aware of the real situation at all." Reminding that the main body of the boundary had already been confirmed by Yi Chung-ha during the 1885–1887 demarcations, the Foreign Ministry criticized the requests of O and others as "extremely and astonishingly ridiculous."[29] Obviously, there was a fairly big perception gap between the central government and local elites.

It was not until Russia occupied Manchuria that Korea for the first time tried to establish its ruling institutions on the northern bank. Some officials in Hamgyŏng suggested Hansŏng take advantage of the Qing–Russian confrontation and make the territorial claim.[30] In August 1900 Korea set up garrison troops along the southern bank of the Tumen, with the headquarters in Chongsŏng and branches in Musan, Hoeryŏng, Onsŏng, Chongsŏng, and Kyŏngwŏn. In 1901 it further established a border police bureau of 200 policemen in Hoeryŏng, with two branches in Musan and Chongsŏng.[31] Korean soldiers and policemen thus regularly crossed the river, patrolling and accepting complaints from local cultivators. Some corrupt officers even robbed Qing and Korean residents.[32] Serious confrontations occurred between the local police forces

---

[28] Several local surveys and reports done from 1897 to 1899 were recorded in Kim, "Pugyŏ yosŏn," pp. 332–370.

[29] "Oebu Naemun," Kyujanggak 17770–1, M/F83-16-22-A.

[30] "Hamgyŏng nambukdo naegŏan," Kyujanggak 17983, no. 1-207-209.

[31] "Kantō Zaijū Kanjin no Shinzoku Kanshū oyobi sonota," Jangseogak Archives, B6B-55 MF35-10492.

[32] QJZRHGXSL, vol. 9, p. 5837. See also "Hamgyŏng nambukdo naegŏan," Kyujanggak 17983, vol. 1, pp. 223–238.

of the Qing and Korea. Through diplomatic channels, the Qing urged the Korean government to constrain its local officials and punish the perpetrators.[33]

In 1902 the Korean government appointed Yi Pŏm-yun as the Surveillance Commissioner of Kando (*Kando kwanch'alsa*) to oversee the Koreans on the Tumen north bank – arguably the first time "Kando" was used in an official title. But Yi Pŏm-yun had ambitions of his own. He tried to install Korean sovereignty over the Kando region by attentively registering local households, lands, and properties.[34] He also suggested establishing an administration to govern local Koreans. The next year he was appointed as the Supervising Commissioner of Kando (*Kando kwanlisa*).

Other than his title, however, Hansŏng provided Yi Pŏm-yun neither concrete power nor specific responsibilities. Nevertheless, Yi intended not just to "protect" Korean cultivators but also to incorporate the north bank into Korean territory. Without permission or support from the central government, Yi carried out a series of radical policies to concentrate his own power in the region.[35] He recruited youth in Musan and organized his own private army. Dismissing the local *xiangyue* appointed by the Qing, he named 180-odd Koreans as administrative staff to supervise dozens of villages in the northern bank society. Using this governing structure, he forbad local residents to shave their hair or pay taxes to the Qing. Instead, every household had to pay him not only tax but also a registration fee, as a way to fund local garrison troops. Moreover, Yi demanded that one young male in every twenty households join his troops, with each of his soldiers supported by five households.[36] This quasi-militarization echoed the half-military, half-agricultural system that was once implemented in Kwanbuk during the Chosŏn dynasty.

Yi compelled his soldiers to cross the river and loot, mainly targeting the residents living opposite Musan, since no Qing troops were stationed. Many households thus were double victims, prey both to Chinese bandits and Korean soldiers.[37] In fact, cross-referencing of records by the Qing authority on the Korean lootings in Musan in 1903 with Korean records on bandit lootings in 1904 shows the startling fact that 67 percent (85

---

[33] Ibid., vol. 9, pp. 5428–5429, 5432. See also *Kantō Zaijū Kanjin no Shinzoku Kanshū oyobi sonota*.

[34] Lhim Hag-Seong, "20segi ch'o 'Kando' chiyŏge kŏjuhan chosŏnine taehan hogujosawa kŭ ŭimi," *Han'gukhak yŏng'u*, vol. 30 (2013), pp. 357–384.

[35] Yi Hŭng-gwŏn, "Ch'ŏngŭi Kandojŏngch'aekkwa Yi Pŏm-yunŭi ijumin kwanli yŏng'u," *Inmungwahak yŏng'u*, vol. 48 (2016), pp. 227–252.

[36] QJZRHGXSL, vol. 9, pp. 5789–5847.

[37] Ibid., pp. 5849–5881.

out of 126) of Korean households that were looted by Korean troops in 1903 were again the victims of Chinese banditry in 1904.[38] Finally at the end of 1903, with an army of more than 1,000 soldiers carrying 500 guns and trained by a Russian advisor, Yi announced that the northern bank of the Tumen was Korean territory. He publicly said he would relocate his headquarters to the north side of the river. At the same time, he ordered his staff to secretly hide guns in villages in preparation for his invasion, scheduled for early 1904. Although some naturalized Koreans disclosed his plan to the Qing, Yi Pŏm-yun went ahead with his invasion in April. The battle lasted around two weeks, until Yi and his troops were routed and had to retreat back to the south.[39]

In response, the Qing government announced a prohibition on grain exportation in the Yanji region to force the Korean government to discharge Yi Pŏm-yun. The strategy worked. Faced with the criticism and complaints against Yi by local officials in Hamgyŏng[40] as well as the vigorous protests from the Qing,[41] the Korean government removed Yi from his position. With nowhere to go, Yi Pŏm-yun, the younger brother of the famous pro-Russian minister Yi Pŏm-jin, planned to seek help from Russia.[42] Unluckily for him, the ongoing Russo-Japanese War prevented him from doing so.

Yi Pŏm-yun's invasion had its legacies. One of them was the signing of the Aftermath Regulation on the Sino-Korean Border (C. *zhonghan bianjie shanhou zhangcheng*) in the summer of 1904. Although not a formal protocol between two states, the regulation was the first codified agreement on the Tumen boundary after the "independence" of Korea.[43] In its twelve articles, local officials from both countries agreed to maintain the status quo of the boundary and wait for the two governments to co-survey the border. They also agreed to deny Yi Pŏm-yun's authority and admit the Qing's right to punish the naturalized Koreans who had assisted him. The agreement allowed civilians to travel across the river freely while prohibiting armed military staff from doing so. It acknowledged that "Kando/Jiandao" was just "a shoal" in front of Guangjiyu, and the Koreans were still allowed to farm on it. Finally, the agreement

---

[38] Ibid. and "Hambuk pyŏn'gye sŏngch'aek."

[39] Yang and Sun, *Zhongchao bianjie shi*, pp. 434–437.

[40] "Hamgyŏng nambukdo naegŏan," Kyujanggak 17983, no. 2-153-156; "Ŭijŏngbu naegŏan," June 13, 1904, Kyujanggak 17887.

[41] "Hwa'an," diplomatic notes from Xu Taishen, the Qing ambassador in Korea, Kyujanggak 18052.

[42] "Naebu naegŏmun" no. 11, Kyujanggak 17794.

[43] Quan Hexiu, "Ri'e zhanzheng dui jindai zhonghan guanxi de yingxiang," *Jindaishi Yanjiu*, no. 23 (2005), pp. 126–128.

enabled coordination on the trial of cross-border homicide cases, and lifted the grain embargo to ease the food shortage in Korea (though the Qing retained the right to impose a grain embargo in the future).[44] During a time when the Russo-Japanese War had put the central governments of both states in a terrible predicament, this kind of local-level regulation played a decisive role in stabilizing the border region.

Another legacy of Yi Pŏm-yun's invasion had to do with Yi himself. Renounced by his own government, defeated by the Qing, and ignored by Russia, Yi and his militia had to flee to Primorsky and seek support from the Korean community there. When Korea fell into Japan's protectorate in 1905, Yi's ultimate enemy became Japan. His troops joined a grand anti-Japanese movement called the Righteous Army (K. Ŭibyŏng), one of the most active non-governmental armed forces in the frontier region. Like many other NGAF leaders, Yi was identified in Japanese documents as a "rogue" or "bandit."

Although the Korean government failed to solidify its authority over the Tumen northern bank, the notion that "Kando" had been a Korean space and should be included in Korean territory spread among the post-"independent" generation of intellectuals, whose views were extensively expressed in the media in the late nineteenth and early twentieth centuries.[45] Newspapers such as *The Korea Daily News* (*Taehan maeil sinbo*) and *Capital Gazette* (*Hwangsŏng sinmun*) repeatedly reported on this territorial dispute, intensifying not only the claim of "our land" but sympathy towards "our people." Several historical-geographic books, combining historical narratives of national glory and contemporary concern for national integrity, called attention to Korea's "northern territory." One of them was *An Investigation of the Territory of the Great Korea* (*Taehan Kangyŏk ko*, 1903), a revised edition of Chŏng Yag-yong's 1811 historical-geographic work, *An Investigation of Our Territory* (*Kangyŏk ko*). The book's editor, Chang Chi-yŏn, editor of the *Hwangsŏng sinmun*, added a new chapter on the issue of the Tumen boundary, making Chŏng's study in the early nineteenth century look like a historical demonstration of Chang's territorial assertion.[46] Another book, *Selected Reports on the Northern Territory* (*Pugyŏ yosŏn*),[47] published in 1903, was funded by Yi Pŏm-yun. The book included several survey reports written by local officials. What was interesting about these reports was

---

[44] QJZRHGXSL, vol. 9, pp. 5952–5953.
[45] For detailed discussion, see Schmid, *Korea between Empires*, pp. 199–215.
[46] Chang Chi-yŏn, "Paektusan chŏnggyebi ko," in Chŏng Yag-yong, *Taehan kangyŏk ko* (Seoul: Hwangsŏng Sinmunsa, 1903).
[47] Kim, "Pugyŏ yosŏn," pp. 332–356.

that, in addition to the conventional discourse of dynastic geography, some of them used a brand-new rhetoric, international law, to argue for Korean ownership over the Tumen north bank. This new rhetoric will be discussed later.

Japan: Leading Asia, Conquering Manchuria, and "Protecting" the Koreans

Japan's intervention in what it called the "Kantō" area served its grand geopolitical strategy of competing against Russia. When the Qing planned to start a new round of demarcation after the military clash with Korea, Japan, which at that point controlled the Korean government, asked the Qing to postpone because of the ongoing Russo-Japanese War. The Qing agreed to resume border negotiations when the war concluded.

With the mediation of US president Theodore Roosevelt, Japan and Russia ended their war with the Treaty of Portsmouth. The treaty redistributed the two powers' spheres of influence in Korea and Manchuria. Russia maintained its interest in northern Manchuria, while Japan took over all the special benefits Russia had enjoyed in southern Manchuria, including the lease of Port Arthur and Dalian and the railway between Changchun and Port Arthur. Japanese troops could station along the railway. On November 11, 1905, two months after the Treaty of Portsmouth, Japan forced Korea to sign the Japan–Korea Protectorate Treaty (Eulsa Treaty), wielding international law to deprive Korea of diplomatic rights and turn the country into Japan's formal protectorate. Itō Hirobumi was appointed the Japanese Resident-General (tōkan) of Korea, the top colonial agency in the peninsula. In Korea the Protectorate Treaty, which was signed by five Cabinet ministers over Emperor Kojong's rejection, triggered anti-Japanese sentiment on a large scale. Facing suppression, many nationalist intellectuals left the country to mobilize an independence movement. Yi Sang-sŏl, founder of the Sŏjŏn (C. Ruidian) Academy in Longjing, was one of them.

Japan's consistent military victories in the years from the Sino-Japanese War to the Russo-Japanese War marked the heyday of the Meiji period. As suggested by the Triple Intervention, tension between Japan and the Western powers mounted as Japan's strength increased in Asia. But, if post-Restoration Japan demonstrated its ambition to become the new leader of East Asia, a Japan-centered regional order was not yet fully determined. Before World War I the Euro-American states also intensified their expansion in the Asian Pacific region. An East–West dichotomy was therefore a key theme in Meiji diplomatic thought. Reviewing Meiji diplomatic history in 1904, veteran diplomat Soejima Taneomi said that two central issues in post-Napoleonic Europe were "the nationalist movement and the Orient."[48] Japan saw itself as both a victim (along with China and Korea) of Euro-America's eastward expansion and a leading defender of the Orient. For Soejima, controlling Korea was not an act of aggression but a means to "protect" both Korea and Japan from being colonized by the West.[49]

Against this backdrop, some of the most famous intellectuals, former samurai, and politicians established various civil organizations dedicated to the integrity of the Orient. These activists were later categorized as "Pan-Asianist." Not necessarily an antithesis of the "Departing Asia" narrative (*Datsu-A Ron*, raised by great thinker Fukuzawa Yukichi), Pan-Asianist thought embraced Japanese hegemony in Asia, insisting that it was not only Japan's right but also its obligation to "civilize" "backward" neighbors in order to fight against white Westerners' colonization.[50] This paradoxical idea, that the old orientalism had to be countered by a new kind of orientalism, inspired Japan's knowledge production on Korea, Manchuria, and the Kantō area.

Japan's Knowledge Regime concerning Manchuria

Among the Pan-Asianist groups, the Kokuryūkai (the Amur Society, or Black Dragon Society) was the most radical in supporting the colonization of Manchuria. Founded in 1901 and named after the Heilong (Amur) River, the Kokuryūkai claimed that it was dedicated to "investigating and explaining all things and issues in Siberia, Manchuria and Korea."[51] Combining nationalist, Pan-Asianist, and colonialist appeals, the society aimed to expel Russia from the Far East, turning the Siberia–Manchuria–Korea region into Japan's resource base.

The core figure of the society, Uchida Ryōhei, vigorously promoted this goal after traveling throughout Manchuria and Siberia alone from 1897 to 1898. Uchida and his comrades lobbied the government to prepare for war with Russia as they propagated their political ideas in printed media. As early as 1901 they had already noticed the strategic value of the Tumen River region and emphasized the integration

---

[48] Soejima Taneomi, "Meiji Gaikōshi," in Okuma Shigenobu, ed., *Kaikoku gojūnenshi*, vol. 1 (Tokyo: Kaikoku gojūnenshi Hakkōjo, 1907), pp. 169–170.

[49] Ibid., p. 209.

[50] See Sven Saaler, "Pan-Asianism in Modern Japanese History: Overcoming the Nation, Creating a Region, Forging an Empire," in Sven Saaler and J. Victor Koschmann, eds., *Pan-Asianism in Modern Japanese History: Colonialism, Regionalism and Borders* (Abingdon, UK: Routledge, 2007), pp. 1–18.

[51] "Kokuryūkai Kiyaku," in *Kokuryūkai kaihō*, vol. 1 (1901), p. 123.

of the two sides across the river. Published in the bulletin of the society (*Kaihō*), an article titled "On Colonizing Manchuria" ("Manshū Shokumin Ron") suggested that two railways should be built to connect Korea with Manchuria. One was to extend the Hansŏng–Pusan railway to Fenghuang City on the Liaodong Peninsula; the other was to connect Pyŏngyang and Hamgyŏng and extend to Hunchun in the Tumen River region. No mention was made of the territorial dispute. It was obvious that the whole of Manchuria was seen as being in Japan's pocket: "What Manchuria means to Japan and Russia now is just like what Korea meant to Japan and the Qing-China prior to the Japan–Qing War. If an unfortunate confrontation happened, the whole area only belongs to Japan and Russia. Other states are not allowed to intervene."[52]

The Kokuryūkai's efforts represented but a portion of Japan's systematic knowledge production on Manchuria. From the turn of the century numerous articles, correspondence, and reports were published to introduce Manchuria's geography, climate, hydrology, geology, history, demography, agriculture, timber and mineral resources, social conditions, and even local bandits in detail. Of course, Russian activity in Manchuria was a major concern. When Russia proposed to establish a coadministrative prefecture in the Tumen borderland, the news attracted huge attention in Japan. Civil groups such as Kokumin Dōmeikai (National United League)[53] and Chōsen Kyōkai (Association of Korea) began to study the issue. The General Staff Office of the Imperial Army also sent investigators to the Tumen border region.[54]

New definitions were proposed to the disputed land. In 1904 *Historical Geography* (*Rekishi Chiri*) magazine published an article titled "The History of the Manchuria–Korean Borderland" ("Man–Kan Kyōkai Rekishi"). Written by Kotō Bunjirō, a geologist trained in Germany, the article outlined the history and the dispute of the borderland. What is worth noticing was that Kotō used the term "neutral area" to describe both the "Kantō" region and the Yalu River region west to Mt. Changbai.[55] Although not directly advocating Korea's territorial claim, the term denied Qing's sovereignty over the region. This idea later developed as a dominant thought in Japan's deterritorialization of Manchuria.

A similar narrative also appeared in *Manchurian Geography* (*Manshū Chishi*), an encyclopedic survey compiled by Morita Toshitō, a lieutenant

[52] Kokubu Tanenori, "Manshū Shokumin Ron," in *Kokuryūkai kaihō*, vol. 2, p. 77.
[53] It was founded by Tōyama Mitsuru, the most famous Pan-Asianist, who was also Uchida Ryōhei's mentor.
[54] Nagai Katsuzō, ed., *Kainei oyobi kantō jijō: Ichimei hokusen kantō no annai* (Kainei: Kaineiinsatsujo, 1923), p. 65.
[55] Kotō, "Kan-Man Kyōkai Rekishi," pp. 1–16.

colonel of the Imperial Army. Written before the Russo-Japanese War but published in 1906, the book has a special section on *Kegai kuiki* – that is, the "area beyond civilization." With *Kegai kuiki*, Morita refers to two areas in the Sino-Korean borderland. One is the Han bianwai, the organization of "gold bandits" who were "entrenched in the east and west sides of Mt. Changbai, just like a state beyond Qing's governance." The other is "Kantō," which "is out of Korea's administrative circle."[56] It should be noted that the "Kantō" in Morita's narrative describes the region between the Tumen and the Hailan Rivers, a large space stretching 250 to 300 kilometers from east to west, and 100 to 150 kilometers north to south. Besides praising the abundant timber and gold resources, Morita also calls for occupying the borderland: "There is a saying that Mt. Changbai is the Alps of East Asia. By dominating this mountain, [we could] conquer Manchuria and Korea, control the real power of East Asia, and guard the peace of the Orient."[57]

A growing recognition that "Kantō" was the key to dominating Manchuria, which was itself the key to dominating East Asia, was echoed in the Japanese military, government, and society. Several investigative teams went to the region around the same time. In November 1905 and March 1906 the Japanese Korean Army completed two reports on Kantō, both confirming the economic and defense values of the place.[58] In 1905 and 1906 the Imperial Army General Staff Office and Ministry of Foreign Affairs, respectively, entrusted journalist Naitō Torajirō (later famous sinologist Naitō Konan) to investigate the Kantō dispute (discussed in Chapter 5).

In early 1906 the Kokuryūkai organized a conference to discuss the Kantō issue in Tokyo. Following the meeting the Imperial Army commissioned Nakai Kitarō (Kinjō), a former journalist of *Yomiuri Shimbun*, to lead a survey team. The Nakai report was submitted directly to the Resident-General, Itō Hirobumi, and the commander-in-chief of the Japanese Korean Army, Hasegawa Yoshimichi. Although it did not support Korea's territorial claim, the report highlighted the economic potential of the area and called for the integration of northern Korea and the Kantō region.[59] Each of these reports differed from one another in many ways, but all tended to see Kantō as an extension of the Korean

---

[56] Morita Toshitō, *Manshū Chish* (Tokyo: Maruzen Kabushiki Kaisha, 1906), p. 428.
[57] Ibid., p. 426.
[58] JACAR, "Kantō kyōkai chōsa zairyō," ref. C06040131500, and "Kantō ni kansuru chōsa gaiyō shintatsu no kudan," ref. C03027067300.
[59] Tsurushima, *Tomankō chiiki kaihatsu*, pp. 199–249; Jiang Longfan, "Riben jieru 'jiandao wenti' de zhanlue gouxiang tantao," *Yanbian daxue xuebao* (shehui kexue ban), no. 1 (1999), pp. 43–48, 40–45.

Peninsula and urged the Japanese government to intervene in the dispute more aggressively for the sake of national interests. The imperial government eventually adopted many of the thoughts and opinions set forth in these reports.

Temporary Kantō Branch of the Japanese
Resident-General of Korea

In November 1906 two events, both of great significance to Japan's colonization of Manchuria, occurred almost simultaneously. One was widely noticed: on the 26th the South Manchuria Railway Company (SMR), the Japanese colonial agency equivalent to the British East Indian Company, was inaugurated in Tokyo. The other event was comparatively inconspicuous: on the 18th the Korean prime minister, Pak Che-sun, submitted an official note to Resident-General Itō Hirobumi raising the issue that "the Koreans are bullied by bandits and rogues" in Kando. Since Japan was hosting Korea's diplomacy according to the Japan–Korea Protectorate Treaty, Pak asked Itō to send officials to "protect the Koreans" there. That the two events happened at roughly the same time might be more than a coincidence. They exposed the fact that Japan's enterprise of colonizing Manchuria was never developed in just one direction but two. While controlling the South Manchuria Railway promised Japan access to the Manchurian hinterland through the Liaodong Peninsula, occupying Kantō would mean opening an eastern gate to this resource-rich frontier. Besides, the Kantō region was to a certain extent geostrategically more critical to Japan, in that it directly adjoined Russia, Japan's longtime and most threatening rival.

In fact, Japanese politicians in Hansŏng and Tokyo had been planning to intervene in the Tumen northern bank long before November. In mid-July 1906 the Japanese ambassador to Korea, Hayashi Gonsuke, advised Itō to send Japanese officials to the Kantō region. Itō, accepting this initiative after meticulous consideration, designed a detailed plan to install a branch of the Resident-General of Korea there. He personally drafted its administrative structure, allocation of staff, and policy orientation. Informed by both Hayashi Gonsuke and the Nakai report, Itō understood that it would be difficult to publicly support Korea's territorial claim. So his plan was to leave the land dispute aside temporarily, but use "the mistreatment of the Korean people" as an excuse for intervention. In September Itō submitted his proposal to foreign minister Hayashi Tadatsu for approval. Around the same time he disclosed this scheme to a pro-Japanese Korean organization, the Ilchinhoe. The latter soon presented a petition to the Korean government, asking it to "protect the Koreans in Kando." A month later Tokyo ratified Itō's project. Immediately, Itō demanded the dispute-related documents from the Korean government. And, as expected, he also received Pak Che-sun's official request in November, which, interestingly, asked not about taking land but guarding people.[60] It is therefore more appropriate to see Pak's action as the completion rather than the initiation of a well-planned colonial agenda.

Itō carefully carried out his plan in secret. After consulting with Hasegawa Yoshimichi, Itō appointed Lieutenant Colonel Saitō Suejirō, a China hand who had served in General Nogi Maresuke's army during the Russo-Japanese War, as the director of the future Kantō Branch. From December 1906 to January 1907 Saitō had returned to Tokyo to recruit his staff. The most important assistant he invited was a jurist, Shinoda Jisaku, who had also served in Nogi's army during the war. One of Shinoda's duties was to study the territorial dispute from the perspectives of history and international law. In their private meeting, Saitō plainly explained the Japanese government's intention: "On the surface, we are there to protect the majority of Korean residents who were bullied by the Qing officials and bandits. But essentially, our aim is to try to solve the Kantō issue in favor of Korea."[61]

Inspired by Saitō's "imperial spirit," Shinoda quit his career as a lawyer and devoted himself to the colonial enterprise. The team was soon composed. Other than Shinoda, major staff members included an agronomist, a mineralogist, and an administrative chief along with Korean clerks, policemen, and interpreters.

Meanwhile, the Japanese and Russian delegations were having secret negotiations in Vladivostok on how to divide their spheres of interest in Manchuria and Mongolia. Worried that the operation on the Tumen northern bank might agitate Russia, Japan decided to postpone the establishment of the Kantō Branch till the negotiations concluded. Saitō and Shinoda took advantage of the time by leading a team in disguise to spy on the area.

From April 18 to 29 the team trespassed across the border and investigated local demographic, topographic, transportation, living, and governmental conditions. Upon their return they formulated some guiding principles for future colonization. First, all policies would be based on the premise that Kantō was Korean territory. Second, the Korean government should entrust the branch to rule all the local Koreans, and the

---

[60] Choi Jangguen, "Kangoku tōkan Itō Hirobumi no Kantō Ryōdo seisaku," vol. 102, nos. 7/8 (1996), pp. 175–202, and vol. 102, no. 9 (1996), pp. 171–187.

[61] Shinoda, "Kantō mondai no kaiko," p. 472.

branch would not confront the Chinese authority at this stage but would leverage its advantage when the occasion came. Third, in case of emergency, the branch could seek support from the nearby Japanese garrison. Fourth, to develop the Kantō region, Ch'ŏngjin in northern Hamgyŏng would be made a trade port connecting with Japanese ports, and railways would be constructed to link Kantō with Ch'ŏngjin and Hoeryŏng. Telegraph wires were to be erected between Hoeryŏng and the branch, and the place where the branch office was located (Longjing) should be urbanized.[62] Itō approved these principles.

The (first) Japanese–Russian agreement on Manchuria and Mongolia was signed in July 1907. With the negotiations settled, on August 19 Saitō Suejirō led the majority of the branch staff and the military police force, including over 300 people, 100 horses, and dozens of carts of cargos, across the Tumen River from Hoeryŏng. With little delay from the astonished Qing troops, the group marched towards Longjing.[63] On the very same day the Japanese deputy ambassador in Beijing, Abe Moritarō, submitted a diplomatic note to the Qing government: "Whether Kantō is Qing territory or Korean territory has been an unsolved problem for a long time. The 100,000-odd Koreans living there are bullied by bandits and rogues. In order to protect them, the [Japanese] Resident-General [of Korea] sends officials to Kantō. Please telegraph local Chinese officials as soon as possible to avoid a misunderstanding."[64] Four days later, on August 23, the Temporary Kantō Branch of the Resident-General (Tōkanfu rinji kantō hashutsujo) was officially announced open.

Japanese Colony Building in Kantō

To a great degree, colonial construction in Kantō was a prototype of Japan's colonial enterprise in East Asia. Even when the Kantō Branch had existed only for two years, many of its projects were considered so successful that the Japanese applied them later in Korea and other parts of Manchuria. The colonial state infiltrated local society mainly through four efforts.

The first was administration and police building. The branch created a three-layer administrative system to counterbalance its Qing counterpart, the Yanji subprefecture. It divided the Kantō realm into

---

[62] Ibid., pp. 476–478.
[63] Ibid., pp. 483–485.
[64] JACAR, "Kantō no hanto ni kanshi seikan ryōkoku fungi ikken," vol. 1, pp. 297–298, ref. B03041192300; Gugong bowuyuan, ed., *Qing Guangxu chao zhong ri jiaoshe shiliao*, vol. 71 (Beiping: Gugong bowuyuan, 1932), p. 10.

four districts (Musan Kantō, Hoeryŏng Kantō, Chongsŏng Kantō, and Hokutokaisho), under which were forty-one communes (*sha*) composed of 290 villages. The branch also appointed pro-Japanese Koreans (many of them Ilchinhoe members) as the heads of villages, communes, and districts. At the same time the colonial agency dispatched altogether 270 military policemen to fourteen locations. Most of these police stations were set up opposite Qing barracks. Their legal authority was clear: these police stations accepted and processed more than 1,000 local civil and criminal cases in two years.[65]

The second means Japan used to work its way into Korean society was to conduct a wide range of local investigations. The branch hosted agricultural, geological/mineral, and commercial research that covered not only the area north of the Tumen River but also that north of the upper Yalu River. The commercial inquiries expanded to neighboring towns such as Jilin, Dunhua, and Hunchun in preparation for future economic integration. Compiled in 1909 in a huge volume containing nearly 1,000 pages and dozens of illustrations, statistical tables, and maps entitled *Investigation on Industries in Kantō* (*Kantō sangyō chōsasho*), the three studies provided painstakingly detailed descriptions/records on almost every aspect of local economic and industrial activities.

Furthermore, in order to legitimize Korea's territorial claim, the branch launched historical and archaeological surveys. The investigators "accidentally discovered" a stele in the Burhatong River, by which they asserted that the Koryŏ kingdom of Korea once expanded to that site. They also inspected the relics of Toyotomi Hideyoshi's invasions (1592–1598) in order to highlight the historical "Japanese existence" in the region. From archaeological findings they employed a racial discourse and argued that the ancient residents in Kantō were not "the race of the northern continent" but belonged to the "lineage of ancient Korea."[66] On top of that, the branch assigned a Korean police officer and Ilchinhoe member, Kim Hae-rong, to survey the customs of local Koreans. The outcome of this was the report *Kinship, Custom, and Other Issues of the Kantō Korean* (*Kantō Zaijū Kanjin no Shinzoku Kanshū oyobi sonota*).[67]

How to evaluate the significance of these investigations? Historians working on twentieth-century China generally agree on the inimitable value of the wide-ranging studies conducted by the research bureau of the South Manchuria Railway Company. But the earlier, groundbreaking

---

[65] Shinoda, *Tōkanfu rinji kantō hashutsujo kiyō*, pp. 165–170, and map 2.

[66] Ibid., pp. 91–94, 151–155.

[67] Tōkanfu kantō hashutsujo, ed., *Kantō Zaijū Kanjin no Shinzoku Kanshū oyobi sonota*, 1917, Academy of Korean Studies, MF35-10492.

Kantō investigations to a large extent foreshadowed many of the later SMR works, such as Manchurian–Korean historical research and custom surveys. Considering that all the Kantō studies were done in just two years with limited resources (in contrast to the nearly forty years of research supported by the SMR), in terms of both quantity and quality they were by no means less remarkable than the famous SMR investigations.

Japan's third colonizing effort involved planting experiments. For Japan, one of the greatest attractions of Manchuria was its immeasurable agricultural potential. In 1907 the Kantō Branch bought about 19,800 square meters of dry land behind its office and established an experimental farm. In 1909 it created a frost-free greenhouse and a garden of 6,000 square meters. Researchers cultivated various grains, vegetables, fruits, and flowers to test their adaptation to local conditions and compared the quality of seeds from both Japan and Korea. They applied cutting-edge cultivation techniques, especially winter-proofing technology.[68] The branch also rented a paddy field in Longjing to test-plant rice.

Finally, the branch actively promoted educational and hygienic projects. Immediately after the branch opened, Saitō shut down the Sŏjŏn Academy, the school founded by Yi Sang-sŏl that gathered many anti-Japanese activists. To replace it, the Kantō Ordinary School was founded, under the supervision and management of the Japanese. The branch also certified more than fifty private schools that promised to follow pro-Japanese guidelines. To reward and ensure their loyalty, the branch either sent staff to attend the opening ceremonies or supplied the schools with free textbooks.[69]

Hygienic projects, ranging from disease control to sewerage, were simultaneously "modern" and colonial. Of all the programs, what the Japanese seemed most proud of was the Jikei (K. Chahye, 慈惠) Hospital in Longjing. During its sixteen months of operation the hospital received a total of 13,533 patients from Kantō and the surrounding areas.[70] Following the successful example in Kantō, more modern hospitals were founded in every province in Korea during the colonial period; all inherited the name "Chahye."[71] This is another example of the colonialist enterprise burgeoning from the periphery and spreading to the interior, not the other way around.

---

[68] *Kantō sangyō chōsasho*, Nōgyō, pp. 389–542.
[69] Shinoda, *Tōkanfu rinji kantō hashutsujo kiyō*, pp. 213–214.
[70] Ibid, p. 229.
[71] Shinoda, "Kantō mondai no kaiko," p. 508.

In sum, Japanese regime building on the Tumen northern bank established almost a norm of state penetration. Under the circumstances of sovereign competition, it stimulated the Chinese to increase their own pace of regime building and strengthen local governance in every aspect: administration, policing, research, infrastructure, education, hygiene, not to mention transportation and communication.[72] The Sino-Japanese rivalry over the Tumen river region soon developed into a major conflict in East Asian politics.

The Coming of International Law: A New Discourse

The 1894 Sino-Japanese War was the last strike on the Qing-centered world order. With Korea detached from the *zongfan* structure, the Qing lost its last and most loyal subordinate state. In theory, the Chinese empire was finally made "perfectly equal" with other states in the world, except that the "equality" was enforced through a series of punishments, including military invasion, coerced reparation, territorial cessions, and unequal treaties.[73] Similarly, Korea gained (or was granted) its "independence" at the price of losing its autonomy in both internal and external affairs. The old hierarchy of "all under heaven" surrendered to a new hierarchy of "international relations" in which "some nations were more equal than others."[74] With the assumption that all nations were made equal, previous notions of land, borders, and people were redefined and recategorized accordingly.

Chinese and Korean Adoptions of Das moderne Völkerrecht der civilisirten Staten

In 1897 a Hamgyŏng official, Cho Chon-u, was dispatched to survey the society and topography of the northern bank. His report was compiled in the aforementioned *Selected Reports on the Northern Territory* (*Pugyŏ yosŏn*), published in 1903. Insisting that the Tumen north bank was Korean territory, he suggested that the Qing and the Korean government hold a public debate in front of the "ambassadors of all nations" to "correct" the boundary. He quoted several articles in a book of international law, *Kongpŏp hoet'ong* (C. *Gongfa huitong*, 公法會通), to show that his

---

[72] Xu Shichang, *Dongsansheng zhenglue*, vol. 1 (Taipei: Wenhai chubanshe, 1965), pp. 54–135.

[73] James Hevia, *English Lessons: The Pedagogy of Imperialism in Nineteenth-Century China* (Durham, NC: Duke University Press, 2003).

[74] Peter Duus, *The Abacus and the Sword: The Japanese Penetration of Korea, 1895–1910* (Berkeley, CA: University of California Press, 1995), p. 13.

arguments were well supported by "the principle of treaty."[75] From then on, several other Korean reports quoted similar articles from the same book to request the redemarcation of the Sino-Korean boundary.[76]

Kongpŏp hoet'ong was published in Korea in 1896, a year after the end of the Sino-Japanese War (and a year before the Cho Chon-u report). The first Korean text on international law, it was a reprint of *Gongfa huitong*, the Chinese translation of *Das moderne Völkerrecht der civilisirten Staten (The Modern International Law of Civilized States)*, written in 1872 by Swiss jurist Johann Caspar Bluntschli. The Chinese version, published in 1880, was itself a translation of the French edition of *Das moderne Völkerrecht*.[77]

Unlike Japan, which imported the Chinese translation within a year,[78] it took Korea sixteen years to print and circulate *Das moderne Völkerrecht*, adding a new preface for the Korean version. Written by Yi Kyŏng-sik (director of the Translation Bureau of the Board of Education), the preface begins with an ancient history of the alliance meeting among the feudal states in China's Spring and Autumn Period (771~476 BC). According to Yi, it shows that the *kongpŏp* (public law) principle was universal and not against the Confucian doctrine. He continues: "Located in the east of Asia, our state always obeys the rituals (*ri*) and laws (*pŏp*) inherited from the sage kings. Our dress and literature are after that of the Three [ancient Chinese] Dynasties."[79] Because Korea is remote, the country had no diplomatic experience and so "was isolated unavoidably." But the time had arrived, according to Yi, in which Emperor Kojong, who "masters the Heavenly Mandate" and "establishes the foundation of autonomy," wanted to make friends with nations of all five continents. At such a moment, every Korean "is thinking about how to [make Korea] step into a world of civilization and accomplish the kingly governance." For that purpose, Yi wrote, no reference was more valuable than the book he was prefacing, *Kongpŏp hoet'ong*.[80]

---

[75] Kim No-gyu, "Pugyŏ yosŏn," pp. 351–352.

[76] One of them was Yi Chonggwan's report in 1899. See ibid., pp. 354–355. The other was Hwang Uyŏng's report, which was submitted to the Japanese government in 1903. See Taehan Min'guk Kukhoe Tosŏgwan, ed., *Kando yŏngyukwŏn kwan'gye palch'we munsŏ* (Seoul: Kukhoe Tosŏgwan, 1975), pp. 1–3.

[77] Rune Svarverud, *International Law as World Order in Late Imperial China: Translation, Reception and Discourse, 1847–1911* (Leiden: Brill, 2007), p. 97.

[78] The Chinese translation was by William A. P. Martin, the president of Qing's Tongwen Guan, an imperial academy dedicated to Western learning. Based on Martin's Chinese translation, the Japanese version, "*Kōhō kaitsū*" (Tokyo: Rakuzendō, 1881), was further annotated by Kishida Ginkō.

[79] The three dynasties are the Xia, Shang, and Zhou dynasties of China, which Confucian scholars often referred to as the golden period of the world.

[80] Yi Kyŏng-sik, "Kongpŏp hoet'ong sŏ," in *Kongpŏp hoet'ong* (Hansŏng: Hakbu P'yŏnjipkuk, 1896).

The preface incorporated two characteristics that by then were not uncommon in East Asian intellectuals' perception of public international law. First, it created an analogy between anarchy in the contemporary international world and the cleavage of the feudal states in China's Spring and Autumn Period. Second, it conflated the principle of international law, based on the Kantian ideal of "perpetual peace," with that of the "Heavenly Mandate" and "kingly governance," based on the neo-Confucian doctrine of *li*, or ritual. In fact, it was the translator of *Das moderne Völkerrecht*, William Martin, who first employed this strategy to persuade the Manchu court to accept the "universal norm" of international law. It was also how late Qing intellectuals, such as Kang Youwei, adopted the new world order regulated by "public law."[81] By 1896 the Korean literati had fully absorbed the hybrid norms of Confucianism and Kantianism from China – in similar historical circumstances, yet applied in different ways. When Martin introduced Henry Wheaton's *Elements of International Law* to China under the title *Wanguo gongfa* (1864) as the first in a series of international law canons, Qing officials clearly indicated that its principles applied only to China's interactions with Western countries. They never intended to implement the principle of *gongfa*, public international law, to revise the tributary relations regulated by the Confucian *zongfan* structure. But, when Korea decided to import the public law, or *kongpŏp*, in the post-"independence" period, it was never hesitant to impose the principle on China, even though Korea still advocated the ideal of a Confucian world order to preserve the "Heavenly Mandate" as what it was.

Many recent scholars have studied Martin and his translation of Wheaton's *Elements of International Law*.[82] However, research on his translation of Bluntschli's *Das moderne Völkerrecht* is comparatively rare. Scholars have noticed that Bluntschli's theory of the modern state had remarkable influence on the formation of nationalist thought in Japan and China.[83] Yet Bluntschli's work on international law, which was

---

[81] See Satō Shin'ichi, *Kindai Chūgoku no chishikijin to bunmei* (Tokyo: Tokyo Daigaku Shuppankai, 1996), especially chapter 1. Satō Shin'ichi also correctly points out the fundamental distinction between the explanations of Martin and Kang Youwei. Also see Liu, *The Clash of Empires*, chapter 4.

[82] In fact, most studies on the introduction of international law in China focused on this book. Other than Satō and Liu's books, see Tian Tao, *Guojifa shuru yu wanqing zhongguo* (Jinan: Jinan chubanshe, 2001); Svarverud, *International Law as World Order in Late Imperial China*.

[83] Liang Qichao, the first intellectual who advocated that China must be rebuilt through *Minzuzhuyi* (nationalism), got his idea of "nation" from the Japanese translation of Bluntschli. See Wang Ke, "'Minzu': yige laizi riben de wuhui," *Ershiyi shiji shuangyuekan*, no. 77 (2003), pp. 73–84.

introduced much earlier to China by Martin, was somewhat neglected. Perhaps this is the case because, before Bluntschli's work, Martin had elaborated the basic principle of international law through the previous three books he translated, especially Wheaton's *Elements of International Law*. He decided to publish the Bluntschli translation, the *Gongfa huitong*, mainly as a handy supplement to the previous works. As Martin explained in the preface, the reason he picked *Das moderne Völkerrecht* was because the book focuses on the concrete legal codes generated from real cases rather than general principles. When dealing with practical problems, it was more convenient to quote the legal provisions from this book.[84] Therefore, its intellectual impact was far less than that of Wheaton's *Wanguo gongfa*. But the Koreans determined that the book was a "good reference" for precisely the same reason Martin had selected it: it was less theoretical and more practical. Given the fact that *Kongpŏp hoet'ong* was repeatedly cited by low-ranking local officials, we may assume that the book once circulated quite widely in Korea.

Korean officials made use of *Kongpŏp hoet'ong* to prove their territorial claims, but did so in a rather loose manner. Their citations concentrated on four provisions, all from the chapter on "Territorial Sovereignty" (*"Gebietshoheit"*). In English, these four articles read:

Article 283: if two states set out to colonize from two neighboring points, and seize [land as their] state territories without taking into account the inherent relationship of two distinct river basins and a mountain range, a middle line between the two territories shall be adopted as the border.

Article 295: if new islands emerge in a large river [*Strom*] or rivers, they belong to the nearest riparian state, unless special treaties prescribe otherwise. If they emerge in the middle of the river, then they are subject to a division in the middle by both riparian states.

Article 296: where two state territories meet, the neighboring states are obligated to arrange the borderline together and to mark it as clearly as possible.

Article 297: if a mountain range constitutes the border between two countries, then in case of doubt the highest ridge and the drainage divide determine the border.[85]

Other than article 296, which was cited to prove the legitimacy of the 1712 Mukedeng investigation, the other three articles referred to general principles of demarcation. That said, the articles were poorly understood and applied, as the interpretations contradicted one another. The

---

[84] Ding Weiliang (William A. P. Martin), "Gongfa huitong xu," in *Gongfa huitong* (Beijing: Tongwenguan, 1884).

[85] Translated from Johann Caspar Bluntschli, *Das moderne Völkerrecht der civilisirten Staaten als Rechtsbuch dargestellt* (Nördlingen: C. H. Beck, 1868), pp. 168–175. Thanks to Hsia Ke-chin for generously providing the English translation.

Tumen north bank was not a "new island" that had emerged in the river (as in article 295), nor a colony between the two countries (as in article 283). And if, as article 297 stated, the highest ridge of Mt. Changbai (Paektu) should determine the Sino-Korean border, then the Mukedeng stele must be discounted as evidence of demarcation, since it was erected south of the summit. In that case, article 296 could not be cited to confirm the authority of the Mukedeng investigation.

Yet, no matter how poorly the *Kongpŏp* principles were engaged with, the episode still presented a remarkable revision from practices of the past: Korean officials were now eager to apply a novel rhetoric to construct Korea's new relationship with the world. Unlike Yi Chung-ha, who adeptly manipulated the *zongfan* doctrine during the 1885–1887 demarcations, Korean officials in the late 1890s were ready to see Qing China as an equal partner and to reevaluate the Sino-Korean connection in light of a novel universal norm.

Sadly, the world at the turn of the twentieth century was not one of Kant but, rather, of Machiavelli. The regime of international law, not as "universal" as it claimed itself to be, was more of a tool for imperial powers to legalize their colonial acquisitions. Rarely was there a colonized people who successfully defended their sovereignty by relying principally upon "public laws." In East Asia, Bluntschli's textbook doctrines were hardly implemented in practice. This perhaps also explained why people later largely neglected the *Gongfa huitong*. Even so, the efforts of grassroots Korean officials demonstrated that, rather than becoming helpless victims of the new international order, some Koreans were proactively pursuing a *raison d'état* by bringing to bear the new principles, just as they had formerly done with the *zongfan* code.

A Korean Emissary and a Japanese Jurist

In May 1907 Yi Sang-sŏl, the founder of the Sŏjŏn Academy in Longjing, left the village for Vladivostok. A few days beforehand the former official of the Korean court had angrily refused to allow a group of Japanese, led by Saitō Suejirō and Shinoda Jisaku in disguise, to stay at his school. Now he headed to the Primorsky to accept a secret mission that shocked Japan and the world.

In Vladivostok Yi Sang-sŏl met Yi Jun, who brought him an appointment letter from Emperor Kojong. The Korean emperor assigned Yi Sang-sŏl as the envoy and Yi Jun as the deputy envoy to attend the Second Peace Conference at The Hague. Kojong asked them to announce to the world that Korea was independent and that Japan had violated international law by depriving Korea's diplomatic rights through the protectorate treaty, which he had not signed. Via the Trans-Siberian Railway, Yi Sang-sŏl and Yi Jun went to St. Petersburg, where they were joined by Yi Wi-jong, a diplomat serving in the Korean consulate in Russia. The three emissaries arrived in the Netherlands in June.

Contrary to their expectations, the "international community" did not even allow their entry in the meeting hall. By definition of international law, Korea was not qualified to attend the conference because it was not a sovereign nation. It was merely a Japanese "protectorate," just like the Belgian Congo, for which the concept was invented in 1885. Meanwhile, Japan skillfully manipulated the international terms and convinced most powers in The Hague that it had acquired Korea by proper means and for noble ends. The regime of international law, on which Koreans thought they could count, had abandoned them. Not only that, but the law literally downgraded the country to a semicivilized or barbaric land. In a word, Korea as a nation was "declared illegal," as Alexis Dudden vividly puts it.[86]

Itō Hirobumi was outraged by the secret mission. Under his pressure, Emperor Kojong, afraid to admit his role in the incident, had to abdicate and pass his throne to his son, Sunjong. Subsequently, the Japan–Korea Treaty (chongmi choyak), which stripped Korea's autonomy in domestic politics, was signed. With no hope of accomplishing his mission, Yi Jun died under mysterious circumstances in The Hague in July. Yi Wi-jong returned to Russia and was killed in 1917 during World War I. Yi Sang-sŏl, having devoted all he had to the anti-Japanese movement in the Primorsky, also died in 1917. He never returned to Longjing, nor his home country. His school was shut down by the Kantō Branch, the Japanese colonial agency in Kando.

Demonstrating the principle that the weak must rely on a norm while the powerful can manipulate it, years after it happened Shinoda Jisaku still liked to talk about his dramatic encounter with Yi Sang-sŏl, a famous "indocile Korean" (J. futei senjin). The two figures, both of whom were engaged in the international law regime yet had entirely different fates, intersected at Kando/Kantō. More than just the chief of the general affairs of the Kantō Branch, Shinoda Jisaku played a key role in the Japanese colonization in both Kantō and Korea. To a large extent, he was a model of how Japan made use of the new "universal" norm to propel its imperialist enterprise.

Born to a peasant family in Shizuoka prefecture, Shinoda graduated from Tokyo Imperial University in 1899, majoring in law. A member of the newly established Japanese Association of International Law, he was

---

[86] Alexis Dudden, *Japan's Colonization of Korea* (Honolulu: University of Hawai'i Press, 2005), pp. 7–26.

a close friend of Akiyama Masanosuke (1866–1937), a pioneering legal scholar in Japan. Following Akiyama's encouragement and recommendation, he joined the Imperial Army during the Russo-Japanese War as a jurist.[87] For Japan, fighting a war against a major world power such as Russia served as proof that Japanese civilization and the Japanese race could not be considered inferior to Western civilization and the white race. Since all European colonial powers were advocating international law as the "universal norm," Japan also needed it to fashion itself as a "civilized" nation – more civilized than Russia. Allocating at least one international law expert to each of its armies, then, was a crucial strategy in ensuring Japan not only victory on the battlefield but also victory in the context of internationally recognized moral and legal standards.

Shinoda served in the Third Army, commanded by General Nogi Maresuke (1849–1912). Most of the battles the Third Army engaged in took place on the Liaodong Peninsula in Manchuria. Involving by far the greatest degree of mechanized warfare, these were arguably the most horrific conflicts in the whole war, with both Russia and Japan suffering massive human casualties. Even General Nogi himself lost two sons. When the Russian troops in Port Arthur finally surrendered in January 1905, Shinoda took part in designing the legal procedure of capitulation. Negotiations mainly drew upon precedents from the Franco-Prussian War, as well as the *Laws and Customs of War on Land* created at the First Peace Conference at The Hague in 1899. To a lesser degree, according to Shinoda, reference was also made to the ceremony that took place in 1636 when the Chosŏn dynasty surrendered to invading Manchu forces.[88] The whole handover process was conducted smoothly and peacefully, which he later boasted as "establishing a new example for international war in the Far East."[89] Shinoda emphasized in particular Japan's extraordinary contribution to the laws of war: "[F]oreign observers at the time, such as military attachés and journalists etc., highly praised the capitulation, to the extent that it established a model for the future."[90]

Indeed, Japan wanted to ensure that every step of its expansion looked "civilized." International law provided the appropriate trappings, though often at the cost of those who were deemed to be "uncivilized." Designating Korea a "protectorate," for example, showed Japan's mastery

---

[87] Shinoda Jisaku, "Ko Akiyama hakuji wo okufu," in Akiyama Masanosuke Denki Hensankai, ed., *Akiyama Masanosuke den* (Tokyo: Akiyama Masanosuke Denki Hensankai, 1941), pp. 403–404.

[88] Shinoda Jisaku, *Nankan Sanjō no kaijōshi: Kyokutō ni okeru capitulation no ichirei* (Keijō: Shinoda Jisaku, 1930).

[89] Shinoda Jisaku, "Ryojunkō kaijō kiyaku," in Oda Sensei Shōju Kinenkai, ed., *Oda sensei shōju kinen chōsen ronshu* (Keijō: Osaka Yagō Shoten, 1934), p. 360.

[90] Ibid., p. 363.

of the colonial discourse embraced by the "international community." It publicly denied Korea's autonomy and deprived the Korean people of their own state. In the case of the Kantō dispute, Japan portrayed local Koreans as the victims of a humanitarian crisis, so that "protecting Koreans" became its noble excuse for encroaching on the territorial sovereignty of another state. However, underneath the surface, what Japan was really worried about was the potential for Kantō, a region adjoining the Japanese-ruled peninsula, with only a loosely controlled border, and already home to the world's largest overseas Korean community, to become a hotbed for anti-Japanese activism. Independent activists and Righteous Army (Ŭibyŏng) militias, which Japan referred to as "indocile Koreans" (*futei senjin*), moved back and forth across the Tumen River, attacking Japanese garrisons and gaining support among local populations, causing major headaches for the Japanese colonial rulers. Therefore, aside from its economic benefits, gaining and maintaining control of Kantō was a key objective for the Japanese in their attempt to eliminate Korean resistance.[91]

But Shinoda Jisaku had other thoughts on the territorial issue. Since the Japanese government never announced definitively that the Tumen northern bank was Korean territory, he, as a jurist, had to figure out a way to ensure that it was justifiable for Japan to claim the land. His strategy was to give Kantō a new definition: no-man's-land.

No-Man's-Land, or Terra Nullius

Shinoda's notion that Kantō was a no-man's-land developed over years and still has great influence today. In 1909 he published his first paper on the dispute in the *Journal of International Law* (*Kokusaihō zasshi*). In order to demonstrate the "fair" and "scientific" basis for his argument, he denounced both Qing and Korean territorial claims, asserting that Kantō was an unused wildland with unclear sovereignty.[92] Later, in an essay titled "Retrospective on the Kantō Issue," he wrote: "Regarding the Kantō Issue, the conclusion of my research is that: 'Kantō belongs neither to the Qing nor to Korea. It is a naturally formed, uninhabited, neutralized zone.'"[93] But this statement needs to be read in context. Shinoda's "Kantō" encompassed a much larger region than the area for which the term was normally used, including not only the lands north

---

[91] Shinoda, "Kantō mondai no kaiko."

[92] Shinoda Jisaku, "Nichiro sensō izen ni okeru kantō mondai," *Kokusaihō zasshi*, vol. 8, no. 3 (1909), pp. 171–199; no. 5 (1910), pp. 361–376; no. 6 (1910), pp. 453–469.

[93] Shinoda, "Kantō mondai no kaiko," p. 485.

of the Tumen River but also those north of the Yalu River. That is to say, his "Kantō" constituted a huge area that covered almost all of southern Manchuria. This move deliberately confused the north bank of the Tumen, which was under dispute, with the north bank of the Yalu, which was not. "Since the land north of the Yalu was recognized as Qing territory," he argues, "it was fair to regard the land north of the Tumen as Korean territory."[94]

What is more, although Shinoda was not the first to try to neutralize the territory under dispute, he did it in a new way. Recall that the early Korean squatters argued that the land in the Tuman north bank was "unused wildland." Certain Japanese researchers before him, for example Kotō Bunjirō and Morita Toshitō, had also viewed Kantō as a "neutralized area" or an "area beyond civilization." However, Shinoda's definition did not simply echo these theories but had a much more subtle implication when taken within the framework of international law. Shinoda explained that the "neutrality" of Kantō was a result of the Manchu–Chosŏn agreement reached in the early seventeenth century following the two Manchu invasions, in which the two regimes swore to maintain their original division. But the original text of the agreement did not indicate where the border was. Taking advantage of this ambiguity, Shinoda cited *Description de la Chine*, an influential encyclopedic record of the history, geography, and society of China published in 1735 by French sinologist Jean-Baptiste Du Halde. Based on one document in this book (discussed below), Shinoda determined that Korean territory extended to the north of the Tumen and Yalu Rivers and that a vast area of southern Manchuria was a "no-man's-land":

Although at that time, the concept of the state boundary was generally vague, with hardly any explicit indications, we could still assume from *this record* that the northeast border of Korea was from Heishan Mountain north of the Tuman River to the mountains containing the Yalu River system and south of Fenghuang City. We could also assume that to the north [of this boundary] existed a *no-man's-land* [*mujinchitai*].[95]

Further, in his 1938 monograph *The Demarcation Stele of the Paktusan* (*Hakutōsan teikaihi*), Shinoda clarified and consolidated this definition, devoting an entire chapter to "the formation of a no-man's-land" (*mujinchitai no seiritsu*).[96] According to Shinoda, since the Qing government had extremely limited civilian access to the borderland area, such a policy presented itself as a form of "territorial abandonment." And,

[94] Ibid., p. 486.
[95] Ibid., pp. 485–490, italics mine.
[96] Shinoda, *Hakutōsan teikaihi*, pp. 20–31.

since no facilities had been established after the Qing "abandoned" the land, he argued that "this place did not belong to the Manchu." This was how the region north of the Yalu and Tumen Rivers "became a complete no-man's-land." Despite the lengthier historical narrative in the monograph, the logic remained essentially the same as that of his previous essay. The most important evidential support, again, was Du Halde's *Description de la Chine*. But Shinoda deliberately conflated two concepts here: a land with few inhabitants and a so-called no-man's-land. It was true that, after invading Korea and conquering China, the Qing made a significant part of Manchuria a royal reserve and forbad Han civilians from entering. Yet the Qing set up banner troops to defend the Jilin frontier and regularly patrolled the border with Korea. Furthermore, the Qing claim to southern Manchuria was well documented by both the Qing and Chosŏn governments. There should be no confusion between a lightly populated place and an ungoverned space. Still, Shinoda insisted there was a no-man's-land and handpicked a single European text to support this argument. Why? What elements of this document did he cite in making his claims? More important, how was the information in this document produced?

Let's start with the document that he cited. *Description de la Chine* gained an enormous reputation in eighteenth- and nineteenth-century Europe and was widely considered as one of the foundation works of Western sinology.[97] But the compiler, Du Halde, never visited China himself. Instead, he composed his masterwork by collecting and drawing upon correspondences and reports written by Jesuit missionaries in China. Du Halde's description of the Korean border was based on a memoir written by Jean-Baptiste Régis (1663–1738), who had been dispatched by Qing emperor Kangxi to survey and map Manchuria in 1709 and 1710. Shinoda used this background in making his case that Régis's account was, in his words, "trustworthy." Quoting from Régis, Shinoda argued that the western boundary of Korea lay to the east of the city of Fenghuang and that an "uninhabited space" lay between the willow palisade and the Korean boundary. Along with Régis's memoir, Shinoda included a published map of Korea edited by French cartographer Jean Baptiste Bourguignon d'Anville (1697–1782). Quoting Régis, Shinoda explained

---

[97] Shinoda noted the book title as its abbreviation: "Description de la Chine" (*Hakutōsan teikaihi*, p. 22). The original whole title is *Description géographique, historique, chronologique, politique, et physique de l'empire de la Chine et de la Tartarie chinoise: enrichie des cartes générales et particulières de ces pays, de la carte générale et des cartes particulières du Thibet, & de la Corée, & ornée d'un grand nombre de figures & de vignettes gravées en tailledouce.*

that the Korean boundary was shown on this map using a broken line (see Map 8).[98]

Shinoda was not the first Japanese who employed these Jesuit documents. It was possible that he got the information from Naitō Torajirō (1866–1934). In 1906 Naitō was commissioned by the Japanese Ministry of Foreign Affairs to investigate the Qing–Korean territorial dispute. In the survey report he submitted to the Ministry of Foreign Affairs in 1907, Naitō mentioned Régis's memoir in order to prove the argument that Kantō was an "uninhabited neutralized zone" and "deserted area" within the Qing boundary.[99] Shinoda, who likely read Naitō's report or even possibly became acquainted with him during the latter's investigation trip,[100] had a slightly different interpretation of Régis's description.

Shinoda used the Japanese term *mujinchitai* (no-man's-land) to interpret Régis's expression of *un espace inhabité* (uninhabited space). But what was involved here was not simply a matter of translation from one language to another. His ultimate purpose was to prove that the "sovereignty" of this space was "undecided," that it belonged "to neither the Qing nor to Korea." In other words, rather than using the phrase "no-man's-land" in its literal meaning, he instead interpreted it in a specific legal sense.

In the language of international law, the land was to Shinoda a *terra nullius*. This Latin term, despite claims that it was derived from the Roman legal term *res nullius*, is arguably a modern invention.[101] Usually translated as "no-man's-land," *terra nullius* actually does not refer to an uninhabited or less populated place but to a land without sovereignty. Appearing first in the form of *territorium nullius*, the term was proposed and discussed by German professor Ferdinand von Martitz at a meeting of the Institut de Droit International (Institute of International Law) in 1888. Aiming to secure the German share of the European colonies in Africa, Martitz defined the term as referring to "any region not effectively under the sovereignty or protectorate of one of the states forming the community of international law, whether inhabited or not."[102]

---

[98] Shinoda, *Hakutōsan teikaihi*, p. 22.

[99] JACAR, "Kantō mondai chōsa-sho," in "Kantō no hanto nikanshi seihan ryōgoku fungi ikken/fuzoku-sho (Naitō Torajirō shokutaku oyobi chōsa hōkoku)," ref. B03041212800 and ref. B03041212500.

[100] Naitō Konan, "Kantō Kirin Ryokōdan," in *Naitō Konan zenshū*, vol. 6 (Tokyo: Chikuma Shobō, 1976), pp. 414–438.

[101] Michael Connor, *The Invention of Terra Nullius: Historical and Legal Fictions on the Foundation of Australia* (Sydney: Macleay Press, 2005); Andrew Fitzmaurice, "The Genealogy of Terra Nullius," *Australian Historical Studies*, vol. 38, no. 129 (2007), pp. 1–15.

[102] Mark F. Lindley, *The Acquisition and Government of Backward Territory in International Law: Being a Treatise on the Law and Practice relating to Colonial Expansion*

Map 8 The Kingdom of Korea
Source: Du Halde, J.-B., A Description of the Empire of China and Chinese-Tartary, Special Collections Research Center, University of Chicago Library.

According to the logic of international law, the term *terra nullius* has a close relationship with one of the basic methods of territorial acquisition: occupation.[103] A land that belongs to no one is a subject for occupation, provided that the occupier is a sovereign state recognized by the "community of international law." As many scholars have argued, although the term per se was rarely used to describe situations as they unfolded, its logic, which derived from the natural law tradition, was widely adopted by European colonial powers in rationalizing their seizure of indigenous lands.[104] The natural law tradition recognizes property rights only by effective use. In the context of land/territorial rights, *terra nullius* concerns not only whether the land had been explored or not but also by whom. If necessary, according to natural law, indigenous land rights must yield to colonial practices. As Martitz argued in the 1888 meeting, it is "an exaggeration to talk about the sovereignty of savage or half-barbarian."[105] By the late nineteenth and early twentieth centuries this logic had become firmly embedded in the legal rhetoric used to retrospectively justify what was essentially the encroachment upon and dispossession of the lands of indigenous peoples.

Around the same time European colonizers manipulated the principle of *terra nullius* to deny the landownership of aboriginal peoples in Africa, Australia, and North America, Japan was quick to adopt this principle in interpreting and justifying its imperial expansion following the Meiji Restoration. As scholars have recently pointed out, during its colonization of the island of Hokkaido (1869) and its expedition to Taiwan (1871) Japan characterized both islands as examples of "no-man's-land" in legitimizing the expulsion of the indigenous Ainu and Taiwanese aborigines.[106] Colonization on a global level was unfolding at the same pace,

(London: Longmans, Green, 1926), p. 16; quoted in Fitzmaurice, "The Genealogy of Terra Nullius," p. 11.

[103] Daniel-Erasmus Khan, "Territories and Boundaries," in Bardo Fassbender and Anne Peters, eds., *The Oxford Handbook of the History of International Law* (Oxford: Oxford University Press, 2014), pp. 225–249.

[104] Lauren Benton and Benjamin Straumann, "Acquiring Empire by Law: From Roman Doctrine to Early Modern European Practice," *Law and History Review*, vol. 28, no. 1 (2010), pp. 1–38; Kaius Touri, "The Reception of Ancient Legal Thought in Early Modern International Law," in Fassbender and Peters, eds., *The Oxford Handbook of the History of International Law*, pp. 1012–1033.

[105] Andrew Fitzmaurice, "Discovery, Conquest, and Occupation of Territory," in Fassbender and Peters, eds., *The Oxford Handbook of the History of International Law*, pp. 840–861.

[106] Michele Manson, *Dominant Narratives of Colonial Hokkaido and Imperial Japan: Envisioning the Periphery and the Modern Nation-State* (New York: Palgrave Macmillan, 2012); Norihito Mizuno, "An Aspect of Modern Japan's Overseas Expansionism: The Taiwanese Aboriginal Territories in the Early Meiji Japanese Perspective," *Archiv Orientální*, vol. 78, no. 2 (2010), pp. 175–193; Shin Kawashima, "China," and Masaharu Yanagihara, "Japan," both in Fassbender and Peters, eds., *The Oxford Handbook of the History of International Law*, pp. 451–474 and 475–499.

under the same logic. In light of this background, it made perfect sense for Shinoda to argue that, on the one hand, "Kantō belongs to neither the Qing nor Korea" while, on the other hand, "it was fair to regard the lands to the north of the Tumen as Korean territory." According to Shinoda's reasoning, because the overwhelming majority of the people of this "no-man's-land" were Korean, and since Korea was no longer a sovereign state but a "protectorate" of Japan, it followed that Japan had every right under international law to govern this region.

Again, however, Shinoda's ambitions extended far beyond the Tumen River region. Citing Régis's report in Du Halde's book, he argued that the Korean border extended all the way to Fenghuang City in the eastern part of the Liaodong Peninsula, meaning that most of the Yalu River region could also be included in his concept of Kantō. The problem was that he was citing Régis outside the original context. To illustrate this point, it is worth quoting Régis at length. The portion Shinoda extracted is marked in bold:

I did not go far enough into the [Korean] Kingdom, as I said before, to be able to speak with any certainty concerning the nature of its soil; but what I saw of it upon the frontiers is very well cultivated after the manner of the Southern Chinese: a Tartar Lord, whom the Emperor hath sent here, attended by one of the inferior Mandarins of the Mathematick Tribunal, gave us an account that the country is good, and produces in great plenty whatever is necessary for life... The same Lord hath brought along with him a map of it, exactly like that in the Royal Palace; as he did not go farther than the court, he only gave us the length of the road which he took thither from the City of *Fong hoang tching* [Fenghuang city], having had it measured by a Line, *Fong hoang tching* is at the East end of the Palisado of *Luang tong* [Liaodong]: we were there, and it is from this very spot that we began to take its dimensions. We found by immediate observations its latitude to be ten degrees, thirty minutes, and twenty seconds; and its longitude appeared to be seven degrees and forty two minutes; **to the East of this city is the western boundary of Corea under the now reigning family; for after the wars of the Koreas with the Mantchuoux [Manchu], who subdued them before they attack'd China, it was at last agreed upon between them that there should be left a certain space uninhabited between the Palisado and the Boundaries of Corea: those boundaries are marked upon the map by prick'd lines**: as I have not myself taken a view of the inward Parts of the Kingdom nor the seacoast, I am far from offering this map as a finished work, but only as the best which has been publish'd, none having either ability or means to take a particular and exact account of the situation of the cities, and of the course of the rivers.[107]

[107] Jean-Baptiste Du Halde, *The General History of China, Containing a Geographical, Historical, Chronological, Political and Physical Description of the Empire of China, Chinese-Tartary, Corea and Thibet*, 3rd edn., corr., trans. Richard Brookes, vol. 4 (London: J. Watts, 1741), pp. 382–383.

It is obvious that Shinoda obscured crucial information in his selective quotation. Régis never ventured beyond the city of Fenghuang, to say nothing of reaching the Korean border. In fact, the Qing emperor did not permit Jesuits serving in the Qing court to approach Korea. Even if the emperor had allowed it, the Chosŏn court would very likely have forbidden missionaries from entering the country. What is more, the account by Régis and the map of the Korean kingdom included in Du Halde's book were provided by a "Tartar lord" who himself had traveled only as far as the capital city. The Jesuit map of Korea was clearly not based on a direct field survey, as Shinoda somehow implied. In stark contrast to what Shinoda was insisting, Régis himself admitted that he was in no position to offer a "trustworthy" depiction of Korea.

But let us not stop here. Régis's narrative provides us with enough clues to cross-examine the relevant Chinese and Korean documents and investigate how the geographic knowledge he received from the "Tartar lord" was formulated in the first place. The "Tartar lord" Régis mentioned was Mukedeng, the same Manchu official who carried out a survey of the Qing–Chosŏn borderlands and mistakenly erected a stele in 1712 that was to play a key role in the entire territorial dispute. The trip that Régis describes took place in 1713, when Mukedeng was sent to Korea once again by Emperor Kangxi as a deputy envoy. While announced as a diplomatic mission, the real purpose of the trip was to collect further geographical data on Korea so as to complete Kangxi's ambitious project of mapping the entire empire using the Jesuits' cartographic techniques. Mukedeng and the Chinese mathematician He Guozhu carried out measurements en route, all the way from the city of Fenghuang to Hansŏng. Upon entering the capital, Mukedeng made a direct request to King Sukchong for detailed hydrographic and geographic data of Mt. Changbai/Paektu, along with a map of the region. But the Koreans claimed that the court did not possess such information either. Mukedeng was not convinced.

Several days later the chief minister, Yi Yu, made a suggestion to King Sukchong: "[Mukedeng] requested a map of our country. Although the interpreters tried to palter with him, it seems we have to give him something... But the maps in the Border Defense Bureau [Pibyŏnsa] are too detailed to present. We just received a map that is neither too precise nor too general, with many errors concerning the rivers in the Mt. Paektu area. We may show him this one."[108] Mukedeng made a copy of this map and returned the original.

---

[108] *Chosŏnwangjo sillok, Sukchong sillok*, 39-6-2.

Exactly which map the Koreans provided Mukedeng is unknown, but it is this map that constituted the basis of the map Régis created and d'Anville in turn produced. In his memoir Régis said that he calculated the geographic location and the shape of the Korean peninsula by cross-referencing his survey of Fenghuang City, Mukedeng's measurement en route to Hansŏng, and of course Mukedeng's copy of the map from the Korean court.

D'Anville, a royal geographer of France, used the Jesuit maps to produce a series of maps for Du Halde's four-volume *Description de la Chine.* Two years later these maps were collected and published in The Hague as a single-volume atlas, *Nouvel atlas de la Chine, de la Tartarie chinoise et du Thibet (New Atlas of China, Chinese Tartary and Tibet).*[109] In the preface to the atlas, the editor praised the quality of the original Korean map: "If any map is correct, it ought to be this one, since it was originally surveyed by Korean geographers, under the orders of the king, and the original map is preserved in his palace. The map given here is based on this original. We understand the missionaries did not discover any significant differences between their own observations at the northern borders of the kingdom and the limits marked on the map. Otherwise they would have mentioned it. This circumstance alone validates the accuracy of the map."[110] Of course, the editor could not have known the story behind the Korean map. But the preface nevertheless confirms that the Jesuit map of Korea published in *Description de la Chine* indeed relied on the flawed map provided by the Korean court.

The quibble between Qing and Chosŏn over the Korean map vividly demonstrates Brian Harley's observation that "cartography was primarily a form of political discourse concerned with the acquisition and maintenance of power."[111] In his work *Cartography in Korea*, historian Gari Ledyard argues that the map given to Mukedeng might be very similar to the "Map of the Eight Provinces" made in the seventeenth century, as the two contain much of the same misinformation. Ledyard even suspects that, "[g]iven the general Korean inclination to deceive the Chinese and other foreigners about their country (and the map episode only represents a pervasive habit, nourished by foreign invasions over the

---

[109] The publication of the volume was not authorized by d'Anville. See Mario Cams, "Jean-Baptiste Bourguignon d'Anville and the Nouvelle atlas de la Chine," in Roberto M. Ribeiro and John W. O'Malley, eds., *Jesuit Mapmaking in China: D'Anville's Nouvelle Atlas de la Chine (1737)* (Philadelphia: Saint Joseph's University Press, 2014).

[110] Ibid., p. 68.

[111] J. Brian Harley, "The Hidden Agenda of Cartography in Early Modern Europe," *Imago Mundi,* vol. 40, no. 1 (1988), pp. 57–76.

centuries), it is not beyond possibility that the map given to Mukedeng could even have been doctored in spots."[112]

It was not only the source of Régis's knowledge that was tainted. Régis himself also wrongly understood the geographic location of the Korean boundary. While he did make mention of the Yalu and Tumen Rivers, describing them as "most considerable rivers, which are its [Korea's] defense as well as its riches,"[113] he depicted the boundary as lying north of the rivers, implying that the realm across both rivers fell within Korean territory. This description contradicted most Chinese and Korean records and could not have been given by Mukedeng, who had just surveyed the boundary a year beforehand. Many European-made maps in the eighteenth and early nineteenth centuries inherited Régis's misinterpretation about the Korean border. How exactly Régis made this mistake is hard to determine, but it is highly likely that he misinterpreted the willow palisade ("Palisado") as the Qing boundary instead of a domestic barrier[114] – a possible explanation related to the fact that the Qing deliberately evacuated the area between Fenghuang City and the Yalu River so that no civilian could inhabit the frontier zone. The Korean emissaries who made the tributary journeys to Beijing were received by the Qing only when they reached the fence gate of Fenghuang City on the willow palisade, typically a few days after crossing the border river from the town of Ŭiju. Fenghuang, as opposed to the river, thus often served as a conceptual division between the two states in terms of communication, psychology, and culture.[115] Yet the Yalu River was repeatedly confirmed as the geographic and political border between the two countries.[116] In *Description de la Chine* there is another document, titled *An Abridgement of the History of Corea*, which clearly indicates that the Yalu River was the

---

[112] Ledyard, "Cartography in Korea," p. 303.

[113] Du Halde, *The General History of China*, vol. 4, p. 383.

[114] In the same memoir, Régis claimed that Korea "borders on the west upon the Chinese province called...Leao tung...which is separated from east Tartary by a wooden Palisado." First, Leao tung (Liaodong) was not a province. It simply referred to the east of the Liao River, or, in most contexts, the Liaodong Peninsula. Second, the willow palisade in eastern Shengjing was neither a provincial nor a state boundary. See ibid., p. 382.

[115] Wang Yuanchong, "Beyond Fenghuang Gate: Chosŏn Korea's Mixed Perception of Qing China in the Late Eighteenth Century," paper presented at the New York Conference for Asian Studies, Poughkeepsie, New York, October 16–17, 2015.

[116] For example, in 1746 King Yŏngjo of Chosŏn petitioned Emperor Qianlong of Qing to stop stationing troops and cultivating wasteland near the Mangniushao post north to the Yalu River. The reason was it would be difficult to stop illegal crossing if people were living in the region. In their exchanges, they reconfirmed that a stone island in the river was the division between the two states. See *Qingshilu Gaozong shilu*, vol. 270 (Beijing: Zhonghua shuju, 1986), pp. 26–28, and vol. 271, p. 710.

division between Korea and Liaodong. But, for Shinoda, Régis's confusion seemed to be more valuable.

To sum up the twisting route of the discourse on the Sino-Korean borderland: in 1713 the Korean court gave Mukedeng false geographic information regarding the country and its frontier in order to safeguard its interests from further Manchu harassment. Based on the material that Mukedeng had collected in Korea, Régis produced a description and a map of Korea that were later reproduced in Du Halde's *Description de la Chine* in 1735. After nearly two hundred years Shinoda Jisaku picked out a specific portion of Régis's transcript and distorted it to align with his colonialist ambitions. After being transmitted in various incarnations from one end of Eurasia to the other and back again over a period of almost two centuries, then, the geographic knowledge that Korea had fabricated in order to protect itself was eventually used by the Japanese as evidence that the lands to the north of the Tumen and Yalu Rivers could be considered a *terra nullius*.

The journey taken by the concept of "no-man's-land" did not stop in the early twentieth century. The 1960s and 1970s, an era in which the Pak Chŏng-hŭi government was vigorously promoting anti-communist nationalism, saw rising nostalgia for the "northern territory" in South Korean society.[117] Nationalist historians and irredentist groups called for the "recovery" of Korean sovereignty in "Kando." On the one hand, modern Korean scholars denounced the 1909 Sino-Japanese treaty relating to the Tumen boundary because Korea was under the illegal colonial rule of the Japanese when it was signed.[118] On the other hand, some of them uncritically adopted Shinoda Jisaku's interpretation of Régis's text. Claiming that the Yanbian region (and a portion of the Russian Far East) was originally a "no-man's-land" until the Koreans occupied it in the late nineteenth century, they failed to excavate (or purposefully ignored) the colonialist provenance and implications of such a concept.[119] The Jesuit map of Korea was also held up as "objective" evidence from a European (hence nonbiased) perspective.[120] The notion of the no-man's-land had thus come full cycle, returning to the place it had started. Only, this time,

---

[117] Andre Schmid, "Rediscovering Manchuria: Sin Ch'aeho and the Politics of Territorial History in Korea," *Journal of Asian Studies*, vol. 56, no. 1 (1997), pp. 26–46.

[118] No Yŏng-don, "Kando Yŏngyukwŏn ŭl dullăssan pŏmjŏk chemunje," *Paeksan Hakpo*, no. 84 (2009), pp. 217–246.

[119] Yu Pong-yŏng, "Paektusan Chŏnggyebi wa Kando Munje," *Paeksan Hakpo*, no. 13 (1972), pp. 73–134; Sin, *Kando yŏngyugwŏn e kwanhan yŏn'gu*, p. 10; Kim Kyŏng-ch'un, "Chosŏnjo hugiŭi kukgyŏngsŏne taehan ilgo," *Paeksan Hakpo*, no. 29 (1984), pp. 5–33.

[120] Kang Hyo-suk, "Kando yŏngyukwŏnae taehan che koch'al: Kando kojido wa kando hyŏbyak chŏnhuŭi ilbunŭi chase pyŏnhwa," *Chŏnbuk sahak*, no. 43 (2013), pp. 179–212.

what was once colonialist discourse was adapted to nationalist needs, constituting an example of a rather ironic collaboration between colonialism, imperialism, and nationalism.

The attempts to conceptualize a multilateral frontier space in East Asia have demonstrated the dynamic of intellectual connections between the two ends of the Eurasian continent. To borrow the words of Lauren Benton, the journey taken by the notion of *terra nullius* suggests the need to "reexamine a prominent and seductive narrative about the progressive rationalization of space in an increasingly interconnected world."[121] During prolonged intercommunication between diverse areas of the globe in the past three centuries, spatial and legal knowledge has been produced, reproduced, and transformed along with competition for power in various forms. The epistemological turn of the Tumen River borderland serves as an example, which helps us construct a more comprehensive understanding of the relationship between Europe and East Asia, especially with regard to how each has contributed to the other's historical evolution.

---

[121] Lauren Benton, *A Search for Sovereignty: Law and Geography in European Empires, 1400–1900* (Cambridge: Cambridge University Press, 2009), p. 9.

5   Boundary Redefined
A Multilayered Competition

On a winter day in 1907, in Hansŏng, Korea, Bai Wenwei, a Chinese in his early thirties, was approached by a Japanese military policeman. "Do you know where I can find this person?" the officer asked, showing him a piece of paper with Bai's name on it. Bai replied: "I don't know."

A member of staff in the Qing Commission of Frontier Affairs, Bai had come to Korea to collect documents in preparation for the territorial debate with Japan. A few days earlier, using 500 silver dollars, he had purchased the *Atlas of the Great East* (*Taedong yŏjido*) from the son of a high-ranking Korean official. The atlas, made by Korean cartographer Kim Chŏng-ho, indicated that the Tuman River was the Qing–Korean boundary (see Chapter 2), making the map a critical piece of evidence supporting China's territorial claim. But the news of this purchase was soon known by the Japanese. Annoyed at losing evidence to the Chinese, the Japanese authority in Korea immediately ordered a search for Bai Wenwei. After encountering the Japanese police, Bai hid in the Chinese consulate before returning to Manchuria via the maritime route.[1]

But the story had a still more intriguing side to it. Although he was serving in the Qing government, Bai was in fact an anti-Qing activist. He first concealed himself in the Jilin local army (Jiqiangjun), then was transferred by his comrade Wu Luzhen, then the assistant administrator of the Commission of Frontier Affairs, to the current position. He spent three years in Yanji trying "to communicate with outlaws in the greenwoods and prepare for the revolution."[2] In twentieth-century Chinese history, Bai was remembered as a renowned military commander and politician in the Nationalist Party (KMT), a veteran revolutionary who stood up to the autocratic rule of Chiang Kai-shek, and a patriot who called for a united front to counter the Japanese invasion in the 1930s. The map story, recorded in his autobiography, was just a small episode reflecting

---

[1] Bai Wenwei, "Wushi nian dashiji," in *Bai Wenwei zishu 1876–1947* (Beijing: Renmin ribao chubanshe, 2011), pp. 1–103, 21.
[2] Bai Wenwei, "Wushinian jingli," in ibid., p. 121.

the sophisticated interaction and overlap of diverse political ideas and forces in the multilateral borderland of the Tumen River region. The current chapter introduces how the complex rivalry of these forces unfolded through the territorial struggle from 1907 to 1909. During this period the dispute shifted from being mainly a population and boundary conflict between Qing China and Korea to a state-building contest between China and Japan.

Compared to the 1885–1887 demarcation between the Qing and Chosŏn, the 1907–1909 Sino-Japanese demarcation was different in both content and means. It was no longer a contest of dynastic geography. Although geography was still a battlefield in the diplomatic struggle, it provided no more than an intellectual context for intensive political negotiation. Neither side raised any new evidence from the topographical perspective, nor was there a joint investigation in the field. The real confrontation here, as mentioned, was over state building in a society composed mainly of the immigrants from a third country. It also included a contest on discursive level: how to reinterpret a border formed hundreds of years ago in accordance with the new regimes of international law and territorial state.

Nor was the new demarcation a bilateral competition between just two states. This was especially evident at the local level. The building of a sovereign state in a given place needs to be responsive to local society, whose objectives may or may not be aligned with the aims of the dominant state. Under the mighty pressures of the Chinese and Japanese states, the Korean community was torn into rival factions. Different factions used the states to pursue their own political agendas, which were not necessarily appendages to either state. In other words, in this competition the Koreans, though not a united force, should be seen as independent actors pursuing what they believed to be the best interests of Korea.

Meanwhile, nonstate actors also participated in the sovereignty struggle, sometimes to a greater degree than the states. Depending on the issue, the relationship between state and nonstate actors could be cooperative or hostile. Added to that, even within the government system, bureaucrats at different levels – central, provincial, and local – did not necessarily understand the state's priorities in the same way. The power structure in the Tumen demarcation was thus entangled in multiple layers, with various agents woven into the nexus of interlaced tensions and coalitions.

During and after the negotiation, the Tumen frontier – or, to a large extent, the whole of Manchuria – was further redefined in accordance with various geopolitical visions. The contention over this space aroused tremendous public attention in Japan, China, and Korea. Leading intellectuals in all three societies enthusiastically constructed new images of Manchuria. Manchuria became a space accommodating almost all important political imaginations in early twentieth-century East Asia. The last part of the chapter analyzes the "Kantō/Jiandao" theses of three representative intellectuals in three countries. It demonstrates not only how a geographic space was conceived according to rival political ideals but also how these diverse concepts, despite conflicting with each other, were mutually influenced and reciprocally shaped.

State and Nonstate Actors in the Contest

When Itō Hirobumi forced the Korean emperor Kojong to abdicate, the news immediately raised alarm for frontier security among Chinese officials. Xu Shichang, a close assistant to Yuan Shikai and a key figure of the Beiyang clique, had just been appointed as the first viceroy of Three Northeast Provinces, the principal administrator of Manchuria. Eight days after the abdication of Kojong, on June 28, 1907, Xu telegraphed the Foreign Ministry:

The coerced abdication of the Korean emperor…is a crucial incident relating to our eastern provinces. The Sino-Korean border issue has been suspended for a long time and will require thorough negotiations. Having no records or documents here, I am afraid we will be short of evidence when facing the challenge. Therefore I ask you to issue an order to our Resident Minister in Korea, asking him to select staff who were familiar with frontier affairs and send them to Fengtian, along with the border maps and selected copies of essential documents, for the purpose of careful consultation. This is of vital importance.[3]

On the very next day Xu secretly appointed a young officer of the New Army, Wu Luzhen, to investigate the Yanji area. A team of nine people, led by Wu, spent seventy-three days thoroughly surveying the southern Jilin area, from Jilin City all the way to Hunchun. The team collected extensive empirical data on the local surroundings, including geography, hydrology, population, industry, and history. Later Wu Luzhen, with the help of his assistant, Zhou Weizhen, compiled the data and wrote a detailed report. *The Report on the Yanji Frontier Affairs* (*Yanji bianwu baogao*) became a cornerstone document, from the Chinese perspective, of the history, geography, and politics of the north Tumen River region.

Just as Xu expected, Japan officially provoked the Kantō issue in late August through the embassy in Beijing, at the same time sending military police across the Tumen River. When Japan announced the establishment of the Kantō Branch on August 23, the Qing Foreign Ministry

---

[3] Xu Shichang, *Tuigengtang zhengshu*, book 5, vol. 48 (Taipei: Wenhai chubanshe, 1968), telegraph 6, p. 2395.

responded with a diplomatic note the next day. Pointing out that the Tumen north bank was under the governance of China's Yanji subprefecture, the Qing firmly denied the name "Kantō/Jiandao" and claimed that Yanji was doubtless Chinese territory. The Koreans who crossed the river should be protected by the Chinese government, and China would absolutely not tolerate Japanese intrusion into the local affairs there. Furthermore, to give the Japanese Kantō Branch tit for tat, the Qing established the Supervising Commission of Frontier Affairs, appointing Chen Zhaochang as the administrator (*duban*) and Wu Luzhen as the assistant administrator (*bangban*). Thus started the two-year-long confrontation and negotiation over the Tumen north bank area.

State Actors: Japan's Colonization and China's New Policy Reform

Although both the Qing and Japanese governments recognized the geopolitical significance of the Tumen River region, they did not necessarily share the same strategic goal. On the offensive side, briefly put, Japan emphasized Kantō's geographic importance in containing Russia, its ample agricultural and mineral production, and its geoeconomic importance to northern Korea. As Xu Shichang summarizes, Japan's strategic considerations regarding Yanji revolved around four points: military significance, transportation, immigration, and industry. That is to say, Japan intended to contest the territory with Russia; integrate Manchuria, northern Korea, northwestern Japan and the Russian Far East into one transportation system; colonize Manchuria; and explore the wealthy resources in Jilin.[4] Indeed, most observers in 1907 would agree that Japan's ambition involved far more than Kantō. Rather, Kantō was merely a springboard to future conquests in Manchuria, Mongolia, and even eastern Siberia. This kind of strategy was well in line with Japan's overall foreign policy of befriending Britain and the United States and opposing Russia.

From 1901 to 1913 two political allies, Katsura Tarō and Saionji Kinmochi, controlled the Japanese Cabinet in turn, and the ambitious Kantō policy was consistently implemented during that time. Another concern, perhaps less critical for Tokyo than for the Resident-General in Hansŏng, was to constrain the Korean resistant movement both within the peninsula and beyond. With the Korean community growing on the Tumen north bank, Kando was clearly a hotbed of more and more "indocile Koreans." Therefore, gaining or losing Kantō directly concerned Japanese rule in the peninsula.

---

[4] Xu, *Dongsansheng zhenglue*, vol. 1, pp. 56–58.

The political concerns of the side on the defensive, the Qing, deserve more elaboration. Realizing the power disparity between itself and Japan, the Qing was worried about safeguarding its own territorial sovereignty. Regarding China as a vulnerable party in the Russian–Japanese–Chinese geopolitical game, Qing officials decided the best hope was to make Yanji a fulcrum for balancing the two other aggressive powers. As Xu Shichang puts it: "Yanji is a corner where the influences of China, Japan and Russia meet each other. Russia could use it to confine Japan; Japan could use it to confine Russia. If we use it well, we could confine both Russia and Japan."[5]

More significantly, the crisis was not happening in just any frontier but in the birthplace of the Qing empire. Occupied by Russia and ravaged in the Russo-Japanese War, Manchuria was hardly a "royal reserve" anymore. Rather, it seemed very likely to be the first domino predicting the fall of the whole empire. With the large scale of exploitation and migration, the banner system now existed only in name. To make matters worse, ever since the suppression of the Hundred Days' Reform (*wuxu bianfa*) in 1898, the influence of Chinese revolutionaries, mingled with anti-Manchu sentiment and anticolonial nationalism, was markedly increasing, gaining popularity among the young generation of elites. Facing these multilayered threats, the late Qing elite officials, both Manchu and Han, responded with a top-down constitutional reform generally known as the New Policy (*xinzheng*). The interiorization of Manchuria was a crucial part of this reform.

Xu Shichang (1855–1939) was one of the most enthusiastic advocates of the New Policy. In 1905 the Qing decided to send five grant ministers abroad to observe the political systems of Europe, Japan, and America in "preparation for the constitutional monarch" (*yubei lixian*). Due to an assassination attempt on the five ministers by a revolutionary, the trip was delayed. Xu, originally among the five, was then reappointed as minister of police and did not participate in the trip. Nevertheless, Xu still committed himself to reforming Qing political institutions in accordance with Western systems. In 1906, after observing the situation in Manchuria, Xu submitted several memorials suggesting changes to its military and political institutions. The Qing government eventually adopted his reforms. In 1907 Beijing announced the provincialization of Fengtian (Shengjing), Jilin, and Heilongjiang, and appointed Xu as the first viceroy of the East Three Provinces.

---

[5] Xu, *Dongsansheng zhenglue*, vol. 1, p. 56.

This was Xu's opportunity to put his New Policy ideas into practice. He immediately made numerous reforms and adjustments: replacing the old administrative system with civil institutions, substituting newly trained armies and policemen for the banner troops, reorganizing administrative divisions, recruiting migrants for cultivation, encouraging industry and commerce, establishing modern schools, and so on.[6] Of course, Xu was not the first reformer in Manchuria. Zhao Erxun, the Fengtian general before the provincialization, had imposed a number of reforms, as had Chongshi and Wu Dacheng before him. Yet Xu pushed the changes to a new level.

Turning Manchuria into provinces meant dissolving the administrative boundary between Manchuria and interior China. The transition would not have been possible without support from both the Manchu and the Han. Other things aside, Xu's appointment itself was revolutionary: a Han minister for the first time became the top governor of Manchuria. Under him, all three provincial governors were Han. Han officials occupied even more middle-ranking positions, including the banner posts. For example, Chen Zhaochang, administrator of frontier affairs, held a concurrent post as vice commander-in-chief of Hunchun, and so was the first (and only) Han to take this Manchu-exclusive title. In a word, the New Policy in the northeast frontier accelerated the integration of Manchuria and China. Yet it came with a price: the Manchus were deprivileged, even marginalized, in their ancestral homeland.

For a new generation of Manchurian officials, frontier building in Yanji was an inseparable part of the new state building in Manchuria and China. It simultaneously served two interrelated goals: to defend a borderland against external threats and to test the effectiveness of the New Policy reforms, which foreshadowed the overall renovation of the whole state. In that sense, the Sino-Japanese conflict over Yanji/Kantō was ultimately a contest for state integration. While Japan attempted to solidify the geographic link between Kantō and Korea by merging the Tumen River region into the Japanese sphere, Qing China saw Yanji as the epitome of northeast China. Failing to bind it with Manchuria meant failing to bind the East Three Provinces with China. To win the game, both parties installed modern statecraft, such as policing, survey, public education, and public health, in this remote ethnic area. Their efforts at frontier building showed more commonalities than differences between the two sides.

---

[6] Zhao Yuntian, *Qingmo xinzheng yanjiu: 20 shiji chu de zhongguo bianjiang* (Harbin: Heilongjiang jiaoyu chubanshe, 2004), pp. 71–139. On Xu's reform and the Manchu people, see Shao, *Remote Homeland, Recovered Borderland*, pp. 52–58.

Although they were inconspicuous, there were also other state actors involved in this competition. Hearing that Japan had sent military police across the river, Russia intended to respond by occupying Hunchun. After the Qing assured Russia that it would negotiate with Japan on the matter, Russia instead stationed an army on the Qing–Russian border to alert Japan.[7] Japan's actions in this trilateral borderland were under close watch by Britain and the United States, which were certainly not eager to see Japan irritate either China or Russia on the issue, nor to let Japan monopolize all the advantages Manchuria offered. The global geopolitical competition was a critical factor in this game. Eventually, the Sino-Japanese conflict was settled not merely on the bilateral level but on a global level.

Nonstate Actors

Often overlooked, three nonstate actors played essential roles in the mapping of the region and boundary: the Japanese Pan-Asianists, the Chinese revolutionaries, and the Korean collaborators (the Ilchinhoe) and resisters. The power of these actors should not be underestimated. With their distinct political agendas (at odds with those of the states), all of them pushed the states to solve the dispute.

Japanese Pan-Asianists: Decolonization through Colonization. Among all the nonstate actors in this contest, the Japanese Pan-Asianists were the most aggressive.[8] A vague umbrella term, "Pan-Asianism" in Meiji Japan might be broadly defined as an ideology that highlighted an "Asian" identity against Western expansion.[9] The paradoxical ideology was combined and intertwined with contradictions: opposing Western colonization by proposing Japanese colonization; rejecting the "Yellow Peril" discourse by advocating the superiority of the "yellow" race; embracing integration of a greater East Asia yet emphasizing Japanese leadership; supporting modern reforms in Korea and revolution in China while denying the full sovereignty of the two neighbors. Emerging from the Freedom and People's Rights movement, which called for civil rights and revision of the unequal treaties, some Pan-Asianists at first attacked the pro-Western policies of the Meiji government and so were

---

[7] Xu, *Dongsansheng zhenglue*, vol. 1, p. 57.

[8] Choi Jang-guen, "Ilbun taeryungnanginŭi kandomunje kaeipkwajŏng," *Paeksan Hakpo*, vol. 71 (2005), pp. 437–472.

[9] Eri Hotta, *Pan-Asianism and Japan's War, 1931–1945* (New York: Palgrave Macmillan, 2007), pp. 2–3.

suppressed by the authorities. Later, the ideology gained the sympathy of more and more government officials, and as a result Pan-Asianists increased their influence in policy-making circles. From the late Meiji period onward, Pan-Asianist organizations and the imperial government cooperated, each using the other party as an instrument to reach their different yet collusive political goals.

Before the Russo-Japanese War Pan-Asianist organizations, especially the Genyōsha (Black Ocean Society) led by Tōyama Mitsuru and the Kokuryūkai (Amur Society) led by Uchida Ryōhei, actively engaged in Manchurian exploration and promoted war with Russia. Claiming to be *shishi*, "patriots with noble ideals," members of these organizations supported the Imperial Army by doing espionage, organizing guerrillas, and recruiting bandits. After Japan expelled Russians from the Korean Peninsula and southern Manchuria, some Pan-Asianists, notably Uchida, found another urgent task for themselves: annexing Korea.

Building a united East Asia was a central ideal for the early Pan-Asianists. A major source for propagating the theme was a book titled *On the Union of the Great East (Daitō gappōron)*, written by Tarui Tōkichi (1850–1922). Tarui was once arrested by the government for organizing the Oriental Social Party. After his release from prison he befriended Tōyama Mitsuru and Hiraoka Kōtaro, both key members of the Genyōsha. Tarui was a fervent supporter of Kim Ok-kyun's reforms in Korea. The failed reforms inspired him to draft his views on the union of Japan and Korea. Because his first manuscript was lost in 1885 when he was again imprisoned, it was not until 1893 that Tarui completed and published *On the Union of the Great East.* Written in classical Chinese to attract the Korean elites, the book calls for the merger of Japan and Korea to create a new state: the Great East. Tarui envisaged that the Great East would then ally with China and save the Asian race and civilization from Western colonization. The book soon gained enormous attention.[10]

When Itō Hirobumi assumed office as the Japanese Resident-General of Korea, he invited Uchida Ryōhei to join his staff. Uchida regarded this as a great opportunity to turn Tarui's idea into reality. Uchida, however, understood *gappō* (union) quite differently from how Tarui did. While Tarui emphasized an equal partnership of the two countries, Uchida wanted to turn Korea into a subordinate part of the Japanese empire. Itō, who did not really favor the idea of immediate annexation, nevertheless needed Uchida and the Kokuryūkai's influence in Korea and Manchuria to implement his colonial projects. Uchida had a decisive impact on the

[10] Kuzū Yoshihisa, *Tōa senkaku shishi kiden*, vol. 3 (Tokyo: Ozorasha, 1997), pp. 281–282.

Ilchinhoe, a Korean populist organization. The Resident-General certainly wished to instigate the Ilchinhoe, through Uchida, to demonstrate the "popular support" for Japanese rule in Korea. He used the strategy on many occasions. The forced abdication of Emperor Kojong and the establishment of the Kantō Branch, for example, were both first petitioned by Ilchinhoe members. In both cases Uchida's role was hidden but crucial.

If the Resident-General and Uchida's Kokuryūkai were not exactly on the same page regarding the issue of annexation, they undoubtedly shared a similar stance on intruding in the sovereignty of northeast China. Uchida and his Kokuryūkai had agitated for the colonization of Manchuria for years. With the Kokuryūkai's powerful network in the government and media, it had successfully promoted the concept that Manchuria would determine the fate of Japan and that the Mt. Changbai area was the key to controlling Manchuria.[11] Other Japanese Pan-Asianists also romanticized the Manchu homeland as a wild and rich new frontier for Japan, and encouraged the Japanese to keep forging ahead to achieve this goal. Under these circumstances, the Kantō dispute provided Japan with a perfect opportunity for state–society collaboration; the Resident-General's assertion of the need to "protect the Koreans" and the Kokuryūkai's expertise in irritating the "popular opinion" of the Koreans could coincide flawlessly.

Like the Japanese government, Pan-Asianists targeted overall Japanese interests in Manchuria, not just the territorial sovereignty of Kantō. They were the first group to suggest the government exchange the Japanese recognition of the Tumen boundary with economic privileges in Manchuria. In January 1909 eight influential figures, including Tōyama Mitsuru, Ioki Ryōzō, Shiba Shirō, and Kōno Hironaga, submitted a secret note to Komura Jutarō, then the foreign minister. Still insisting Kantō was a "Korean territory," they nevertheless proposed dealing with this "minor problem" flexibly. Given the condition that the Qing agreed to satisfy Japan on the privilege of consular jurisdiction, the autonomy of the Korean immigrants, the right of building the Jilin–Changchun railway, and the opening of forest and mining resources, they suggested that "Japan could yield the territorial right" to the Qing. "We should follow the principle of acquiring substantial [interest] while keeping away from [what exists only in] name."[12] Eight months later the Japanese government resolved the Kantō dispute in that exact spirit.

[11] Uchida Ryōhei, *Mankan kaimu hiken* (Keijō: Uchida Ryōhei, 1906), p. 144.
[12] JACAR, "Kantō no hanto nikanshi seihan ryōgoku fungi ikken," vol. 13, no. 1, pp. 20–23, ref. B03041205800.

The Chinese Revolutionaries: Working with the Enemy. The Japanese Pan-Asianists had a remarkable influence on political developments in East Asia in the late nineteenth century and early twentieth. They created an alluring discourse that promised a "progressive" East Asia as opposed to the colonial modernity of the West, without acknowledging that it was precisely the dichotomy of progressiveness versus backwardness that was an inseparable part of the spirit of colonial modernity. They kept searching for allies in Korea and China and provided them with generous aid. In Korea they first supported reformists (*gaehwapa*) such as Kim Ok-kyun, then the pro-Japanese Ilchinhoe. In China they gave their initial hope to reformists (*weixindang*) such as Kang Youwei and Liang Qichao, then saw the Chinese revolutionaries, notably Sun Yat-sen and Huang Xing, as their comrades.

With direct help from Tōyama Mitsuru and Uchida Ryōhei, Sun and Huang found in 1905 the Tongmenghui (United Allegiance Society), the leading revolutionary organization that later developed into the Chinese Nationalist Party (KMT). The Tongmenghui merged several organizations, including Sun's Xingzhonghui (Revive China Society) and Huang's Huaxinghui (China Arise Society). Targeting the Manchu government, it regarded "the expelling of the Tartar barbarians" (*quchu dalu*) as the first step to building a Chinese republic. Many of the early revolutionaries were known to be anti-Manchu and advocated driving the Manchus "back" to Manchuria. These racist attitudes gained them much sympathy from both anti-Qing secret societies and young nationalist elites. Many Japanese Pan-Asianists, for their own geopolitical interests, also supported the idea of separating Manchuria from China.

The dominant historical narrative of the Chinese revolution, centered on Sun and Huang, rarely puts Manchuria at the core of modern China's nation-building scheme. This marginal and ethnic frontier, it seems, is usually treated as estranged from – if not opposite to – the Han-oriented revolution. Indeed, according to various historical records, Sun Yat-sen in his early career repeatedly suggested to his Japanese friends that he would trade the advantages (even sovereignty) of Manchuria for Japanese support of his revolution.[13] However, if we shift our focus away from Sun or Huang in this complex historical process called "revolution" and restore Manchuria to what it was during the process, the revolutionaries' attitudes towards this Manchu homeland would appear much more diverse. Especially during the Yanji/Kantō crisis, many Chinese revolutionaries sided with their enemy, the Qing government, and protected

---

[13] Yang Tianshi, "Sun Zhongshan yu 'zurang manzhou' wenti," *Jindaishi yanjiu*, no. 6 (1988), pp. 61–74.

Manchurian sovereignty against Japan. Two of the most prominent figures here were Wu Luzhen (1880–1911) and Song Jiaoren (1882–1913).
Technically speaking, Wu Luzhen's role in the Jiandao dispute was as
more of a state than nonstate actor. In 1907 Wu was assigned by Xu
Shichang to cope with the Yanji crisis. During two years of Sino-Japanese
confrontation, as the de facto principal Qing official in charge of local
affairs, Wu established himself as a legendary patriot because of his reso-
lute resistance against Japanese penetration. Xu would not have known
that Wu, a talented New Army officer who was among the first group of
Qing graduates at the Imperial Japanese Army Academy, was also a prime
leader of the local Tongmenghui branch. In fact, both an early member
of Sun Yat-sen's Xingzhonghui and a founding member of Huang Xing's
Huaxinghui, Wu knew Sun and Huang long before the two leaders met
each other. At the time he was assigned the job in Yanji, Wu, along with
Bai Wenwei (who starts this chapter), was trying to expand revolutionary
influence in the New Army in preparation for a future uprising.

Unlike Sun and Huang, Wu was against the idea of "racial revolution." During his military study in Japan he established a profound
friendship with Gioro Liangbi, a Manchu royal and a fellow student who
later became the core leader of the Qing royalists. Despite their polarized opinions on revolution, Wu and Liangbi appreciated one another's
talent and cherished each other like brothers. Wu used to say, "The only
Manchu we should be worried about is Liangbi, and the only Han who
could counter him is me."[14] According to his biography, Wu criticized
Huang Xing's anti-Manchuism on the grounds that it would split China
into pieces:

If the theory of racial revolution prevails, it will give the Manchus an excuse. The
Manchus will certainly join hands with the Mongols and the Hui-Muslims to
fight against the Han. Wars and disasters will follow and the state will fall apart.
[...] Having been born and raised in South China and having never travelled
north of the Yellow River, Huang Keqiang [Huang Xing] is not able to understand this situation.[15]

Wu himself had traveled to the northwest provinces as a New Army
officer before assuming his office in Yanji. This experience provided him
a comprehensive understanding of the strategic, economic, societal, and
political significances of the borderlands. Published in 1908 during the

---

[14] Wu Zhongya, "Wu Luzhen de yisheng," in Yunmeng zhengxie wenshi ziliao weiyuanhui,
ed., *Yunmeng wenshi ziliao*, vol. 1 (Yunmeng: Yunmeng zhengxie wenshi ziliao weiyuanhui, 1985), p. 18.

[15] Qian Jibo, "Wu Luzhen zhuan," in Zhengxie Shijiazhuang shi weiyuanhui, ed., *Wu
Luzhen shiliao ji* (Shijiazhuang: Zhengxie Shijiazhuang shi weiyuanhui, 1991), p. 86.

apogee of the Jiandao conflict, his *Report on the Yanji Frontier Affairs* is still regarded as both a classic study of Manchurian historical geography and representative of nationalist frontier thinking. One particularly interesting demonstration of Wu's nationalist logic is the way in which he sorts out a perfectly linear sequence in the Yanji-Manchurian history and traces this history all the way back to the semimythological era of the Central Plains. In so doing, Wu not only binds Yanji tightly to Manchuria but also integrates Manchuria into a grand concept of "China":

The realm of the Yanji subprefecture has developed over more than four thousand years from Tangyu to our Dynasty. Regimes like Sushen, Mohe, Bohai [Parhae], Liao, and Jin occupied this place by establishing their kingdoms in Manchuria. Regimes like Han, Yuan, Ming, and our Dynasty owned this place by unifying China.[16]

He also rejects the historical link between Manchuria and the Korean Peninsula and denies the Koryŏ/Chosŏn regimes as the legitimate successors of the Kokuryŏ kingdom, whose realm crossed the peninsula–Manchuria division. By doing so, he further demarcates a clear-cut boundary between the history of "China" and that of "Korea." Seeing the Sino-Korean geographic border as an absolute state-to-state divide, he harshly criticizes the conciliation policy towards the Korean cultivators under the *zongfan* principle. Regarding it as a "mistake," he believes the policy "forgot the real danger of opening the door to the wolves for just a vain reputation of 'cherishing the inferior.'" The consequence, says Wu, was that "the foundation area of our Dynasty...has become almost a Korean colony."[17]

If Wu Luzhen became involved in the Kantō/Yanji dispute quite dramatically, Song Jiaoren engaged in this conflict in even more striking fashion. A founding member and leading activist of the Tongmenghui, Song Jiaoren first learned about the term "Kantō/Jiandao" when he was studying politics in Tokyo. According to his diary, from May 1906 onward he had repeatedly read in Japanese media the stories of "Kantō" and "the Han bianwai." Describing "Kantō" as an "independent state" run by a "bandit (*bazoku*) leader" named Han Dengju, the Japanese media portrayed Han as a Chinese Robin Hood who governed a resource-rich realm with his own troops and stood against the Qing state. For Chinese revolutionaries, who desperately needed any kind of military support, such an alluring picture was too tempting to overlook. Hoping he could induce Han to aid the revolution, Song did more research and found

[16] Wu, "Yanji bianwu baogao," p. 19.
[17] Ibid., p. 65.

Lieutenant Colonel Morita Toshitō's *Manchurian Geography* (*Manshū Chishi*). Dissatisfied with the contradictory information in Japanese literature, he sent an inquiry to Morita and received a response from one of Morita's assistants. Although it clarified some of Song's questions, the reply did not resolve all his points of confusion. So Song made a decision. "If we want to know it exhaustively," he wrote in his diary, "I think the only way is to travel there and investigate the realm myself."[18]

After raising funds from a friend, Song departed from Japan in March 1907 and arrived in Andong, Fengtian. With the help of a Japanese contact and under a Japanese pseudonym, he arranged to meet several local bandit leaders and persuaded them to collaborate with the rebellion. His Tongmenghui comrades Wu Luzhen and Bai Wenwei also provided him funds. But in May the plan for the uprising was leaked, and Song had to flee back to Japan. Three months later the Kantō conflict occurred. Having witnessed the situation in Manchuria, Song determined to study the issue in depth. He took advantage of the Japanese collection of Korean archives and documents and drafted a thesis he called *The Jiandao Issue* (*Jiandao wenti*). Buttressed mainly by international law theory, the thesis aimed to prove Chinese "sovereignty" over the Yanji area.

As these events were developing, the Qing government was trying to find students to investigate the boundary dispute. After some consideration, Song, under the pseudonym "Song Lian," sent his manuscript to Yuan Shikai through the Qing legation in Japan.[19] Yuan was so impressed by this excellent and timely work that he immediately asked the legation in Tokyo to invite the author to join the government. A middle-ranking position along with a fat reward were also granted. Song turned down the title but accepted the money and distributed it to fellow Chinese students.[20] How did Song reconcile revolution and sovereignty? An open letter he wrote to the Qing ministers to Japan rejecting his appointment revealed the answer:

To whom it may concern. It is unfortunate that I have always held a doctrine that is extremely antagonistic to your government. When the "Jiandao" problem occurred, I was afraid that muddleheaded and ignorant government officials like you men would sit by and watch the Japanese grab tens of thousands *li* of land. *I object to this government, but every citizen* [*guomin*] *shall cherish state territory.* [...]

---

[18] Chen Luxu, ed., *Song Jiaoren ji*, vol. 2 (Beijing: Zhonghua shu ju, 1981), pp. 514–726.

[19] According to the Kokuryūkai materials, Song thought about selling the manuscript to the Japanese Foreign Ministry. See Kuzū, *Tōa senkaku shishi kiden*, vol. 2, p. 437.

[20] Matsumoto Hideki, *Sō Kyōjin no kenkyū* (Kyōto: Kōyō Shobō, 2001), pp. 105–107; Wu Xiangxiang, *Song Jiaoren zhuan: zhongguo minzhu xianzheng de xianqu* (Taipei: Zhuanji wenxue chubanshe, 1985), pp. 44–49.

Since I know more about this subject than you government officials, it is particularly inappropriate if I do nothing about it. Therefore I spent several months writing "The Jiandao Issue" and discovered the evidence to prove that the place was indeed Chinese territory. I hoped this could assist the government diplomacy.[21]

Wu Luzhen and Song Jiaoren were leading revolutionaries who, at this critical moment, chose to cooperate with the Qing government to save state sovereignty. Both in their mid-twenties, they represented a new generation of Chinese elites who embraced a nationalist view on what state, nation, boundary, and territory meant to a country. The two themes, anti-Qing revolution and the protection of state sovereignty, enhanced one another, with Manchuria understood not only as a part of China but also as a key factor determining the fate of the future Chinese nation. More importantly, in the formation of their nation state consciousness, both Wu and Song adopted intellectual influence from Japan.[22] Wu graduated from the Imperial Japanese Army Academy, the same school from which his main Japanese rival, Saitō Suejirō, the director of the Kantō Branch, had graduated several years earlier. It was at least partially due to this experience that Wu dared to confront Saitō face to face with an iron fist attitude. Song generated his initial impressions of Jiandao/Yanji through the Japanese media and relied on sources in Japan to study the issue. As many historians have pointed out, his friendship with Japanese Pan-Asianists facilitated, in an obscure way, his belief in the sovereign integrity of China, unlike his comrade Sun Yat-sen.

The Ilchinhoe and Its Opponents: Same Bed, Different Dreams.   On the local level, the Japanese Kantō Branch tried not to provoke the Chinese authority directly. Rather, it encouraged the Ilchinhoe Koreans in the Kando region to sabotage Qing governance by, for example, ceasing to pay taxes and refusing the grain levies for the local troops. This did not mean, however, that the Koreans were merely a tool of Japan with no political agendas of their own. Even the pro-Japanese Ilchinhoe organization had its own political vision for modernizing Korea, one that was fundamentally different from that of its Japanese advisors.[23]

---

[21] Song Jiaoren, "Zhi Li, Hu er xingshi shu," italics mine; quoted in Yang Tianshi, "Song Jiaoren yiwen gouchen," in Yang Tianshi, ed., *Cong dizhi zouxiang gonghe: xinhai qianhou shishi fawei* (Beijing: Shehui kexue wenxian chubanshe, 2002), pp. 699–700.

[22] Gao Shihua, "Kindai Chūgoku niokeru Kokkyō ishiki no keisei to Nihon: Kantō mundai omeguru Sō Kyōjin to Go Rokutei Katsudō o chūshin toshite," Ph.D. dissertation, Tokyo University, 2003.

[23] For example, the Ilchinhoe mobilized a large-scale tax resistance movement and substantially controlled tax administration in some areas. See Moon Yumi, "Immoral Rights: Korean Populist Collaborators and Japanese Colonization of Korea, 1904–1910," *American Historical Review*, vol. 118, no. 1 (2013), pp. 20–44.

From its establishment in August 1904 to its dissolution in September 1910, the Ilchinhoe (Advanced in Unity Society) remained the largest and most active civil organization in preannexation Korea, claiming to have 800,000 to 1,000,000 members during its heyday. Although it is often baldly labeled as a "traitor" and "anti-nation" group, recent studies have complicated the popular image of this notorious collaborative organization.[24] The Ilchinhoe was a combination of two civil groups. One, the original Ilchinhoe founded by Song Pyŏng-jun in 1904, inherited the main body of the former Independence Club (1896–1898). The other, the Chinbohoe (Progressive Society), led by Yi Yong-gu, developed from the Tonghak (East Learning) peasant movement and its religious successor, Ch'ŏndogyo (Religion of the Heavenly Way). The Independence Club was composed largely of the literati officials in Hansŏng, who advocated reforming Korean political institutions and "civilizing" the country in accordance with "modern" (i.e., Western) political systems. The Tonghak movement, in contrast, was made up mainly of peasants, who embraced policies more favorable to the rural population. Chinbohoe members, though spread countrywide, were more concentrated in the northern provinces of P'yŏngan, Hamgyŏng, and Hwanghae.[25] Despite their different bases, both the Ilchinhoe and the Chinbohoe believed that Korean politics was corrupt and needed a complete overhaul in order for Korea to become a civilized, enlightened, and progressive country.[26] The two notable leaders, Song and Yi, also shared the belief that, given the domestic and geopolitical circumstances, Korea was incapable of reaching this goal on its own. It had to rely on the help of Japan, the only "civilized" country in East Asia.

The rise of Pan-Asianism in Japan triggered great hope among the Ilchinhoe leaders. Yi Yong-gu himself was an ardent reader and enthusiastic believer of Tarui Tōkichi's *On the Union of the Great East*. He once told Uchida Ryōhei: "The ideal of my whole life is also what Mr. Tanhō [Tarui's pen name] called the Union of the Great East."[27] He even gave his son a Japanese name, Ohigashi Kunio, meaning "the boy of the Great East State." After the establishment of the Resident-General, some Japanese Pan-Asianists and officials, such as Uchida Ryōhei, Kōmuchi

---

[24] See Hayashi Yusuke, "Nichiro sensō to Chōsen shakai," in *Higashiajia kindaishi gakukai*, ed., *Nichiro sensō to Higashi ajia sekai* (Tokyo: Yumani Shobō, 2008), pp. 127–146.

[25] Hayashi Yusuke, "Undō dantai toshite no Isshinkai – minshū tono sesshoku yōsō o chūshin ni," *Chosen Gakuho*, no. 171 (1999), pp. 43–67.

[26] Kim Dong-Myung, "Isshinkai to nihon – 'seigappō' to heigō," in *Chōsenshi Kenkyūkai*, ed., *Chōsenshi kenkyūkai ronbunshū*, vol. 31 (Tokyo: Ryokuin Shobō, 1993), pp. 97–126.

[27] Kuzū, *Tōa senkaku shishi kiden*, vol. 3, p. 31.

Tomotsune, and Kunitomo Shigeaki, were invited to become advisors to the Ilchinhoe.

The cooperation between the Ilchinhoe and the Japanese government began during the Russo-Japanese War. Song Pyŏng-jun worked as an interpreter for the Japanese army, and the Ilchinhoe provided Japan its fervent support. When Japan could not find enough labor to build the military railway between Hansŏng and Ŭiju (a northern border town) the Ilchinhoe mobilized thousands of members in P'yŏngan and Hwanghae provinces and helped finish the project in just four months. It also organized a team to deliver materials to the north and even conducted espionage for the Japanese army.[28] To return the favor and further manipulate the domestic politics of Korea after Kojong's forced abdication, Resident-General Itō granted many Ilchinhoe members official positions in the puppet Yi Wan-yong government. Song Pyŏng-jun was assigned minister of agriculture, commerce, and industry; others took offices at the provincial and prefectural levels.

In Kantō/Kando the local Ilchinhoe readily colluded with the Kantō Branch. Many Ilchinhoe members were poor peasants desperate for land of their own. It was in their best interest if Korea held the sovereignty of the Tumen north bank, no matter by what means. When the Kantō Branch opened in August 1907 it recruited nineteen Ilchinhoe members as staff, including the chairmen of the Ilchinhoe branches in North Hamgyŏng province and Kando. The Japanese appointed Ilchinhoe members as village and commune heads to countervail those assigned by the Qing. Taking advantage of the Japanese support, Ilchinhoe expanded across the Kando region, counting over 10,000 members at its peak and establishing thirteen private schools.[29]

However, the Japanese soon recognized the Ilchinhoe as a potential threat. Witnessing the group's extraordinary ability to mobilize, Itō and other Japanese politicians were vigilant about its growing influence. Following Kojong's abdication, Itō started to consider how to restrain Ilchinhoe before it escaped his control. In 1907 Uchida Ryōhei brought up a grand immigration project: to move all the Ilchinhoe members to Kantō and turn this political organization into an industrial cooperative. The plan would kill two birds with one stone: it would both confine the power of the Ilchinhoe in Korea and increase the pro-Japanese population in Kantō.[30] The scheme was immediately approved by Itō, who

---

[28] Ibid., vol. 2, pp. 26–27.
[29] Hayashi Yusuke, "Kantōni okeru Isshinkai," in Higashiajia Ninshiki Kenkyūkai, ed., *Nikkan rekishi kyōdō kenkyū purojiekuto shinpojiumu hōkokusho*, no. 7 (Kunitachi: Higashiajia Ninshiki Kenkyūkai, 2005), pp. 19–35.
[30] Ibid., pp. 25–26.

had prime minister Katsura Tarō's endorsement to fund the project. This was arguably Japan's first attempt to systematically move the Koreans to Manchuria. In the end, however, the Japanese had no need to take such measures.

In 1910 Yi Yong-gu, in the name of the Ilchinhoe, made his most notorious move: to petition for the union (*gappō*) of Japan and Korea. As some scholars point out, Yi's original intention was to call for an equal confederation that promised both the same status for the Korean emperor and the Japanese emperor, as well as the same rights for Korean and Japanese citizens alike.[31] When the Japanese accepted the petition and maneuvered the annexation process, Korea was deprived of its entire sovereignty and was belittled further: from a protectorate to a colony. The Japanese government then paid the Ilchinhoe ¥150,000 and disbanded it, along with all other civil organizations – though by that time a number of Ilchinhoe members had already renounced the group, many of them later becoming anti-Japanese activists.[32] Yi Yong-gu died just two years after the annexation, having lived out his life in deep regret at his proposal to unify Japan and Korea.

After 1906 the Ilchinhoe had gradually become isolated: it not only failed to win the complete trust of the Japanese but had also made itself a public enemy of all anti-Japanese Koreans. The opponents of the Ilchinhoe varied in form, ideology, political ideal, and mass base and did not share a common view of what "Korea" meant to the Koreans. Yet all of them identified Japan as their main foe, not a supporter of the integrity of Korea.

As colonial rule tightened, resistant activities moved northward to Manchuria and Primorsky Russia. Adjoining both northern Korea and Primorsky, "Kando" was especially attractive to Korean resisters for its strategic geographic location. Religious and schooling networks spread further into the region, sometimes with the encouragement of the Chinese government. The Japanese Kantō Branch was well aware of this development because the influence of the Ilchinhoe among Koreans was largely constrained by the anti-Japanese movements. What alerted the branch most was not religious or educational activities but the Korean militia called the Righteous Army (Ŭibyŏng), active in Primorsky and the Sino-Korean borderland. Since 1907 the branch had repeatedly

---

[31] Kim Dong Myung, "Isshinkai to nihon – 'seigappō' to heigō," pp. 107–133. Also see Ogawara Hiroyuki, "Isshinkai no nikkan gappō seigan undō to Kankoku gappei," in Chōsenshi Kenkyūkai, ed., *Chōsenshi Kenkyūkai ronbunshū*, vol. 43 (Tokyo: Ryokuin Shobō, 2005), pp. 183–210.
[32] Kim, "Isshinkai to nihoñ," p. 118; Hayashi, "Undō dantai toshite no Isshinkai," pp. 47–48.

reported intelligence to the Resident-General on the Righteous Army, which the branch defined as the "mob" (*bōto*), concerning its link with local Koreans. Yi Pŏm-yun, the militia leader who was once a trouble-maker for the Qing, now became a headache for the Japanese. The Righteous Army was in fact a general title for different factions of anti-Japanese militia. Borrowing the name of the Korean resistance militia during Toyotomi Hideyoshi's invasion in the late sixteenth century, the first Righteous Army rebellion started in 1895, when the Japanese murdered Queen Min, and the pro-Japanese Kim Hong-ji Cabinet issued an order forcing all Korean males to cut their hair and change to Western hairstyles. The conservative *yangban* and local Confucian scholars, notably Yu In-sŏk, led the first round of the Righteous Army movement. When the pro-Japanese Cabinet was replaced by a pro-Russian one in 1896, the hair-cutting order was suspended and most of the Righteous Army disbanded. Yet Yu In-sŏk insisted that it was still unbearable for Korea to rely on a "Western barbarian." For Yu, a representative of the political school of "defending the [Confucian] doctrine and expelling the [Western] heterodoxy [*wijŏngch'ŏksa*]," the only right way for Korea was to restore the Confucian world order in the peninsula. In other words, Yu wanted to continue embracing Korea's traditional status as "a small China."

Emperor Kojong's abdication triggered the second wave of the Righteous Army movement. This time Yu's militia was quickly defeated by the Japanese. He retreated to Primorsky, where he united all the Righteous Army leaders, including Yi Pŏm-yun and Yi Sang-sŏl, and was elected as the chief commander of the army. In 1909 Yu wrote a letter to Wu Luzhen, the Qing official in charge of Yanji frontier affairs. Expressing his admiration of Wu's courage in confronting the Japanese, Yu asked Wu to urge the Chinese government to help Korea. Employing an orthodox Confucian ideology, he said:

Since Kija [C. Jizi] came to king Korea, we have always complied with China. The big and small Chinas are essentially one country. [...] There are big and strong states in today's world. However, which country can Korea rely on? The only country Korea could rely on is the one we always depended upon and were affinitive with: China.[33]

No record shows whether Wu Luzhen responded to, or even received, Yu's letter.

---

[33] Yu In-sŏk, "Yŏ O ŏsa Rokchŏng," in Yu In-sŏk, *Ŭiamjip*; quoted in Du Honggang, ed., *Hanguo wenji zhong de qingdai shiliao*, vol. 17 (Guilin: Guangxi shifan daxue chubanshe, 2008), pp. 330–331.

Although Yu In-sŏk was a highly respectful leader, his Confucian political ideology represented only one of many political visions of the Righteous Army movement. Just as the Chinese revolutionaries had diverse understandings of Manchu, Manchuria, and China, the Korean resisters did not have a unanimous perception about Korea and its position in East Asia. Yi Pŏm-yun, for example, renounced the traditional *zongfan* order by militarily challenging Qing's authority in Kando. An Chung-gŭn, another Righteous Amy leader, who gained worldwide fame by assassinating Itō Hirobumi in Manchuria in 1909, belonged in an altogether different part of the political spectrum. With a Catholic background and Pan-Asianist ideals, An believed that Japan had betrayed its promise to build a peaceful East Asia against the "white peril." By bringing about Itō's death, he hoped East Asian countries could be integrated successfully.[34]

Korean nationalist attitudes towards the Kando dispute were even more complicated in public media. As historians Lee Sung-Hwan and Lee Myeong-Jong observe, the views of one of the leading newspapers at the time, the *Korean Daily News* (*Daehan Maeil Sinbo*), were not consistent during the dispute. Initially advocating Korean sovereignty over Kando, the *News* shifted its tone beginning in early 1908 and accepted Chinese sovereignty instead. It made the change not only because the new position was more realistic but also because it did not want to justify the Japanese invasion of Kando. If Japan controlled this largest overseas Korean community, the cradle of the Korean independence movement would be destroyed.[35]

In sum, in the Sino-Japanese competition over Kantō/Yanji, the Koreans were far from voiceless. "Kando" was seen as the epitome of Korea. Various political forces participated in this bilateral contest as they brought in their own political blueprints. The Ilchinhoe placed its hope for modernizing Korea on Japan. Others, despite regarding Japan as the cause of Korea's misery, were not necessarily all pro-China. Indeed, even though the Koreans in the two rival camps formed alliances, consciously or unconsciously, with either Japan or China, neither side abandoned its core political ideal of constructing a strong Korea. Katsura Tarō, then the Japanese prime minister, once commented: "Even the Ilchinhoe would not give up the idea of a state. Its members also have patriotic emotions, which were only constrained by the misery they suffered. [...] Japan

---

[34] Nakano Yasuo, *An Jungun: Nikkan kankei no genzō* (Tokyo: Aki Shobō, 1984).
[35] Lee Sung-Hwan, "T'onggambu sigi taehanjeguk ŭi kandomunje insik," *Yŏksawa kyŏnggye*, no. 65 (2007), pp. 63–92; Lee Myeong-Jong. "Taehanjegukki kandoyŏngt'oronŭi tŭngjanggwa chongsik," *Tongasia munhwayŏn'gu*, no. 54 (2013), pp. 311–344.

teaches them the doctrine of 'being loyal to the throne and patriotic to the state,' and lets them bathe in the grace of civilization. The time they graduate is the day Korea gains its independence."[36] In this sense, both pro- and anti-Japanese Koreans shared the same dream of building what they believed to be an ideal Korean state, only they chose completely different paths, which eventually alienated the Korean community.

Towards the Jiandao Convention: Three Layers of Confrontation

The Sino-Japanese dispute over Yanji/Kantō is better reviewed in at least three spatial layers. On the capital level (Beijing versus Tokyo), it was one part of the overall geopolitical and geoeconomic struggle, a local leverage point for the contest between a dying and a rising empire. On the provincial level (Xu Shichang versus Itō Hirobumi), it was a competition for frontier building, a tug-of-war between two kinds of borderland integration: interiorization or colonization. On the local level, matching the wits of Wu Luzhen versus Saitō Suejirō, it was a direct cut-and-thrust involving endless vocal and physical confrontations. The narrative below unfolds these struggles, looking first at the provincial, then the local, and finally the capital.

Qing's Reactions in Jilin

To a large extent, Japanese intrusions, the installation of Japanese colony building in Kantō (addressed in Chapter 4), provided Xu Shichang an opportunity to implement numerous reforms in various areas. His military reform in Jilin was an integrated part of the overall modern military building in Manchuria. Corruption and malpractice were age-old problems that severely damaged the frontier defense capacity. Reforms were implemented for local standing armies in Jilin, which had scattered and lacked a unified command. Xu concentrated the main forces of Jilin province in Yanji, put them under the command of the Commission of Frontier Affairs, and restructured the old military organization. In order to ensure that the transition went smoothly, he stationed two troop units of the New Army in the area.[37] Xu established new logistical and armament systems and consolidated existing military schools and several army academies of topography. He issued new standards of topography: longitude/latitude

---

[36] Masumi Junnosuke, *Riben zhengzhi shi*, trans. Dong Guoliang, vol. 2 (Beijing: Shangwu yinshuguan, 1988), p. 406.
[37] Xu, *Dongsansheng zhenglue*, vol. 1, pp. 110–111.

cartography was finally enforced in Jilin to satisfy military needs. As a result, a novel style of army with relatively strong combat capacity came to be found not only in Jilin but in all the northeast provinces.[38] The unprofessional and inefficient local police system in Yanji underwent similar improvements. Xu transferred 180 newly trained police soldiers from the provincial capital to Yanji, dissolved the old institution, and merged the remaining police force into the new organization.[39]

Other policies included establishing a hospital, constructing buildings around the Commission of Frontier Affairs to attract merchants, registering the population and cultivated land, supporting farming by the garrison troops, and exploiting forest resources. Reforms made in education merit special attention. The Japanese Kantō Branch funded a public school and encouraged the Ilchinhoe to set up private schools in the Korean community. As a countermeasure, the Commission of Frontier Affairs, too, funded a few public primary schools and fostered the coeducation of Chinese and Korean children. The Yanji government also turned a private Korean school run by anti-Japanese activists, the Yangzheng Academy, into a public school. Chinese textbooks were used in those schools where the Chinese-language course was one of the mandatory classes. The political aim was crystal clear here. As Xu Shichang remarked, "The effect of popularizing education cannot be seen immediately. Yet if we want the Korean children to get rid of their old customs and assimilate into our country, education is the only remedy."[40] Cultural assimilation, for the first time, became an official Qing policy towards Korean immigrants.

Local Conflicts

On the local level, confrontations occurred frequently. The Kantō Branch submitted both special and periodic reports to the Resident-General.[41] The Commission of Frontier Affairs was also in close communication with the viceroy of the East Three Provinces. Thanks to the adoption of the telegraph, a trivial incident could cause a tremendous flurry of exchanges between borderlands and capitals. Xu Shichang described the situation: "When there was a new problem, it often generated dozens of rounds of verbal debate; when there was a new case, it often needed tens of thousands of words of arguing in official documents."[42]

---

[38] Zhao, *Qingmo xinzheng yanjiu*, pp. 111–126.
[39] Xu, *Dongsansheng zhenglue*, vol. 1, pp. 114–115.
[40] Ibid., p. 124.
[41] For the exchanged documents between the Japanese Resident-General and the Kantō Branch, see "T'ongbyŏl Kando Kwan'gye Wangbongmun," Kyujanggak 17858.
[42] Xu, *Dongsansheng zheng lue*, vol. 1, p. 74.

Generally speaking, the competition at the local level could be divided into two phases. Before the autumn of 1908 the two sides tried to avoid direct physical struggle and usually sparred through Korean agents. Saitō Suejirō, for his part, appointed the Ilchinhoe Koreans to his staff in addition to heads of the local community and incited them to stop Korean peasants from paying tax to the Qing government. In a proclamation, the Ilchinhoe borrowed the rhetoric of international law and asserted that, "for a long time, our fellow men have known neither public law nor public opinion in the world. The fact that we cultivate our land but pay tax to another state has never been seen in public law nor been heard in public opinion in the world."[43] The local Ilchinhoe leader, Kim Hae-rong, urged Korean peasants to pay money to the branch instead.

On the Qing side, the local government refuted the village heads named by the Japanese and continued to tax through the Qing-assigned *xiangyue* system. The tension between the Korean agents serving the different states immediately escalated. State interventions, in turn, sabotaged agent institutions on both sides. Wu Luzhen expelled Kim Hae-rong, who had no choice but to flee back to Hoeryŏng. Saitō responded by arresting Hyŏn Tŏk-sŭng, a naturalized Korean who was positioned by the Qing as the administrative chief of all communes (*zong xiangyue*), with the excuse that Hyŏn "extorted the local Koreans." Both sides claimed in their reports that their actions were supported by the local residents.

The indirect political confrontations also expanded to the economic field. The state-run Tianbaoshan silver mine, one of the largest silver producers in China, suspended operations in 1899. In 1906, with the Japanese consulate in Fengtian as intermediary, the official manager of the mine, Cheng Guangdi, secretly signed a joint venture contract with a Japanese firm and put the Tianbaoshan mine under the control of Japanese capital. When Wu Luzhen came to Yanji, he forcibly closed down the mine and insisted the contract was illegal, ignoring the repeated protests of the Japanese government. Furthermore, Qing officials imposed an old economic strategy, crop embargos, to constrain the Japanese/Korean actions on the northern bank. Similar policies included forbidding private ferries and bridges and unapproved land transactions. The resulting crop price inflation in northern Hamgyŏng put enormous pressure on the local government.[44]

---

[43] Taehan Min'guk Kukhoe Tosŏgwan, *Kando yŏngyukwŏn kwan'gye palch'we munsŏ*, pp. 188–189.

[44] Fengtian gongshu dang, JC10-1-20585, Liaoning Provincial Archive. See also JACAR, "Kantō no hanto nikanshi seihan ryōgoku fungi ikken," vol. 9, no. 7, pp. 36–39, ref. B03041201900.

In spring 1908 the Korean Righteous Army in Primorsky, led by Yi Pŏm-yun, attacked a Japanese barrack in Musan Kantō. Rumor had it that Yi would cross the Tumen River and gather more anti-Japanese forces in the border region. The situation granted the Japanese an excuse to bolster military personnel in Kantō. With the numbers of stationed soldiers increasing on both sides, from autumn 1908 onward the local confrontations entered a new phase that witnessed more and more low-intensive yet direct conflicts between the Kantō Branch and the Commission of Frontier Affairs. With a few casualties on both sides, the protests and verbal exchanges were no longer simply matters of diplomacy. In 1909 *North China Herald*, a Shanghai-based English-language newspaper, reported a violent conflict that resulted in the death of a Chinese government staff member. "In that no testimony by any disinterested witness can be procured," the unnamed author wrote, "it is impossible to arrive at the exact truth; ...even official reports are probably coloured by the efforts of petty bureaucrats to justify their actions."[45]

In consideration of the ongoing negotiations between Beijing and Tokyo and constrained by the counteractions of the local Qing government, the Japanese did not immediately make more provocative moves. Both sides carefully maintained the status quo until the debate was closed at the capital level.

New Territorial Discourses in the Negotiation

Japan invaded Kantō on the argument that the sovereignty of Kantō was not yet decided. Qing China rejected the Japanese intervention by denying there was a dispute over sovereignty. The central point of this debate was territorial rights. Diplomatic negotiations between Beijing and Tokyo, therefore, focused largely on the legitimacy of the Tumen River boundary. From late 1908 to May 1909 Wu Luzhen was temporarily transferred to Beijing to assist the Foreign Ministry on the Yanji issue. His historical and geographic understandings greatly influenced the ministry. As Shinoda Jisaku mentioned in one of his reports, Wu's standpoint was "completely adopted" by the Qing government.[46] For their part, Shinoda and Saitō contributed much to the Japanese stance on the territory. As several rounds of talks did not produce any new empirical evidence, it became very clear that the debate was not about geography. Rather, the debate was about how to relocate historical territorial rights within the

---

[45] "Unrest in Chientao," *North China Herald*, July 31, 1909.
[46] JACAR, "Kantō no hanto nikanshi seihan ryōgoku fungi ikken," vol. 17, no. 1, p. 10, ref. B03041210700.

modern nation state conceptual framework and how to interpret the East Asian past within the new hegemonic terms of international law.

This conflict was explicitly demonstrated in two documents. The first was a long memorandum (over 3,000 words) that the Japanese minister in Beijing, Ijūin Hikokichi, sent to the Qing Foreign Ministry in January 1909. The second was a still more lengthy reply (10,000 words) by the Qing Ministry a month later.[47] The key controversy was a very old one: whether Túmen/Tuman (圖們/豆満) and Tŭmen (土門) were the same river. The Japanese not only re-raised all the clichés once held by the Chosŏn – that the Mukedeng stele defined a northern river instead of the Tuman as the boundary – but also entirely denied there was a bilateral agreement, that the main stream of the Tumen/Tuman was indeed the division, reached in the 1885–1887 demarcations. "Since no boundary treaty was established," stated the Japanese memorandum, "the case of the joint demarcation in the thirteenth year [of Guangxu's reign: 1887] was a mere scrap of paper." The Qing memorandum, drafted by Wu Luzhen, refuted the Japanese argument nearly sentence by sentence.

It is not necessary to summarize the long-winded debate; most of the points just repeated what the Chosŏn and Qing demarcation delegates had brought up twenty years earlier. What is worth noticing is that several historical principles that had never been questioned beforehand were now under severe challenge. For example, the Japanese memorandum said nothing about the *zongfan* relationship between the Middle Kingdom and the Korean Peninsula, a fundamental departure from Yi Chung-ha's strategy. Rather, it rejected the legitimacy of such a historical connection: "You [the Chinese government] said: history proves that the land north of the Tuman River is Chinese territory. It is, however, only decided by China alone. China claims that before [sic] the Tang Dynasty, [local regimes such as] Bohai [K. Parhae] and Jurchen were *jimi* [affiliates] of China. Yet the term *jimi* does not have the same meaning of 'governance' or 'territorial sovereignty.' Besides, the so-called China at that time has no connection with the Qing state today." Here Japan highlighted the rupture, while rejecting the continuity, of Chinese history: the historical *zongfan* hierarchy was repudiated by the principle of modern sovereignty, and the Qing, a Manchu regime, was denied as a successor of the Middle Kingdom.

This kind of anachronistic strategy was not employed by the Japanese alone. The Qing, too, reinterpreted the historical event using the standard of modern international practices. Insisting that the Mukedeng stele

---

[47] Both memorandums are recorded in Xu Shichang, *Dongsansheng zhenglue*, vol. 1, pp. 97–108.

was not sufficient evidence, the Qing denied that the 1712 Mukedeng survey mission was intended as a demarcation. Emperor Kangxi's edict, argued the Qing memorandum, "only said to send an official to 'survey the border' (查邊, *chabian*) rather than 'draw the boundary.' It also said that this mission 'is to survey our borderland (查我邊境, *cha wo bianjing*) and will not involve your country (與彼國無涉, *yu biguo wushe*).'" Besides, since neither Mukedeng nor his Korean escorts were granted the title to determine the boundary, the Qing Foreign Ministry said, the 1712 mission was "definitely not a joint demarcation." Here, two original ambiguous and multivocal characters, *cha* (查, which could mean "survey," "investigate," or "examine") and *bian* (邊, "border," "borderland," "boundary") were deliberately disambiguated and univocalized. The term *chabian*, which could simultaneously refer to "survey the border region" and "settle the boundary" in the eighteenth-century context, was purposefully translated only as the former in light of the early twentieth-century terminology. Using contemporary international law standards, the Qing implied that a recognizable demarcation project could be conducted bilaterally only by equal partners with proper official appointment, forgetting that rarely had the empire ever clarified a boundary with a subordinate state in this fashion.

Intense as this debate was, however, Japan realized it was in the weaker position in the argument even before this round of exchanges. Government documents show that as late as December 1907 Japan had acknowledged that the Korean delegate Yi Chung-ha had settled most parts of the Tumen River boundary with the Qing in 1887, no matter how Japan later tried to distort this fact.[48] Several investigation papers done by the Japanese, such as the Nakai Kitarō report, did not favor the Japanese claim either. In a telegraph sent to the Japanese minister in Beijing in April 1908, foreign minister Hayashi Tadasu, though he had consulted with Saitō Suejirō and figured out the diplomatic rhetoric, admitted that "the basis of the Korean territorial claim is weak."[49]

Up to late 1908 and early 1909 Japan felt more and more pressure in Korea and Manchuria. Anti-Japanese activities transferred largely to the Sino-Russian–Korean borderlands. But, unless the stability of the Korean hinterland was secured, Itō Hirobumi was reluctant to invest more military resources to cope with the Righteous Army movement. Hilary Conroy points out: "The best he [Itō] could do, beyond issuing

---

[48] JACAR, "Kantō no hanto nikanshi seihan ryōgoku fungi ikken," vol. 5, no. 1, pp. 7–10, ref. B03041196900.
[49] JACAR, ref. B03041200700, p. 35. Kantō no hanto nikanshi seihan ryōgoku fungi ikken, vol. 8, no. 6.

occasional reminders to his troops that gentleness was to be preferred, was to try to set geographical limits at the Korean border."[50] Besides, while Russia was watching the Japanese expansion in Manchuria closely, other Western countries, especially the United States, showed increasing interest in investing in Manchuria and cutting a share of the Japanese privilege there. Japan now eagerly desired to solve the Kantō dispute with the Qing as soon as possible.

Resolution: Regional and Global

The Kantō/Jiandao problem was not resolved as a freestanding issue. Rather, it was settled in a package deal that included five other deadlocked conflicts between the Qing and Japan in Manchuria. Those conflicts, which concerned rights to construct railways and build coal mines, were closely associated with the Japanese capitalist/imperialist expansion implemented through the South Manchuria Railway Company. Besides China and Japan, other major global powers of the early twentieth century, especially the United States, were also involved in the disputes. In the course of bringing differences to closure, a local problem was woven into a network of global power politics, a territorial issue was knotted in with modern capitalist development, and the redemarcation of an old boundary was drawn into an overall revolution of reterritorialization.[51]

Before the turn of the new century the huge economic potential of Manchuria had already attracted enormous attention among the world capitalist powers. Seeing Manchuria as the next new frontier after the westward movement, the United States insisted on an open-door policy and prevented any player from monopolizing any opportunity in this vast borderland. After the Russo-Japanese War, American entrepreneurs and politicians expressed particular interest in the business of railroad construction in Manchuria. Railway tycoon E. H. Harriman did his utmost to expand his railway kingdom to northeast China. Willard Straight, the first American consul general in Fengtian, also aggressively preached the benefit of American investment in this resource-rich region. Their thoughts were readily received by Chinese officials, who wanted to bring

---

[50] Hilary Conroy, *The Japanese Seizure of Korea, 1868–1910: A Study of Realism and Idealism in International Relations* (Philadelphia: University of Pennsylvania Press, 1960), p. 368.

[51] My references include Paul Hibbert Clyde, *International Rivalries in Manchuria, 1689–1922* (Columbus, OH: Ohio State University Press, 1928); Moriyama Shigenori, *Kindai Nikkan kankeishi kenkyū: Chōsen shokuminchika to kokusai kankei* (Tokyo: Tokyo Daigaku Shuppankai, 1987); Wang Yunsheng, ed., *Liushinianlai zhongguo yu riben*, vol. 5 (Beijing: Shenghuo dushu xinzhi sanlian shudian, 1979), pp. 72–94; Wang Xueliang, *Meiguo yu zhongguo dongbei* (Changchun: Jilin wenshi chubanshe, 1991).

in American or British powers to balance both Japan and Russia. "It is not surprising," wrote historian Paul Hibbert Clyde in the 1920s, "that in the year immediately following the Russo-Japanese War the subject of railway politics played such an all-important part in the Manchurian question."[52]

When Harriman's attempt to purchase the South Manchuria Railway was rejected, Straight, who never concealed his disgust for the Japanese economic monopoly of southern Manchuria, made a proposal to Xu Shichang and the Fengtian governor Tang Shaoyi, suggesting an extension of the Qing's Imperial Railway from north China to northeast China. The railway would first connect Xinmintun and Fakumen (both in Fengtian) and lead eventually to Qiqihar and Aihui in Heilongjiang. The Qing government soon approved the plan. Because the 1907 economic crisis constrained Harriman's financial ability to make this investment, the Qing assigned the project to British contractor Pauling & Co. Since the planned railway was essentially parallel to the South Manchuria Railway, it immediately caused fierce objections from Japan. For Japan, the SMR was the foundation as well as the promise of its success in Manchuria – both economically and strategically. It was absolutely intolerable that the Xinmintun–Fakumen railway excluded the SMR. From the Japanese point of view, all other existing or planned railway projects, along with the coal mines affiliated to them, had to be merged into the SMR system.

Nor did the US administration back the idea of competing with the SMR in Manchuria. President Theodore Roosevelt believed that the importance of the US–Japanese alliance overrode the open-door doctrine. Besides, to gain American support for the SMR construction, Japan had agreed to purchase tracks, engines, and trains from the United States. During the first year of its operation (1907–1908) the SMR imported nearly ¥20 million worth of materials, or 67 percent of its total imports, directly from the United States.

But Washington's tolerance of Japan's actions ended with the election of William Howard Taft in 1908. Taft, who had had a long talk with Straight during his visit to Vladivostok in 1907, was extremely interested in the idea of investing US capital in northeast China. After assuming the presidency, he soon included Manchuria as one of the key sites to promote his "dollar diplomacy," using foreign relations to extend American economic interests. Meanwhile, SMR imports from the United States dropped drastically, to less than ¥100,000, or 15 percent of total imports,

---

[52] Clyde, *International Rivalries in Manchuria*, p. 174.

in just one year (1908–1909). The American consul in Fengtian sent increasing reports to the State Department accusing Japan of discriminating against American merchants.

Western media started to notice the ongoing territorial dispute between Japan and China. On September 5, 1907, the *New York Sun* published an article suggesting the Kantō issue could be settled by international arbitration. Given the context that "Japan, Great Britain, France and Russia have recently bound themselves by treaty to respect the territorial integrity of China," it pointed out: "Japan will violate those compacts if she insists upon settling by force a claim of long standing made by China to an important frontier district. [...] On one pretext or another Russia might do in northern Manchuria or in Mongolia what Japan has assumed to do on the border of Corea." The Japanese ambassador to America, Aoki Shūzō, responded, in a two-page exclusive interview published four days later in *The New York Herald*. He assured the Americans that the Japanese action "does not mean war" and "both Japan and China will come to some understanding." He also emphasized that "there never has been any question or controversy between the American people and the people of Japan."[53]

When the Sino-Japanese conflict was turning white hot in 1909, the *North China Herald*, which closely affiliated with the British consulate in China, published a long article about the matter and called on the two parties to treat the problem as "an entirely separate dispute" – "separate," of course, meaning distinct from other Sino-Japanese controversies in Manchuria, such as railroads and mining.[54] On March 24 *The Times* in London published a story that China was considering submitting the whole Manchurian dispute with Japan to The Hague. The report certainly encouraged such a move, saying that "it is difficult to imagine how Japan can decline the proposal."[55] The Japanese intelligence agencies reported to the Foreign Ministry that behind China's plan were the British, who had interests in the Xinmintun–Fakumen railway project, and the Americans, whom China would entrust to submit the arbitration request.[56] On June 2 *The Times* published another lengthy report noting that "Great Britain would not remain indifferent to any controversy likely to affect Chinese and Japanese relations." Written by a

---

[53] JACAR, "Kantō no hanto nikanshi seihan ryōgoku fungi ikken," vol. 3, no. 2, pp. 4–7, ref. B03041194900.
[54] JACAR, "Kantō no hanto nikanshi seihan ryōgoku fungi ikken," vol. 16, no. 2, pp. 17–18, ref. B03041209800.
[55] "Japan and Manchuria," *The Times* (London), March 24, 1909, p. 5.
[56] Li Huazi, "Zhong ri jiandao wenti he dongsansheng wu'an de tanpan xiang xi," *Shixue jikan*, no. 5 (2016), pp. 49–64.

"special correspondent from Tokio" with "very full and authoritative information," this article disclosed that "Japan is...prepared to resume direct negotiation with Peking with the sincerest desire for a reasonable settlement."[57]

Indeed, facing enormous pressure, Japan was eager to work out the railway issues with the Qing before America or Britain intervened. In February 1909 Ijūin Hikokichi presented a note to the Qing Foreign Ministry, suggesting that the "six cases of the East Three Provinces" be settled together.[58] The first five deadlocked cases concerned the following.

No. 1, The Xinmintun–Fakumen Railway. Japan objected to the plan and proposed two alternatives; both highlighted the SMR involvement.

No. 2, The Branch of the Dashiqiao Railway. Japan proposed to maintain this branch and let the SMR manage it.

No. 3, The Extension of the Beijing–Fengtian Railway. Japan proposed to merge the Fengtian station of this railway with the Fengtian station of the South Manchuria Railway so as to connect the Beijing–Fengtian Railway with the SMR.

No. 4, The Fushun and Yantai Coal Mines. Japan asserted that these two collieries were either affiliated with or run by the South Manchuria Railway during the Russian occupation. Therefore, Japan should inherit the mining rights.

No. 5, The Mines along the Andong–Fengtian Railway. Japan urged China to reconfirm that all the coal and iron mines along this railway were under the joint administration of the Japanese and the Chinese.

The sixth and last case of this bundle of conflicts was "the Kantō/ Jiandao affair." Here Ijūin emphasized the issues of commerce, consular jurisdiction, and the railway connecting Changchun and Hoeryŏng, while implying that Japan might agree to Chinese sovereignty over the area. He suggested several points: if the land north of the Tuman River was determined to be Korea's, Japan should allow the Chinese to live and do business there and let the Chinese government establish consulates there. If it was decided the land was China's, China should allow Japan to do the same, with the Japanese consulates having jurisdiction over the Koreans and Japanese. In addition, the Jilin–Changchun Railway would be extended to Hoeryŏng in Korea.

To negotiate the above "six cases" with China individually, Japan believed, would cost tremendous effort. Yet, by bundling them together,

[57] "Japanese Policy in Manchuria," *The Times* (London), June 2, 1909, p. 7.
[58] Wang, *Qingji waijiao shiliao*; quoted in Wang Yunsheng, *Liushinianlai zhongguo yu riben*, vol. 5, pp. 178–182.

the Japanese were confident that China might be more willing to trade the railway/mine issues for Japanese recognition of its territorial sovereignty in Yanji. They were right. During several rounds of negotiation in the next months, despite objections from Wu Luzhen and Xiliang (the new viceroy of the East Three Provinces), the Qing Foreign Ministry made significant concessions on the first five cases and bargained for the judicial rights and consulate issues only in the Jiandao/Kantō case. China also agreed not to bring the cases to The Hague for arbitration.

Finally, on September 4, 1909, the two sides settled all the "Manchurian six cases" with two separate bilateral conventions.[59] The first, the Negotiation Protocols concerning the Five Cases of the East Three Provinces (C. Dongsansheng wuan jiaoshe tiaokuan), confirmed the railway and mine privileges held by Japan. The second, the Protocols regarding the Sino-Korean Boundary of the Tumen River (C. Tumenjiang zhong han jiewu tiaokuan, also known as the Jiandao/Kantō Convention), dealt exclusively with the Tumen boundary dispute. In this latter convention, the two sides confirmed that the Tumen River was the Sino-Korean boundary and the headwater was defined as the Shiyi stream. The Chinese government allowed Japan to open four consulates and permitted the Koreans to live and farm on the north side of the river. China had the authority to protect, and the judicial rights over, the Korean residents. The Japanese consuls could participate in the court hearing when a Korean was brought to trial. Furthermore, China should extend the Jilin–Changchun Railway to Hoeryŏng to connect the Korean railways.

The Tumen River border was eventually determined in line with international law. On November 2, 1909, the Japanese Kantō Branch withdrew to Korea and disbanded. Ultimately, the redemarcation of the boundary was not at all about territory. The *Osaka Daily News* in Japan commented, "The Japanese government gave up the nominal territorial right, yet acquired substantial interests. This is a huge diplomatic success."[60] Saitō Suejirō, too, expressed his joy at the result. In one of his final reports, he said the establishment of the Kantō Branch had three purposes: to determine the ownership of Kantō; to protect the Koreans in Kantō; and to acquire the railway right to link northern Korea and

---

[59] The English translation of the two conventions, titled "Agreement concerning Mines and Railways in Manchuria" and "Agreement relating to the Chientao Region," are collected in Carnegie Endowment for International Peace, Division of International Law, ed., *Manchuria: Treaties and Agreements* (Washington: Carnegie Endowment for International Peace, 1921), pp. 129–130, 135–136.

[60] JACAR, "Kantō no hanto nikanshi seihan ryōgoku fungi ikken," vol. 17, no. 3, p. 3, ref. B03041210900.

Jilin, thus building up the great passageway connecting northern Japan, Korea, and Manchuria. "The problem is now settled," said Saitō; "the main purposes are accomplished. This is something most worth celebrating."[61] In other words, a state division line was reconfirmed, yet such a line was more like a channel of capitalist/colonialist penetration rather than a barrier to defend against such a penetration. "The settlement is well received by the members of the Diplomatic Corps here," *The New York Times* reported on September 5. "The Japanese are pleased with it, but the Chinese describe themselves as being in the position 'of a man coerced by successive blows.'"[62]

Spatial Imaginations: Naitō Konan, Song Jiaoren, and Sin Ch'ae-ho

From 1907 to 1910 the Manchurian frontier drew tremendous attention in Japan, China, and Korea. Historical geographic studies about the Tumen River, Mt. Changbai, as well as Manchuria in general boomed in all three countries. Multiple political interests or anxieties were embedded in the narratives as each side constructed its own spatial imagination of the region. These imaginings, though competing, were in fact mutually influenced and enhanced. More importantly, with the popularization of print media, the intellectual constructions over this borderland to a significant extent predicted the entangled nationalist and colonialist discourses developed in twentieth-century East Asia. This section lays out these discourses and analyzes the works of three influential intellectuals: Naitō Torajirō of Japan, Song Jiaoren of China, and Sin Ch'ae-ho of Korea. Far from a full-scale investigation of the historical geographic narratives generated in the early 1900s about the Tumen region, my comparison highlights the close alliance between knowledge and politics, as well as the intellectual symbiosis of nationalism and colonialism.

Naitō Torajirō (Konan): Japanese Orientalism

Naitō Torajirō (1866–1934), or, as he is more famously known, Naitō Konan, is remembered today as one of the pioneers of modern Japanese sinology.[63] The founder of the Kyōto School of Oriental (Tōyō)

---

[61] Ibid., p. 36.
[62] "Japan in Manchuria: Agreement Signed with China on Disputed Points," *New York Times*, September 5, 1909, p. C3.
[63] For a detailed introduction in English, see Joshua Fogel, *Politics and Sinology: The Case of Naito Konan, 1866–1934* (Cambridge, MA: Harvard University Press, 1984).

historiography, Naitō did not work in academia until he was forty-one. Before joining Kyōto Imperial University, in 1907, he had been an established journalist for twenty years. For a short period he also worked as a secretary to Takahashi Kenzo, the chief Cabinet secretary in the second Matsukata Masayoshi Cabinet (1896–1898). Responsible for drafting policy outlines for the Cabinet, he became involved in various political activities. His experience as a journalist and social activist distinguished him from most of his peers at the university – though other Japanese sinologists were just as affected by the imperialist/colonialist zeitgeist. All scholarship is political, and this was especially true for the Japanese Oriental studies emerging in the late nineteenth and early twentieth centuries.[64] Yet perhaps nothing was more revealing of the academic-political collaboration in late Meiji Japan than Naitō's engagement in the Kantō conflict.

A thorough analysis of the Naitō historiography is beyond the scope of this study, so I will just briefly present his intellectual position within the late Meiji context. Born to a Confucian scholar family in Akita, Naitō studied the Chinese canon with his father. After graduating from the Akita Normal School, the highest formal education he achieved, Naitō first became a primary school teacher then went to Tokyo to pursue a career in journalism. As a newsman, he cultivated his interest in politics and wrote many political commentaries. During this time he developed his own understanding of Japan's "heavenly mandate" (*tenshoku*) in human history. Unlike Fukuzawa Yukichi, who regarded Western civilization as the right direction of human development, Naitō embraced Chinese culture wholeheartedly and rejected claims of European culture as superior. He believed that Oriental civilization had its own historical logic and vitality. Both civilizations, East and West, were part of a "universal civilization" (*konyo bunmei*). It was Japan's heavenly mandate to revive a China-centric Oriental culture and let "Japan's civilization and Japan's aesthetics (*shumi*) be popular in the world, illuminating the whole universe (*konyo*)."[65] It was to this end that he supported both the Sino-Japanese War and the Russo-Japanese War. For him, the aim of the wars was not to show that Japan was more "civilized" than China and Russia but to demonstrate Japan's duty to revive East Asian culture and Japan's arrival at the center of universal civilization.

[64] Stefan Tanaka, *Japan's Orient: Rendering Pasts into History* (Berkeley, CA: University of California Press, 1993).
[65] On Naitō's theory of Japan's mandate, see Yamada Shingo, "'Kinsei bungaku shiron' ni'itaru 'zenshi': Naitō Konan no 'tenshoku ron' no imi," *Kenkyū Ronshū (Kawai Bunka Kyōiku Kenkyūjo)*, vol. 3 (2006), pp. 203–226.

In 1902 the *Ōsaka Daily News* sent Naitō to Manchuria to investigate the local situation under the Russian occupation. While there, in Mukden/Fengtian he discovered a great number of precious Qing documents in multiple languages (Han, Mongolian, and Manchu). After the Russo-Japanese War, in order to collect more multilingual historical materials preserved in the royal libraries (Wenyuange and Chongmoge) of the Mukden Imperial Palace, he applied to the Foreign Ministry for funding in the name of "surveying civil affairs." The ministry approved his proposal and granted him ¥1,500, even instructing the local Japanese army to provide necessary assistance.[66] This 1905 trip was the first of his three government-funded trips to Manchuria in the next three years. Although this expedition was not directly related to the Kantō dispute, after Naitō returned the General Staff Office (sanbō honbu) commissioned him to write a report about the Sino-Korean boundary dispute. Using Korean governmental documents and the Qing texts he found in Mukden/Fengtian, Naitō submitted his first report on the history of Kantō, which supported Korea's territorial claim.[67]

In 1906 Naitō quit his job in journalism and devoted most of his time to the investigation the Foreign Ministry had entrusted to him. In July Naitō began his second journey to study the Kantō problem. He began by spending more than a month in Hansŏng, collecting Korean archives and meeting with Korean sources, including officials, Ilchinhoe members, and intellectuals. There he talked with Chang Chi-yŏn and fellow investigator Nakai Kitarō. Through Pyongyang and Andong, he once again visited Mukden/Fengtian and copied numerous Manchu and Mongolian documents.[68] A few months later he handed over his second Kantō report to the Foreign Ministry. More a thesis of historical geography, the second report quotes exhaustively from various Chinese and Korean sources to explain the development of the Sino-Korean border and completely overthrows the argument of the first report. Reading the secret memorials that Yi Chung-ha submitted to King Kojong during the 1880s demarcations, Naitō adopts the view that the Tumen/Tuman River was indeed the Qing–Chosŏn border.[69] That said, Naitō does not come

---

[66] Note that, in 1905, ¥1,500 was more than two times the annual salary of a lecturer at the Imperial University. See Naitō Torajirō, "Yū Sei daisanki," in *Naitō Konan zenshū*, vol. 6 (Tokyo: Chikuma Shobō, 1976), pp. 369–391.

[67] JACAR, "Kantō no hanto nikanshi seihan ryōgoku fungi ikken/fuzoku-sho (Naitō Torajirō shokutaku oyo chōsa hōkoku)," ref. B03041212500.

[68] Naitō Torajirō, "Kanman shisatsu ryokō nikki," in *Naitō Konan zenshū*, vol. 6, pp. 369–404.

[69] JACAR, "Kantō no hanto nikanshi seihan ryōgoku fungi ikken/fuzoku-sho (Naitō Torajirō shokutaku oyo chōsa hōkoku)," ref. B03041213700.

to the clear conclusion that "Kantō" was historically Chinese territory. He blurs his view by raising some "interesting material" he discovered in Mukden: a Jesuit map and memos compiled by Jean-Baptiste Régis, who marked a vast land north to the Yalu and Tumen Rivers as "uninhabited space."

Meanwhile, the year 1906 marked a turning point in Naitō's professional life. Dissatisfied with Tokyo Imperial University's domination of historical studies (which drew heavily from the German historiography of Leopold von Ranke), Kyōto Imperial University established the College of Letters in 1906 and recruited Naitō as a lecturer of Chinese history. Since Naitō had no college degree, the Ministry of Education indicated it would not grant its approval unless Naitō could present a paper to demonstrate his academic qualifications. Within a short time Naitō delivered a thesis titled "An Investigation of the Korean Northeastern Border" ("Kankoku tōhoku kyōkai kōryaku"), similar in content and structure to the Kantō report he submitted to the Foreign Ministry a month later.[70] He not only won a position in one of the most prestigious universities in Japan but received another three years of funding for his study: ¥4,500 annually from the Foreign Ministry.[71]

During the summer vacation in 1908 Naitō made his third and last investigative trip. This time he actually visited Kantō and personally experienced the local conditions: harsh weather, rough topography, and rampant banditry. Since this was his first survey in the field, he paid great attention to geography and recorded topographic data in detail. Shinoda Jisaku, the legal consultant and director of general affairs for the Kantō Branch, offered his help. He met with Wu Luzhen to get his travel certificate.[72] Although it is unclear whether they exchanged opinions on other matters, once back in Japan Naitō did get copies of both Wu Luzhen's *Report of the Yanji Frontier Affairs* and Song Jiaoren's *Jiandao Issue*. After carefully studying the Chinese views, he submitted his policy suggestions to the Foreign Ministry in early 1909 under the title "Personal View on the Kantō Issue" ("Kantō mondai no shaken"). It was this article that explained Naitō's geopolitical perception of the Tumen region.

"Personal View" is nothing like the previous two reports: it is short, succinct, and straightforward, without tedious historical analysis and textual references. The article is composed of four parts. The first,

---

[70] Naitō Torajirō, "Kankoku tōhoku kyōkai kōryaku," in *Naitō Konan zenshū*, vol. 6, pp. 506–563.

[71] Nawa Etuko, "Naitō Konan to 'Kantō mondai,' 1," *Okayama Daigaku Daigakuin Shakai Bunka Kagaku Kenkyūka kiyō*, no. 6 (1998), pp. 99–117.

[72] Osato Buhachirō, "Hokkan Kirin Ryokō Nikki," in *Naitō Konan zenshū*, vol. 6, pp. 407.

"Kantō's Topography," introduces the area's geographic situation with the expectation of developing the local economy and trade. It concludes: "From the perspective of terrain, it is more convenient if Kantō belonged to Korea than if it belonged to the Qing." The second part, "Advice on the Kantō Railway," focuses on the strategic importance of connecting the Ch'ŏngjin port in northern Korea with the Jilin–Changchun Railway in China. Such a railway is not only a necessity to exploit resources in Manchuria, Naitō says, but would significantly deter the Chinese Eastern Railway run by Russia. In the third part, "Personal Opinion on the Kantō Agreement," Naitō lists nine conditions the Qing government would need to meet in exchange for Japan's admission of its territorial sovereignty. These conditions, briefly put, would turn Kantō into a special economic and judiciary zone where Koreans and Japanese would enjoy various economic rights and consular jurisdiction. Finally, in his "Additional Remarks," Naitō deals with the sovereignty issue over two islands in the lower Yalu River (which was not directly related to the Kantō issue).[73] The article gives no mention about the nature of the boundary, nor its historical development.

It is quite impressive how closely Naitō's suggestions coincide with the actual treaty finally agreed by the two governments; they were not identical but exceedingly similar. The extent to which Naitō's advice affected the Japanese government's Kantō policy is debatable. Some people argue that his impact was decisive; others disagree.[74] Nevertheless, no one denies that Naitō Torajirō, as either an independent historian or a government-hired scholar, involved himself deeply in Japan's colonial enterprise and played a critical role.

What exactly did Kantō mean to Naitō? For Naitō the historian, Kantō was a fantastic topic of Oriental studies, an intricate history worth enormous time and energy in pursuit of the truth and, more important, the starting point of a brilliant academic career. For Naitō the imperial investigator, Kantō meant a "convenient" access point for penetrating Manchuria from Korea, a promise of imperial prosperity, and a strategic point for Japan's geopolitical competition. As shown in his "Personal View," Naitō somehow hid his opinion on the territorial dispute. Another

---

[73] JACAR, "Kantō no hanto nikanshi seihan ryōgoku fungi ikken/fuzoku-sho (Naitō Torajirō shokutaku oyo chōsa hōkoku)" no. 9, ref. B03041213200.

[74] See Naitō Boshin, ed., "Naitō Konan, Kitsurin Kantō ryokōdan," in *Ritsumeikan bungaku*, vol. 216 (1963), pp. 100–113; Nawa Etuko, "Naitō Konan to 'Kantō mondai,' 1," and "Naitō Konan to 'Kantō mondai,' 2," *Okayama Daigaku Daigakuin Shakai Bunka Kagaku Kenkyūka kiyō*, no. 7 (1999), pp. 235–253; Kawatani Yuichirō, "Naitō Konan to Kantō mondai ni kansuru jakkan saikentō," *Chūgoku kenkyū geppō*, vol. 55, no. 4 (2001), pp. 39–46.

episode exposed his stand. In 1909 historian Shidehara Taira published a thesis on the Kantō border dispute in which he employed the same materials (Yi Chung-ha's memorials) Naitō used in his second report.[75] Because Shidehara introduced those "disadvantageous" sources to the public, Naitō criticized him as "being very imprudent in diplomatic issues," even though Shidehara shared Naitō's views on the boundary issue.[76]

The two Naitōs, outstanding historian and "prudent" assistant of imperial enterprise, were reconciled by what he understood as the "heavenly mandate" of Japan. The unification of scholarship and politics was revealed in the Naitō historiography and so-called Kyōto School of Oriental Studies, which combined empirical studies with textual research and a historical approach with contemporary concerns. Not only Kantō but also Manchuria, Mongolia, "China Proper," and the whole Orient were seen as both subjects of and channels to the eventual glorious domination of the Japanese empire over civilization. The center of world civilization shifted constantly, and now it was Japan's turn. As Stefan Tanaka puts it, the Orient (Tōyō) rendered "a unitary language that gave Japan a new sense of itself and its relations with the outside. Through this concept, ...the Japanese created their modern identity."[77]

In addition, the valuable multilingual documents that Naitō collected in his investigative trips contributed significantly to the increased presence of Japanese Oriental studies, which had the tendency to separate "China" (*shina*) from its frontiers and integrate Manchuria and Korea into one historical-geographic unit. With energetic government investment, "Manchurian-Korean history" (*mansenshi*) was exploited as a new territory of imperial historical studies. A pioneer institution of this new field was the Investigation Department of the Manchurian-Korean History and Geography (Mansen rekishi chiri chōsabu), funded by the South Manchuria Railway Company. One of Naitō's most distinguished disciples, Inaba Iwakichi, who accompanied Naitō during his second Kantō investigation, joined the sector in 1908 and became a prominent member.[78]

---

[75] Shidehara Taira, "Kantō kokkyō mondai," in Tōyō Kyōkai, ed., *Tōyō Kyōkai Chōsabu gakujutsu hōkoku*, vol. 1 (Tokyo: Tōyō Kyōkai, 1909), pp. 207–235.

[76] Nawa Etuko, "Naitō Konan to 'Kantō mondai,' 2," pp. 241–242.

[77] Tanaka, *Japan's Orient*, p. 11.

[78] Inaba Iwakichi, "Yoga Mansenshi kenkyū katei," in Inaba Hakushi Kanreki Kinenkai, ed., *Inaba Hakushi kanreki kinen Man-Sen shi ronsō* (Keijō-fu Nishikomon-chō: Inaba Hakushi Kanreki Kinenkai, 1938), pp. 1–28.

Song Jiaoren: Saving Sovereignty by International Law

The founding father of the Guomindang Party (one of the predecessors of the KMT), Song Jiaoren is widely recognized as a pioneer bourgeois revolutionary, a highly respected leader (second only to Sun Yat-sen and Huang Xing), and a martyr of Chinese constitutional democracy. He led the Guomindang to success in the first parliamentary election after the Qing emperor was forced to pass his power to Yuan Shikai. Just as everyone expected him to assume the office of the prime minister of the Republic of China, Song was assassinated at the age of thirty-one in March 1913, many people believing it to be a plot by Yuan. Song's *The Jiandao Issue* (*Jiandao wenti*), written during his asylum/study in Japan in 1908, is a rare academic work of a leading revolutionary. Precisely for that reason, it offers an excellent insight into a constitutional revolutionary's view on national sovereignty.

The most distinguished feature of *The Jiandao Issue*, compared to Wu Luzhen and others' theses on the same topic, was its highlight of the principles of international politics and international law.[79] The thesis did inevitably go on at some length discussing geography and history, but it repeatedly claimed that territorial sovereignty was first and foremost regulated by a new universal order and thus could only be effectively saved by such an institution. When a "forcible approach" was not the best option for China, a "peaceful approach" was a passable form of self-preservation. Song's opinion, shaped both by his theoretical studies in Japan and his empirical experience in Manchuria, departed remarkably from previous and contemporary views on Manchuria in two ways. First, consistent with the policy to decentralize Manchuness in practice, Song further removed Manchuria as a time-spatial concept in imperial symbolism. The dynastic geographical rhetoric presenting the place as "a land of dragon rising" no longer provided territorial legitimacy. Second, compared to frontier officials (Wu Dacheng, Xu Shichang, and Wu Luzhen), Song placed more hopes on the intervention of international law in resolving the Yanji/Jiandao problem. As expressed in the preface of *The Jiandao Issue*, he believed that "military might is not real power; public opinion is." In light of this view, he published the book hoping to arouse public opinion to protect "Jiandao," a land roughly the size of Taiwan, from being taken from China.[80]

---

[79] Song Jiaoren, "Jiandao wenti," in Li Shutian, *Guangxu dingwei Yanji bianwu baogao*, pp. 267–344.
[80] Ibid., pp. 269–270.

After introducing the origins of the dispute and the arguments of the rival sides, Song uses a whole chapter "to observe the Jiandao problem from the perspective of international law." A state, says Song, acquires its territory by two main methods: original acquisition and derivative acquisition. Original acquisition takes three forms: accretion (e.g., emerged islands or alluvion); prescription (as when Japan took over Sakhalin Island from China); and occupation (as when Spain "discovered" South America or Portugal "discovered" Africa). Derivative acquisition has five forms: exchange (Japan and Russia exchanged Sakhalin for the Kuril Islands); presenting (Italy gave Nice to France); purchase (the United States purchased Alaska); cession (Japan took Taiwan from China); and annexation (the United States annexed Hawaii and the Philippines). In addition, a state is demarcated by two kinds of boundaries: a natural boundary, such as a mountain, river, desert, and wildland; or an artificial boundary, regulated by bilateral treaties. "These types of territorial acquisition and demarcation," says Song, "are necessary forms to establish state territorial sovereignty, which is affirmed by international law." Therefore, a territorial dispute could not be settled by force. Instead, "we must examine who acquired sovereignty first, to whom the natural geography is more convenient, and how the border treaty is regulated."[81] In other words, all three elements – history, geography, and political treaty – are necessary conditions for a resolution of any border dispute.

He then goes on to apply these three elements to the Jiandao dispute. For history, he traces Jiandao sovereignty back to the mid-Tang dynasty and employs a narrative of racial lineage. The conclusion: Jiandao sovereignty is a derivative acquisition that China (*zhonggou*) took from the Tungusic peoples (the Mohe, Jurchens, and Manchus). "It has absolutely nothing to do with either the Korean state or the Korean nation [*minzu*]."[82] For geography, he argues that Mt. Changbai and the Yalu and Tumen Rivers comprise a natural divide between the Korean Peninsula and the Manchurian Plain, "as if they are deliberately [posited] to separate the Manchu race [*renzhong*] and the Korean race." Here, Song repeatedly imposes racial discourse, which was popular in the early twentieth century, to demarcate East Asian history and geography. Regarding political treaties, he admits that international law in Eastern countries was not developed. Yet, when countries adjoined, there were de facto demarcations even if no treaty was ever signed. Unlike the Qing Foreign Ministry, Song actually sees the 1712 Mukedeng survey as a demarcation mission and regards the stele and barriers as boundary marks. But

---

[81] Ibid., pp. 285–286.
[82] Ibid., p. 290.

back then, argues Song, "there was not what we now know as the 'scientific boundary line.' And because Chosŏn was China's subordinate state, there was neither a treaty signed by equal partners, nor a way to establish it."[83] (Having no access to the inside documents of the 1880s demarcations, he was unaware that the boundary marks left by the Mukedeng mission had already been proved in error.) Song concludes: "Given the situation of the three elements, Jiandao completely meets the requirements of a Chinese territory. The best resolution of the Jiandao issue is to judge it as a Chinese territory; the criteria are very clear."

The regime of international law, according to Song, not only defines the territorial nature of Jiandao but also provides China with the opportunity to use "peaceful" approaches to solve the territorial conflict with Japan. Song's attitude was more defensive than aggressive: "Peaceful approaches," says Song, "use principles of law as armor and facts as shields." Within the three peaceful approaches – mediation by a third party, international investigation, and arbitration – the latter two were more suitable for settling a boundary dispute. If diplomatic negotiations failed, China could suggest international investigation and confine the Jiandao issue to a pure boundary problem. Even if the international investigation had no stopping power, it would nonetheless prevent Japan from using Jiandao as an excuse to invade Manchuria. If this method also failed, China could call for arbitration by either The Hague Convention or a European state. To support his argument, Song employs two cases in South America (the 1881 Chile–Argentina territorial dispute and the 1889 Brazil–French Guianan dispute, arbitrated by Britain and Switzerland, respectively) to exemplify the "international precedents."[84]

Other than reframing Jiandao's history and geography to place it in accordance with the doctrines of international law, what else did this space – remote and strange to most Chinese as it was – mean to Song Jiaoren? He situates this corner of the territory in the grand game of international politics, seeing it as "a buffer zone for the three spheres of influence of China, Japan and Russia. [...] If one state got it first and managed it well, it could at best counter the influences of the other two, or at least solidify its own frontier."[85] By the same token, the reason Japan coveted this place "lies half in Jiandao and half beyond." Japan's strategic aim was to compete with Russia for economic and military benefits in Manchuria. Therefore, the best interest for China, argues Song, is to maintain a balance of power between Russia and Japan, so that China

[83] Ibid., p. 294.
[84] Ibid., p. 342.
[85] Ibid., p. 335.

could win time to strengthen itself. Power balance is the only reason that China survived without being carved up. If Japan, by taking over Jiandao, occupied the whole of Manchuria, such a balance would no longer exist.[86] For Song, the reason to preserve Jiandao, too, lies half in and half beyond Jiandao itself. Jiandao involves the integrity of China's territorial sovereignty: what happens to it affects the fate of the Chinese nation.

At the end of his book, Song lists China's territorial losses in previous decades and attributes these tragedies to "the failure of diplomacy." This assertion, of course, was only half true: China suffered first and foremost because of its failure to contain the aggression of global capitalism and imperialism. Yet, considering his initial passion to make Manchuria a source of anti-Qing revolution, it seems obvious that he expected Jiandao to be a departing point for the old China and a starting point for a new China. Nevertheless, Song's Jiandao thesis revealed his foresight as well as his wishful thinking. On the one hand, he was right in predicting the Japanese ambition: in 1931, a little more than two decades after Song wrote his book, the Japanese Kwantung Army fabricated the Mukden incident and occupied Manchuria. On the other hand, he was wrong to lay the greatest hope in "peaceful approaches." Although China in 1931, unlike Korea in 1905, did get moral and legal support from an international investigation (when the Lytton Commission of the League of Nation denounced Japan's aggression), the international law regime still failed to protect China from being devastated by Japanese colonialism.

Sin Ch'ae-ho: Saving the Nation through History

Between 1905, when Korea became a Japanese "protectorate," and 1910, when Korea was officially annexed, a new historical studies movement arose in the country. Generally tagged as "enlightenment historiography," this trend of rewriting history was essentially an intellectual resistance to Japanese colonization. Ironically, as many scholars have pointed out, it established itself by heavily borrowing theories and discourses of Meiji Japanese historiography, either directly from Japan or indirectly from China.[87] Certain features were common to this historiography across all three East Asian countries: the highlight of nation (C.

---

[86] Ibid., pp. 333–338.
[87] Schmid, "Rediscovering Manchuria"; Sassa Mitsuaki, "Dankun nashonarizumu no keisei: kankoku aikoku keimō undōki wo chūshinni," *Chōsen Gakuhō*, no. 174 (2000), pp. 61–107.

minzu; J. *minzoku*; K. *minjok*) as the main actor, a linear and progressive narrative, an appeal to revive the national glory of the past, and the identification of mythical figures as national progenitors. Korean historians adopted and adapted these new elements in their own history rewritings, propagating nationalist sentiments in newspapers such as *Capital Gazette* and the *Korean Daily News*. Notable representatives of the movement were Pak Ŭn-sik, Chang Chi-yŏn, and Sin Ch'ae-ho.

Among them, Sin Ch'ae-ho (1880–1936) was arguably the most influential. Sin did not write specifically about Kando, at least not under his name. Given that he worked as an editor and regular writer for the *Korean Daily News*, and that the *News* published many anonymous reports and comments on Kando from 1907 to 1909, Sin was hardly a bystander on the issue. But Sin's more remarkable contribution was that he constructed a tight connection between Korean history and Manchuria. Not only did he create a novel narrative about the Korean nation, but his narrative had a huge impact on modern and contemporary Korean societies in both the north and south.

For Sin, the nation (*minjok*), rather than the state, is the subject of history. In order to arouse nationalist nostalgia towards the past greatness of the "Korean nation," he revolutionizes conventional historiography and shifts the geographic center of the Korean history from the peninsula to Manchuria. In so doing, he creates a vision of a historical Korean space that certainly contained the Tumen River region as well as much more. Sin believed that in historical studies both time and space exist to serve the subject of a nation, as is apparent in his famous definition of history:

What is history? It is the records of the state of mental activity in human society wherein the struggle between "I" [*a*] and "non-I" [*pi-a*] develops through time and expands through space. World history, then, is a record of such a state for all of mankind, whereas Korean history is a record of such a state of the Korean people [*Chosŏn minjok*].[88]

Several key notions make up the critical characteristics of Sin's historiography. First, the antithesis of "I" versus "non-I" constructs a perpetual theme in human history. For Sin, this "I" transcends states and dynasties. It is a community bound by a shared blood line – a people as a racial/ethnic unit as opposed to a people as subjects of a king. Second, the historical time/space is the arena of the I/non-I clash. History and geography

---

[88] Sin Ch'ae-ho, "Chosŏn sanggosa," in *Tanjae Sin Ch'ae-ho chŏnjip*, vol. 1 (Seoul: Tanjae Sin Ch'ae-ho Sŏnsaeng Kinyŏm Saŏphoe, 1987), p. 31. The translation is quoted from Henry H. Em, "*Minjok* as a Modern and Democratic Construct: Sin Ch'ae-ho's Historiography," in Gi-Wook Shin and Michael Robinson, eds., *Colonial Modernity in Korea* (Cambridge, MA: Harvard University Press, 1999), pp. 336–362, 357.

were united, and together they mirrored the trajectory of a nation's evolution. Third, and most important, Sin's philosophy of history is one of subjective idealism. Because he believed history is entirely concerned with "the state of mental activity," it is more of a spiritual product than a material outcome.

Such a definition functions more as a political manifesto than an academic approach. Facing the crisis of Korea's exclusion as a (nation) state, Sin hoped to create an independent "Koreanness" from history, so as to save the "national soul" from being encroached upon. In his early writings, he excoriates traditional Confucian historiography precisely because it embraced a superior China while casting Korea as a sinicized barbarian. The official history, according to Sin, was nothing but a humiliating narrative of *Sadaejuŭi* (serving-the-great-ism) and therefore had to be completely abandoned. By the same token, he was also against Pan-Asianist ideology, because it replaced the primary target (Korean independence) with the secondary (reviving Asia) and would essentially exterminate the Korean nation.[89]

Sin's historiography grew out of its own historical context. It inherited the self-consciousness from the *silhak* (practical learning) school of philosophy of the late Chosŏn period. Yet unlike *silhak* scholars, who advocated solving sociopolitical problems via pragmatic and materialistic approaches, Sin seems to emphasize a spiritual and cultural resistance. Another theoretical source of his historiography was social Darwinism, which he probably borrowed from Chinese enlightenment thinker Liang Qichao, albeit merely on a subjective level. Unlike Liang, Sin never valued "rational" and "scientific" methods in his new historical studies. On the contrary, since orthodox literature was not sufficient to serve the needs of pursuing an independent "Koreanness," Sin had to base many of his arguments on unofficial history, myths, even pseudographs.

From August to December 1908 Sin published a series of articles in the *Korean Daily News*. Titled "A New Reading of History" ("Toksa sinlon"), these articles reveal the basic outline of his national historiography.[90] Lamenting that Korean history was always treated as a portion of other nations' histories, Sin first identifies the "race" and "geography" with which his new narrative would be concerned. He asserts that there were six nations in the "Eastern countries." Among them, "the race (*jok*) of Puyŏ (C. *Fuyu*) is our holy race, the descendants of the Tan'gun, and the master of the Eastern land for 4,000 years." The other five nations

---

[89] Hwang Hyo-Kang, "Kanmatsu kokugaku no seiji shisō: Shin Saikō wo chūshin nishite," *Kanagawa Hogaku*, vol. 29, no. 2 (1994), pp. 1–88.
[90] Sin Ch'ae-ho, "Toksa sinlon," in *Tanjae Sin Ch'ae-ho chŏnjip*, vol. 1, pp. 467–513.

(i.e., the Xianbei, Chinese, Mohe, Jurchen, and the aboriginals in the peninsula) conquered and assimilated with each other. As a result, only the Puyŏ occupied a persistent position in the East. Therefore, "the 4,000-year history of the Eastern countries is the history of the rise and decline of the Puyŏ race." In terms of geography, Sin says "our nation" originated in Mt. Paektu and the Yalu River region, then spread to the whole of Manchuria and the Korean Peninsula. As a result of external and internal turbulence, "our nation" withdrew to the peninsula, thereby constraining itself to this "iron jar."

In traditional Korean historiography, the Confucian historical lineage embraced Kija (Jizi), an aristocrat in exile from China's Shang dynasty (around the sixteenth century BC to 1046 BC), as the first sage ruler of the country. After the ancient period of "the Kija Chosŏn" the northern peninsula was under the jurisdiction of the Four Commanderies of the Chinese Han (漢) dynasty, while the southern part was ruled by the small confederations of the Three Han (韓) people. The Three Kingdoms – Kokuryŏ, Paekche, and Silla – emerged in the north and south, respectively, until the southern Silla (53 BC–935 AD), with the help of the Chinese Tang dynasty, eventually unified the peninsula in 668 AD.

Sin, however, refuted this Sinocentric lineage. He instead claimed that the Tan'gun, a mythical figure born in the Mt. Paektu area, initiated the first Korean kingdom. The Puyŏ people inherited this kingdom and later established all of the Three Kingdoms. In contrast to most historians, who praised Silla's achievement of unification, Sin condemns the Silla king who sought help from a foreign state (i.e., the Tang China) to slaughter the people of his own nation (*minjok*) and caused Korea to lose its Manchurian territory for "more than 900 years." He further condemns Korean historians, who overwhelmingly embraced the legitimacy of the Silla and ignored the real national glory in the north, namely, the Kokuryŏ (37 BC–668 AD) of the Three Kingdoms and its successor, the Parhae (698–926 AD), to the extent that few details about them appear in official histories.

By highlighting the "Tan'gun–Puyŏ–Kokuryŏ" lineage, Sin inevitably sees Manchuria as the holy cradle and sacred homeland of the nation. Manchuria had not only witnessed the rise of the Korean nation in the past but would also determine the resurgence of the nation in the future. Published in July 1908, Sin's famous thesis on "Korea and Manchuria" paints the picture:

How close is the relationship between Korea and Manchuria? When the Korean nation obtained Manchuria, the Korean nation was strong and prosperous. When other nations obtained Manchuria, the Korean nation was weak and backward.

Among other nations, if a northern nation obtained Manchuria, the Korean nation was incorporated into this northern nation's sphere of influence. Whereas if an eastern nation obtained Manchuria, the Korean nation was incorporated to that eastern nation's sphere of influence. Alas! This is an unchangeable iron rule that has lasted for four thousand years.[91]

He then shifts his focus from history to contemporary politics. "Ever since the opening of East–West communication," says Sin, "this place has been a particular focus of the East Asian competition. Russia and Japan have fought over Manchuria for more than a decade, and Korea just looked on indifferently. Today, Manchuria is what Korea was." In other words, Manchuria and Korea comprised a community of shared destiny under imperialism and colonialism.

Sin's later commentaries on Manchuria extended his concern to international politics. In light of the fact that all major capitalist powers were competing with Japan for the benefits of Manchuria, Sin predicted that "the problem of acquiring or losing Manchuria is a problem of life or death for Japan."[92] As for the Korean nation, he took an irredentist stand and claimed Korea's future lay in stepping northward to "demand the return of the old territory of Kokuryŏ and revive the glory of the Tan'gun."[93]

In January 1910 Sin published his most comprehensive and systematic discussion on Manchuria. In a *Korean Daily News* essay titled "Further on the Manchurian Issue" ("Manju munje e ch'wihayŏ chaeron ham"), Sin expresses three interrelated visions of Manchuria.[94] First, he analyzes the past and current conflicts in Manchuria and divides Manchurian history into three phases: ancient, medieval, and modern. In the first phase the land was ruled by the Puyŏ race. In the second the territory was conquered by different races in East Asia (*Tongyang*, the same characters of the Japanese word "Tōyō") and became the center of East Asian history. The period after the rise of the Qing empire witnessed the last and current phase, in which Manchuria served as an arena for world competition. "Alas! We do not know into whose hands Manchuria will fall in the future," Sin says; "World competition today is concentrated in East Asia. And Manchuria is the wellspring of East Asian problems."

Sin goes on to address the significance of Manchuria to the destiny of the Korean nation. He draws a parallel between Manchuria and the

---

[91] Sin Ch'ae-ho, "Han'guk kwa Manju," in ibid., vol. 4, p. 234.
[92] Sin Ch'ae-ho, "Manju wa Ilbon," in ibid., vol. 4, p. 235.
[93] Sin Ch'ae-ho, "Han'guk minjok chirisang palchŏn," in ibid., p. 198.
[94] Sin Ch'ae-ho, "Manju munje e ch'wihayŏ chaeron ham," in ibid., pp. 238–243.

Balkans, a strategic area that often decided the fate of European countries. He singles out the Italian nationalist Conte di Cavour to show how, by proactively intervening in the Balkan issue, he accelerated the unification of his home country. In other essays as well, Sin compares Korea to Italy and Mt. Paektu to the Alps. Sin's interest in modern Italy, aside from the geopolitical similarity between the two peninsular countries, directly concerns his political appeal for the independence of Korea. For him, Italy is a model for Korea. Sin laments, "If only Korea had men like…Conte di Cavour."

At the end of his essay, Sin envisions Manchuria as a major overseas settlement for Koreans. He raises three hopes for Korean immigrants in Manchuria. First, they must be "noble-minded," be patriotic, and support each other in establishing "institutions of civilization" such as schools and newspapers. Second, they must work hard to "preserve national essences" such as religion, customs, and language, so as to prevent their assimilation by other races. Third, they must "cultivate political ability." In Africa and Australia, Sin says, the white people built new states in colonies because they had strong political capability: they were united, free, and would not tolerate their own oppression. The "red and black races," in contrast, suffered from their weak political capability. He calls on Korean immigrants to "awaken their neglected consciousness and bring their political nature into full play," then "make a contribution to the home country in the future." In other words, Sin expected modern Korean nationals to be formed first in Manchuria.

Sin's visions demonstrated the huge influence of Chinese thinker Liang Qichao, an important source of Korean nationalism in the early twentieth century. Liang revolutionized traditional Chinese historiography with nationalist narrative. In his 1901 essay "On Chinese History" ("zhongguo shi xulun"), Liang describes Chinese history as having three stages: ancient, medieval, and modern. Liang suggests that ancient history is about the "China of the Chinese"; the medieval stage is the "China of the East Asians"; and the modern stage the "China of the world."[95] Sin's three phases of the Manchurian history obviously directly copied Liang's framework. Moreover, in 1907 Sin translated Liang's *Biographies of the Three Heroic Founders of Italy* (*yidali jianguo sanjiezhuan*), which introduces stories of Giuseppe Mazzini, Giuseppe Garibaldi, and of course Conte di Cavour. Sin's notion of Korean nationals, too, is very much in debt to Liang's theory of the "new citizen" (*xinmin*) of China. The only difference is that Liang believes that individual rights are as important

---

[95] Liang Qichao, "Zhongguo shi xulun," in *Liang Qichao quanji*, vol. 2 (Beijing: Beijing chubanshe, 1999), pp. 453–454.

as public spirit in creating the "new citizen," whereas Sin places more emphasis on the public aspect in making new Korean nationals.[96]

Aside from the tight intellectual linkages between Sin and his Chinese counterparts, there was an internal coherence between his theory and that of the Japanese *mansenshi* (Manchurian-Korean history) school. Of course, the political nature of Sin's historiography and the *mansenshi* school (of which Naitō Konan could be regarded as a scholarly source) couldn't be more opposite: one was resistive, the other aggressive. Nevertheless, each highlighted a new image of Manchuria and Korea as highly integrated in terms of both history and geography, past and future. Jun Uchida points out the nationalist connotations of this similarity: "Where writers like Sin Ch'ae-ho had pinned their hopes for the resurgence of their *minjok* on 'the northern lands' occupied by Korea's ancient dynasties, the Japanese writers appropriated the ethnic vigor of the Korean 'brethren' to promote the continental expansion of their own *minzoku*."[97]

Upon finishing "Further on the Manchurian Issue," Sin fled to China before the annexation. He lived out the remainder of his life in Manchuria, Beijing, Shanghai, and Vladivostok, engaging in the Korean resistance movements and dying in a Japanese prison in Fushun, Fengtian Province. Sin never returned to Korea and never again wrote about Manchuria. His sojourn in Manchuria was an exile, not a homecoming. Yet, in the first half of the twentieth century, a great number of Koreans, nationalists or not, immigrated to Manchuria. Kando/Yanji did become a new home for most of them. As Pak Ŭn-sik comments: "For Koreans who migrated outside their country, this place [Kando] is their favorite."[98] Just as Sin predicted, the Korean community in Manchuria, a base of the Korean independence movement, did become a source of new Korea.

So what exactly did Manchuria represent for Sin? It was a visionary homeland that bore all the past glories of an imagined community that had fallen into crisis; it was a spiritual ballast for a stateless nation. Or, as Andre Schmid puts it, Manchuria was "an implicit territorial standard to measure the *minjok*'s position in a world of racial struggle."[99] No Koreans before Sin had considered land and people in this way, not the *silhak* scholars in the eighteenth and nineteenth centuries, and certainly

[96] Moon Dae-il, "Liang Qichao 'xinmin' sixiang dui Shen Caihao 'xinguomin' sixiang de yingxiang," *Dongfang luntan*, no. 2 (2002), pp. 9–15.
[97] Jun Uchida, *Brokers of Empire: Japanese Settler Colonialism in Korea, 1897–1945* (Cambridge, MA: Harvard University Press, 2011), p. 313.
[98] Pak Ŭn-sik, *Han'guk t'ongsa*, vol. 3 (Seoul: Pagyŏngsa, 1974), p. 175.
[99] Schmid, "Rediscovering Manchuria," p. 35.

not Yi Chung-ha in the 1880s. In fact, it is probably because of Sin's brand of historiography that Yi Chung-ha, a Confucian official, is now often wrongly portrayed as a pioneer nationalist.

Korean nationalists inherited – and twisted – Sin's legacy. The most recognizable of Sin's intellectual heirs is historian and writer Ch'oe Nam-sŏn (1890–1957), who drafted the Korean Declaration of Independence in 1919. Ch'oe developed Sin's admiration for the Tan'gun and Mt. Paektu but radically romanticized and religionized these national icons. He even invented the concept of the *pulham munhwa* (Mt. Paektu culture), arguing that nations in Manchuria, Korea, and Japan belonged to the same sphere of ancient culture centered on Mt. Paektu. He further claimed that the Tan'gun myth shares roots with the Japanese myth of *tenson kōrin*, the grandson of Amaterasu, the sun goddess, who descended to earth to rule Japan. Although its purpose was to show that Korean culture was not inferior to its Japanese counterpart, this vacuous theory catered to the Japanese colonialist discourses of *nissen dōzo* ("Japan and Korea share the same ancestor") and *naisen iitai* ("Japan and Korea are one"), which Japan manipulated to justify its colonial rule. Because of that, after World War II the Republic of Korea (ROK) accused Ch'oe of being a pro-Japanese collaborator.[100]

The resurgence of nationalist sentiment in South Korea in the 1960s and 1970s boosted the popularity of Sin's historiography, which served the political needs of the Pak Chŏng-hŭi government (1962–1979). Studies of Kokuryŏ and Parhae, previously considered of little importance, gradually took on weight. The irredentist idea of recovering the old territory of Kando or Manchuria, though not yet a mainstream view in government or academia, was fanatically discussed from time to time among populist historians and the media.

Sin was also a critical source of inspiration to Kim Il Sung, the North Korean leader who was a communist guerrilla fighter in Manchuria in the 1930s and 1940s. In his reminiscences he lauds Sin's patriotic spirit and his philosophy of struggle.[101] Not at all surprisingly, the official historiography in North Korea (DPRK) adopts the Mt. Paektu-centered narrative and emphasizes the glory of the Tan'gun and Kokuryŏ (as opposed to Kija and Silla). Popular images of Kim Il Sung and his heir, Kim Jong Il, are often associated with Mt. Paektu to demonstrate their

---

[100] Chi Myong-Kwan, "Sin Saikō sigaku to Sai Nanzen sigaku," *Tōkyo Joshi Daigaku Hikaku Bunka Kenkyūjo kiyō*, vol. 48 (1987), pp. 135–160.
[101] Kim Il-sŏng, *Jin Richeng huiyi lu: yu shiji tongxing*, vol. 2 (P'yŏngyang: Oemun ch'ulpansa, 1992), pp. 6–7.

anti-Japanese legends as well as historical legitimacy to lead the nation.[102] To further solidify the Kim family's rule, in June 2013 the DPRK under Kim Jong-un (the third generation of the Kim regime) revised *The Ten Principles*, a foundational political document of the regime, and swore to uphold the "Mt. Paektu bloodline" forever.[103] Under the official ideology of *chuch'e* (self-reliance), history textbooks in the DPRK stress that the Korean nation is the subject of Korean history, a history of struggling against foreign invasion. One could easily see in such rhetoric the reverberation of Sin's historiography.[104]

Along with the territorial competition over Kando/Kantō and Manchuria, the multilateral frontier underwent an intellectual deterritorialization and reterritorialization. Bringing to the table their own political ideals, leading intellectuals in Japan, China, and Korea sketched a scheme and vision for this space – colonialist, institutionalist, and nationalist. Each vision absorbed the intellectual sources from its opponents, inspiring, nourishing, and enhancing one another even as they competed. Through this multilateral and interactive process, perceptions of Manchuria, and especially that of Mt. Changbai/Paektu, were simultaneously disenchanted, rationalized, and reenchanted. In this sense, Manchuria occupied a complex, critical, and unique position in the spiritual history of twentieth-century East Asia.

---

[102] Charles K. Armstrong, "Centering the Periphery: Manchurian Exile(s) and the North Korean State," *Korean Studies*, vol. 19, no. 1 (1995), pp. 1–16.

[103] Dennis P. Halpin, "Welcome to North Korea's Game of Thrones," *The National Interest*, April 23, 2014, http://nationalinterest.org/feature/welcome-north-koreas-game-thrones-10298.

[104] As Michael Robinson noted: "Because of the emergence of an almost hysterical cult of personality centered on Kim Ilsong, it is difficult for the North Koreans to give credit to alternate sources of inspiration for their own dogma. Nevertheless, Sin's early writing on the concepts of *sadaejuŭi* and *chuch'e* must be considered as important precedents for the development of the highly nationalistic strain in Kim Ilsong's thought." Michael Robinson, "National Identity and the Thought of Sin Ch'ae-ho: Sadaejuŭi and Chuch'e in History and Politics," *Journal of Korean Studies*, vol. 5 (1984), pp. 121–142.

6 People Redefined
Identity Politics in Yanbian

The 1909 Sino-Japanese Jiandao/Kantō Convention temporarily settled the territorial dispute over the Tumen River boundary. Yet the reconfirmation of the China–Korea border was hardly the end of the frontier crisis. With the Japanese annexation of Korea in 1910, wave after wave of Koreans left their homes for Manchuria or Russia. The physical boundary was essentially meaningless in practice. Under the circumstances, an old problem – the problem of people – reemerged, in a whole new sociopolitical setting.

Fast-forward to December 1928. In that month the head of a Korean peasant family living in Wuchang County, Jilin province, submitted a petition to become a Chinese national. In standardized format and language, the document reads:

The petitioner: Chang Sang-u,
    (originally from: Yŏnghae Prefecture, Kyŏngsang province of Korea)
    (now living in: Yushuchuan, the fifth district of Wuchang County, Jilin province)
    is 26 years old and his occupation is farming.
He submitted this petition of naturalization. This expatriate (*qiao min*) is currently 26 years old and has been living in China for over 5 consecutive years. In accordance with Article Four of the Revised Nationality Law of the Republic of China, he is willing to acquire the nationality of the Republic of China, and obey all Chinese laws. The petition is submitted to the Ministry of Interior.

Aside from Chang Sang-u himself, the paper also lists his wife (surname Chŏn, 22 years old), a daughter (Sun-i, 2), and a younger brother (Sang-in, 19) as derivative applicants. Together with this document was a separate certificate of guarantee, signed by two fellow farmers living in the same county. Supposedly, both were Chinese or ethnic Koreans with Chinese nationality.[1]

Other than this petition, we know little about Chang's story. Wuchang, like Yanji, accommodated many Korean immigrants in the twentieth

---

[1] Zhongguo bianjiang shidi yanjiu zhongxin, *Dongbei bianjiang dang'an xuanji*, vol. 116, pp. 2–3.

century. In part because of these Korean immigrants, it became one of the most famous rice-producing regions in Manchuria. But what drove Chang and his family to Wuchang? Why did they seek Chinese nationality? Was their petition voluntary or coerced? Were there other options for them? Was naturalization an economic choice to acquire landownership, a political gesture to resist the Japanese colonization, or simply a survival strategy to get China's protection? Moreover, before they wanted to turn themselves into Chinese, did they have any "nationality" at all (given that Korea had no longer been a state since 1910)? In other words, what did "nationality" mean to the Koreans living in Chinese Manchuria in the early twentieth century? And, equally important, what did the naturalization of the Koreans mean to early twentieth-century China?

With the collapse of the Qing empire in 1912, the identity of the Manchurian Koreans was an even more challenging problem than it had been in the 1880s. Both China and Japan attempted to create a clear-cut boundary between "us" and "them," while the Koreans had their own worries. Before 1910 most Chinese censuses call the Koreans *Han min* ("Korean civilians") and distinguish them from "foreigners," a category saved for the Japanese and Russians. In 1911, a year after the annexation, the local authority in Yanji issued the *Arrangements to Naturalize the Korean Expatriates* (*Hanqiao ruji banfa*). The gist of the regulation was that the Koreans, now seen as "expatriates," were not allowed to own land. "For those who already own land, we should persuade them to register [as Chinese]. [...] For those who have lived here for a long time but do not want to naturalize, our government will take back their land at a proper price, regard them as foreigners, and order them to leave."[2] But, in the early republic period, local Chinese governments defined "Korean" quite loosely. Compiled in 1914, *The Gazetteer of Yanji County*, for example, categorized any Korean as "foreigner," along with "Japanese" and "other nationalities."[3] In contrast, a census of Yanji Circuit (*dao*) in 1927 dichotomized the local population as either "Chinese" (*hua min*) or "expatriates" (*qiao min*). The naturalized Koreans belonged to the "Chinese," while the unnaturalized were "expatriates."[4] In the very same year the *Gazetteer of Hunchun County* classified local *minzu* (nationalities or ethnicities) in this way: the "Han" (Chinese), "Manchu," "Hui" (Muslim), "cultivators" (*ken min*, referring to Koreans), and "expatriates" (*qiao min*, referring to Japanese and Russians).[5] According to this

[2] Yanbian chaoxianzu zizhizhou dang'anguan, ed., *Qingchao moqi ge bumen de zhangcheng guitiao*, pp. 7–8.
[3] *Yanji xian zhi*, vol. 10, "waijiao," 1915.
[4] Yanbian chaoxianzu zizhizhou dang'anguan, ed., *Yanji dao gaikuang*, p. 11.
[5] Li Shutian, ed., "Hunchun xianzhi," in *Hunchun shi zhi*, pp. 99–106.

document, the Korean/cultivator was neither "us" nor "them" but something in between. This chapter introduces the continued trilateral tensions on the north Tumen River bank between the Chinese state, the Japanese state, and the Korean society in the 1910s. My investigation moves from geographic boundaries to ethnic, national, and psychological boundaries, focusing on the identity politics surrounding the Manchurian Koreans. It examines the competing efforts to redefine the Manchurian Koreans by the Japanese government, the Chinese government, and local Koreans themselves. How did sovereignty and identity shape each other? How did colonialism and nationalism unfold and become entangled in this multilateral frontier? With these questions in mind, perhaps we will be in a slightly better position to contextualize the diverse identities that Koreans such as the Chang family tried to make for themselves.

Yanbian Society: New Developments

In the second decade of the twentieth century several watershed events marked a new beginning in East Asian history. These sweeping changes occurred almost simultaneously, once again reshaping the political ecologies of China, Japan, and Korea. On October 26, 1909, Itō Hirobumi was assassinated in Manchuria by An Chung-gŭn, a member of the Korean Righteous Army. Itō's death helped accelerate the Japanese annexation of Korea. In August 1910, with the signing of the Japan–Korea Annexation Treaty, Korea became a colony of the Japanese empire. Terauchi Masatake, the last Japanese Resident-General of Korea, was inaugurated as the first Japanese Governor-General of Korea. By February 1912 the aftereffects of the 1911 Wuchang uprising (in Hubei Province) ended both the Qing's 268-year rule over the Middle Kingdom and the imperial system that had lasted more than two millennia in China. But, within the newly founded Republic of China, the power fell not to the revolutionaries but to Yuan Shikai and his Beiyang clique. In Manchuria, where the Beiyang clique had for years built up its power base, the impact of the 1911 revolution was relatively trivial. When the Beiyang was split among several rival warlords after Yuan's death in 1916, the East Three Provinces were under the governance of Zhang Zuolin, a shrewd bandit-turned-warlord who had accumulated his power by maintaining a cooperative yet distant relationship with Japan.

In Japan the great Meiji period concluded in 1912 with the death of Emperor Meiji. In the first half of the ensuing Taishō period (1912–1926) Japan integrated itself more deeply into the global capitalist system. The Japanese economy experienced both unprecedented prosperity during World War I and a great depression thereafter. As a result, Japan had to continue its expansion in the continent and further monopolize its privileges in Korea and China. Manchuria became the base for Japan to realize its geopolitical strategy.

A new spatial concept, "Yanbian," came to indicate the immigration region along the north bank of the Tumen River. Starting in the 1910s the term appeared repeatedly in Chinese documents, though it was not yet an official administrative division. During 1909 and 1910 several new counties were installed in the region, and the Yanji subprefecture (*ting*) was promoted to the level of full prefecture (*fu*). The title of this prefecture changed several times until it was renamed the Yanji Circuit (*dao*) in 1914. The circuit contained eight counties: Yanji, Helong, Hunchun, Wangqing, Dunhua, Emu, Ning'an, and Dongning.[6]

Meanwhile, the Japanese and Koreans still used "Kantō/Kando" to refer to the Tumen northern bank where Korean immigrants were mostly concentrated. The realm of Kantō/Kando was tantamount to the three Chinese counties of Yanji, Helong, and Wangqing. Additionally, Japanese documents often listed Hunchun County in the lower Tumen River region along with Kantō as two districts belonging to the same socioeconomic zone. Chinese documents, too, frequently addressed the four border counties of Yanji, Helong, Wangqing, and Hunchun together, seeing them as an integrated zone. Thus, a new Chinese term, Yanbian (*Yan* from Yanji, plus *bian*, meaning "border" or "frontier"), was created to refer to these four counties. In Japanese contexts it was the equivalent of "Kantō + Hunchun."

The number of Korean immigrants in the northern Tumen region skyrocketed after the annexation. According to the Japanese census, the number of Koreans in Yanbian grew from 109,500 in 1910 to 127,500 the next year and 163,000 the year thereafter. By 1919 Koreans residing in this area numbered 297,150. In other words, the Korean population almost tripled in just ten years. Meanwhile, Chinese immigrants also kept flooding into the area; the number rose from 33,500 in 1910 to more than 72,000 in 1918.[7] The Yanbian region having been developed for decades, there was less space for the newcomers; many Korean resettled elsewhere, either crossing the Yalu River to southern Fengtian or moving further north to other places in Jilin or Heilongjiang.[8] Figure 2

---

[6] Yanbian chaoxianzu zhizhizhou dang'anju, ed., *Yanjidao gaikuang (chugao)* (1984).

[7] Chōsensōtokufu keimukyoku, ed., *Kantōmondai no keika to ijūsenjin* (Keijō: Chōsensōtokufu keimukyoku, 1931), table between pp. 64 and 65.

[8] From 1912 to 1915 the total Korean population in Manchuria went from around 238,400 to around 282,000. Kantōtotokufu minseibu, ed., *Manmō keizai jijō 3* (Dairen: Kantōtotokufu minseibushomuka, 1916), pp. 187–188.

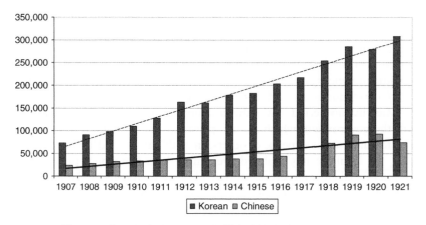

Figure 2 Population increase in Yanbian (1907–1921)
Sources include: Chōsensōtokufu keimukyoku, ed., *Kantōmondai no keika to ijūsenjin*, p. 65; and Takenaka Ken'ichi, "Seimatsu mingokuki no chūgoku no kantō niokeru chōsenjin kyōiku seisaku nitsuite no ichikōsatsu," *Jinbun Ronshū*, no. 37 (1998), pp. 83–120. The data on the Chinese population in 1917 are incomplete.

shows the Korean and Chinese population increases in Yanbian from 1907 to 1921.

Although most new immigrants were engaged in agricultural production, their arrival had a significant impact not only on land distribution but also on social stratification, economic structure, local culture, and ideology. Class division in the region was increasingly notable. As immigrants flooded the area, arable land gradually became a scarce resource. In terms of land redistribution, only a few wealthy households purchased land directly from local Han and Korean landowners. The majority, lacking financial means, became tenant farmers. The *Jilin Korean Ethnographic Investigation* records that in Taixing village there was no arable land left uncultivated in the early republic period. Peasants who arrived during this time had to lease land from the "mountain occupiers." A new type of landlord emerged:

Land trading appeared after the wildlands were all privatized. [...] Some buyers accumulated their wealth from diligence and frugality. They bought small pieces of land and farmed them themselves, hence, they became owner-peasants. There were also wealthy people who purchased large pieces of land. They were called *maishanhu*, the "mountain buyers."[9]

[9] Jilinsheng minzu yanjiusuo, eds., *Jilinsheng Chaoxian zu shehui lishi diaocha* (Beijing: Minzu chubanshe, 2009), p. 226.

Naturally, when land became scarce, the price for leased land rose higher and higher. Wealth gradually concentrated into the hands of a few big landlords, both Korean and Han. In Taixing village, where Korean peasants arrived in great numbers, a Shen family that initially had only a small piece of wildland rapidly accumulated wealth. The family's property expanded to 150 *shang* of land in the early 1930s, then further increased to 370 *shang* in the Manchukuo period.[10] Wealthy landlords had more avenues to collude with the government, which in turn provided them channels to augment their fortunes at the expense of others. In both Taixing and Taipinggou villages, the local wealthy grabbed even more land from poor peasants by bribing official land surveyors. More fields were then registered under their names, which they were able to rent out at higher prices.[11] Censuses done by the Japanese also show the trend of social stratification. Recall that in 1907 80 percent of Han households and 60 percent of Korean households in "Kantō" were categorized as "landlords." In 1925, by contrast, only 47 percent of Han and 8 percent of Korean households belonged to the same category. More than half (55 percent) of Korean households in 1925 were tenant families. The rest (37 percent) were categorized as owner-peasants.[12]

New immigrants came from all over Korea. Unlike the pioneers, who were mainly from the Hamgyŏng region, many of the new immigrants were from southern provinces, such as Kyŏngsang or Chŏlla, where rice was the main crop. A more diverse demography gradually altered the original structure of agricultural production. Although millet, soybeans, and corn remained the primary products, there was an appreciable increase in rice plantations. Combining the advantages of local agrarian conditions, advanced paddy plant experience, and improved rice seed imported from Japan, Korean peasants tested and expanded paddy fields in Manchuria. In just a short period Manchuria became one of the best rice producers in China. The overwhelming majority of rice peasants in Manchuria were Koreans, to the extent that "the history of Korean immigration to Manchuria is the history of the flourishing of the paddy field," as a Japanese document suggests.[13] The Yanbian region became the largest rice provider in the East Three Provinces. Until 1930 more than 22 percent of all paddy fields in northeast China were in Yanbian.[14]

---

[10] Ibid.

[11] Ibid., pp. 314–315, 226.

[12] *Kantōmondai no keika to ijūsenjin*, p. 68.

[13] Minami Manshū Tetsudō Kabushiki Kaisha Kōgyōbu, ed., *Manshū no suiden* (Dairen: Minami Manshū Tetsudō Kōgyōbu Nōmuka, 1926), p. 6.

[14] Yi Baozhong, *Chaoxian yimin yu dongbei diqu shuitian kaifa* (Changchun: Changchun chubanshe, 1999), p. 113; Yu Chunying and Yi Baozhong, *Jindai dongbei nongyelishi de lishibianqian* (Changchun: Jilin daxue chubanshe, 2009), pp. 77–78.

The success of the Korean rice planters encouraged their Chinese counterparts, who had previously had questioned the feasibility of growing
rice in such a high latitude, to join the paddy business.

Rice in early twentieth-century Manchuria was more than just food.
It was a cash crop as well. With World War I, rice prices in world markets inflated remarkably. Profits from rice topped those of other crops.
Comparing rice with the most important export of Manchuria, soybeans,
in the early 1920s, the price of rice in Yanbian was nearly three times that
of soybeans. Profits from rice were double those from soybeans growing
in the same area. Since rice was so marketable, in the late 1920s 75 percent of rice produced in Yanbian was sold to the market, supplying not
only China but also Korea, Japan, and Russia.[15] Korea was a particularly
important market for Manchurian rice, since Korean rice, better in quality at that time, was largely exported to the Japanese market rather than
consumed locally.

For the Japanese market particularly, rice was a strategic commodity.
Starting in the 1910s Japan showed great interest in investing in the paddy
enterprise in Manchuria. It did so mainly through Korean peasants, who
were the primary source of labor in this business and were regarded by
Japan as Japanese "subjects." However, the fact that few Koreans owned
land, combined with the cautiousness of the Chinese government to sell
land to the Koreans, presented a dilemma and became a source of fre-
quent political conflict between Japan and China.

In addition to economic changes associated with accelerated class
division and a new agricultural economy, the new immigrants also created a significant political impact. Newcomers came to Yanbian with
relatively distinct political sentiments. Many of them, like the early
immigrants, had been rural residents in their home countries. But,
unlike the early refugees, the main factor that pushed them out was
the Japanese colonization of Korea, not natural disasters. A large portion of these people were forced to leave after losing their farms to the
Japanese colonial agency, notably the Oriental Development Company
(Tōyōtakushoku kabushikikaisha, abbr. Tōtaku). In other words, their
exile was caused mainly by political, as opposed to pure economic,
reasons.

On top of that, the new wave of northward migration included a great
number of social elites, including former *yangban*, or intellectuals, who
strongly opposed the harsh Japanese rule. Many of them were driven

---

[15] Wang Guochen, *Jindai yanbian jingji fazhanshi* (Yanji: Yanbian daxue chubanshe, 2010),
pp. 48–49.

out by the Japanese suppression of Korean nationalist education and media in the 1910s. For them, Manchuria, especially Kando, was the base of resistance – or at the very least a place that allowed them to preserve Koreanness beyond Korea. They further expanded the religious and educational networks in Yanbian, through which they fostered anti-Japanese sentiment and laid a solid foundation for nationalist movements. This political tendency was observed in an official report of the Jilin provincial government in 1915. Based on their political attitudes, the report divided Koreans in Yanbian into three groups: "the pro-Chinese faction" (*qinhua pai*), "the pro-Japanese faction" (*qinri pai*), and "the fence sitters" (*qiqiang pai*). The first group, according to the report, was "especially large."[16] This observation reflects fairly accurately the ideological inclination among the Yanbian Koreans, even though the term "pro-Chinese" more or less misinterpreted what was essentially anti-Japanese.

Being Japanese: Colonial Economy and Politics

After the annexation, Japan announced that all Koreans in Korea were "Japanese subjects." But were "subjects" citizens? How were Koreans living outside Korea to be understood in terms of their nationality? Were they under the jurisdiction of Japanese consuls? What about those who had a foreign nationality? Should there be different policies towards overseas Koreans who were foreign nationals from those who were not? These questions were not really legal questions but primarily political questions concerning Japanese colonial interests. The nationality of the Koreans exiled in Russia or the United States rarely created serious diplomatic problems between Japan and those two major powers. Even that of the Koreans in interior China did not present much of a dispute, since the Japanese colonial influence did not yet stretch that far. It was precisely because Manchuria – the primary base of overseas Koreans – was now regarded as a strategic area for Japanese colonialism that the legal status of local Koreans emerged as a crucial issue that exacerbated Sino-Japanese tensions.[17]

---

[16] Zhongguo bianjiang shidi yanjiu zhongxin, *Dongbei bianjiang dang'an xuanji*, vol. 43, p. 376.
[17] Quite a number of scholars have explored this topic; my narrative is much in debt to their studies. Some of the most important examples include: Inoue Manabu, "Nihon teikoku shugi to kantō mondai," *Chōsenshi kenkyūkai ronbunshū*, vol. 10 (1973), pp. 35–83; Jiang, *Jindai zhongchaori sanguo dui jiandao chaoxianren de zhengce yanjiu*; Bai, *Higashi Ajia seiji gaikōshi kenkyū*; Park, *Two Dreams in One Bed*.

The Treaty of Southern Manchuria and Eastern Mongolia

The Jiandao/Kantō Convention stipulated that the Chinese government would allow Korean cultivators to live and work in the northern bank region and that those Koreans would submit to Chinese authority. The challenge came in 1915. In this year the Japanese government coerced Beijing into accepting a series of new requests, generally known as "the Twenty-One Demands," to enlarge Japan's privileges in China. Although Japan did not get all it wanted, it nevertheless successfully forced the Yuan Shikai government to sign a treaty promising Japan special benefits in southern Manchuria and eastern Mongolia. According to the Treaty of Southern Manchuria and Eastern Mongolia, "Japanese subjects" enjoyed the right to lease lands for agricultural and industrial investments. In all civil and criminal cases, they were subject to the Japanese consulates as opposed to the Chinese authority.

The key issue here was whether the new treaty applied to Koreans in Yanbian and, if so, how to coordinate the contradiction between this new agreement and the Jiandao/Kantō Convention. Even the Japanese government at first had no consistent opinion on this matter. In June 1915, right after the new treaty was signed, Suzuki Yōtarō, then the Japanese Consul-General of Kantō, asked the Foreign Ministry whether certain articles in the Kantō Convention that admitted the Chinese juridical power over local Koreans were still valid. The Foreign Ministry replied that they were. The judgment was made in accordance with the new Treaty of Southern Manchuria and Eastern Mongolia: article eight clearly indicated that "other current treaties between China and Japan...will be implemented as usual." However, the Governor-General of Korea challenged the Foreign Ministry's position, as it raised three concerns: first, if the old and new treaties were carried out indiscriminately, it would apply Japanese exterritoriality to some Manchurian Koreans but not others. Second, it would put a Manchurian Korean who moved from one place to another under different juridical systems. Third, and perhaps most important, those "indocile Koreans" would take advantage of the legal loophole and turn Kantō into an anti-Japanese breeding ground.[18]

After an intensive internal discussion the Foreign Ministry eventually adopted the position of the Governor-General and agreed that the new treaty applied to the Kantō Koreans. In August 1915 the Japanese Cabinet decided that, in light of the Treaty of Southern Manchuria and Eastern Mongolia, the related protocols in the Kantō Convention were

[18] Gaimushō, *Kando kwangye (kaebang kup chosa)*, vol. 2 (Seoul: Koryŏ Sŏrim, 1990), pp. 93–95.

now to be regarded as null and void. Soon the Japanese consulates in Manchuria received an order from Tokyo that indicated that all legal cases in which Koreans were defendants must be trialed by the Japanese consulates.[19] China soon issued its strong objection to this policy.

Defining Koreans as Japanese was not, of course, to extend "imperial benevolence" to the colonized. Rather, the policy was tightly woven into Japan's overall colonial scheme of controlling Manchuria. It aimed at two goals. As the Governor-General of Korea put it, it sought to contain the booming anti-Japanese movements among Manchurian Koreans and criminalize those "indocile Koreans." The policy also used the Manchurian Koreans as a vehicle to expand Japanese economic and political interests. If a piece of land was owned or leased long term by Koreans, it would be perfectly justifiable for the Japanese authority to extend its power there.

Three Pillars for Penetrating Manchuria

Of course, imposing Japanese jurisdiction on the Manchurian Koreans alone was not sufficient to implement Japan's colonialist plan. Japan established three institutions to respond to the political, financial, and social situations of the Korean community – what we might call the three pillars of Japanese policy in Manchuria.

The political pillar was embodied in the Japanese consulates. The 1909 Jiandao/Kantō Convention allowed Japan to have four consulates on the Tumen north bank: Longjing, Juzijie, Toudaogou, and Baicaogou. In 1910 Japan established a further consulate, in Hunchun. These five consulates constituted the Consulate-General of Kantō. In the 1910s the administrative realm of the Consulate-General of Kantō covered the main area where Koreans had settled in southern Manchuria, including both the Yanbian region in Jilin province and the neighboring Fusong and Antu counties in Fengtian province.[20] While the Japanese consulates in other countries/regions reported only to the Foreign Ministry in Tokyo, the consulates in Kantō were cosupervised by both the Foreign Ministry and the Governor-General of Korea in Kyŏngsŏng (Seoul). The officials appointed as general consuls in Kantō held concurrent posts as secretaries of the Governor-General of Korea. If there were important matters, the general consul had to consult with the Governor-General first, rather than the Foreign Ministry. In addition, half of the policemen serving in these consulates (many of them Korean) were not on the

---

[19] Chedŭng Sil munsŏ, *Chosŏn Ch'ongdok sidae kwan'gye charyo*, vol. 10, pp. 743–765.
[20] Tōyō Takushoku Kabushiki Kaisha, *Kantō jijō*, p. 76.

payroll of the Foreign Ministry but were transferred from Korea by the Governor-General.[21] The dual administrative system revealed that the Japanese consulates in Kantō were not just diplomatic institutions but an extension of the Japanese colonial government in Korea. The consulates had extensive intelligence networks, which paid special attention to local Koreans' political attitudes and Chinese policy trends towards the Koreans. Detailed information was routinely collected and reported to both the Korean Governor-General and Foreign Ministry.[22]

After 1915 the Japanese consulates confronted the Chinese government over jurisdiction of the Koreans and even expanded their power to local policing. Japanese police forces stepped up their presence on Chinese soil, intervening aggressively in various civil and public security affairs. They even patrolled beyond the so-called trading ports areas, which were de facto Japanese concessions around the consulates. The Japanese consulates acted in the name of suppressing "indocile Koreans," and they urged the Chinese government to "cooperate." The connotation was clear: if China was reluctant to outlaw anti-Japanese activities in Yanbian, Japan would do it itself, with or without Chinese permission.

The financial pillar consisted of various Japanese financial agencies in the region. Among them, perhaps the most salient was the Oriental Development Company, or Tōtaku.[23] Founded in 1908, Tōtaku was one of two national colonial enterprises in imperial Japan (the other being the South Manchuria Railway Company). One of Tōtaku's main concerns in the 1910s was a countrywide cadastral survey in Korea, which it conducted from 1910 to 1918. Through this project, Tōtaku annexed numerous lands owned by Koreans and leased them to Japanese agricultural immigrants. At the same time, it turned tens of thousands of Korean landlords or owner-peasants into tenants and squeezed many of them out of the country.[24]

In Yanbian Tōtaku established its first local branch in 1918 when it took over a relief society originally run by the Consulate-General. It made low-interest loans to local peasants, usually taking their land as collateral. Since land in Manchuria was sold or rented much more cheaply

[21] Li Hongxi, *Riben zhu zhongguo dongbei diqu lingshiguan jingcha jigou yanjiu* (Yanji: Yanbian daxue chubanshe, 2008).
[22] See, for example, JACAR, "Chōsen henkyō Kiyokuni ryōdo-nai kyojūno Chōsenjinni taisuru kiyokuni seifuno kaijū seisaku kankei zassan," ref. B03030255200.
[23] See Park, *Two Dreams in One Bed*, pp. 102–103.
[24] In Mark Driscoll's words, the Tōtaku, with its financial power, and Japanese garrison army, with its military threat, constituted "the two headed monster grotesqueing Korea." See *Absolute Erotic, Absolute Grotesque: The Living, Dead, and Undead In Japan's Imperialism, 1895–1945* (Durham, NC: Duke University Press, 2010), p. 116.

than in Korea, a Tōtaku loan was especially attractive to Korean immigrants, who, ironically, were forced to resettle here precisely because the very same colonial agency had deprived them of their lands at home. Aside from making loans, Tōtaku also invested in agricultural development, urban building, and gas and electricity construction. Within a few years Tōtaku surpassed all local financiers and became the biggest loan provider in the region. It acquired a large amount of land by either confiscating default mortgages or purchasing them indirectly via naturalized Korean-Chinese. An investigation in 1927 found that Tōtaku was known to own the titles to 58,170 *mu* of land in the four counties of Yanbian, 72 percent of them paddy fields. At least another 50,000 *mu* were secretly purchased with Tōtaku capital. Combining these two figures shows that the company alone substantially controlled more than 3 percent of cultivated lands in Yanbian.[25]

Japanese commercial capital gradually monopolized the commodity market of Yanbian in the 1910s. This was another reason why Japanese investors such as Tōtaku were so successful in manipulating the local economy. From 1910 to 1914 the Japanese established 118 companies in Yanbian. This integrated the local economy into the world capitalist system, at the cost of destroying the existing commercial structures. As early as 1911 Chinese local officials had already sensed the danger. The Yanji prefect reported to the Jinlin provincial government: "Not only was landownership gradually transferred to foreigners, but businessmen gradually lost their livelihoods." He counted that, in recent years, "[n]early 1,000 rural households returned to inland China after selling their farms to the Koreans; dozens of merchants closed their businesses after they lost their profits to the Japanese."[26] In Longjing alone, the value that the Japanese businesses took in the import/export trade increased twenty-one-fold in eight years, going from 130,000 custom taels in 1910 to 2.7 million custom taels in 1918, amounting to 80 percent of the total value.[27]

The last pillar of Japan's triangular colonial power structure, the social pillar, rested on the Korean People's Society, or Minhoe (K. Chosŏnin minhoe; C. Chaoxianren minhui). Founded in Longjing in 1917, the Minhoe claimed to be a "self-governing organization" dedicated to "enhancing the common benefit for local Koreans." In practice, it was subsidized and supervised by the Japanese consulates and functioned

---

[25] Shen Ruqiu, "Yanbian diaocha shilu," in Yanbian lishi yanjiusuo, ed., *Yanbian lishi yanjiu*, vol. 2 (Yanji: Yanbian lishi yanjiusuo, 1986), pp. 157–228.

[26] Zhongguo bianjiang shidi yanjiu zhongxin, *Dongbei bianjiang dang'an xuanji*, vol. 46, p. 462.

[27] Yang Zhaoquan et al., *Zhongguo chaoxianzu geming douzheng shi* (Changchun: Jilin renmin chubanshe, 2007), p. 114.

as a grassroots institution of Japanese governance. Within ten years the Minhoe had installed fourteen branches in Yanbian. Wherever a consulate police branch was established, there was a local branch of the Minhoe. One of the main jobs of the Minhoe was to conduct household censuses. It collected exhaustive local information – from income and harvests to public sentiment and even personal political inclinations –and reported them to the Japanese consulates. The Minhoe was also entwined in public and civil affairs such as postal services, medical care, communication facilities, and local education. The Minhoe established several schools in Yanbian, using both the dues it charged members and the Japanese subsidy. All these schools adopted Japanese curricula and textbooks and propagated pro-Japanese ideas.[28] Not surprisingly, in the eyes of the Governor-General of Korea, the Minhoe was "the most important institution regarding the protection of Korean residents."[29]

Together, the three pillars influenced and shaped local life. For example, the Kantō Financial Department (Kantō Kin'yū-bu), a microcredit agricultural loan provider in the region, funded by the Japanese government and supervised by the Consulate-General, became an affiliated enterprise of the Minhoe in the 1920s. Shen Ruqiu (K. Sim Yŏ-ch'u), a Yanbian Korean writer, published a detailed investigation in 1928. According to his report, one of the reasons the Minhoe was attractive to Korean peasants was that the interest the Kantō Financial Department charged on its loans was significantly lower than that of private lenders. Any application for such a loan, however, had to be accompanied by a recommendation from the Minhoe.[30] Joining the Minhoe also averted suspicion of being "anti-Japanese." According to a 1931 census, 47,493 Korean households were members of the Minhoe. Among them, 30 percent had acquired ¥846,910 in loans from the Kantō Financial Department.[31] Considering that in 1930 the total number of Korean households in Kantō was 68,200,[32] it is clear that joining the Minhoe was a widespread survival strategy for the majority (nearly 70 percent) of the local Korean population.

In sum, the identification of Koreans as "Japanese subjects" in the 1910s was a key component in the overall Japanese colonial scheme in both Korea and Manchuria. The political, economic, and social institutions were comprehensive forces of colonial penetration. While using

---

[28] Shen, "Yanbian diaocha shilu," p. 222.
[29] Chōsensōtokufu keimukyoku, eds., *Kantōmondai no keika to ijūsenjin*, pp. 190–192.
[30] Shen, "Yanbian diaocha shilu," p. 221.
[31] Gaimushō, *Kando kwangye*, vol. 2, p. 632.
[32] Chōsensōtokufu keimukyoku, ed., *Kantōmondai no keika to ijūsenjin*, table between pp. 64 and 65.

Koreans as pawns in its colonial strategy, Japan was also extremely cautious about the "indocile Koreans" and their anti-Japanese activities in northeast China. Defining the Koreans in China as "Japanese subjects" granted Japan a legal excuse to suppress those who threatened the stability of Japan's colonial rule. However, for Koreans, "being Japanese" never meant being equal to the Japanese. This was especially the case for the Koreans living in Korea. Thus, migrating to China provided at least the possibility of a bearable life.

Being Chinese: The Inclusion and Exclusion of Koreans

Turning Korean cultivators into Chinese subjects was a consistent policy goal of the Chinese government throughout the decades-long Tumen demarcation process. In different historical contexts, however, the same policy did not necessarily mean the same thing. As addressed in previous chapters, in the 1880s, when the imperial frontier officials (e.g., Wu Dacheng) talked about including the Koreans with the Qing's household registrations (*bantu*), they aimed at fulfilling imperial authority over the yet-to-be-developed borderland, which was under severe foreign threat. The Koreans were seen as members of the Celestial Dynasty. As long as they were living and working on Chinese land, they could be regarded as "the people of the Central Plains," and it was just a matter of time before they would truly assimilate into the Chinese political and cultural system. In the 1890s, when the China-centered *zongfan* hierarchy collapsed, the Korean cultivators were recognized as more "other" than "us." Yet this otherness could be moderated, for example, by changing men's hairdos and attire. At this stage, the identity issue was mainly associated with the economic rights of landownership. Other than that, the identity politics (involving "shaving hair and changing dress") did not affect the livelihood of the Koreans: many found ways to bypass the rule and own land. It was not until Japan's intervention that the issue of Korean identity became a political crisis concerning China's sovereignty. In the 1910s the Japanese annexation of Korea and consequent massive Korean immigration put great strains on the land–people relationship. The Chinese government started to crack down in its efforts to naturalize the Koreans. On the surface the policy still focused on landownership. Yet the identity politics during this phase was far deeper than the matter of property rights or taxation, as it developed into a critical means of sovereignty building.

In fact, even before the Jiandao/Kantō Convention, Chinese officials realized that the Sino-Japanese struggle over Yanbian was essentially a competition to win over the Korean people. Naturalizing Koreans was no longer a purely economic policy but first and foremost a political strategy. In March 1908 Xu Dewei, the registrar of Helongyu, visited a Korean village school and spoke with the villagers about cultural assimilation and political rights:

> Before, Korea was a subordinate state of the Great Qing Emperor. The relation between the two states was very amicable. The pundits of your elder generations knew that. [...] Please consider: you got land and came across the border to farm, so in this respect you are Chinese subjects [*zhongguo zimin*]. Being common people, though, you are enjoying the same rights as the Chinese. The only difference is that you could not be appointed as Chinese civil or military officials. Why? This is all because our languages and cultures are different, and you do not change your apparel. To make a remedy for this shortcoming, I invited a Chinese teacher for you. [...] After you go on to graduate from middle school, those who studied well could be appointed as Chinese officials. The purpose of my speech is to persuade you to make up your mind to submit to China and break away from the influence of tiger-and-wolf-like Japan.[33]

The legacy of the *zongfan* ideology was notable in this statement: the tributary past was recalled; culture (language) and apparel (hairdo and dress) remained the precondition of being "Chinese." But there was a rupture: the meaning of being Chinese had switched from one based mainly on economic rights to one based mainly on political rights (possibility to take positions in the government).

In just a few months this Chinese grassroots official went further and talked about a breakthrough reform in governing the Korean cultivators. On January 3, 1909, Xu Dewei submitted a long report to the Jilin governor stating his opinions on frontier defense, beginning with the flaws of past policies. Xu believed that previous regulations focused too heavily on taxation while neglecting the problem of state sovereignty: "[W]e issued orders to make Koreans naturalized [*ruji*]; however, none of these orders – household registration, farmland taxation, shaving hair and changing dress – had the authority to completely outlaw [illegal immigration]. Up to today, the number of Koreans grows larger and larger, and it is more and more difficult to manage them." He offered ten suggestions to enhance frontier governance, including creating a civil bureaucratic system, promoting education, bolstering the police force, and developing public welfare. Although pursuing Chinese language study was one of his suggestions, it followed from a prior need "to establish and determine nationality" (*bian ding guo ji*):

---

[33] JACAR, "Kantō no hanto nikanshi seihan ryōgoku fungi ikken," vol. 8, no. 8, pp. 26–27, ref. B03041200700.

I observe: the household census is the basis of good civil politics; establishing and determining nationality is the basis for governing people. [However], our state always sees the household census as but a mere scrap of paper; it pays even less attention to the nationality law. The consequences: outsiders secretly purchased our land and assaulted our sovereignty; rebels came and went freely while escaping from the punishment of state law – these are all because we lack a nationality law as protection. Once the Yanji border dispute is settled, we should immediately dispatch competent staff to conduct a field survey in divided areas, and forbid someone else from doing the job on their behalf. They should register naturalized Koreans in detail and house by house, then report the census to the Ministry of Civil Affairs. [We should also] submit a memorial to the Emperor, petitioning his order to establish a code about naturalizing foreigners. After the legislative ministers have codified and issued the nationality law, we could register the life and death, arrival and departure of the foreigners accordingly.[34]

The continuity and rupture of history were delicately demonstrated in this registrar's statements. Two parallel logics coexisted in his hybrid recognition of the Koreans. In his speech to the Korean students and villagers, he called them "Chinese subjects" who lacked political rights only due to barriers of language and costume. Behind this definition was the cosmology inherent in a traditional family–state genealogy that had regulated Sino-Korean interactions for hundreds of years. In his report to the Jilin governor, however, he categorized Koreans as "foreigners" who needed to be restrained and naturalized by nationality law. Behind this definition was the logic of the sovereign state and international law. These two understandings had become entangled and resulted in a rather ambiguous and contradictory policy towards the Korean immigrants. Such a policy, emphasizing ethnic inclusiveness, cultural assimilation, and economic exclusiveness simultaneously, was implemented through diverse and pragmatic local variations. This was how the boundary of being Chinese was demarcated in early twentieth-century Yanbian. The intention and outcome of this demarcation echoed, and was profoundly shaped by, the geopolitical contest in Manchuria.

Nationality Law

When Xu Dewei, a low-ranking registrar in Yanbian, called for the codification of a nationality law in 1909 he probably did not know that Beijing had already initiated the legislative process in the previous year.

On March 28, 1909, the first nationality law in China, the Nationality Protocols of the Great Qing (Daqing gouji tiaoli), was submitted by the

---

[34] Zhongguo bianjiang shidi yanjiu zhongxin, *Dongbei bianjiang dang'an xuanji*, vol. 102, pp. 240–241.

Constitutional Compilation Bureau to the emperor for approval. Its preamble states that the traditional concept of *ji* (registration) needs to be updated, from registering households for the purpose of taxation to registering nationality for the purpose of protecting "national rights" (*guoquan*) – that is, sovereignty:[35]

> We believe: people are the basis of the state; compiling registration [*zhu ji*] is the basis of [governing] people. When talking about "household registration" [*hu ji*], we always mean nothing but investigating the population and distinguishing the elder and the younger, in so doing to impose taxation and duty of labor. The law of "national registration" [*guo ji*], [however], is in charge of the affairs of expatriation and naturalization. On a higher level, it matters to the gain and loss of national rights; on a lower level, it concerns the compliance or incompliance of people's will.

That being said, the Qing legislators made it clear that the Chinese nationality law was different from those of other countries: it emphasized the "preservation" of Chinese emigrants (i.e., to prevent overseas Chinese from being naturalized as foreign nationals) more than the "inclusion" of foreigners:

> The state competition today is more and more a contest of territorial expansion and colonization. Only in China, because of our large population, people [have to] migrate around the world to trade and farm. Considering the different situations between China and other countries, and what is important and what is not, it is not necessary [for China] to prioritize the inclusion and submission [of other people]. We instead must value the cherishing and preservation of the [Chinese] emigrants. This is the real intention of the current legislation.

It further explains that there are two legislative principles in nationality laws: *jus soli* (right of soil, *shudi zhuyi*), which determines an individual's nationality by place of birth, and *jus sanguinis* (right of blood, *shuren zhuyi*), which determines an individual's nationality by the nationality of parents. The Qing legislators state that the current protocols lay particular stress on *jus sanguinis*.

The first nationality law in China, unlike what Xu Dewei would have wished for, did not aim to naturalize foreign immigrants. Rather, this law was an attempt to resolve two contemporary issues in totally different sociopolitical settings. First, many Chinese living in China's foreign concessions or leased territories naturalized themselves as foreign nationals. In so doing, they either profited from the new identity or evaded Chinese jurisdiction. Second, the colonial government in the Dutch East Indies was forcing Chinese immigrants to denounce their Chinese nationality in order to

---

[35] HCFDTYMD, vol. 234, pp. 371–384.

constrain nationalist movements.[36] The Qing law highlighted the principle of *jus sanguinis*, which reflected that the Qing was more anxious about the pressing issue that Chinese subjects, willingly or unwillingly, were turning themselves into foreign citizens, not the other way around. This concern, interestingly, resonates with the Korean king's worry in the 1880s when the Qing tried to put Korean squatters under the Qing's jurisdiction.

That being said, the Qing nationality law did formulate the circumstances that allowed foreigners to apply for Chinese nationality. According to the protocols, foreign persons – to be more specific, adult males – who met certain basic requirements could petition for naturalization (*ru ji*, or "join the registration"): they had to (1) have lived in China for more than ten consecutive years; (2) be at least twenty years old and have a disposing capacity according to the law of their home country; (3) be of good virtue and conduct; (4) possess sufficient assets or talents to support themselves; and (5) cancel their original nationality upon being naturalized, according to the law of their home country. Aside from these five basic requirements, the protocols listed additional conditions for those who made special contributions to China, women, adopted children, illegitimate children, and others.[37]

The nationality law provided only basic principles of naturalization. For the Koreans in China, the law departed from past policies in two significant ways. First, cultural symbols such as the Manchu style of queue and dress were no longer a precondition for being Chinese. One of the main social barriers for naturalization was now eliminated. Second, the length of residence was established to limit opportunity. Borrowing from the nationality laws of other countries (especially Japan), this protocol was particularly unfavorable to new Korean immigrants, who had come to Yanbian in great numbers in an attempt to escape Japanese rule. In practice, however, the local government in Yanbian made efforts to cope with the issue flexibly. In 1909, for example, a great number of Koreans in Helong County petitioned to be naturalized. Since "more than half of them were disqualified because of the requirement of the length of residence," local authorities proposed making an exception and reducing the required length to five years.[38]

---

[36] Miu Changwu and Lu Yong, "'Daqing guoji tiaoli' yu jindai 'zhongguo' guannian de chongsu," *Nanjing shehui kexue*, no. 4 (2012), pp. 151–154.

[37] For example, the wife of a Chinese national would be seen as a naturalized Chinese, but a married woman could not petition for naturalization separately from her husband. HCFDTYMD, vol. 234, p. 375.

[38] *Helongxian yamen dang'an*, no. 3-1-266, Yanbian Archive; Zhongguo bianjiang shidi yanjiu zhongxin, *Dongbei bianjiang dang'an xuanji*, vol. 40, pp. 471–472. It also worth mentioning that, in Fengtian province, the local limit on residential periods was even more

Nonetheless, the breakthrough on the criteria for "joining the registration" still caused a certain tension in local practice. There was disagreement among Chinese officials on how to demarcate the boundary between naturalized and unnaturalized Koreans. Some officials insisted that culture, as opposed to assets or years of residency, was a more effective way to draw the line. In September 1911 the deputy magistrate of Yanji Prefecture submitted a report to Zhao Erxun, the viceroy of the East Three Provinces, addressing his concern about the naturalization standards. He observed that, even though the shaving and dress code had been in place for years, most Koreans still maintained their own customs. This showed, he said, that those Koreans did not "yearn sincerely for our civilization" (*qing yin xiang hua*). He therefore suggested:

Neither assets nor the number of years [of residency] is passable to count as the criterion of naturalization. As long as [the applicant] learns our language, our way of living, and dresses like us, and he submits the petition that is confirmed by officials, we should grant him a naturalization certificate. Otherwise, if only one [in a family] has changed [his hairdo and dress], even if he has had his property for more than five years, we should not approve his naturalization petition readily.[39]

Zhao Erxun, a banner man himself, replied that he sympathized with the magistrate's concern. However, the other provincial officials, whom he consulted, argued against the proposal on the grounds that it was but a long-term ideal that could not solve the current crisis. Besides, they said, "among all foreign countries, no one prescribed a limit to language and dress in its naturalization protocols. Insisting on this matter does not accord with the public [international] law (*gongli*)." They requested the local official "to permit the naturalization first, and then pursue further progress gradually." In the eyes of these provincial officials, being a Chinese national was primarily a legal issue. Cultural assimilation, if it still mattered at all, was only secondary. The discussion shed light on a turning point in the history of "becoming Chinese."

After overthrowing the Qing regime in 1912, the newly founded republican government repeatedly revised the nationality law. In 1912 and 1914 Yuan Shikai's Beiyang government issued the Nationality Law of the Republic of China and its revision. Further, in 1929, the

---

flexible. According to the *Regulations on Protecting the Korean Expatriates* (*Hanqiao bao'an tiaoli*), established in 1910, Koreans who had already owned immovable property before the issue of this regulation could be exempted from the ten-year residency requirement. Zhongguo bianjiang shidi yanjiu zhongxin, *Dongbei bianjiang dang'an xuanji*, vol. 36, p. 359.

[39] Zhongguo bianjiang shidi yanjiu zhongxin, *Dongbei bianjiang dang'an xuanji*, vol. 40, pp. 345–346 and p. 472.

Nationalist government set forth a new Nationality Law of China. Both laws, in the naturalization section, inherited the basic principles of the Nationality Protocols of the Great Qing. One remarkable change was that the laws reduced the residency requirement from ten years to five. To compete with the Japanese infiltration, local governments in the Sino-Korean border areas constantly simplified the naturalization procedure for qualified Korean immigrants. At the prefectural and county levels, regulations were made more flexible to accommodate local conditions. Stimulated by China's new policy as well as the Japanese annexation of Korea, the number of naturalized Koreans in Yanbian rapidly increased. Before the fall of the Qing, thousands of Korean households submitted their petitions. Sometimes the petitions were filed collectively. For example, after Korea was annexed, 2,289 Korean households in Helong County applied for naturalization together. Petitioning for Chinese nationality sometimes became a symbolic act of Korean resistance. In 1914 two Koreans, Yi Tong-ch'un and Kim Nip, who claimed to represent 10,000 "cultivators" in Yanbian, went to Beijing and submitted a collective naturalization petition directly to the Department of Domestic Affairs.[40]

Naturalization and Landholding

The Chinese policy towards Korean immigrants was never merely inclusive and containing. The nationality issue was never about an abstract identity. Rather, it was always a means to solve another problem: landholding. The original target was simple: if land was exclusively owned by those with Chinese nationality, Japan would not find an easy excuse to interfere with frontier sovereignty. But not every Korean could, or was willing to, be naturalized. Therefore, in the early 1910s the Chinese local government carried out a dual policy: encourage Korean landowners to be naturalized, on one hand, and prevent landownership from being transferred to unnaturalized Koreans, on the other. Neither policy was satisfactory. New immigrants soon outnumbered those who had resettled there decades ago. Most of the newcomers did not want to be naturalized – and they were not qualified anyway. But, since farming was their main survival strategy, these Koreans, as a Chinese official reported,

---

[40] *Helongxian yamen dang'an*, Foreign Affairs, vol. 47, and *Jilin dongnanlu guanchashi gong-shudang*, vol. 68, 1914, Yanbian Archive; quoted in Jiang, *Jindai zhongchaori sanguo dui jiandao chaoxianren de zhengce yanjiu*, p. 186.

"demand nothing but lands they could cultivate."[41] Despite the repeated prohibition, illegal land transactions or rents never stopped.[42]

In 1915 the controversy between nationality and landholding suddenly intensified with the signing of the Sino-Japanese Treaty of Southern Manchuria and Eastern Mongolia. Japan denied that Koreans had the right to choose to become Chinese. It quoted the Chinese nationality law that one could be naturalized only by canceling the original nationality in accordance with the law in the country of origin. Since the Koreans "had no right" to denounce their original nationality, Japan insisted, they could not be recognized as Chinese nationals, no matter how long ago they had been naturalized. However, according to the Japanese nationality law itself, Japanese citizens canceled their nationality automatically when they chose another nationality. To this question, Japan's answer was that "the current Japanese nationality law did not apply to the Koreans." At the same time, the Japanese consulates in Manchuria refused to issue Japanese passports to the Koreans who resettled in Jilin or Fengtian.[43] In other words, although Japan asserted that all Koreans in Manchuria were "Japanese subjects," Japan neither considered the Koreans Japanese citizens nor allowed them to choose to become Chinese citizens.

Since diplomatic protest would be useless against such a deliberate provocation, the Chinese government decided to compromise. The Jilin provincial government proposed a negotiation strategy later adopted by the Foreign Ministry of the Beiyang government. It suggested China first hold the firm position that the 1909 Jiandao/Kantō Convention was still effective and that all the Koreans in Yanbian had the right to naturalize at will. If Japan rejected this argument, China would step back and suggest that all Koreans who had resettled before the new treaty in 1915 had the freedom to petition for naturalization. If Japan still disapproved of this, the bottom line was that the Koreans who had settled in Yanbian before the annexation (1910) had to be allowed to become Chinese nationals if they so chose.[44] According to this strategy, "being Chinese" was neither a matter of culture nor of geographic boundary but a matter of timing. The strategy faltered, however, because of Japan's colonial infiltration in Manchuria.

Another problem that troubled local Chinese officials was the constant land purchasing and leasing by the Koreans. According to the 1915

---

[41] Zhongguo bianjiang shidi yanjiu zhongxin, *Dongbei bianjiang dang'an xuanji*, vol. 43, p. 292.
[42] Jin, *Yanbian diqu chaoxianzu shehui de xingcheng yanjiu*, pp. 203–212.
[43] Zhongguo bianjiang shidi yanjiu zhongxin, *Dongbei bianjiang dang'an xuanji*, vol. 43, pp. 363–364.
[44] Ibid., pp. 450–458.

treaty, Japanese subjects (here, Koreans) had the right to buy or rent land for agricultural purposes in southern Manchuria. Assisted by the loans provided by Japanese financial institutions, lands owned or rented by the Koreans were rapidly expanded in Yanbian and other regions. Furthermore, in 1916 intelligence from the Chinese Consul-General in Korea showed that the Minhoe, the Korean People's Society, was planning to purchase a large expanse of paddy fields in Manchuria as a way to solicit more members. Deeply disturbed by this message, the Chinese officials in Fengtian and Jilin provinces secretly issued several orders to prevent arable land from being sold, mortgaged, or leased long term to Koreans. At the same time, they encouraged Chinese peasants to develop paddy fields as another method to counter the expansion of the Korean rice farmers.[45]

Under pressure from aggressive Japanese penetration, officials in Jilin and Fengtian debated whether to reform the overall policy towards the Manchurian Koreans. Both sides agreed that two interrelated issues, naturalization and the right of landholding, were the keys to sovereignty integration. Their opinions differed, however, over which should be the primary concern. Officials in Fengtian believed that the most urgent task was to solve the land problem. Lands owned by Koreans who were disqualified for naturalization should either be confiscated or converted to land for lease, whereas "persuading [the Koreans] to be naturalized," they said, "should be the last option." For the Fengtian officials, having "hundreds of thousands people with alien minds living in our borderland" was extremely dangerous. Their counterparts in Jilin disagreed. They pointed out that Korean immigrants in Yanbian numbered over 200,000. Forced nationalization or other changes in land policy would cause a huge diplomatic conflict. Besides, many Korean landowners were not naturalized because the process was too complex and time-consuming. The most urgent mission, then, was to "properly relax" the naturalization restrictions. Such a move must be gradual and flexible so as to avoid irritating Japan. "In sum," said the Jilin officials, "if one more Korean was naturalized, there will be one less dispute over land. If the [naturalization] procedure could be completed one day earlier, the danger of conflict will be remitted for one day." Zhang Zuolin, then the governor of the East Three Provinces, agreed with the Jilin officials and ordered their counterparts in Fengtian to be in line with Jilin on the immigrant issue.[46]

---

[45] Ibid., pp. 459–471; vol. 44, pp. 32–47.
[46] Ibid., vol. 43, pp. 291–320.

Zhang Zuolin's overall policy towards the Manchurian Koreans was complex, controversial, and rather ambiguous. While it was well aware that Japan had expelled most Koreans to Manchuria, the government was extremely cautious about the fact that Japan was using them as an instrument to colonize Manchuria. In addition, despite urging Koreans to be naturalized, even culturally assimilated, Zhang's government was afraid of extended Korean ownership over arable lands. Even though local officials tried every method to obstruct the expansion of the pro-Japanese Minhoe, at the same time they were on guard against anti-Japanese activities among the immigrants in order to avoid irritating Japan and causing diplomatic trouble.

A Japanese census in 1927 showed that, among 368,827 Koreans in Yanbian, 55,684 were naturalized Korean-Chinese. The ratio was slightly over 15 percent.[47] Although this was a significant portion, "being Chinese" was in general never easy for the Koreans. Especially in the 1910s and 1920s, they were regarded by local Chinese officials as neither "us" nor "the enemy" but a little bit of both.

Being Korean: Minjok Politics beyond Korea

The Koreans in Yanbian in the early twentieth century were generally categorized, by both China and Japan, along the lines of their political inclinations. In Chinese documents, they were often classified according to their stand in the Sino-Japanese geopolitical competition. As mentioned earlier, terms such as "pro-Chinese," "pro-Japanese," and "fence-sitters" were used to distinguish their subidentities. Japanese documents employed a similar logic and divided them according to their attitudes towards Japanese rule. Hence, "indocile Korean" became a common category, as opposed to the "(normal) Korean." Yet neither classification had much to do with how the Yanbian Koreans defined themselves. True, the political tension between China and Japan was the single most important factor determining the shape of identity politics in Yanbian. But the Korean immigrants did not simply ally with one side or the other. Participation in anti-Japanese activities, for instance, did not necessarily mean they were "pro-China." They would certainly have animosity towards China when the local government restrained their right to land-holding. Even among those who claimed to identify with China, what "China" meant was quite divergent in their minds.

---

[47] *Kantōmondai no keika to ijūsenjin*, pp. 65, 71.

Internal Conflict

On January 7, 1914, around 700 Korean peasants gathered at the Yanji County yamen.[48] They asked the local government to punish the leaders of the Kanminhoe (C. *Kenminhui*; Society of Cultivators), accusing them of charging membership fees and coercing Koreans to become naturalized Chinese. The protest was organized by a rival group, the Nongmugye (C. *Nongwuqi*; Association for Agricultural Affairs). The demonstration turned into a violent scuffle between the supporters of the two civil organizations. Chinese officials transferred 100 soldiers and 60 policemen to suppress the riot and arrested 200 protesters. In the following days the Nongmugye mobilized thousands of peasants from surrounding areas to Yanji, urging the government to release those arrested and chastise the Kanminhoe.[49] Under this pressure, the Yanji government discharged the protesters from prison and agreed to investigate the case.

The Kanminhoe argued that it had collected dues only from members who gave voluntarily. Although the Nongmugye failed to present sufficient evidence to support its accusation of coerced membership, the top official in Yanbian, Tao Bin, hoped to avoid further social turbulence by ordering the Kanminhoe to stop taking in fees. The Kanminhoe ignored his order. In the next two months the hostility between the groups turned white hot, each claiming that its members were under death threats from the other side. The Jilin government forced the two societies to disband immediately on the grounds that both were functioning as "self-governing" organizations (*zi zhi tuan ti*). By an order of President Yuan Shikai, all regional autonomous groups in China were suspended. The two pioneer civil groups of the Korean immigrants thus existed for only a short period before internal friction brought about their dissolution.

Although the nominal cause of this conflict was dues collection, the real controversy between the two groups centered on naturalization. The Kanminhoe advocated making Korean immigrants Chinese nationals, while the Nongmugye was against it. Surprisingly, perhaps, the rift on this matter had little to do with opposing attitudes towards Japan. It was not a struggle between a pro-Chinese and a pro-Japanese clique. Although the more radically anti-Japanese Kanminhoe often accused the Nongmugye of being "a running dog of the Japanese," neither group collaborated with the Japanese consulates. Not only did the Nongmugye see

---

[48] My narrative on the incident is based on Jiang, *Jindai zhongchaori sanguo dui jiandao chaoxianren de zhengce yanjiu*, pp. 193–238; Jin, *Yanbian diqu chaoxianzu shehui de xingcheng yanjiu*, pp. 147–168.
[49] "Qingyuanshu," Yanjixian jingcha shiwusou, Yanbian Archive.

China as the sole authority, but the local government tended to have conciliatory policies towards the Nongmugye, in sharp contrast to the manner in which it later treated the pro-Japanese Korean People's Society.

The feud between the Kanminhoe and the Nongmugye reflected the split view among the immigrant elites on how to be Korean in China. For the Kanminhoe, turning themselves into Chinese nationals was the only way for the Koreans to be free from Japanese rule. Led by intellectuals who adopted Western values and nationalist ideas (many of whom were Christian), the Kanminhoe welcomed the Chinese revolution and saw the newly founded republic as a progressive force that could truly protect the rights of Koreans.[50] It established several modern schools to advocate nationalist and modern education, and even suggested that the local government allow the Koreans to purchase land so that 10 percent of the property transaction fee would be invested in local education. As a governmental report concluded, the ultimate goal of the Kanminhoe was to "promote republican civil rights and to break away from the fetters of annexation."[51]

In contrast to the Kanminhoe, the Nongmugye was composed mainly of upper-class Confucian gentry who had long lived in Yanbian. From their point of view, to be Korean was to maintain the orthodox Confucian values and the Korean way of life. As conservatives living a relatively stable and wealthy life in China, they regarded reformist behaviors such as wearing new dress and promoting a new style of education as no less a threat than annexation. A Chinese report described the Nongmugye members: "Their apparel did not change, and their customs remained pure. When they saw a reformist who cut his hair and wore Western-style clothes, they would fight to resist."[52] To confront the Kanminhoe, they allied with the local branch of the Confucian Society (Kongjiaohui), a civil group dedicated to promote Confucianism as the "national religion." Not only did "being Korean" mean different things to the two rival groups, then, but their views of China were also widely divergent: one embraced "China" as a republic nation state, the other as an ideal Confucian civilization whose long-lost values were preserved only by the Koreans.

It would be easy to assume that, for the Yanbian Koreans who were trapped in the geopolitical contest between China and Japan, identity

---

[50] "Kenmin Jin Yueyuan qingyuanshu," no. J101-02-0905, Jilin Provincial Archive.
[51] "Wei chengfushi," February 11, 1914, Jilin Dongnanlu guanchashishu dang'an, Yanbian Archive; quoted in Jiang, *Jingdai zhongchaori sanguo dui jiandao chaoxianren de zhengce yanjiu*, p. 218.
[52] Ibid., p. 219.

politics was simply a matter of siding with one or the other country; they could either turn themselves into Chinese citizens or remain unnaturalized and in theory become Japanese subjects. However, the real situation was far more nuanced. The conflict between the Kanminhoe and the Nongmugye was not one between pro-China and pro-Japan groups but, rather, between reformists and conservatives. When "being Korean" was not a legal option for them, local Korean elites still had various alternatives to affirm their unique identity socially, politically, ethnically, and culturally. Moreover, this identity was itself in constant flux, and not all immigrants always agreed on it. To be or not to be naturalized, in certain contexts, was a way to constructively answer – rather than passively avoid – the tough question of how to be Korean in China.

The Network of Religion and Education

In the 1910s churches and schools remained as dynamic social networks among the Yanbian Koreans. At the same time that Catholicism and Protestantism were expanding, various other religions or quasi-religions indigenous to the Koreans also took root in the immigrant society. Compared to Buddhism, these newly arrived religions, both Western and indigenous, were more aggressive in intervening in sociopolitical life in Yanbian. As a result, they had more public appeal, social influence, and potential to mobilize. The Kanminhoe, for example, was developed on the basis of the local Christian circle, which also partially explains why it was so opposed by the Confucian gentry. The recently imported faiths were easily attached to or associated with various political ideologies and functioned as channels for the Koreans to consolidate their identities. Some religions, such as Catholicism and Protestantism, were the source of reformist knowledge and thoughts. Others, such as those that enshrined the Tan'gun, were colored by nationalist motivation. Many Korean independent activists were religious believers. The unfolding of indigenous religions – their establishment, differentiation, and derivation – was also tightly linked with local political ecology.

In January 1913 the Jilin provincial government received a petition from a group of Korean immigrants complaining that their churches in Yanji and Helong Counties had been shut down by the local authorities. "There are no fewer than hundreds of thousands of Korean expatriates in the East Three Provinces," stated the petition, "and they all rely on the might of your honorable country and are willing to entrust themselves to your protection." The purpose of establishing churches in Yanbian was to "promote education, enrich wisdom and virtue, so that people are instructed to be good. [We] have nothing to do with politics." Yet these

Koreans were now deprived of the freedom of religion because they had been framed by "evil people." The petitioners lamented: "[U]nder your gracious governance, [another] powerful country could hurt and expel us arbitrarily but you could do nothing about it. Not only does your gracious country lose the right of freedom, but it is not what our humble people expect: that we could rely on your comfort."

Although the petition provides no more detail about the incident, the provincial government's comment on the petition does shed light on the closing of the churches. It mentions the different Korean religions in Yanji, among them the Sich'ŏngyo ("Religion of Serving Heaven") and the Taejonggyo ("Great Ancestor Religion"), and goes on to say that members of the Sich'ŏngyo mostly "ingratiate themselves with Japan," serving as the eyes and ears of the Japanese consulates in Yanbian. In contrast, the Taejonggyo members were basically anti-Japanese. When the Sich'ŏngyo protested to the Japanese consulate about the actions of the Taejonggyo, the Japanese in turn complained to the Chinese government, accusing the Taejonggyo of "compelling people to join." Under this pressure, the Chinese government instructed local officials to "restrain them in a civilized manner."[53] The petition, therefore, must have been made by Taejonggyo members after the local Chinese government intervened.

Both Sich'ŏngyo and Taejonggyo emerged during the Japanese colonization of Korea. They belonged, respectively, to two rapidly expanding indigenous religious systems: the Tonghak (Eastern Learning) system, which developed from the Tonghak peasant movement, and the Tan'gun system, which revived the Tan'gun worship. The most influential religion in the Tan'gun system was the Taejonggyo, while in the Tonghak system the Ch'ŏndogyo ("Religion of the Heavenly Way") had the greatest reach.

On December 1, 1905, the third-generation patriarch of the Tonghak movement, Son Pyŏng-hŭi (1861–1922), decided to change the Tonghak into a purely religious organization. He renamed it Ch'ŏndogyo and announced that it was the orthodox inheritor of the Tonghak. Son did this for two reasons: to avoid Japanese persecution against the Tonghak political movement and to expel Yi Yong-gu and his Ilchinhoe followers from the Tonghak. To counter Son's action, Yi Yong-gu and other Ilchinhoe members in September 1906 founded Sich'ŏngyo, with Japanese support. Both Ch'ŏndogyo and Sich'ŏngyo claimed to be the legitimate

[53] "Hanqiao Lixisoudeng wei zai Yanji, Helong dengchu sheli jiaotang beifeng quzhu qingxing de binwen ji Jilinxingsheng de xunling," Jilin Provincial Archive, no. J101-02-0896.

successor of the Tonghak. Aside from polarized political ideologies, the two sects differed little in terms of religious doctrine.[54] After the annexation all civil organizations in Korea were disbanded. The Ilchinhoe survived only in its religious form. In Yanbian the Sich'ŏngyo thrived with the expansion of the Ilchinhoe. A Japanese investigation shows it had 7,500 adherents in Kantō during its heyday. When the Tumen boundary dispute was settled, however, its influence soon declined. By 1915 it had only 1,300 members, and most remained so in name only.[55]

The Taejonggyo was founded in 1909 by Na Ch'ŏl (1863–1916), an anti-Japanese activist, in Hansŏng. Originally called the Tan'gungyo ("Religion of the Tan'gun"), it called itself the oldest Korean religion and claimed that its progenitor was the Tan'gun himself. Na Ch'ŏl insisted that he had only "revived" (*chung'gwang*), as opposed to founded, the religion. As he told the story, Na Ch'ŏl began his revival after he was given a set of holy scriptures by an old man. Those scriptures, he claimed, had been rediscovered in a temple to the north of Mt. Paektu by the old man's teacher, who received a revelation from the Tan'gun. Taejonggyo reveres the Tan'gun as the god of the Korean people. Clearly a nationalist (*minjok*) belief, its theology nevertheless mingled the Trinitarianism of Christianity, the ethical principles of Confucianism, the practices of Taoism, and the historiography of Sin Ch'ae-ho. On the eve of the annexation this new religion attracted a great number of followers and grew rapidly. Fearing Japanese persecution, Na changed the religion's name to the Taejonggyo and moved its headquarters to Yanbian, China. Until 1946 Yanbian was the most important base of its preaching activities. The Taejonggyo never concealed its distinct political stand. As a critical force in the Korean independence movement, it had many nationalist converts, including intellectuals such as Sin Ch'ae-ho, Pak Ŭn-sik, Yi Sang-sŏl, and Yi Tong-nyŏng. In 1915 the Japanese Governor-General of Korea declared the Taejonggyo illegal.[56]

Aside from the Ch'ŏndogyo, Sich'ŏngyo, and Taejonggyo, Yanbian also accommodated other new indigenous (quasi-)religions, such as the Ch'ŏnglimgyo, Cheugyo, and Suungyo of the Tonghak system and the Tan'gungyo of the Tan'gun system. These (quasi-)religions were less influential than the first three, and, in terms of number of churches, Protestantism and Catholicism outdid them all. An official investigation by the Governor-General of Korea shows that in 1915 there were 268

[54] Kim Tŭk-hwang, *Hanguo zongjiaoshi*, trans. Liu Xuefeng (Beijing: Shehui kexue wenxian chubanshe, 1992), pp. 338–354.
[55] Chōsen sōtokufu, "Kokkyō chihō shisatsu fukumeisho," in Yuk Nak-hyŏn, *Kando yŏngyukwŏn kwan'gye charyojip* (Seoul: Paeksan Munhwa, 1993), vol. 1, p. 283.
[56] Kim To-jong and Liu Xuefeng, "Hanguo dazongjiao," *Dangdai Hanguo*, Spring issue (1999), pp. 70–73; Kim Tŭk-hwang, *Hanguo zongjiaoshi*, pp. 55–59.

Table 3 *Numbers of adherents of religious groups in "Kantō" (1917)*

	Yanji County	Helong County	Wangqing County	Total
Sich'ŏngyo	1,232	466	36	1,714
Catholicism	3,713	837		4,550
Protestantism	2,383	1,356	197	3,936
Ch'ŏndogyo	460			460
Taejonggyo	602		85	687
Buddhism	51			51

Sources: Chōsengun Shireibu, "*Kantō oyobi Konshun*" (Chōsengun Shireibu, 1921), p. 39; Tōyō Takushoku Kabushiki Kaisha, *Kantō Jijō*, pp. 854–874.

Catholic churches, 429 Protestant churches, 165 Taejonggyo churches, and 108 Ch'ŏndogyo churches in the Kantō area (excluding Hunchun County).[57] Another census, conducted by the Japanese in 1917, arguably exaggerated the scale of the Sich'ŏngyo but gives an idea of the numbers of believers in Kantō (see Table 3).

Going back to the petition of 1913, it is obvious that the Taejonggyo followers told the Jilin provincial government only half the truth in saying their purpose was purely education. Certainly, one of the most important activities of not only the Taejonggyo but all churches was running schools. However, in 1910s Yanbian, education itself was hardly exempt from intense political rivalry. This was the case both for the public schools established by the Chinese and Japanese governments and for most private schools funded by religious groups.

Many scholars have studied the emergence of modern education in Yanbian.[58] Most regard early schooling in the Korean immigrant community as the cradle of "anti-Japanese nationalism." A survey done by the Ministry of Education of Manchukuo in 1934 frankly admitted that "the first step of education in Kantō was anti-Japanese nationalism; the educational institutes established later, too, were largely nationalistic."[59]

---

[57] Chōsen sōtokufu, "Kokkyō chihō shisatsu fukumeisho," pp. 284–285.
[58] See Piao Kuican, *Yanbian Chaoxian zu jiao yu shi gao* (Changchun: Jilin jiaoyu chubanshe, 1989); Tsukinoki Mizuo, "Chūgoku kindai kyōiku no hassei to shijuku," and "Chūgoku kantō niokeru chōsenzoku gakkō no tenkai," *Higashi ajia kenkyū* (1999), no. 24, pp. 29–40, no. 25, pp. 73–85; Takenaka Ken'ichi, *Manshū ni okeru kyōiku no kisoteki kenkyū*, vol. 5 (Tokyo: Kashiwashobō, 2000); Piao Jinhai, "20 segi ch'o Kando Chosŏnin minjok kyoyuk undongŭi chŏngaewa Chunggukŭi tae Chosŏnin kyoyukchŏngch'aek," *Han'guk kŭnhyŏndaesa yŏn'gu*, vol. 48 (2009), pp. 70–114.
[59] Manchoukuo wen jiao bu, xue wu si, *Manshūkoku shōsū minzoku kyōiku jijō* (Sinkyō: Bun kyōbu Gakumushi, 1934), p. 24.

Only recently have scholars been rethinking the static nationalist model and paying more attention to the impetus of religions, especially Protestantism, in promoting immigrant education.[60] To be fair, Korean nationalism, religion, and education were so intertwined in the 1900s and 1910s that they could hardly be separated from one another.

As shown in Chapter 3, one of the first Korean private schools in the Tumen northern bank, the Sŏjŏn (C. Ruidian) Academy, was founded by nationalist Yi Sang-sŏl with the help of local Korean Christians. After the Jiandao/Kantō Convention the Japanese influence temporarily waned as the pro-Japanese Ilchinhoe/Sich'ŏngyo schools were largely closed down. At the same time, numerous new schools, mostly private, were established. Local Christians and nationalists such as Kim Yak-yŏn and Yi Tong-ch'un organized the Education Society of Cultivators (K. Kanmin Kyoyukhoe), the predecessor of the Kanminhoe, in 1910. It worked closely with the Chinese government and provided financial and intellectual support for dozens of Korean private schools.[61] Moreover, to solidify its educational sovereignty, the Chinese government made some Korean private schools public. Many of them had previously been associated with churches; thus, even some public schools run by the state had religious backgrounds. A Japanese investigation in 1915 revealed the overwhelming role that religion played in the local schooling enterprise: of the twelve public schools, five were affiliated with Protestantism and one with Catholicism. Among the seventy-eight Korean private schools, forty-seven were established by religious groups (thirty-eight Protestant, four Catholic, one cofounded by the two churches, two Ch'ŏndogyo, and two Taejonggyo).[62]

The year 1915 marked a watershed for Korean education in Yanbian. After signing the Treaty of Southern Manchuria and Eastern Mongolia, both Japan and China took radical steps to intervene in local schools. The Japanese Governor-General in Korea, through the Minhoe, expanded the Japanese schooling network in Yanbian and subsidized some Korean private schools. In return, these schools were required to adopt the same curriculum in colonial Korea. Some religious schools with poor management were taken over by the Japanese system. With attractive subsidies and scholarships, the number of schools run or funded by Japan grew rapidly. Up to 1918 Japan had controlled about 17 percent of the total schools in Kantō. Meanwhile, the Chinese local government issued "The Unified

---

[60] For example, see Yu, *Zhongguo guomin guojia gouzhu yu guomin tonghe zhi licheng*, p. 424.
[61] JACAR, ref. B03030257300, "Kantō tzaijū senjin kiyokuni kika oyo chihatsu ekifuku ni kantsuruken hōkoku," pp. 93–97, Chōsen henkyō Kiyokuni ryōdo-nai kyojūno Chōsenjinni taisuru kiyokuni seifuno kaijū seisaku kankei zassan.
[62] Chōsen sōtokufu, "Kokkyō chihō shisatsu fukumeisho," pp. 292–300.

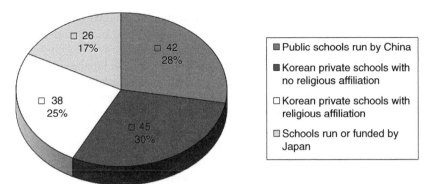

Figure 3 Public and private schools in Kantō (1918)
Source: Tōyō Takushoku Kabushiki Kaisha, *"Kantō jijō,"* pp. 816–845.

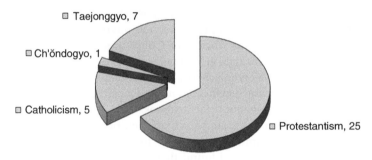

Figure 4 Religion-affiliated schools in Kantō (1918)
Source: Tōyō Takushoku Kabushiki Kaisha, *"Kantō jijō,"* pp. 816–845.

Measurements for Cultivators' Education" ("Huayi kenmin jiaoyu banfa"),
which requested all schools to consolidate Chinese language studies, adopt
the Chinese curriculum, and gradually reduce religious influence. The
Chinese government, like its Japanese rival, lured private schools by providing education allowances. Figures 3 and 4 show the situation in 1918.

  Figure 3 demonstrates that, although the Chinese public school system and the Japanese school system expanded remarkably in terms of
numbers, there were still more Korean private schools in Kantō. Among
the private schools, those with religious affiliations made up a significant
portion. Figure 4 reveals the main religious groups that backed those
schools. The Japanese investigators made an observation that points out
the nuanced interactions among religion, education, and nationalism
in Yanbian: "Of the religions popular among the Koreans, these three

religions, Catholicism, Protestantism, and the Taejonggyo, for the convenience of their preaching, invested their main efforts in education and attempted to advocate dangerous thoughts."[63]

Moreover, aside from the twenty-six schools in the Japanese system, the other schools were adopting the Chinese curriculum, which, once it had been negotiated and compromised, was more favorable to the local Korean teachers and students for several reasons. Korean language training, for one, was strengthened. Also, although at least six hours per week of Chinese language courses were mandatory, the Korean language course – called "national language" (K. *kugŏ*) – had much more weight in the curriculum. Textbooks originally in Chinese were also translated and taught in Korean.[64] This was in contrast to the Japanese system, which posited Japanese as the "national language" and reduced the Korean and Chinese training to only six hours per week for the first and second grade and even less in higher grades.[65] A more significant difference was that the Japanese system largely excluded classes on Korean history and geography in the primary schools, whereas in Yanbian all private schools offered these courses. Organized through the Education Society of Cultivators, textbooks were compiled by nationalist intellectuals in Yanbian, notably Kye Pong-u, and were uniformly used by all Korean schools in the Chinese system before 1920. Not surprisingly, an anti-Japanese tone and nostalgia for the lost homeland were marked throughout these textbooks.

In December 1916 Suwa Hikarutama, a staff member of the Japanese consulate in Toudaogou, submitted a report to the foreign minister. During a local investigation he had found that a primary school (subsidized by the Chinese government) was using an "anti-Japanese textbook" in its "moral cultivation" (K. *susin*; C. *xiushen*) classes. He made a copy of the book and submitted a translation along with his report.[66] Titled "Never Forget Our Vendetta" ("Osubulmang"), the book traced the history of Japanese aggression all the way back to the Silla period and painstakingly listed the invasions, suppressions, and humiliations Korea had suffered at the hands of the Japanese in recent years. The title straightforwardly expressed the message to "never forget" what Japan had done to Korea. The Japanese seemed unaware that the author was Kye Pong-u, one of the most renowned "indocile Koreans" under their surveillance.[67]

---

[63] Tōyō Takushoku Kabushiki Kaisha, "*Kantō jijō*," p. 851.
[64] Ibid., p. 849.
[65] Yu, *Zhongguo guominguojia*, p. 403.
[66] JACAR, "Chōsen henkyō Kiyokuni ryōdo-nai kyojūno Chōsenjinni taisuru kiyokuni seifuno kaijū seisaku kankei zassan," ref. B03030261100.
[67] Kim Dae-Yong, "Kye Pong-u ŭi minjogundong ch'ogi hwaltong kwa 'Osubumang' ŭi pyŏnch'an'," *Han'guk Sasang kwa Munhwa*, vol. 68 (2013), pp. 145–174.

Like many other nationalist educators, Kye was a Christian and a former journalist. He wrote the book in Kando in 1912 and continued compiling many other school books aimed at arousing nationalist consciousness among young Koreans. One of his most influential textbooks, *The Reader of National Language* (*Kugŏ tokpon*), had this paragraph:

Our state [*kuk*] is composed of 20 million people and 3,000 *ri* of land. Although since the time of our ancestors up to our own we have always lived on this land, Japan took it away in the [Tan'gun's] year of Four Thousand Two Hundred and Forty-Three. Now that we have become a stateless people, in what way could we love our state? Both 20 million people and 3,000 *ri* still exist; therefore, loving our state is like loving our body. We could not forget the sovereignty we lost, just as we could not stop remembering our parents who passed away. Whether working or studying, we can only revive our state again if we do not abandon this spirit.[68]

At least among nationalist elites, their identity as a "stateless people" came from the deepest hearts and minds of the Yanbian Koreans. This identity was inculcated in school upon Korean young men and women who found themselves stuck between Japan and China. The state they identified with was defined by neither nationality law nor certificate of naturalization but the integration of land and people. This kind of integration was in fact new in Korean history; it no longer indicated the legitimacy of dynastic governance but appealed to the continuity of the common spatiotemporal experience (however fictional) of all Korean people (*minjok*). When land and people were separated, and nation (*minjok*) and state torn apart, Yanbian provided these "stateless people" a space to construct their "imagined community." Thus, from the standpoint of education alone, Yanbian in the 1910s was a place perhaps more "Korean" than Korea itself.

The March First and March Thirteenth Movements

Before 1920 the joint frontier area of Yanbian, northeastern Korea, and Primorsky Russia had already formed a base for the Korean resistance movement. Religious leaders, independent activists, and militia fighters frequently contacted each other and tried to consolidate their forces. Their longing for an independent Korea was greatly encouraged by both the Bolshevik revolution in Russia and the end of World War I in Europe. As most studies point out, the self-determination principle that emerged from the Russian Revolution and the "Fourteen Points" announced by

---

[68] Quoted in Yu, *Zhongguo guominguojia*, p. 231.

US president Woodrow Wilson inspired the Korean independence move-ment by the end of the 1910s. Korean expatriates began to discuss a joint anti-Japanese action, including a plan to send delegates to the Paris Peace Conference. In early 1918 several key members of the Taejonggyo, led by patriarch Kim Kyo-hŏn and Sŏ Il, organized a resistance group in Yanbian. They employed a typical Taejonggyo term, *chung'gwang* ("revival"), to name the group: the Chung'gwangdan (or Revival Association). On November 13 thirty-nine highly influential expatriate Korean activists signed a Korean independence declaration initiated by the Chung'gwangdan members in Manchuria.[69] The declaration was drafted by Cho So-ang, later the for-eign minister of the provisional government of the Republic of Korea. Among the signers were not only Taejonggyo members such as Kim Kyo-hŏn, Sŏ Il, Sin Ch'ae-ho, and Pak Ŭn-sik but also Righteous Army leaders such as Yi Pŏm-yun (who had invaded "Kando" in 1904) and Christians such as An Ch'ang-ho and Yi Sŭng-man (generally known as Syngman Rhee, later the first president of South Korea).[70] This docu-ment, later known as the Mu-u Declaration of Independence (after the name of the year in the Stems-and-Branches calendar), became the first of a series of proclamations of Korean independence.

In Tokyo, Korean students gathered at the Korean YMCA on January 6, 1919, and decided to petition for the independence of Korea on February 8. Possibly inspired by the Mu-u Declaration, the students issued a similar announcement, known as the February 8th Declaration of Independence. The main drafter of this document was Yi Kwang-su, arguably one of the most controversial figures in Korean modern his-tory. (Yi was then a progressive independent activist converted from Ilchinhoe; he would later become a progenitor of modern Korean litera-ture as well as a notorious collaborator.)

Both declarations foreshadowed the coming of a more radical nation-alist storm. On January 22 the Japanese announced that the abdicated emperor Kojong was dead. Rumors soon spread that he had been poi-soned by his Japanese guards. Across the Korean boundary, independent activists prepared to take this opportunity to launch a large-scale anti-Japanese demonstration. Religious leaders were at the vanguard of the movement. During a Christian church service on January 25 in Yanbian,

[69] "November 13, 1918," in *Korean History Database*, Kuksa P'yŏnch'an Wiwŏnhoe, http://db.history.go.kr/url.jsp?ID=tc_md_1918_11_13_0010, accessed February 17, 2013.

[70] Yu Sŏk-chae, "Uri minjok ch'ŏt tongnipsŏnŏnsŏ wŏnbun palkyŏn," *The Chosunilbo*, Feb-ruary 14, 2009, http://news.chosun.com/site/data/html_dir/2009/02/13/2009021300951.html, Chosun.com, accessed February 17, 2013.

more than thirty delegates were selected to lead the local campaign. They decided that all churches and organizations should be consolidated in this movement. Some delegates went to Primorsky to unify the action on the Russian side. Meanwhile, two teachers secretly returned to Korea to coordinate with the action in Seoul. In early February news arrived that the Ch'ŏndogyo and Christian leaders in Seoul were planning a protest on March 1st. Teachers and students in Yanbian Korean schools, both private and public, soon organized their own mass demonstration.[71]

One Protestant school, the Mingdong (K. Myŏngdong) Academy, played a pivotal role in this event.[72] Founded in 1908 by the Confucian scholar Kim Yak-yŏng (1868–1942), Mingdong was another pioneer nationalist school in the region. Kim promoted modern curriculums and divided the academy into primary and secondary sections. In order to persuade a Christian educator to join, Kim agreed to add a Bible class to the curriculum and even converted to Protestantism. Around the same time he organized the Education Society of Cultivators, and, later, became the head of the Kanminhoe. The academy often invited nationalist scholars (including Chang Chi-yŏn) as lecturers, attracting students not only from Manchuria but also from northern Korea and Primorsky.

In February 1919 a new Korean declaration of independence, drafted by Ch'oe Nam-sŏn, was sent to the Mingdong Academy under the cover of commercial goods. Teachers and students at Mingdong mimeographed the document and sent copies all over Yanbian. Meanwhile, in the peninsula, tens of thousands of copies of the declaration were distributed around the country through the Ch'ŏndogyo and Christian channels.

On March 1 in Seoul, fifteen Ch'ŏngdogyo members (including Son Pyŏng-hŭi), sixteen Protestant preachers, and two Buddhist monks gathered at the city center and read the declaration. As planned, the nonviolent demonstration triggered a countrywide mass protest against Japanese rule in Korea. The colonial government reacted with an iron fist, transferring military forces to suppress the protests. According to Japanese sources, the total death toll was over 500; according to Korean sources, it reached more than 7,500.[73]

Thereafter, Japan not only clamped down its control of Korea but also became more vigilant of the situation in Yanbian. On March 10 the Japanese Consul-General of Kantō asked the Chinese Yanji government

[71] Yang et al., *Zhongguo chaoxianzu geming douzheng shi*, pp. 135–136.
[72] Li Hongjun, "Fanri minzu jiaoyu de yaolan: mingdong xuexixao," Zhengxie Longjing weiyuanhui, eds., *Longjing wenshi ziliao*, vol. 2 (Longjing: Longjing xian weiyuanhui wenshi ziliao yanjiu weiyuanhui, 1988), pp. 87–92.
[73] Bruce Cumings, *Korea's Place in the Sun: A Modern History* (New York: W. W. Norton, 2005), pp. 154–155.

to quash any anti-Japanese actions brewing among Korean immigrants. If China failed to do so, the Consul-General threatened, Japan would send troops to "provide the stability" for the region. Under pressure, the prefect of Yanji issued a public bulletin to prohibit "any behavior that diminishes the Sino-Japanese relationship" and persuaded Korean leaders to abandon plans to protest. On March 12 the government transferred more than forty soldiers, led by infantry commander Meng Fude, to Longjing in preparation for the mass demonstration.

The Koreans, however, ignored the warning. In the early morning of March 13 around 20,000 Koreans gathered at Longjing from nearby regions, including students and teachers from the Mingdong and other schools. At noon a local Catholic church tolled its bell, the signal to begin the rally. Leaders of the demonstration read the declaration of independence and made speeches, and the crowd paraded towards the Japanese general consulate, waving the *taegukgi* flag and shouting angry slogans.[74] As the demonstrators approached the consulate, they were blocked by Chinese soldiers. The two sides were drawn into physical confrontation. Meng Fude ordered his men to shoot. In the end seventeen people were killed, forty-eight injured, and ninety-four arrested. The slaughter, however, did not stop the movement. Until the end of April forty-seven more parades and demonstrations took place in Yanbian.

Not only Koreans but also Chinese took part in the protests.[75] The flames of the Korean anti-Japanese sentiment were fanned by another great mass movement in another capital: the May Fourth Movement in Beijing. The call to return the sovereignty of Shandong, the native province of the majority Chinese migrants in Manchuria, aroused enormous sympathy among the Chinese in Yanbian. Chinese nationalists saw no obstacle to joining hands with Korean nationalists to fight their common enemy.

In this round of mass campaigns, students and the bourgeois elites decided on a more substantial form of struggle: boycotting Japanese goods. But not all activists had faith in peaceful methods. After the events of March 1st and March 13th, many came to believe that neither demonstrations nor boycotts could achieve their goals; the only effective strategy was armed resistance. Quite a few militias were organized in Yanbian in 1919, their members ranging from several hundred to several thousand. Acquiring supplies and ammunitions from the Korean communities in Yanbian and Russia, they shuttled across the border to attack Japanese troops and police. Along with the remnants of the Righteous

---

[74] Yanbian chaoxianzu zizhizhou dang'anguan, eds., *Sanyisan fanri yundong*, 1985.
[75] Yang et al., *Zhongguo chaoxianzu geming douzheng shi*, pp. 136–137.

Army in Primorsky, they were called by a joint name: the Independent Army (Tongnipkun). A Chinese witness in 1920 wrote: "This army occupies mountains as defense, is equipped with sufficient weapons, and is solidly united."[76] In the following decades these anti-Japanese guerrillas developed into a major part of the Korean nationalist movement in Manchuria.

Few scholars doubt the historic significance of the March First Movement. It was the same sort of turning point in Korean history as was the May Fourth Movement in China. Less widely acknowledged is the dynamic transborder linkage between March 1 in Seoul and March 13 in Yanbian. One well-compiled anthology, for example, says that "preparation for the [March 1] demonstration involved only a handful of activists and a surprisingly short period of time."[77] This is certainly not the most accurate description if we take into account the larger picture of the Korean resistant movement. Indeed, the March First Movement launched an age of Korean nationalism, an age labeled "modern." Perhaps it is fair to say that this "modern" age actually began and was fomented in Yanbian, beyond the Korean boundary, to the north of the Tumen River.

---

[76] Yanbian chaoxianzu zizhizhou dang'anguan, ed., *Chaoxian dulijun zai yanbian jiqi fujin huodong shiliao* (1985).

[77] Yŏng-ho Ch'oe, Peter H. Lee, and W. Theodore de Bary, eds., *Sources of Korean Tradition*, vol. 2: *From the Sixteenth to the Twentieth Centuries* (New York: Columbia University Press, 2000), p. 335.

Conclusion
Our Land, Our People

The Tumen River demarcation left indelible traces on the processes of nation and state transitions in East Asia. Its occurrence, negotiation, transfiguration, and (temporal) resolution were tightly woven into a complex network of geopolitics, economy, and culture, within which the history of twentieth-century East Asia unfolded. In turn, the making of border and people in Yanbian contributed remarkably to the construction of this multilateral and multilayered network. To illustrate this point, let us briefly examine the careers and orbits of some of the main figures of the demarcation. These individuals provide a sketch of how a local story organically connects to a larger picture of regional history.

After negotiating the border dispute with the Qing in 1885 and 1887, Yi Chung-ha, the leading Korean delegate, was assigned to government positions at the central and provincial levels. He displayed excellent administrative and diplomatic skills during the Tonghak Rebellion, the Sino-Japanese War, and the Russo-Japanese War. Despite serving his country well, Yi resigned when Japan annexed Korea in 1910, retreating into farming and reading. When Tokyo issued him a medal to commemorate the annexation, he resolutely rejected it.[1] Yi died in 1917.

Wu Luzhen, who helped to solidify the Yanji frontier against Japan, later became the military commander of one of the most elite corps of the Qing. When the Wuchang uprising broke out in his native province of Hubei in October 1911, Wu, who was stationing his army in northern China, plotted an uprising to echo the revolution. Unfortunately, the plan was leaked. On November 17, under the secret order of Yuan Shikai, Wu was assassinated at the age of 31.[2] His life ended in almost the same way as that of his comrade Song Jiaoren two years later. Today Wu is widely remembered as a revolutionary martyr.

Xu Shichang, the viceroy of the East Three Provinces during the frontier dispute, returned to Beijing in 1909. When the Qing finally reformed

---

[1] Yi Pŏm-se, "Sŏn kobi haengsang."
[2] Qian, "Wu Luzhen zhuan."

the administrative system, replacing the Grand Council with the first Western-style Cabinet in China, Xu was one of only four Han ministers in this Manchu-dominated "royal Cabinet." After the abdication of the Qing emperor he became first the premier of the Yuan Shikai government, then in 1918 the president of the Republic of China. It was during his presidency that the May Fourth Movement took place. Failing to reconcile the civil wars among the Beiyang warlords, Xu resigned and withdrew from politics in 1920. In 1937 Japan occupied north China and tried to lure Xu to join the puppet government. Xu declined and died two years later.[3]

Saitō Suejirō, the head of the Kantō Branch, resumed his service in the Imperial Army after the demarcation. Promoted to a lieutenant general, he took office as commander of the Japanese China Garrison Army in 1915. Later he worked in the Japanese legation in China as a military attaché. During the Allied intervention in the Russian Civil War (1918–1922) Saitō, then the commander of the 11th Division, stationed his troops in Vladivostok. When the Allied troops withdrew, in 1920, Japan alone continued supporting the White movement against the Bolsheviks, until 1924. Saitō died of illness in Vladivostok in 1923.[4]

The Tumen River demarcation completely changed the career path of Shinoda Jisaku, the legal advisor and director of general affairs of the Kantō Branch. Although he published several works on international law, he worked mainly as a colonial bureaucrat in Korea for the rest of his life. In the 1920s and 1930s he served as the minister of the Korean royal household (J. Riōshiki, K. Iwangchik), supervising the everyday lives of members of the (former) Chosŏn royal family. While in this position he presided over the compilation of the last two Veritable Records of The Annals of the Chosŏn Dynasty: that of Kojong (Kojong Sillok) and Sunjong (Sunjong Sillok). Contemporary Korean scholars generally criticize these two volumes as being heavily tarnished by Japanese censorship and distortion.[5] From 1940 to 1944 Shinoda was appointed as the ninth principal of Keijō Imperial University, a predecessor of today's Seoul National University and one of only two imperial universities in the Japanese colonies.[6] During this period he was awarded the

---

[3] Jing Min, *Xu Shichang* (Taipei: Wenhai chubanshe, 1967).
[4] Kuzū, *Tōa senkaku shishi kiden*, vol. 3, p. 626.
[5] See, for example, Kang Jae-eun, *The Land of Scholars: Two Thousand Years of Korean Confucianism*, trans. Suzanne Lee (Paramus, NJ: Homa & Seka Books, 2005), p. 218; Chang Yong-suk, "Iwangji ue 'Kojong Sunjong sillok' pyŏnch'an sayŏp kwa kŭ silsang," *Sahak yŏn'gu*, no. 116 (2014), pp. 105–142.
[6] The other was Taihoku Imperial University, the predecessor of today's National Taiwan University.

Grand Cordon of the Order of the Rising Sun, a distinguished honor for his service in Korea.[7]

Through these lives, salient historical themes of the nineteenth and twentieth centuries in East Asia – the Sino-Japanese conflicts, the Russo-Japanese feud, the prolonged Chinese revolution, and Japanese colonialism and imperialism – were linked and integrated. The greater historical dramas rehearsed themselves on the local stage of the Tumen frontier. China, for example, suffered a painful metamorphosis from Celestial Empire to vulnerable member of the international system. The Tumen region witnessed the unremitting efforts of the Koreans, who became a stateless people in the first half of the twentieth century, to find their "place in the sun." For Japan, the dual task of joining the club of civilized nations and protecting Asia from Western colonization constituted a fundamental dilemma in its pursuit of modernity. This dilemma could be resolved only by consistent colonial expansion in the region. The making of the Japanese "Kantō" to a large degree predicted the Japanese imperialist dream of a "co-prosperous" Asia, which was both finalized and failed in the 1940s. Referring to Japan's attempt to build a multiethnic state, Manchukuo, in Manchuria in the 1930s and 1940s, Prasenjit Duara suggests that Manchukuo "served as a laboratory" that had profound influence in the formation of "Japanese modernity."[8] Using the same metaphor, it could be argued that the Tumen River demarcation was an experiment that preceded both Manchukuo and East Asian modernity.

The Loss of the Mukedeng Stele and the Transformation of Manchuria

The Mukedeng stele standing on the Sino-Korean boundary was stolen in July 1931. Who took it, why it was taken, where it went, and whether it was destroyed is unknown. Less than two months later the Japanese Kwantung Army fabricated the Mukden incident that led to Japan's invasion and occupation of Manchuria. The next year Japan set up Manchukuo (1932–1945) and installed the last Qing emperor, Pu Yi, as the head of this puppet state. In 1934 the Manchukuo government established ten provinces. One of them was Jiandao, composed of the five Korean-majority counties (Yanji, Helong, Wangqing, Hunchun,

---

[7] Arima Manabu, Matsubara Takatoshi, and Takano Shinji, "Shinoda Jisaku Bunsho," *Kankoku kenkyū sentā nenpō*, vol. 8, no. 3 (2008), pp. 87–116.

[8] Prasenjit Duara, *Sovereignty and Authenticity: Manchukuo and the East Asian Modern* (Lanham, MD: Rowman & Littlefield, 2003), p. 250.

and Antu) in the Tumen River region. Aside from the first governor (Cai Yunsheng, a Manchu), all the governors of this province were either Korean or Japanese.[9] This was the only period that the Chinese term *Jiandao* was applied to an official administrative district. The disappearance of the Mukedeng stele in 1931 implied that the border was now essentially null. Korea and Manchuria were integrated under the domination of Japanese imperialism and capitalism.

Following the voiding of the boundary, the Korean population increased dramatically in Manchuria, especially in Yanbian. In the fifteen years before 1931 the average growth of the Korean population in Yanbian was 13,000 per year, already a rather astonishing number. Yet after 1931 the number exploded to roughly 30,000 per year. By 1942 Yanbian was home to more than 634,000 Koreans.[10]

Not all of them arrived of their own accord. In the mid-1930s Japan endorsed a national policy to move Japanese and Korean populations to Manchuria. In 1935 the government of Manchukuo and the South Manchuria Railway, along with some financial conglomerates, established the Manchuria Colonization Corporation. The MCC was in charge of an ambitious plan to recruit and settle 5 million Japanese agricultural emigrants in Manchuria over fifteen years. Meanwhile, the Governor-General of Korea and Manchukuo cofounded the Manchuria and Korea Colonization Company in order to move 150,000 Korean households to Manchuria, also over fifteen years. Systematically resettling Koreans to Manchuria was part of the overall strategy for imperial colonization. As Japan saw it, Korea and Manchuria were like two provinces of the empire, divided by a provincial border rather than a state boundary. From 1936 to 1943 tens of thousands Korean peasants were moved into "collective hamlets" in Manchuria. Among them, more than 29,700 settled in eighty-six collective hamlets in Jiandao province.[11]

In 1923 Russia closed the free port of Vladivostok and blockaded the border with Manchuria, leaving Japan the only foreign trade partner to Yanbian.[12] Starting in the 1930s the volume of foreign trade in Yanbian/Jiandao skyrocketed with the Japanese monopoly. Agricultural products and timber in Yanbian were transported to Japan through Korea, in exchange for Japanese industrial products. Foreign trade in Jiandao province was always in adverse balance, in contrast to the situation

---

[9] Yanbian chaoxianzu zizhizhou dang'anguan, ed., *Wei Jiandaosheng gaikuang*, p. 10.
[10] Ibid., p. 5. Aside from the Koreans, there were nearly 202,000 Chinese (including Han and Manchu) and 24,000 Japanese.
[11] Ibid., p. 33.
[12] Hunchunshi difangzhi bianzuan weiyuanhui, *Hunchun shizhi* (Chuangchun: Jilin renmin chubanshe, 2000), p. 460.

that prevailed in the rest of Manchukuo. With the border wide open, Yanbian – and Manchuria – joined the Japanese imperial capitalist system seamlessly.

In the first half of the twentieth century multiple governments practiced various forms of statecraft in Manchuria. The Qing, Russia, Japan, Beiyang, and Manchukuo governments all facilitated the transition of this land from a frontier to a hinterland. Driven by the accelerated demands of war, during the Japanese occupation the wild frontier was simultaneously agriculturalized and industrialized, though this colonial economic growth was remarkably unbalanced.[13] As a center of wartime development, Manchuria absorbed primary sources and labors from north China, Mongolia, and Korea. By the end of World War II it was one of the most vibrant and "modernized" regions in East Asia in terms of the value of industrial output, the commercialization of agriculture, the density of railways, and urban construction.

The Identity of the Korean Chinese

The Koreans in Manchuria were a group of transboundary people, literally and figuratively. After the March 13th movement, this community was riven by the forces of imperialism, colonialism, nationalism, and international communism simultaneously. In October 1920 around 400 bandits attacked Hunchun for the second time that year. They ransacked the city, looted, kidnapped hundreds of hostages, and burned the Japanese consulate. Japan insisted the riot was coordinated by "indocile Koreans," "radical Russians" (the Japanese term for Bolsheviks), and "Chinese horse bandits," although neither the Chinese official investigation nor testimonies of the hostages supported the assertion that Koreans participated in the plunder.[14] Nevertheless, Japan transferred armies from Korea, Vladivostok, and the Kwantung Territory to Kantō. With the collaboration of Zhang Zuolin government's troops, from October 1920 to January 1921 Japanese soldiers raided local villages, slaughtering more than 3,000 Koreans, including teachers, students, and many

---

[13] See Louise Young, *Japan's Total Empire: Manchuria and the Culture of Wartime Imperialism* (Berkeley, CA: University of California Press, 1998); Yu and Yi, *Jiandai dongbei nongyelishi de lishibianqian*.

[14] However, some members from the Independent Army took advantage of the situation to rescue dozens of anti-Japanese activists from the Japanese consul's prison. The Chinese materials on this event include Yanbian chaoxianzu zizhizhou dang'anguan, ed., *Hunchun shijian "Gengchennian taofa"* (1985); Cui Xisheng, "Hunchun shijian," in Zhengxie Hunchun wenshi weiyuanhui, ed., *Hunchun wenshi ziliao*, vol. 2 (Hunchun: Hunchun renmin chubanshe), pp. 55–70. The Japanese reports on the incident are: JACAR, "Konshun jiken ni tsute," ref. C06031229300.

women and children, as well as hundreds of Chinese. Japan followed up with a crackdown on the independence movements in Yanbian. Most guerrilla fighters had to flee to Russia.[15]

In the 1920s the political divergence between Zhang Zuolin and Japan intensified. Zhang, tired of being manipulated by Japan, tried to impede Japanese colonial attempts by launching his own state-building projects. Seeing Manchurian Koreans as Japan's colonial tools, Zhang altered his previously conciliatory policy and instead restricted their rights of both naturalization and landownership. Many Korean landlords in Manchuria (except in Yanbian) were deprived of their land;[16] qualified Koreans were denied naturalization; some Korean dwellers were forced to resettle or repatriate. The tension intensified when Japan assassinated Zhang in 1928, which induced his heir, Zhang Xueliang, to join Chiang Kai-shek's Nationalist government. Within this context, the infamous Wanbaoshan incident ignited a conflict between Chinese and Korean farmers. In 1931 a Chinese broker illegally subleased paddy fields in Wanbaoshan, a village near Changchun, to a group of Korean peasants recruited from elsewhere in Manchuria. A long ditch the Koreans dug to irrigate their fields triggered a dispute with local Chinese farmers. Hundreds of Chinese tried to stop the irrigation project, while the Japanese consulate sent a police force to "protect" the Koreans. The Japanese-controlled media in Korea played up this confrontation, which caused no casualties, as a Chinese massacre of Koreans and stirred up anti-Chinese sentiment. Several anti-Chinese riots broke out in Inchoen, Pyongyang, and Wonsan. Hundreds of local Chinese were either killed, injured, or went missing. As it happened, the incident occurred in July, around the same time the Mukedeng stele was stolen and two months before the Japanese occupation of Manchuria.

During the Japanese occupation the identity of the Manchurian Koreans was complex and multifaceted. In Manchukuo's racial hierarchy, Koreans were caught in the middle: lower than Japanese yet higher than Chinese. Many Korean elites took privileged positions as civil bureaucrats, military officers, managers, or professionals. Most of these collaborators continued their services in South Korea after Japan surrendered in 1945.[17] In contrast, a great number of Koreans chose to resist and comprised a major force of the anti-Japanese struggle in

---

[15] Shen, "Yanbian diaocha shilu."
[16] See Minami Manshū Tetsudō Kabushiki Kaisha Chōsaka, ed., *Zaiman chosenjin atsupaku jijō* (Dairen: Minami Manshū Tetsudō Kabushiki Kaisha Chōsaka, 1928).
[17] Lee Chae-Jin, *China's Korean Minority: The Politics of Ethnic Education* (Boulder, CO: Westview Press, 1986), pp. 26–27.

northeast China. But the majority of Korean peasants simply struggled to live. They strategically maintained an ambiguous identity to survive the highly intense sociopolitical environment.[18]

After the Japanese expedition of Hunchun in 1920, the leading force of the Korean resistance movement in Manchuria was the communists.[19] Initially a loose organization divided into different factions, the Korean communists expanded rapidly. In 1930, under the instruction of the Communist International (Comintern), nearly all Korean communists in Manchuria joined the Chinese Communist Party (CCP). They constituted the main body of the Manchurian Committee of the CCP. Against the background of international communist movements, Korean communists in China were fighting the Japanese alongside their Chinese counterparts. Theirs was a "dual mission": to struggle for the independence and liberation of both the Chinese nation and the Korean nation.[20]

Meanwhile, the Chinese communists came up with a new understanding of the Koreans in Manchuria. Declaring that "the issue of ethnic minorities in Chinese territory has critical significance to the revolution," the Sixth National Congress of the CCP, held in Moscow in 1928, passed the "Resolution regarding the Nationalities Issue." In this historic document, the CCP recognized the "Koreans in Manchuria" as one of the ethnic minorities in China, along with the Mongols and Hui Muslims in the north, Manchu, Taiwanese in Fujian province, "southern primitive ethnics" such as Miao and Li, the inhabitants of Xinjiang, and Tibetans.[21] As many scholars have noted, the Korean communists made tremendous sacrifices and contributions in both the Second Sino-Japanese War and the Chinese Civil War. The cross-boundary revolutionary bond went on to shape PRC–DPRK relations in the Cold War era.[22]

However, the trust between Korean and Chinese communists was not without its cracks. From 1933 to 1936 a brutal internal purge – the

---

[18] Ahn Chong-Eun, "From Chaoxian ren to Chaoxian zu: Korean Identity under Japanese Empire and Chinese Nation-State," Ph.D. dissertation, University of Washington, 2013.

[19] The introduction below is paraphrased from Jin Chenggao, "Chaoxian minzu gongchanzhuyizhe zai zhongguo dongbei kangri douzheng zhongde diwei he gongxian," *Shijie lishi*, no. 3 (2012), pp. 13–20.

[20] Quan Hexiu, "'Shuangchongshiming' shi zhongguo chaoxianzu gemingshi de genbentexing," *Manzu yanjiu*, vol. 97, no. 4 (2009), pp. 126–128.

[21] "Guanyu minzuwenti de jueyi," Zhongguo gongchandang lici quanguo daibiao dahui shujuku, *People's Daily Online*, http://cpc.people.com.cn/GB/64162/64168/64558/4428424.html, accessed February 27, 2013.

[22] See, for example, Charles K. Armstrong, *The North Korean Revolution, 1945–1950* (Ithaca, NY: Cornell University Press, 2003); Bruce Cumings, *North Korea: Another Country* (New York: New Press, 2004).

anti-Minsaengdan campaign – seriously damaged the solidarity between the two. The Minsaengdan (People's Livelihood Corp) was a pro-Japanese group installed shortly after the Japanese occupation of Manchuria. Claiming to "pursue the autonomy of the Korean community," the Minsaengdan participated in collaborative and anti-communist activities before being disbanded by the colonial authority. The Special Committee of the CCP in Eastern Manchuria, however, mistakenly believed that Minsaengdan spies had infiltrated the party organization. A witch-hunt targeted the ethnic Korean cadres.[23] The consequence was atrocious: no fewer than 2,000 Koreans were falsely executed. Many Korean CCP members, including Kim Il Sung, were detained or unjustly convicted. The purge not only destroyed the local CCP committee but ravaged the Korean mass base of the anti-Japanese guerrillas.[24]

It was not until the end of World War II that Manchurian Koreans finally acquired full freedom to clarify their nationality. With the Japanese withdrawal, Yanbian was taken over by the CCP as a "liberation zone" in Manchuria. Unlike the Nationalist government, which regarded Koreans in China as "foreign expatriates," the CCP regime in Manchuria acknowledged the "dual nationality" of the local Koreans and allowed them to choose their own citizenship. More importantly, through the land reform launched by the CCP, Korean peasants in Yanbian acquired landownership and became solid supporters of the party. Numerous Korean poor peasants or tenants joined the People's Liberation Army (PLA) and fought in the Chinese Civil War.[25] From 1945 to 1949 the Korean population in Yanbian decreased by about 116,000, or 18.2 percent. Aside from those who returned to Korea, many were PLA soldiers transferred to north or south China. The majority, however, stayed. In 1952 the Korean population in Yanbian was nearly 520,000.[26]

In November 1948 the PLA defeated Nationalist troops and took over the whole of Manchuria. Within just two months the Jilin Provincial Committee of the CCP convened a symposium on "ethnic works" to determine what form the government should take in Yanbian. Some argued for a Soviet-style ethnic republic. Zhu Dehai (K. Chu Tŏk-hae, 1911–1972), an ethnic Korean CCP cadre, rejected this idea and

---

[23] See Cumings, *North Korea: Another Country*, pp. 109–111; Park, *Two Dreams in One Bed*, pp. 201–207.

[24] Guo Yuan, "Dongman tewei yu 'minshengtuan' shijian," *Dong jiang xuekan*, vol. 25, no. 4 (2008), pp. 49–53.

[25] Jin Meihua, "Manshūkoku Hōkai atono Enpen Chōsenzoku Jichishū no Tochi Kaikaku," *Higashi Ajia kenkyū*, no. 36 (2003), pp. 31–50.

[26] Wang, *Jindai yanbian jingji fazhanshi*, p. 46.

convinced others that an ethnic autonomous district was the most suitable form of government. In September 1949 Zhu participated in the first National Congress of the People's Consultative Conference as one of the ten "domestic ethnic minority delegates," representing the Korean-Chinese (Chaoxianzu). In 1952 the People's Republic proclaimed the establishment of the Yanbian Korean Autonomous District. Three years later the name changed from "district" to "prefecture." As the first prefect, Zhu, along with other Korean socialists, enthusiastically promoted the idea that "Yanbian is an inseparable part of our great socialist homeland; the ethnic Koreans are members of the great family of the Chinese nation."[27]

Soon after the founding of the People's Republic of China the new socialist state launched a national project of "ethnic identification" in order to fulfill the political representation of ethnic minorities.[28] The first phase of the project, from 1949 to 1954, determined thirty-eight ethnic minorities. The Chaoxianzu, who had moved to the north side of the Sino-Korean border only a few decades ago, were recognized as one such minority. It is generally agreed among contemporary scholars that the Chaoxianzu retain both a clear national identity (as Chinese citizens) and a strong ethnic identity. The Chaoxianzu in Yanbian are especially keen to preserve the distinctiveness of their language, culture, and customs in a multiethnic Chinese nation.[29]

The reconstruction of "our land" and "our people" in Yanbian redefined China and the Chinese. The land was transformed from a royal reserve to part of a territorial sovereignty, and the Koreans from "newborn babies to the Celestial Empire" to an ethnic minority. But in the end what was essentially changed was the notion of "we": from "We the sovereign" to "we the nation."

---

[27] Jin Donghe, "Zhu Dehai shengping jilue," *Yanbiandaxue xuebao*, no. 3 (1982), pp. 46–66.

[28] About the ethnic identification project in China, see Thomas Mullaney, *Coming to Terms with the Nation: Ethnic Classification in Modern China* (Berkeley, CA: University of California Press, 2011).

[29] Choi Woo-Gil, "The Korean Minority in China: The Change of Its Identity," *Development and Society*, vol. 30, no. 1 (2001), pp. 119–141; Mia Qing Xie, "Border Crossing and Linguistic Authenticity: Transnational and National Views of the Chinese-Korean Writer Kim Hak-ch'ŏl," paper presented at the annual conference of the Association for Asian Studies, Toronto, March 19, 2017. However, from the 1990s onward the maintenance of ethnic culture in Yanbian has been facing great challenges from the increasingly capitalized economy. See Steven Denney and Christopher Green, "How Beijing Turned Koreans into Chinese," *The Diplomat*, June 9, 2016, http://thediplomat.com/2016/06/how-beijing-turned-koreans-into-chinese, accessed April 4, 2017.

Boundary Redrawn

The Korean Peninsula was divided immediately after World War II. Having now lasted for over seven decades, the division is simultaneously geographic, political, economic, social, and psychological. During the Cold War the boundary between North and South Korea separated not only two states that both claimed to be the authentic "Korea" but also two antagonistic camps, led by the Soviet Union and the United States. In the socialist camp, China and North Korea maintained an intimate relationship, at least on the surface. Before 1960 the Sino-Korean border was never a serious problem. The Koreans living on both sides of the boundary came and went freely. During China's great famine in the late 1950s and early 1960s a great number of people in Yanbian crossed the border to seek help and were received by the North Korean government.[30]

From 1958 onward the PRC moved to resolve boundary disputes with neighboring countries and established the Commission of Borders to oversee the task. Compared to other more urgent boundary issues (especially those with India and Burma), the Sino-Korean boundary was considered secondary and uncomplicated. However, this assumption was soon proved wrong. When, in 1962, the North Korean government suggested resolving the demarcation problem, the PRC leaders suddenly realized how unprepared they were for the discussion.[31] Nonetheless, the two countries approved a boundary treaty in only a few months. We are not exactly sure what stands, disputes, and bargaining tactics the two sides undertook due to the limited available sources. Yet the documents leaked by South Korea, as well as recent studies based on other declassified papers, reveal some clues.

On October 12, 1962, the Boundary Treaty of the People's Republic of China and the Democratic People's Republic of Korea was signed by Zhou Enlai and Kim Il Sung. Further, on March 20, 1964, the Protocols regarding the Sino-Korean Boundary between the PRC and the DPRK were signed by the foreign ministers of the two countries, Chen Yi and Pak Sŏng-ch'ŏl. According to both documents, the Yalu and Tumen Rivers were reconfirmed as the border. But the disputed territory involving the region between the headstreams was completely redemarcated. The new division line connected the Tumen and the Yalu passes through the middle of Heaven Lake and the Hongtushan/Hongt'osan Water. That is to say, China not only accepted Korea's position in the inconclusive

---

[30] Shen Zhihua and Dong Jie, "Zhongchao bianjie zhengyi de jiejue 1950–1964," *Ershiyishiji shuangyuekan*, vol. 124, no. 4 (2011), pp. 34–51.

[31] Ibid., pp. 40–41.

1887 demarcation, which appointed the Hongtushan as the Tumen headwater, but yielded more than half (54.5 percent) of Heaven Lake as well as the southern part of Mt. Changbai to North Korea. The historical Mukedeng stele was now irrelevant. To accurately delimit the border, the two countries erected twenty-eight boundary markers between the Yalu and Tumen headwaters. Their locations were regulated according to precise longitude and latitude degrees and confirmed in rigorous "scientific" terms.

From the standpoint of Korea, no doubt, it was a huge diplomatic success. The state territory now officially extended to the peak of Mt. Paektu, the symbol of the Korean nation. None of the previous Korean governments ever raised such a territorial request. Why did China agree to make concessions? In the late 1950s and early 1960s the Sino-Soviet split tore the socialist camp apart. The ideological divergence between the two communist parties soon intensified to a confrontation between the two states. China regarded the Soviet Union as the major threat to its national security. Internationally, each party tried to draw more socialist countries over to its side. With most eastern European states standing with the Soviets, China desperately needed the support of North Korea, which, in China's eyes, was not only a socialist comrade and an anti-imperialist ally but, perhaps more important, a geostrategic partner with a long history of interactions. Yielding land was a time-honored way for China to demonstrate its commitment to regional leadership. For Korea, when the two big neighboring powers were in fierce competition with each other it was always the best time to maximize its own national interests.[32]

The situation mirrored that of the 1880s: an external threat (i.e., Russia) made China anxious to secure the stability of the Sino-Korean border. As in the old days, China ceded its interest in exchange for Korea's promise to their special security alliance.[33] One could certainly sense the persistence of the *zongfan* logic here. Of course, the PRC leaders denounced the traditional Sino-Korean *zongfan* relations. At the discursive level, they repeatedly emphasized the absolute equality of sovereignty. However, at the practical level, the *zongfan* genealogy recurred in the form of a socialist brotherhood. No matter how much the two states denied it, the PRC–DPRK partnership during the Cold War might

---

[32] Ibid. See also Nishi Shigenobu, "Chūchō kokkyō nitsuiteno ichikōsatsu," *Hokutōajia chiiki kenkyū*, no. 14 (2008), pp. 41–52; Yang Zhaoquan, "Zhongchao bianjie wenti," unpublished article, provided by the author, 2010.

[33] Song Nianshen, "'Tributary' from a Multilateral and Multilayered Perspective," *Chinese Journal of International Politics*, vol. 5, no. 2 (2012), pp. 155–182.

well be seen as a socialist *zongfan* relationship, or a modern tributary order within communist internationalism.

It is worth mentioning that South Korea had a rather ambivalent attitude towards the Tumen River boundary. Scholars in the ROK generally deny the legitimacy of the 1909 Kando Convention on the basis that Japan had illegally deprived Korea of its diplomatic sovereignty at the time.[34] Regarding the current China–North Korean boundary, many insist the treaty is invalid and proclaim that a future reunified Korea should renegotiate and recover the Kando sovereignty from China.[35] The South Korean government, however, never officially challenges the Tumen River boundary. In 2011 the Ministry of Foreign Affairs and Trade, in a document submitted to the congress, declared that the 1909 convention was null. But it also suggested that the issue of Kando sovereignty is "complex and sensitive" and should be dealt with prudently.[36]

Boundary and History

Through the lens of demarcation, this study has explored the formation of modern East Asian states, nations, and international relations in a local space. Boundaries, as "lines drawn to demarcate states' sovereignty," have usually been regarded as a modern product. Anthony Giddens, for example, believes that only a nation state has borders while a traditional state has but frontiers.[37] In Thongchai Winichakul's words, "It is the concept of a nation in the modern geographical sense that requires the necessity of having boundary lines."[38] The Sino-Korean boundary contests this

---

[34] See, for example, Loh Keie-hyun, "Kando hyŏbyak e kwanhan oegyosajŏk koch'al," *Kukchepŏp hakhoenonch'ong*, vol. 11, no. 1 (1966), pp. 155–182; Loh Yeong-Don, "Sowi Chungil kando hyŏbyak ŭi hyoryŏkkwa han'guk ŭi kando yŏngyukwŏn," *Kukchepŏp hakhoenonch'ong*, vol. 40, no. 2 (1995), pp. 61–84. Although rare, some scholars did take the opposite position. See Lee Sung-Hwan, "Kando yŏngyukwŏn munje haegŏlŭl wihan sironjŏk yŏn'gu: 'Kandohyŏbyak' ŭi chegŏmt'orŭl t'onghaesŏ," *Tongbuga munhwayŏn'gu*, vol. 14 (2008), pp. 563–588.

[35] Loh Yeong Don, "Pukhan-Chunggukŭi kukkyŏnghoekchŏng sanghwangŭi koch'al," *Paeksan Hakpo*, no. 86 (2008), pp. 229–261; Lee Beom-Gwan et al., "Chungil kando hyŏbyak ŭi pudangsŏngwa kando yŏngyukwŏn munjeoe haegyŏl pangan," *Han'guk chijŏkhakhoeji*, vol. 26, no. 1 (2010), pp. 265–281. Again, there are voices that call for a positive attitude towards the China–North Korean boundary treaty; see Lee Hyun-Jo, "Cho-Chung kukkyŏng choyak-Ch'e chaeae kwanhan kukchepŏpchŏk koch'al," *Kukchepŏp hakhoenonch'ong*, vol. 52, no. 3 (2007), pp. 177–202.

[36] "Waijiaobu: 1909nian qing ri jiandao xie yue wu xiao," *Yonhapnews*, September 9, 2011, http://chinese.yonhapnews.co.kr/domestic/2011/09/19/0401000000ACK2011 0919002700881.html, accessed April 4, 2017.

[37] Anthony Giddens, *The Nation-State and Violence*, vol. 2 of *A Contemporary Critique of Historical Materialism* (Berkeley, CA: University of California Press, 1987), p. 51.

[38] Thongchai, *Siam Mapped*, p. 56.

understanding. The physical border existed throughout the "traditional" and "modern" phases, bridging the division between pre-national and national states.

In that sense, the (re)making of this border challenges classical theories on the origins of modern states that underline the departure from the past. Modern, according to these theories, was either "born" or "made" out of various novel institutions: war mobilization, surveillance, coerced taxation, and legal or financial systems.[39] Intriguing as they are, these theories create a divorce between past and present. Modern states in East Asia were transformed from an imperial ruling system that was pervasive in China, Korea, and Japan. Confucian political philosophy saw land and people as the two basic components of governance. It is true that we could observe quite a few institutional renovations in late-nineteenth and early-twentieth-century East Asia that were comparable to the European cases. Yet most of these renovations – new knowledge, new practices – still concerned the basic questions regarding land and people: how to redefine and rearrange these two elements so as to overcome severe internal and external challenges. What the "modern" version inherited from the past was no less than what it left behind.

But temporal continuity was just one aspect of the formation of "modern" in East Asia. Another is spatial interactivity. Duara emphasizes the "regional" context of China's nation formation, saying it has never been independent of the same processes in other East Asian countries, especially Japan and Korea.[40] The same argument could be applied to Japan and Korea. The geographic and historical affinity of the three states determines that any significant change to one of them would immediately redefine its relations with the others, just as a redrawn boundary simultaneously reshaped the territories of all adjacent countries. The Tumen River demarcation demonstrated this synchronicity: nation and state building in the three countries overlapped and mutually enhanced one another. The intertwined nation makings in China, Japan, and Korea significantly shaped the East Asian world order; an inter*national* relation was transformed out of, rather than replaced, the *zongfan* hierarchy.

Political scientist Alexander Wendt points out that "the construction of state boundaries is never a finished affair."[41] He denounces territories

[39] See, for example, Joseph Strayer, *On the Medieval Origins of the Modern State* (Princeton, NJ: Princeton University Press, 2016); Charles Tilly, *Coercion, Capital and European States, AD 990–1992* (Malden, MA: Blackwell, 1992); Giddens, *The Nation-State and Violence*.

[40] Prasenjit Duara, *The Global and Regional in China's Nation-Formation* (New York: Routledge, 2009).

[41] Alexander Wendt, *Social Theory of International Politics* (Cambridge: Cambridge University Press, 1999), p. 213.

and borders as fixed entities and regards demarcation as an ongoing process. The functions of boundaries are not just segmentation but also encompassment. A "state's territorial nature does not preclude expanding their sense of Self to include other states, and thus defining their interest in more collective terms."[42] This is particularly true for the *zong-fan* structure, in which the Qing manipulated boundary policy either to include a neighboring country within its cosmological realm (*tianxia*) or to exclude it therefrom. It is also true for the Japanese imperialist system, through which Japan virtually canceled the Manchuria–Korea border and integrated the two colonies. Along with the consistent construction and reconstruction of territorial boundaries, the identities of people encompassed by boundaries – the question of who "we" are – also keeps changing. In a word, no matter whether empires or nation states, and no matter whether in the *zongfan* hierarchy or the international law system, boundaries for both territories and people are relative rather than absolute, flexible rather than rigid.

Any historical narrative of boundaries, therefore, must consider the continuity, interactivity, fluidity, and relativity of transboundary relations and discover their diverse social and humane meanings in a dialectic of the local, regional, and global. "To draw a boundary around anything," says Fernand Braudel, "is to define, analyse, and reconstruct it, in this case select, indeed adopt, a philosophy of history."[43] Situating the Tumen frontier at the center, this study draws attention to the historicity of this "multilateral local," while at the same time stressing the localness of diverse historical voices. Seeing from frontiers and boundary crossers, history does not have to be either linear or bifurcated. Rather, it can be polyphonic: a local integration of the multiplicity.

---

[42] Ibid., p. 212.
[43] Fernand Braudel, *The Mediterranean and the Mediterranean World in the Age of Philip II*, vol. 1, trans. Siân Reynolds (New York: HarperCollins, 1973), p. 18.

Epilogue
Tumen River, the Film

In 2010 Korean-Chinese director Zhang Lü released the film *Tumen River*.[1] A contemporary crisis informs the plot: forced by hunger and poverty, many North Koreans in the 1990s and early 2000s secretly crossed the Sino-Korean boundary seeking food, medicine, or opportunities for a better life. They easily reached the Korean communities in northeast China, especially Yanbian. Some of them returned after getting supplies; some stayed without legal status. While most of them were vulnerable in a foreign environment, some committed crimes and caused serious social problems. South Koreans called these people "North Korean defectors" (*t'albukcha*). But China and South Korea disagree whether they are illegal immigrants for economic purposes or political refugees.

While governments and the media understand the issue mainly through the lens of politics, artists choose a totally different perspective. Born and raised in Yanbian, Zhang Lü employs a harsh realism to probe into the stories of the people and the river, with which he is extremely familiar. Set in a Chaoxianzu village north of the border, his film focuses on a typical family in rural Yanbian.

Changhao, a twelve-year-old boy, lives with his mute elder sister and their grandfather. The children's father has died, and their mother, like most of the young adults in the village, has gone to South Korea as a foreign laborer. Living near the Tumen River, Changhao and other villagers often encounter North Korean refugees, alive or dead. Despite the North Korean and Chinese governments' strict prohibition on border crossing, the villagers usually offer help to the refugees. Changhao makes friends with a North Korean teenager, Chŏng-jin, who sneaks back and forth across the river looking for food to support his family. Changhao and other village boys gave Chŏng-jin food and ask him to play soccer with them in return. Chŏng-jin promises to come again for a game, at the risk

---

[1] The official English title of the film is *Dooman River*. However, to avoid more confusion about the name of the river, I will use "Tumen" instead of "Dooman."

of being shot by North Korean soldiers or repatriated by the Chinese border guards.

One day the grandfather welcomes a young refugee into their house. When the latter rapes Changhao's sister and runs away, the crime overshadows the friendship between the two teenagers. A boy in the village, whose father was arrested for smuggling refugees, informs the authorities about the soccer game, and Chŏng-jin is arrested by the Chinese police. While Chŏng-jin is being taken away, Changhao climbs up on a roof and jumps off, compensating his friend for keeping their promise. Meanwhile, the pregnant sister, who is lying in a hospital ready for an abortion, suddenly cries out Changhao's name. The film ends with a surreal scene in which an old village woman suffering from Alzheimer's disease walks onto a bridge over the Tumen River. She eventually finds her way back to her native home in North Korea, a place once so easy to return to.

In an extremely calm and cold style, the film portrays an unbreakable connection between the two communities estranged by state borders. More than that, it bypasses the layers of society, ethnicity, nation, and state and directly questions the meaning of boundary for individual and family. In the world of nation states, how can we transcend various kinds of boundaries? Zhang Lü's answer in *Tumen River* is humanistic: through sympathy, friendship, commitment, kinship, and even nostalgia.

In an interview with a South Korean news website, Zhang was asked about the Chinese title of the film, whether it would be *Tumen* (图们) *River* or *Douman* (豆满, i.e. Tuman) *River*. "No matter Tumen or Tuman," replied the director, "aren't they after all one and the same river?"[2]

---

[2] Chaoxianribao zhongwenwang, "Tumenjiang hao, Doumanjiang yehao, nadoubushi yitiaojiang ma," cn.chosun.com, March 11, 2011, http://cn.chosun.com/site/data/html_dir/2011/03/11/20110311000028.html, accessed March 2, 2013.

Selected Bibliography

Unpublished Archival Sources

First Historical Archives of China. Beijing, China. "Ningguta Fudutong Yamendang." Quanzong. 31.
"Hunchun Fudutong Yamen Dang'an." Quanzong. 33.
Harvard-Yenching Library. Cambridge, MA. Hamgyŏng-pukto Musan-gun p'yŏn. "Hamgyŏng-pukto Musan-bu ŭpchi." 19–. Microfilm FK400.
Jilin Provincial Archive. Changchun, China. Miscellaneous archives.
Jangseogak Archives. Seongnam, Korea. "Kantō Zaijū Kanjin no Shinzoku Kanshū oyobi Sonota." 1917. # B6B-55 / MF35-10492.
Japan Center for Asian Historical Resource. www.jacar.go.jp. "Chōsen Henkyō Kiyokuni Ryōdo-Nai Kyojūno Chōsenjinni Taisuru Kiyokuni Seifuno Kaijū Seisaku Kankei Zassan." Ref. B03030255200 etc.
"Kantō Kyōkai Chōsa Zairyō." Ref. C06040131500.
"Kantō Mondai oyobi Manshu Go Ankennikantsuru Nisei Kyōyaku Ikken/ Kantō Mondai Chōsho." Ref. B04013458500 etc.
"Kantō ni kansuru chōsa gaiyō shintatsu no kudan." Ref. C03027067300.
"Kantō no hanto nikanshi Seihan ryōgoku fungi ikken." Ref. B03041191900 etc.
"Konshun jiken ni tsute." Ref. C06031229300 etc.
Kyujanggak Archives. Seoul, Korea. "Ch'ŏngsang Saan." # 19571.
"Ch'ŏngwŏnsŏ." # 17848.
"Hambuk Pyŏn'gye Sŏngch'aek." # 17194-v.1–2.
"Hamgyŏng Nambukto Naegŏan." 1901. # 17983.
"Hamgyŏng Pukto Musanbu Ŭpchi." # 17539.
"Hamgyŏng Pukto Musangun Ŭpchi." 1899. # 10999.
Hong Ŭi-yŏng. *Pukkwan Kisa*. 1783. # 4221.
"Hwaan." # 18025.
"Kantō ni Kansuru Shōjō-Gun Kyōchō Komonjo." # 20295.
"Kongmun Tŭngnok." 1894. # 5710.
"Naebu Naegŏmun." # 17794.
"Oebu Naemun." Ŭijŏngbu. 1896–1902. # 17770.
"Sojang." # 18001.
"T'ongbyŏl Kando Kwan'gye Wangbongmun." # 17858.
"Ŭijŏngbu Naegŏan." #17793.
Yi Chung-ha. "Kamgyesa Kyosŏp Pogosŏ." # 26302.
"Yŏnggodap pukchŏngji." # 951.054-Y42.

Liaoning Provincial Archive. Shenyang, China. "Fengtiansheng Gongshudang." "Jundubutang dang."
Yanbian Prefectural Archive. Yanji, China. "Helongxian yamendang." # 1, no. 3.
Yanbian Prefectural Library. Yanji, China. "Yanji Xianzhi." 1914.

Published Primary Sources

Agui. *Qinding Manzhou yuanliu kao.* Taipei: Wenhai chubanshe, 1967.
Atō Inga Kyōkai. *Atō ingashū,* vol. 1, no. 15. Tokyo: Atō Inga Kyōkai, 1926.
Bai Wenwei. *Bai Wenwei zishu, 1876–1947.* Beijing: Renmin ribao chubanshe, 2011.
Bluntschli, Johann Caspar. *Das moderne Völkerrecht der civilisirten Staten als Rechtsbuch dargestellt.* Nördlingen: C. H. Beck'sche buchhandlung, 1868.
Gongfa huitong. Translated by William A. P. Martin. Beijing: Tongwenguan, 1884.
Kongpŏp hoet'ong. Translated by William A. P. Martin. Hansŏng: Hakbu P'yŏnjipkuk, 1896.
Carnegie Endowment for International Peace, Division of International Law, ed. *Manchuria: Treaties and Agreements.* Washington: Carnegie Endowment for International Peace, 1921.
Chŏng Yag-yong. *Chŏng Tasan chŏnsŏ.* Seoul: Munhŏn P'yŏnch'an Wiwŏnhoe, 1960.
Chŏng Yun-yong. *Pungno Kiryak.* Seoul: Asea Munhwasa, 1974.
Ch'oe Chong-bŏm. "Kangbuk Ilgi." *Paeksan Hakpo,* no. 34 (1987): 193–213.
Chōsengun Shireibu. *Kantō oyobi Konshun.* Chōsengun Shireibu, 1921.
Chōsensōtokufu keimukyoku. *Kantōmondai no keika to ijūsenjin.* Keijo: Chōsensōtokufu keimukyoku, 1931.
Chōsensōtokufu. "Kokkyō chihō shisatsu fukumeisho." *Paeksan Hakpo,* no. 9 (1970): 167–246; no. 10 (1971): 194–248; no. 11 (1971): 170–239.
Chosŏnwangjo-sillok. Kuksa p'yonch'an wiwonhoe. http://sillok.history.go.kr.
Dashengwula zhidian quanshu. Changchun: Jilin wenshi chubanshe, 1988.
Du Halde, Jean-Baptiste. *The General History of China, Containing a Geographical, Historical, Chronological, Political and Physical Description of the Empire of China, Chinese-Tartary, Corea and Thibet,* 3rd edn., corr. edn., vol. 4. Translated by Richard Brookes. London: Printed for J. Watts, 1741.
Fang Lang. "Jichao Fenjie an." In *Qingmo bianjing jiewu dang'an,* edited by Chen Zhanqi. Beijing: Quanguo tushuguan wenxian suowei fuzhi zhong xin, 2008.
Gaimushō, ed. *Kando kwangye (kaebang kup chosa).* Seoul: Koryŏ Sŏrim, 1990.
Gaimushō Gaikō Shiryōkan, ed. *Gaimushō keisatsushi: Gaimushō Gaikō Shiryōkan-zō.* Tokyo: Fuji Shuppan, 1996.
Gugong bowuyuan, ed. *Qing Guangxu chao zhong ri jiaoshe shiliao.* Beiping: Gugong bowuyuan, 1932.
Guo Tingyi and Li Yushu, eds. *Qingji zhongrihan guanxi shiliao.* Taipei: Zhongyang yanjiuyuan jindaishi yanjiusuo, 1978.
Haiguan zongshuiwusi shu, ed. *Treaties, Conventions, etc. between China and Foreign States.* Shanghai: Statistical Department of the Inspectorate General of Customs, 1917.
Hong Se-dae. "Paektusan ki." *Paeksan Hakpo,* no. 17 (1974): 225–229.

Hong Yang-ho. "Puksae Kiryak." In *Kando yŏngyukwŏn kwan'gye charyojip*, edited by Yuk Nak-hyŏn. 301–317. Seoul: Paeksan Munhwa, 1976.

Huangchao tong dian. 1787. Qinding siku quanshu (Wenyuange).

Huangchao wen xian tong kao. 1787. Qinding siku quanshu (Wenyuange).

Ilsŏnglok. Seoul: Sŏul Taehakkyo Tosŏgwan, 1982.

"Japan and Manchuria." *The Times*, March 24, 1909.

"Japan in Manchuria: Agreement Signed with China on Disputed Points." *The New York Times*, September 5, 1909.

"Japanese Policy in Manchuria." *The Times*, June 2, 1909.

Jilinsheng dang'an guan and Jilin shifan xueyuan guji yanjiusuo, eds. *Hunchun fudutong yamen dang'an xuanbian.* Changchun: Jilin wenshi chubanshe, 1991.

Jilinsheng minzu yanjiusou, ed. *Jilinsheng Chaoxianzu shehui lishi diaocha.* Beijing: Minzu chubanshe 2009.

"Kando kŏmin hosu kanťo sŏngch'aek." Kyujanggak 17191. *Paeksan Hakpo*, no. 5 (1968): 262–270.

"Kando kŏmin kanbyŏk sŏnch'aek." Kyujanggak 17194. *Paeksan Hakpo*, no. 5 (1968): 256.

Kantō totokufu minseibu. *Manmō keizai jijō 3.* Dairen: Kantōtotokufu minseibushomuka, 1916.

Kim Chi-nam. "Pukchŏngnok." *Paeksan Hakpo*, no. 16 (1974): 195–246.

Kim Chŏng-ho. *Taedong chiji.* Seoul: Asea Munhwasa, 1976.

Kim Hyŏng-jong, ed. *1880-yŏndae Chosŏn-Ch'ŏng kukkyŏng hoedam kwallyŏn charyo sŏnyŏk.* Seoul: Sŏul Taehakkyo Ch'ulp'an Munhwawŏn, 2014.

Kim Yong-jik, ed. *Ŭpchi, hamgyŏng-do.* Seoul: Asea Munhwasa, 1986.

"Ko Kando chŏn'gyol sŏngch'aek." Kyujanggak 17192. *Paeksan Hakpo*, no. 5 (1968): 257.

"Ko Kando Chŏnmin Sŏngch'aek." Kyujanggak 17193. *Paeksan Hakpo*, no. 5 (1968): 259–261.

Kokuryūkai, ed. *Hakkin kokuryūkai kaihō, 1,2-shū.* Tokyo: Kōkyokusha Shuppanbu, 1989.

Kuksa P'yŏnch'an Wiwŏnhoe, ed. *Yŏji tosŏ*, vol. 20. Seoul: Taehan Min'guk Mun'gyobu Kuksa P'yŏnch'an Wiwŏnhoe: pŏngakpanp'och'ŏ T'amgudang, 1973.

"Kyŏngwŏn-gun Wŏlbyŏn hanminho ch'ong chŏn'gyŏl sŏngch'aek." Kyujanggak 17195. *Paeksan Hakpo*, no. 5 (1968): 258.

Li Shutian, ed. *Hunchun shi zhi.* Chuangchun: Jilin wenshi chubanshe, 1990.

Li Tingyu, ed. *Changbai si zhong.* Taipei: Tailian guofeng chubanshe, 1969.

Liu Minsheng, Meng Xianzhang, and Bu Ping, eds. *Shiqi shiji sha'e qinlue Heilongjiang liuyu shi ziliao.* Harbin: Heilongjiang jiaoyu chubanshe, 1992.

Manchoukuo wen jiao bu, xue wu si. *Manshūkoku shōsū minzoku kyōiku jijō.* Sinkyō: Bunkyōbu Gakumushi, 1934.

Manzhou shilu. Liaohai Shushe, 1934.

Minami Manshū Tetsudō Kabushiki Kaisha, ed. *Manshū no suiden.* Dairen: Minami Manshū Tetsudō Kōgyōbu Nōmuka, 1926.

Minami Manshū Tetsudō Kabushiki Kaisha Chōsaka, ed. *Zaiman chosen-jin atsupaku jijō.* Dairen: Minami Manshū Tetsudō Kabushiki Kaisha Chōsaka, 1928.

Naitō Konan. *Naitō Konan zenshū*, vol. 6. Tokyo: Chikuma Shobō, 1976.

Oemubu, ed. "Kando: Sŏbuk pyŏn'gyŏng kwisok munje kwan'gye saryo palch'we." *Paeksan Hakpo*, no. 12 (1972): 178–257; no. 13 (1972): 187–261; no. 15 (1973): 197–246.

Pak Kwan. "Pukchŏng ilgi." *Paeksan Hakpo*, no. 16 (1974): 247–262.

Qinding Da Qing hui dian. 1787. Qinding siku quanshu (Wenyuange).

Qinding Da Qing yi tong zhi. 1842. Qinding siku quanshu (Wenyuange).

Qing shi lu. Beijing: Zhonghua shu ju, 1986.

Qi Zhaonan. *Shui dao ti gang*. 1761. Qinding siku quanshu (Wenyuange).

Quanguo tushuguan wenxian suowei fuzhi zhongxin, ed. *Qing waiwubu shoufawen yilei cungao*. Beijing: Quanguo tushuguan wenxian suowei fuzhi zhongxin, 2003.

Quan Hexiu, ed. *Jindai zhonghan guanxi shiliao xuanbian*. Beijing: Shijie zhishi chubanshe, 2008.

Shengjing tong zhi. 1779. Qinding siku quanshu (Wenyuange).

Shinoda Jisaku. *Hakutōsan teikaihi*. Tokyo: Rakurō Shoin, 1938.

"Kantō mondai no kaiko." In *Chedŭng Sil munsŏ: Chosŏn Ch'ongdok sidae kwan'gye charyo*, vol. 9, edited by Koryŏ Sŏrim, 469–531. Seoul: Koryŏ Sŏrim, 1999.

"Ko Akiyama hakuji wo okufu." In *Akiyama Masanosuke den*, edited by Akiyama Masanosuke Denki Hensankai. Tokyo: Akiyama Masanosuke Denki Hensankai, 1941.

Nankan Sanjō no kaijōshi: Kyokutō ni okeru capitulation no ichirei. Keijō: Shinoda Jisaku, 1930.

"Nichiro sensō izen ni okeru kantō mondai." *Kogusaihō zasshi*, vol. 8, no. 3 (1909): 171–199; no. 5 (1910): 361–376; no. 6 (1910): 453–469.

"Ryojunkō kaijō kiyaku." In *Oda sensei shōju kinen chōsen ronshu*, edited by Oda Sensei Shōju Kinenkai, 359–378. Keijo: OsakaYagō Shoten, 1934.

ed. *Tōkanfu rinji kantō hashutsujo kiyō*. Seoul: Ajia Bunkasha, 1984.

Sin Ch'ae-ho. *Tanjae Sin Ch'ae-ho chŏnjip*. Seoul: Tanjae Sin Ch'ae-ho Sŏnsaeng Kinyŏm Saŏphoe, 1987.

Song Jiaoren. "Jiandao wenti." In *Guangxu dingweiYanji bianwu baogao;Yanji ting lingtu wenti zhi jiejue*, edited by Li Shutian, 267–344. Changchun: Jilin wenshi chubanshe, 1986.

Sun Xuelei and Liu Jiaping, eds. *Guojia tushuguan qingdai guben waijiao dang'an*. Beijing: Quanguo tushuguan wenxian suowei fuzhi zhongxin, 2003.

Sŭngjŏngwŏn ilgi. Kuksa p'yonch'an wiwonhoe. http://sjw.history.go.kr/main.do.

Taehan Min'guk Kukhoe Tosŏgwan, ed. *Kando yŏngyukwŏn kwan'gye palch'we munsŏ*. Seoul: Kukhoe Tosŏgwan, 1975.

Tōyō Takushoku Kabushiki Kaisha, ed. *Kantō jijō*. Keijō: Tōyō Takushoku Kabushiki Kaisha, 1918.

Tōkanfu Rinji Kantō Hashutsujo Zanmu Seirijo, ed. *Kantō sangyō chōsasho*. Tokyo: Takashima Kappanjo, 1910.

Uchida Ryōhei. *Mankan kaimu hiken*. Keijō: Uchida Ryōhei, 1906.

Ushimaru Junryō and Murata Shigemaro, eds. *Saikin kantō jijō: Fu roshi ijū senjin hattatsushi*. Keijō: Chōsen Oyobi Chōsenjinsha, 1945.

Wang Yanwei, ed. *Qingji waijiao shiliao*. Beijing: Shumu wenxian chubanshe, 1987.

Wu Dacheng. "Huang hua ji cheng." In *Songmo ji wen; Hucong dong xun rilu; Qidong lu; Huanghua jicheng; Bianjiang pan ji.* Changchun: Jilin wenshi chubanshe, 1986.

"Jilin kanjie ji." In *Jinxiandai zhongguo bianjiang jiewu ziliao,* 4087–4090. Hong Kong: Fuchi shuyuan chuban youxian gongsi, 2007.

Wu Luzhen. "Yanji bianwu baogao." In *Guangxu dingwei Yanji bianwu baogao; Yanjiting lingtu wenti zhi jiejue,* edited by Li Shutian, 9–165. Changchun: Jilin wenshi chubanshe, 1986.

Wu Zhenchen. *Ningguta ji lue.* Shanghai: Shanghai guji chubanshe, 2002.

Xiao Dehao and Huang Zheng, eds. *Zhongyue bianjie lishi ziliao xuanbian.* Beijing: Shehui kexue wenxian chubanshe, 1993.

Xu Shichang. *Dongsansheng zhenglue.* Taipei: Wenhai chubanshe, 1965.

Tuigengtang zhengshu. Taipei: Wenhai chubanshe, 1968.

Yanbian chaoxianzu zizhizhou dang'anguan, ed. *Chaoxian dulijun zai yanbian jiqi fujin huodong shiliao,* 1985.

——— ed. *Hunchun fudutong yanjiting gaikuang,* 1983.

——— ed. *Hunchun Shijian "Gengchennian taofa,"* 1985.

——— ed. *Kangri jiuguo jun; Sanyisan fanri yundong,* 1985.

——— ed. *Minguo shiqi xingzheng jigou biange,* 1983.

——— ed. *Qingchao moqi gebumen de zhangcheng guitiao,* 1984.

——— ed. *She dongnanlu bingbeidao; Caiche Hunchun fudutong; Yanjiting sheng yanjifu,* 1983.

——— ed. *Wei jiandaosheng gaikuang,* 1984.

——— ed. *Yanbian diqu zuzhi jigou yange (1714–1945 nian),* 1986.

——— ed. *Yanbian qingdai dang'an shiliao huibian,* 2004.

——— ed. *Yanji bianwu gongshu youguan bianwu wenti de gezhong shiliao,* 1984.

——— ed. *Yanjidao gaikuang (chugao),* 1984.

——— ed. *Yanjiting zhengzhi dili zhizhang,* 1983.

——— ed. *Youguan dongnanludao jiben tongji; Xuantong yuannian xingzheng dashiji; Yanjifu jiben qingkuang,* 1994.

Yang Zhaoquan and Sun Yumei, eds. *Zhongchao bianjie yange ji jiewu jiaoshe shiliao huibian.* Changchun: Jilin wenshi chubanshe, 1994.

Yi Sŏ-haeng and Chŏng Ch'i-yŏng, eds. *Ko chido wa sajin ŭro pon Paektusan.* Sŏngnam: Han'gukhak Chungang Yŏn'guwŏn Ch'ulp'anbu, 2011.

Yi Chung-ha. "Chohoe Tamch'o." Kyujanggak 21039. *Paeksan Hakpo,* no. 2, (1967): 192–210.

Iadang chip. Seoul: Yi Hŭng-jong, 1975.

"Kamgyesa Mundap." Kyujanggak 20138. *Paeksan Hakpo,* no. 4 (1968): 257–259.

"Kamgyesa tŭngnok." *Paeksan Hakpo,* no. 18 (1975): 221–253.

"Mundapki." Kyujanggak 21041. *Paeksan Hakpo,* no. 4 (1968): 260–274.

"Pokkam Tomun tamnok." Kyujanggak 21035-v.1–3. *Paeksan Hakpo,* no. 2 (1967): 183–191.

"T'omun kamgye." Kyujanggak 21036. *Paeksan Hakpo,* no. 2 (1967): 169–182.

Yi Ik. *Sŏngho sasŏl.* Seoul: Kyŏnghŭi Ch'ulp'ansa, 1967.

Yi T'ae-jin and Yi Sang-t'ae, eds. *Chosŏn sidae sach'an ŭpchi.* Seoul: Han'guk Inmun Kwahgwŏn, 1989, 1990.

Yu In-sŏk. "Ŭiamjip." In *Hanguo wenji zhongde qingdai shiliao*, edited by Du Honggang. Guilin: Guangxi shifan daxue chubanshe, 2008.

Yuk Nak-hyŏn, ed. *Kando yŏngyukwŏn kwan'gye charyojip*. Seoul: Paeksan Munhwa, 1993.

Zhao Erxun, ed. *Qing shigao*. Beijing: Zhonghua shuju, 1976–1977.

Zhongguo bianjiang shidi yanjiu zhongxin, ed. *Dongbei bianjiang dang'an xuanji*. Guilin: Guangxi shifan daxue chubanshe, 2007.

Zhongguo bianjiang shidi yanjiu zhongxin and Zhongguo diyi lishi dang'an guan, eds. *Hunchun fudutong yamen dang*. Guilin: Guangxi shifan daxue chubanshe, 2006.

Zhongguo diyi lishi dang'anguan, ed. *Guangxu chao zhupi zouzhe*. Beijing: Zhonghua shuju, 1996.

Zhu Shoupeng, ed. *Donghua xulu*. Shanghai: Shanghai guji chubanshe, 2002.

Selected Secondary Sources

Ahn Chong-Eun. "From Chaoxian ren to Chaoxian zu: Korean Identity under Japanese Empire and Chinese Nation-State." Dissertation, University of Washington, 2013.

Akerman, James R., ed. *The Imperial Map: Cartography and the Mastery of Empire*. Chicago: University of Chicago Press, 2009.

Akizuki Nozomi. "Chōchū kankai kōshō no hottan to tenkai." *Chōsen Gakubō*, no. 132 (1989): 79–108.

Amelung, Iwo. "New Maps for the Modernizing State: Western Cartographical Knowledge and Its Application in 19th and 20th Century China." In *Graphics and Text in the Production of Technical Knowledge in China: The Warp and the Weft*, edited by Francesca Bray, Vera Dorofeeva-Lichtmann, and Georges Métailie, 685–726. Leiden: Brill, 2007.

Arima Manabu, Matsubara Takatoshi, and Takano Shinji. "Shinoda Jisaku Bunsho." *Kankoku kenkyū sentā nenpō* 8, no. 3 (2008): 87–116.

Armstrong, Charles K. "Centering the Periphery: Manchurian Exile(s) and the North Korean State." *Korean Studies* 19, no. 1 (1995): 1–16.

The North Korean Revolution, 1945–1950. Ithaca, NY: Cornell University Press, 2003.

Bai Qianshen. "Composite Rubbings in Nineteenth-Century China: The Case of Wu Dacheng (1835–1902) and His Friends." In *Reinventing the Past: Archaism and Antiquarianism in Chinese Art and Visual Culture*, edited by Wu Hung, 291–319. Chicago: Paragon Books, 2010.

Bai Rongxun. *Higashi ajia seiji gaikōshi kenkyū: "Kantō kyōyaku" to saiban kankatsuken*. Osaka: Osaka Keizai Hōka Daigaku Shuppanbu, 2005.

Bassin, Mark. *Imperial Visions: Nationalist Imagination and Geographical Expansion in the Russian Far East, 1840–1865*. Cambridge: Cambridge University Press, 1999.

Benton, Lauren. *A Search for Sovereignty: Law and Geography in European Empires, 1400–1900*. Cambridge: Cambridge University Press, 2009.

Benten, Lauren, and Benjamin Straumann. "Acquiring Empire by Law: From Roman Doctrine to Early Modern European Practice." *Law and History Review* 28, no. 1 (2010): 1–38.

Brophy, David. *Uyghur Nation: Reform and Revolution on the Russia–China Frontier*. Cambridge, MA: Harvard University Press, 2016.

Cams, Mario. "Jean-Baptiste Bourguignon D'Anville and the Nouvelle Atlas de la Chine." In *Jesuit Mapmaking in China: D'Anville's Nouvelle Atlas de la Chine (1737)*, edited by Roberto Ribeiro and John O'Malley, 37–49. Philadelphia: Saint Joseph's University Press, 2014.

Chang Yong-suk. "Iwangji ue 'Kojong Sunjong sillok' pyŏnch'an saŏp kwa kŭ silsang." *Sahak yŏn'gu*, no. 116 (2014): 105–142.

Chaoxianribao zhongwenwang. "Tumenjiang hao, Doumanjiang yehao, nadoubushi yitiaojiang ma." cn.chosun.com, March 11, 2011, http://cn.chosun.com/site/data/html_dir/2011/03/11/20110311000028.html, accessed March 2, 2013.

Chen Hui. *Mukedeng bei wenti yanjiu*. Beijing: Zhongyang bianyi chubanshe, 2011.

Chi Myong-Kwan. "Sin Saikō sigaku to Sai Nanzen sigaku." *Tokyo Joshi Daigaku Hikaku Bunka Kenkyūjo kiyō* 48 (1987): 135–160.

Cho Byung-Hyun. "Kangdo yŏngyukwŏn chujang ŭi chijŏkhakjŏk pŏmwi punsŏk." *Paeksan Hakpo*, no. 90 (2011): 185–211.

Choi Jang-guen. "Kangoku tōkan Itō Hirobumi no Kantō ryōdo seisaku." *Hogaku shimpo* 102, nos. 7/8, 9 (1996): 175–202, 171–187.

Choi Woo-Gil. "The Korean Minority in China: The Change of Its Identity." *Development and Society* 30, no. 1 (2001): 119–141.

Chung, Henry, ed. *Korean Treaties*. New York: H. S. Nichols, 1919.

Clyde, Paul Hibbert. *International Rivalries in Manchuria, 1689–1922*. Columbus, OH: Ohio State University Press, 1928.

Connor, Michael. *The Invention of Terra Nullius: Historical and Legal Fictions on the Foundation of Australia*. Sydney: Macleay Press, 2005.

Conroy, Hilary. *The Japanese Seizure of Korea, 1868–1910: A Study of Realism and Idealism in International Relations*. Philadelphia: University of Pennsylvania Press, 1960.

Crampton, Jeremy W., and Stuart Elden, eds. *Space, Knowledge and Power: Foucault and Geography*. Aldershot, UK: Ashgate, 2007.

Crossley, Pamela Kyle. *A Translucent Mirror: History and Identity in Qing Imperial Ideology*. Berkeley, CA: University of California Press, 1999.

Cui Xisheng. "Hunchun shijian." In *Hunchun wenshi ziliao*, vol. 2, edited by Zhengxie Hunchun wenshi weiyuanhui, 55–70. Hunchun: Hunchun renmin chubanshe, 1987.

Cumings, Bruce. *North Korea: Another Country*. New York: New Press, 2003.

Korea's Place in the Sun: A Modern History, updated edn. New York: W. W. Norton, 2005.

Denney, Steven, and Christopher Green. "How Beijing Turned Koreans into Chinese." *The Diplomat*, June 9, 2016, http://thediplomat.com/2016/06/how-beijing-turned-koreans-into-chinese.

Di Cosmo, Nicola. "Qing Colonial Administration in Inner Asia." *International History Review* 20, no. 2 (1998): 287–309.

Diao Shuren. *Dongbei qi di yan jiu*. Changchun: Jilin wenshi chubanshe, 1993.

"Lun qian ming shiqi Eduoli nüzhen yu ming chaoxian de guanxi: jianlun nüzhen dui chaoxian xiang tumenjiang liuyu tuozhan jiangyu de dizhi yu douzheng." *Zhongguo bianjiang shidi yanjiu* 12, no. 1 (2002): 44–54.

Ding Yizhuang. *Qingdai baqi zhufang yanjiu*. Shenyang: Liaoning minzhu chubanshe, 2003.

Ding Yizhuang and Hu Hongbao. "Cong zupu bianzuan kan manzu de minzu rentong." *Minzu Yanjiu*, no. 6 (2001): 58–65.

Dong-A Ilbo. "Urittang Urihun yŏngt'obunjaeng hyŏnjangŭl kada (10) Ichhyŏjin sŏm Nokt'undo." June 10, 2004, http://news.donga.com/3//20040610/8070989/1.

Driscoll, Mark. *Absolute Erotic, Absolute Grotesque: The Living, Dead, and Undead in Japan's Imperialism, 1895–1945*. Durham, NC: Duke University Press, 2010.

Duara, Prasenjit. *The Global and Regional in China's Nation-Formation*. New York: Routledge, 2009.

———. *Rescuing History from the Nation: Questioning Narratives of Modern China*. Chicago: University of Chicago Press, 1995.

———. *Sovereignty and Authenticity: Manchukuo and the East Asian Modern*. Lanham, MD: Rowman & Littlefield, 2003.

Dudden, Alexis. *Japan's Colonization of Korea: Discourse and Power*. Honolulu: University of Hawai'i Press, 2005.

Duus, Peter. *The Abacus and the Sword: The Japanese Penetration of Korea, 1895–1910*. Berkeley, CA: University of California Press, 1995.

Elliott, Mark. "The Limits of Tartary: Manchuria in Imperial and National Geographies." *Journal of Asian Studies* 59, no. 3 (2000): 603–646.

———. *The Manchu Way: The Eight Banners and Ethnic Identity in Late Imperial China*. Stanford, CA: Stanford University Press, 2001.

———. "Frontier Stories: Periphery as Center in Qing History." *Frontiers of History in China* 9, no. 3 (2014): 336–360.

Em, Henry H. "*Minjok* as a Modern and Democratic Construct: Sin Ch'aeho's Historiography." In *Colonial Modernity in Korea*, edited by Gi-Wook Shin and Michael Robinson, 336–362. Cambridge, MA: Harvard University Press, 1999.

———. *The Great Enterprise: Sovereignty and Historiography in Modern Korea*. Durham, NC: Duke University Press, 2013.

Ertman, Thomas. *Birth of the Leviathan: Building States and Regimes in Medieval and Early Modern Europe*. Cambridge: Cambridge University Press, 1997.

Fassbender, Bardo, and Anne Peters, eds. *The Oxford Handbook of the History of International Law*. Oxford: Oxford University Press, 2014.

Feng Erkang. "Qing chu Jilin manzu shehui yu yimin." In *Qing shi lun cong*, 117–132. Shenyang: Liaoning guji chubanshe, 1995.

Fitzmaurice, Andrew. "The Genealogy of Terra Nullius." *Australian Historical Studies* 38, no. 129 (2007): 1–15.

Fogel, Joshua. *Politics and Sinology: The Case of Naito Konan, 1866–1934*. Cambridge, MA: Harvard University Press, 1984.

Gao Shihua. "Kindai Chūgoku niokeru Kokkyō ishiki no keisei to Nihon: Kantō mundai omeguru Sō Kyōjin to Go Rokutei Katsudō o chūshin toshite." Dissertation, Tokyo University, 2003.

Ge Xiufeng. "Hunchun zaoqi duiwai maoyi." In *Xiri Yanbian jingji*, vol. 7, edited by Zhengxie Yanbian chaoxianzu zizhizhou weiyuanhui, Wenshi ziliao weiyuanhui, 207–214. Yanji: Yanbian renmin chubanshe, 1995.

Giddens, Anthony. *A Contemporary Critique of Historical Materialism*, vol. 2: *The Nation-State and Violence*. Berkeley, CA: University of California Press, 1987.

Giersch, Charles Patterson. *Asian Borderlands: The Transformation of Qing China's Yunnan Frontier*. Cambridge, MA: Harvard University Press, 2006.

Gu Tinglong, ed. *Wukezhai xiansheng nianpu*. Peiping: Hafo yanjing xueshe, 1935.

Guo Yuan. "Dongman tewei yu 'minshengtuan' shijian." *Dong jiang xuekan* 25, no. 4 (2008): 49–53.

Halpin, Dennis P. "Welcome to North Korea's Game of Thrones," *The National Interest*, April 23, 2014, http://nationalinterest.org/feature/welcome-north-koreas-game-thrones-10298.

Hamashita Takeshi. "Tribute and Treaties: Maritime Asia and Treaty Port Networks in the Era of Negotiation, 1800–1900." In *The Resurgence of East Asia: 500, 150 and 50 Year Perspectives*, edited by Giovanni Arrighi, Hamashita Takeshi, and Mark Selden, 17–50. London: Routledge Curzon, 2003.

Higashi Ajia sekai no chiiki nettowāku. Tokyo: Kokusai Bunka Kōryū Suishin Kyōkai, 1999.

Han Shengzhe. "'Yingguogang': Longjing jidujiao zhanglaopai jiaohui shimo." In *Yanbian wenshi ziliao*, vol. 8, edited by Zhengxie Yanbian chaoxianzu zizhizhou weiyuanhui, 93–113. Yanji: Yanbian wenshi ziliao weiyuanhui, 1997.

Han Shengzhe and Jin Shi. "Longjing kaifa shilue." In *Longjing wenshi ziliao*, vol. 1, edited by Zhengxie Longjing xian weiyuanhui, Wenshi ziliao yanjiu weiyuanhui, 1–28. Longjing: Longjing wenshi ziliao weiyuanhui, 1986.

Harley, J. Brian. "The Hidden Agenda of Cartography in Early Modern Europe." *Imago Mundi* 40, no. 1 (1988): 57–76.

Hayashi Yusuke. "Kantōni okeru Isshinkai." In *Nikkan rekishi kyōdō kenkyū purojiekuto shinpojiumu hōkokusho*, no. 7, edited by Higashiajia Ninshiki Kenkyūkai, 19–35. Kunitachi: Higashiajia Ninshiki Kenkyūkai, 2005.

"Nichiro sensō to Chōsen shakai." In *Nichiro sensō to Higashi ajia sekai*, edited by Higashiajia Kindaishi Gakukai, 127–146. Tokyo: Yumani Shobō, 2008.

"Undō dantai toshite no Isshinkai – minshū tono sesshoku yōsō o chūshin ni." *Chosen Gakuho*, no. 171 (1999): pp. 43–67.

He Fei. "Qingdai dongbei tudi kaifa zhengce de Yanbian ji yingxiang." *Dongbei shidi*, no. 5 (2006): 56–60.

Herman, John. *Amid the Clouds and Mist: China's Colonization of Guizhou, 1200–1700*. Cambridge, MA: Harvard University Press, 2007.

Hevia, James. *Cherishing Men from Afar: Qing Guest Ritual and the Macartney Embassy of 1793*. Durham, NC: Duke University Press, 1995.

English Lessons: The Pedagogy of Imperialism in Nineteenth-Century China. Durham, NC: Duke University Press, 2003.

Hostetler, Laura. *Qing Colonial Enterprise: Ethnography and Cartography in Early Modern China*. Chicago: University of Chicago Press, 2001.

"Contending Cartographic Claims: The Qing Empire in Manchu, Chinese, and European Maps." In *The Imperial Map: Cartography and the Mastery of Empire*, edited by James R. Akerman. Chicago: University of Chicago Press, 2009.

Hotta, Eri. *Pan-Asianism and Japan's War, 1931–1945*. New York: Palgrave Macmillan, 2007.

Hou Renzhi. *Lishi dili xue si lun*. Beijing: Zhongguo kexue jishu chubanshe, 1991.

Huang Guoxin. "'Miaoli': Qing wangchao Hunan xinkai miaojiang diqu de falu zhidu anpai yu yunzuo shijian." *Qingshi yanjiu* 8, no. 3 (2011): 37–47.

Huang Jinfu. "Chuyi jindai maoyi zhongzhen, Hunchun." In *Yanbian lishi yanjiu*, vol. 3, edited by Yanbian lishi yanjiusuo, 21–31. Yanji: Yanbian lishi yanjiusuo, 1988.

Hwang Hyo-Kang. "Kanmatsu kokugaku no seiji shisō: Shin Saikō wo chūshin nishite." *Kanagawa Hogaku* 29, no. 2 (1994): 1–88.

Inaba Iwakichi. "Yoga Mansenshi kenkyū katei." In *Inaba Hakushi kanreki kinen Man-Sen shi ronsō*, edited by Inaba Hakushi Kanreki Kinenkai, 1–28. Keijō-fu Nishikomon-chō: Inaba Hakushi Kanreki Kinenkai, 1938.

Inoue Manabu. "Nihon teikoku shugi to kantō mondai." *Chōsenshi kenkyūkai ronbunshū* 10 (1973): 35–83.

Jang Yoo-seung. "Regional Identities of Northern Literati: A Comparative Study of P'yǒngan and Hamgyǒng Provinces." In *The Northern Region of Korea: History, Identity, and Culture*, edited by Sun Joo Kim, 62–92. Seattle: University of Washington Press, 2011.

Jiang Changbin. *Zhong'E guojie dongduan de Yanbian*. Beijing: Zhongyang wenxian chubanshe, 2007.

Jiang Longfan. *Jindai zhongchaori sanguo dui jiandao chaoxianren de zhengce yanjiu*. Mudanjiang: Heilongjiang chaoxianminzu chubanshe, 2000.

"Riben jieru 'jiandao wenti' de zhanlue gouxiang tantao." *Yanbian daxue xuebao (shehui kexue ban)*, no. 1 (1999): 43–48.

Jiang Tiesheng and Lü Jixiang. "Kangxi 'Taishan shanmai zi Changbaishan lai' yiwen de lishixue jiedu." *Shehui kexue zhanxian*, no. 6 (2008): 140–146.

Jin Chenggao. "Chaoxian minzu gongchanzhuyizhe zai zhongguo dongbei kangri douzheng zhongde diwei he gongxian." *Shijie lishi*, no. 3 (2012): 13–20.

Jin Chunshan. *Yanbian diqu chaoxianzu shehui de xingcheng yanjiu*. Changchun: Jinlin renmin chubanshe, 2001.

Jin Donghe. "Zhu Dehai shengping jilue." *Yanbian daxue xue ao*, no. 3 (1982): 46–66.

Jin Guangxi. "Yanbian tianzhujiao de yange yu xianzhuang." In *Yanbian wenshi ziliao*, vol. 8, edited by Zhengxie Yanbian chaoxianzu zizhizhou weiyuanhui, Wenshi ziliao weiyuanhui, 1–24. Yanji: Yanbian wenshi ziliao weiyuanhui, 1997.

Jin Meihua. "Manshūkoku Hōkai atono Enpen Chōsenzoku Jichishū no Tochi Kaikaku," *Higashi Ajia kenkyū*, no. 36 (2003): 31–50.

Jin Yufu. *Dongbei tongshi: Shangbian*. Chongqing: Wushu niandai chubanshe, 1943.

"Qingdai tongzhi dongbei zhi erchong tixi." *Dongbei jikan* 2 (1941).

Jing Min. *Xu Shichang*. Taipei: Wenhai chubanshe, 1967.

Kang Hyo-suk. "Kando yǒngyukwǒn'ae taehan che koch'al: Kando kojido wa kando hyǒbyak chǒnhuǔi ilbonǔi chase pyǒnhwa." *Chǒnbuk sahak*, no. 43 (2013): 179–212.

Kang Jae-eun. *The Land of Scholars: Two Thousand Years of Korean Confucianism*. Translated by Suzanne Lee. Paramus, NJ: Homa & Seka Books, 2005.

Kang Sǒk-hwa. "Chosǒn hugi Paektusan e taehan insigǔi pyǒnhwa." *Chosǒn sidae sa hakpo* 56 (2011): 195–224.

Kawatani Yuichirō. "Naitō Konan to Kantō mondai ni kansuru jakkan saikentō." *Chūgoku kenkyū geppō* 55, no. 4 (2001): 39–46.

Kim Dong-Myung. "Isshinkai to nihon – 'seigappō' to heigō." In *Chōsenshi kenkyūkai ronbunshū*, vol. 31, edited by Chōsenshi Kenkyūkai, 97–126. Tokyo: Ryokuin Shobō, 1993.

Kim Dae-Yong. "Kye Pong-u ŭi minjogundung ch'ogi hwaltunggwa "Osubulmang" ŭi pyŏnch'an." *Han'guk Sasang kwa Munhwa* 68 (2013): 145–174.

Kim Il Sung. *Jin Richeng Huiyilu: Yu Shiji Tongxing*. P'yŏngyang: Oemun ch'ulpansa, 1992.

Kim, Kwangmin. "Korean Migration in Nineteenth-Century Manchuria: A Global Theme in Modern Asian History." In *Mobile Subjects: Boundaries and Identities in the Modern Korean Diaspora*, edited by Yeh Wen-Hsin, 17–37. Berkeley, CA: University of California Press, 2013.

Kim Kyŏng-ch'un. "Chosŏnjo hugiŭi kukgyŏngsŏn'e taehan ilgo." *Paeksan Hakpo*, no. 29 (1984): 5–33.

"Observations géographiques sur le royaume de corée, tirées des mémoires du Père Regis. Haeje." *Paeksan Hakpo*, no. 29 (1984): 235–238.

"Tumangang Hanyuŭi KOREA IRREDENTA e tae ilgo." *Paeksan Hakpo*, nos. 30/31 (1985): 167–214.

Kim Seonmin. "Ginseng and Border Trespassing between Qing China and Choson Korea." *Late Imperial China* 28, no. 1 (2007): 33–61.

Kim Sŏn-ju, ed. *The Northern Region of Korea: History, Identity, and Culture*. Seattle: University of Washington Press, 2010.

Kim Tŭk-hwang. *Hanguo zongjiaoshi*. Translated by Liu Xuefeng. Beijing: Shehui kexue wenxian chubanshe, 1992.

Kim To-jong and Liu Xuefeng. "Hanguo dazongjiao." *Dangdai Hanguo*, no. Spring (1999): 70–73.

Kotō Bunjirō. "Kan-Man Kyōkai Rekishi." *Rekishi Chiri* 6, no. 12 (1904): 1–16.

Kuzū Yoshihisa. *Tōa senkaku shishi kiden*. Tokyo: Ozorasha, 1997.

Kwon Nae-hyun. "Changes in the Perception of Baekdusan during the Late Period of Joseon." *Review of Korean Studies* 13, no. 4 (2010): 73–103.

Larsen, Kirk W. *Tradition, Treaties, and Trade: Qing Imperialism and Chosŏn Korea, 1850–1910*. Cambridge, MA: Harvard University Press, 2008.

Lattimore, Owen. *Manchuria, Cradle of Conflict*. New York: Macmillan, 1932.

Inner Asian Frontiers of China. Boston: Beacon Press, 1967.

Ledyard, Gari. "Cartography in Korea." In *The History of Cartography*, vol. 2, book 2: *Cartography in the Traditional East and Southeast Asian Societies*, edited by J. Brian Harley and David Woodward, 235–345. Chicago: University of Chicago Press, 1994.

Lee Beom-Gwan, Hong Young-Hee, Cho Byung-Hyun, Kim Jong-Nam, Lee Eui-Jong, and Lee Ji-Eun. "Chungil kando hyŏpyak ŭi pudangsŏngwa kando yŏngyukwŏn munjeoe haegyŏl pangan." *Han'guk chijŏkhakhoeji* 26, no. 1 (2010): 265–281.

Lee Chae-Jin. *China's Korean Minority: The Politics of Ethnic Education*. Boulder, CO: Westview Press, 1986.

Lee Hyun-Jo. "Cho-Chung kukkyŏng choyak ch'eje'e kwanhan kukchepŏpchŏk koch'al." *Kukchepŏp hakhoenonch'ong* 52, no. 3 (2007): 177–202.

Lee Myeong-Jong. "Taehanjegukki kandoyŏngt'oronŭi tŭngjanggwa chongsik." *Tongasia munhwa yŏn'gu* 54 (2013): 311–344.

Lee, Robert H. G. *The Manchurian Frontier in Ch'ing History.* Cambridge, MA: Harvard University Press, 1970.

Lee Sung-Hwan (Yi Sŏng-hwan). *Kindai Higashi Ajia no seiji rikigaku: Kantō o meguru Nichi-Chū-Chō kankei no shiteki tenkai.* Tokyo: Kinseisha, 1991.

"T'onggambu sigi taehanjegukŭi kandomunje insik." *Yŏksawa kyŏnggye* 65 (2007): 63–92.

"Kando yŏngyukwŏn munje haegŏlŭl wihan sironjŏk yŏn'gu: 'Kandohyŏbyak' ŭi chegŏmt'orŭl t'onghaesŏ." *Tongbuga munhwayŏn'gu* 14 (2008): 563–588.

Lhim Hag-Seong. "20segi ch'o 'Kando' chiyŏke kŏjuhan chosŏnine taehan hokujosawa kŭ ŭimi." *Han'gukhak yŏn'gu* 30 (2013): 357–384.

Li Fengqiu. "Yanbian diyisuo xiandai xuetang: Ruidian Shushu." In *Yanbian wenshi ziliao*, vol. 5, edited by Zhengxie Yanbian chaoxianzu zizhizhou weiyuanhui, Wenshi ziliao weiyuanhui, 1–5. Yanji: Yanbian wenshi ziliao weiyuanhui, 1988.

Li, Gertraude Roth. "State Building before 1644." In *Cambridge History of China*, vol. 9, part 1: *The Ch'ing Dynasty to 1800*, edited by Willard J. Peterson, 9–72. Cambridge: Cambridge University Press, 2002.

Li Hongxi. *Riben zhu zhongguo dongbeidiqu lingshiguan jingchajigou yanjiu.* Yanji: Yanbian daxue chubanshe, 2008.

Li Huazi. "17, 18 shiji zhong chao weirao chaoxianren yuejing wenti de jiaoshe." *Hanguoxue lunwenji* 13 (2004): 76–87.

Qingchao yu chaoxian guanxi yanjiu. Yanji: Yanbian daxue chubanshe, 2006.

"Chaoxian wangchao de Changbaishan renshi." *Zhongguo bianjiang shidi yanjiu* 17, no. 2 (2007): 126–135.

"Mingchu yu chaoxian zhijian tieling shewei zhizheng." *Hanguoxue lunwenji* 16 (2007).

Ming–Qing shiqi zhongchao bianjieshi yanjiu. Beijing: Zhishi chanquan chubanshe, 2011.

"Zhong ri jiandao wenti he dongsansheng wu'an de tanpan xiang xi." *Shixue jikan* 5 (2016): 49–64.

Li Jiancai. *Mingdai Dongbei.* Shenyang: Liaoning renmin chubanshe, 1986.

Li Shutian, ed. *Han bianwai.* Changchun: Jilin wenshi chubanshe, 1987.

Li Xingsheng. *Dongbei liuren shi.* Harbin: Heilongjiang renmin chubanshe, 1990.

Liang Qichao. "Zhongguo shi xulun." In *Liang Qichao quanji*, 453–454. Beijing: Beijing chubanshe, 1999.

Lin Shixuan. *Qing ji dongbei yimin shibian zhengce zhi yanjiu.* Taipei: Guoli zhengzhi daxue lishixue xi, 2001.

Lindley, Mark F. *The Acquisition and Government of Backward Territory in International Law: Being a Treatise on the Law and Practice relating to Colonial Expansion.* London: Longmans, Green, 1926.

Liu, Lydia. *The Clash of Empires: The Invention of China in Modern World Making.* Cambridge, MA: Harvard University Press, 2004.

Liu Yuantu. *Zaoqi zhong'E dongduan bianjie yanjiu.* Beijing: Zhongguo shehui kexue chubanshe, 1993.

Loh Keie-hyun. "Kando hyŏbyak e kwanhan oegyosajŏk koch'al." *Kukchepŏp hakhoenonch'ong* 11, no. 1 (1966): 155–182.

Loh Yeong-Don (No Yŏng-don). "Kando yŏngyukwŏn ŭl tullassan pŏmjŏk che-munje." *Paeksan Hakpo*, no. 84 (2009): 217–246.

"Pukhan-Chunggukŭi kukkyŏnghoekchŏng sanghwangŭi koch'al." *Paeksan Hakpo*, no. 82 (2008): 229–261.

"Sowi Chungil kando hyŏbyak ŭi hyoryŏkkwa han'gukŭi kando yŏngyukwŏn." *Kukchepŏp hakhoe nonch'ong* 40, no. 2 (1995): 61–84.

Lukin, Alexander. "Russian Views of Korea, China, and the Regional Order in Northeast Asia." In *Korea at the Center: Dynamics of Regionalism in Northeast Asia*, edited by Charles K. Armstrong, Gilbert Rozman, Samuel S. Kim, and Stephen Kotkin, 15–34. New York: M. E. Sharpe, 2006.

Ma Dazheng, ed. *Zhongguo bianjiang jinglue shi*. Zhengzhou: Zhongzhou guji chubanshe, 2000.

Manson, Michele. *Dominant Narratives of Colonial Hokkaido and Imperial Japan: Envisioning the Periphery and the Modern Nation-State*. New York: Palgrave Macmillan, 2012.

Masumi Junnosuke. *Riben zhengzhi shi*. Translated by Dong Guoliang. Beijing: Shangwu yinshuguan, 1988.

Matsumoto Hideki. *Sō Kyōjin no kenkyū*. Kyōto: Kōyō Shobō, 2001.

Mezzadra, Sandro, and Brett Neilson. *Border as Method, or, the Multiplication of Labor*. Durham, NC: Duke University Press, 2013.

Millward, James. "Coming onto the Map: 'Western Regions' Geography and Cartographic Nomenclature in the Making of the Chinese Empire in Xinjiang." *Late Imperial China* 20, no. 2 (1999): 61–98.

Miu Changwu and Lu Yong. "'Daqing guojitiaoli' yu jindai 'zhongguo' guannian de chongsu." *Nanjing shehui kexue*, no. 4 (2012): 151–154.

Mizuno Norihito. "An Aspect of Modern Japan's Overseas Expansionism: The Taiwanese Aboriginal Territories in the Early Meiji Japanese Perspective." *Archív Orientální* 78, no. 2 (2010): 175–193.

Moon Dae-il. "Liang Qichao 'xinmin' sixiang dui Shen Caihao 'xinguomin' sixiang de yingxiang." *Dongfang luntan*, no. 2 (2002): 9–15.

Moon Soon-sil. "Hakutōsan teikaihi to juhasseiki Chōsen no Kyōikikan." In *Chōsen Shi Kenkyūkai ronbunshū*, vol. 40, edited by Chōsenshi Kenkyūkai, 39–66. Tokyo: Rykuin Shobō, 2002.

Moon, Yumi. "Immoral Rights: Korean Populist Collaborators and Japanese Colonization of Korea, 1904–1910." *American Historical Review* 118, no. 1 (2013): 20–44.

Moriyama Shigenori. *Kindai Nikkan kankeishi kenkyū: Chōsen shokuminchika to kokusai kankei*. Tokyo: Tokyo Daigaku Shuppankai, 1987.

Mullaney, Thomas S. *Coming to Terms with the Nation: Ethnic Classification in Modern China*. Berkeley, CA: University of California Press, 2011.

Nagai Katsuzō, ed. *Kainei oyobi kantō jijō: Ichimei hokusen kantō no annai*. Kainei: Kaineiinsatsujo, 1923.

Nagano Akira. *Shinahei dohi Kōsōkai*. Tokyo: Sakagami shoin, 1938.

Nakano Yasuo. *An Jungun: Nikkan kankei no genzo*. Tokyo: Aki Shobō, 1984.

Nawa Etuko. "Naitō Konan to 'Kantō mondai,' 1." *Okayama Daigaku Daigakuin Shakai Bunka Kagaku Kenkyūka kiyō*, no. 6 (1998): 99–117.

"Naitō Konan to 'Kantō mondai,' 2." *Okayama Daigaku Daigakuin Shakai Bunka Kagaku Kenkyūka kiyō*, no. 7 (1999): 235–253.

Naitō Konan no kokkyō ryōdoron saikō: 20-seiki shotō no Shin-Kan kokkyō mondai "Kantō mondai" o tōshite. Tokyo: Kyūko Shoin, 2012.

Neis, Dr. P. The Sino-Vietnamese Border Demarcation, 1885–1887. Translated by Walter E. J. Tips. Bangkok: White Lotus Press, 1998.

Nelson, M. Frederick. Korea and the Old Orders in Eastern Asia. New York: Russell & Russell, 1967.

Nishi Shigenobu. "Chūchō kokkyō nitsuiteno ichikōsatsu." Hokutōajia chiiki kenkyū, no. 14 (2008): 41–52.

"Tomankō (Tomonkō) chiiki kaihatsu niokeru 'NET (Natural Economic Territory)' ron no igi." Kan Nihonkai kenkyū, no. 7 (2001): 14–23.

Norman, E. Herbert. Japan's Emergence as a Modern State: Political and Economic Problems of the Meiji Period, 60th anniversary edn. Vancouver: UBC Press, 2000.

Ogawara Hiroyuki. "Isshinkai no nikkan gappō seigan undō to Kankoku gappei." In Chōsenshi Kenkyūkai ronbunshū, edited by Chōsenshi Kenkyūkai, 183–210. Tokyo: Ryokuin Shobō, 2005.

Okamoto Takashi. Zokkoku to jishu no aida: Kindai Shin-Kan kankei to Higashi Ajia no meiun. Nagoya: Nagoya Daigaku Shuppankai, 2004.

Oye, David Schimmelpenninck van der. "Russian Foreign Policy: 1815–1917." In Cambridge History of Russia, vol. 2: Imperial Russia, 1689–1917, edited by Dominic Lieven, 554–574. Cambridge: Cambridge University Press, 2006.

Pae Sŏng-Jun. "Han·chunggŭi kantomunje insikkwa kaltŭnggujo." Tongyanghak 43 (2008): 339–357.

Pak Ŭn-sik. Han'guk t'ongsa. Seoul: Pagyŏngsa, 1974.

Palais, James B. Politics and Policy in Traditional Korea. Cambridge, MA: Harvard University Press, 1975.

Park, Alyssa. "Borderland Beyond: Korean Migrants and the Creation of a Modern State Boundary between Korea and Russia, 1860–1937." Dissertation, Columbia University, 2009.

Park, Hyun Ok. Two Dreams in One Bed: Empire, Social Life, and the Origins of the North Korean Revolution in Manchuria. Durham, NC: Duke University Press, 2005.

Park Sung-Soon. "Hanch'ŏngan kando yŏngyukwŏn punjaengŭi yŏksajŏk chŏn'gaewa chŏnmang." Tongyanghak 56 (2014): 73–101.

Park Sun-Young. "Chunghwamin'guk sitaeŭi 'Kando' insik." Chungguksa yŏn'gu 69 (2010): 425–465.

"Kando hyŏpyakŭi yŏksajŏk chaengjŏm kwa ilbonŭi ch'aegim." Chonggoksa yŏn'gu 63 (2009): 167–204.

Patrikeeff, Felix, and Harold Shukman. Railways and the Russo-Japanese War: Transporting War. London: Routledge, 2007.

Peng Qiaohong. "Zhongyue lidai jiangyu bianqian yu zhongfa yuenan kanjie yanjiu." Dissertation, Xiamen University, 2006.

Perdue, Peter. "Boundaries, Maps, and Movement: Chinese, Russian, and Mongolian Empires in Early Modern Central Eurasia." International History Review 20, no. 2 (1998): 263–286.

China Marches West: The Qing Conquest of Central Eurasia. Cambridge, MA: Belknap Press of Harvard University Press, 2005.

"Eurasia in World History: Reflections on Time and Space." World History Connected, 2008, http://worldhistoryconnected.press.illinois.edu/5.2/perdue.html.

"Boundaries and Trade in the Early Modern World: Negotiations at Nerchinsk and Beijing." *Eighteenth-Century Studies* 43, no. 3 (2010): 341–356.

Perry, Elizabeth J. *Rebels and Revolutionaries in North China, 1845–1945.* Stanford, CA: Stanford University Press, 1980.

Piao Jinhai. "20 segi ch'o Kando Chosŏnin minjok kyoyuk undongŭi chŏngaewa Chunggukŭi tae Chosŏnin kyoyukchŏngch'aek." *Han'guk kŭnhyŏndaesa yŏn'gu* 48 (2009): 70–114.

Piao Kuican. *Yanbian Chaoxian zu jiao yu shi gao.* Changchun: Jilin jiaoyu chubanshe, 1989.

Qian Jibo. "Wu Luzhen zhuan." In *Wu Luzhen shiliao ji,* edited by Zhengxie Shijiazhuang shi weiyuanhui, 84–88. Shijiazhuang: Zhengxie Shijiazhuang shi weiyuanhui, 1991.

Quan Hexiu. "Jindai zhonghan guanxi shi de yiduan neimu." *Wenxian jikan,* no. 1 (2003): 178–196.

"Ri'e zhanzheng dui jindai zhonghan guanxi de yingxiang." *Jindaishi yanjiu,* no. 23 (2005): 126–128.

"'Shuangchongshiming' shi zhongguo chaoxianzu gemingshi de genbentexing." *Manzu yanjiu* 97, no. 4 (2009): 126–128.

"Wanqing duiwai guanxi zhongde 'yige waijiao liangzhong tizhi' xianxiang chuyi." *Zhongguo bianjiang shidi yanjiu* 19, no. 4 (2009): 70–83.

Rawski, Evelyn. *Early Modern China and Northeast Asia: Cross-Border Perspectives.* Cambridge: Cambridge University Press, 2015.

The Last Emperors: A Social History of Qing Imperial Institutions. Berkeley, CA: University of California Press, 1998.

Rhoads, Edward J. M. *Manchus and Han: Ethnic Relations and Political Power in Late Qing and Early Republican China, 1861–1928.* Seattle: University of Washington Press, 2000.

Robinson, Michael. "National Identity and the Thought of Sin Ch'aeho: Sadaejuŭi and Chuch'e in History and Politics." *Journal of Korean Studies* 5 (1984): 121–142.

Saaler, Sven. "Pan-Asianism in Modern Japanese History: Overcoming the Nation, Creating a Region, Forging an Empire." In *Pan-Asianism in Modern Japanese History: Colonialism, Regionalism and Borders,* edited by Sven Saaler and J. Victor Koschmann, 1–18. Abingdon, UK: Routledge, 2007.

Sahlins, Peter. *Boundaries: The Making of France and Spain in the Pyrenees.* Berkeley, CA: University of California Press, 1989.

Sassa Mitsuaki. "Dankun nashonarizumu no keisei: kankoku aikoku keimō undōki wo chūshinni." *Chōsen Gakuhō,* no. 174 (2000): 61–107.

Satō Shin'ichi. *Kindai Chūgoku no chishikijin to bunmei.* Tokyo: Tokyo Daigaku Shuppankai, 1996.

Schmid, Andre. "Rediscovering Manchuria: Sin Ch'aeho and the Politics of Territorial History in Korea." *The Journal of Asian Studies* 56, no. 1 (1997): 26–46.

"Colonialism and the 'Korea Problem' in the Historiography of Modern Japan: A Review Article." *Journal of Asian Studies* 59, no. 4 (2000): 951–976.

Korea between Empires, 1895–1919. New York: Columbia University Press, 2002.

"Tributary Relations and the Qing–Choson Frontier on Mount Paektu." In *The Chinese State at the Borders,* edited by Diana Lary, 126–150. Vancouver: UBC Press, 2007.

Shao Dan. *Remote Homeland, Recovered Borderland: Manchus, Manchoukuo, and Manchuria, 1907–1985.* Honolulu: University of Hawai'i Press, 2011.

Shen Ruqiu. "Yanbian diaocha shilu." In *Yanbian lishi yanjiu,* vol. 2, edited by Yanbian lishi yanjiusuo, 157–228. Yanji: Yanbian lishi yanjiusuo, 1986.

Shen Zhihua and Dong Jie. "Zhongchao bianjie zhengyi de jiejue 1950–1964." *Ershiyi shiji shuangyuekan* 124, no. 4 (2011): 34–51.

Shibutani Yuri. *Bazoku de miru "Manshū": Chō Sakurin no ayunda michi.* Tokyo: Kōdansha, 2004.

Shidehara Taira. "Kantō kokkyō mondai." In *Tōyō Kyōkai Chōsabu gakujutsu hōkoku,* edited by Tōyō Kyōkai, 207–236. Tokyo: Tōyō Kyōkai, 1909.

Sin Ki-sŏk. *Kando yŏngyukwŏn e kwanhan yŏn'gu.* Seoul: T'amgudang, 1979.

Smith, Richard J. *Mapping China and Managing the World: Culture, Cartography and Cosmology in Late Imperial Times.* New York: Routledge, 2013.

Soejima Taneomi. "Meiji Gaikōshi." In *Kaikoku gojūnenshi,* vol. 1, edited by Okuma Shigenobu, 169–170. Tokyo: Kaikoku gojūnenshi Hakkōjo, 1907.

Son Sŭng-ch'ŏl. "Chōsen kōki jitsugaku shisō no taigai ninshiki." *Chōsen Gakubō,* no. 122 (1987): 115–144.

Song, Nianshen. "'Tributary' from a Multilateral and Multi-Layered Perspective." *Chinese Journal of International Politics* 5, no. 2 (2012): 155–182.

——— "Centralising the 'Far East': Historical Dynamic of Northeast Eurasia." In *The Political Economy of Pacific Russia: Regional Developments in East Asia,* edited by Jing Huang and Alexander Korolev, 53–76. London: Palgrave Macmillan, 2016.

——— "Imagined Territory: Paektusan in Late Chosŏn Maps and Writings." *Studies in the History of Gardens and Designed Landscapes* 37, no. 2 (2017): 157–173.

Stephan, John J. *The Russian Far East: A History.* Stanford, CA: Stanford University Press, 1994.

Sun Chunri. *Zhongguo chaoxianzu yi min shi.* Beijing: Zhonghua shu ju, 2009.

Sun Hongnian. *Qingdai zhongyue zongfan guanxi yanjiu.* Harbin: Heilongjiang jiaoyu chubanshe, 2006.

Sutton, Donald S. "Ethnic Revolt in the Qing Empire: The 'Miao Uprising' of 1795–1797 Reexamined." *Asia Major 3rd Series* 16, no. 2 (2003): 105–152.

——— "Violence and Ethnicity on a Qing Colonial Frontier: Customary and Statutory Law in the Eighteenth-Century Miao Pale." *Modern Asian Studies* 37, no. 1 (2003): 41–80.

Svarverud, Rune. *International Law as World Order in Late Imperial China: Translation, Reception and Discourse, 1847–1911.* Leiden: Brill, 2007.

Takenaka Ken'ichi. "Seimatsu mingokuki no chūgoku no kantō niokeru chōsenjin kyōiku seisaku nitsuite no ichikōsatsu." *Jinbun Ronshū,* no. 37 (1998): 83–120.

——— *Manshū ni okeru kyōiku no kisoteki kenkyū,* vol. 5. Tokyo: Kashiwashobō, 2000.

Tan Qixiang. ed. *Zhongguo lishi ditu ji.* Beijing: Zhongguo ditu chubanshe, 1982.

——— *Changshui ji.* Beijing: Renmin chubanshe, 1987.

——— "Qingdai dongsansheng jiangli zhi." In *Chang Shui Ji,* edited by Tan Qixiang, 167–168. Beijing: Renmin chubanshe, 1987.

——— *Chang shui cui bian.* Shijiazhuang: Hebei jiaoyu chubanshe, 2000.

Tan Qixiang and Gu Jiegang. "Fa kan ci." *Yu Gong,* no. 1 (1934).

Tanaka, Stefan. *Japan's Orient: Rendering Pasts into History*. Berkeley, CA: University of California Press, 1993.

Tang Xiaofeng. *From Dynastic Geography to Historical Geography: A Change in Perspective towards the Geographical Past of China*. Beijing: Commercial Press International, 2000.

Thongchai, Winichakul. *Siam Mapped: A History of the Geo-Body of a Nation*. Honolulu: University of Hawai'i Press, 1994.

Thrower, Norman J. W., and Kim Young Il. "Dong-Kook-Yu-Ji-Do: A Recently Discovered Manuscript of a Map of Korea." *Imago Mundi* 21, no. 1 (1967): 31–49.

Tian Tao. *Guojifa shuru yu wanqing zhongguo*. Jinan: Jinan chubanshe, 2001.

Tian Zhihe and Gao Lecai. *Guandong mazei*. Changchun: Jilin wenshi chubanshe, 1992.

Tsurushima Setsurei. *Chūgoku chōsenzoku no kenkyū*. Suita: Kansai Daigaku Shuppanbu, 1997.

Tomankō chiiki kaihatsu. Suita: Kansai Daigaku Shuppanbu, 2000.

Uchida, Jun. *Brokers of Empire: Japanese Settler Colonialism in Korea, 1897–1945*. Cambridge, MA: Harvard University Press, 2011.

Wada Sei. *Tōa shi kenkyū: Manshū hen*. Tokyo: Tōyō Bunko, 1955.

Wang Dongfang. "Guanyu Mingdai zhongchao bianjie xingcheng de yanjiu." *Zhongguo bianjiang shidi yanjiu*, no. 3 (1997): 54–62.

Wang Guochen. *Jindai yanbian jingji fazhanshi*. Yanji: Yanbian daxue chubanshe, 2010.

Wang Hui. *Xiandai zhongguo sixiang de xingqi*. Beijing: Shenghuo, dushu, xinzhi sanlian shudian, 2008.

Dongxi zhijian de "Xizang wenti": wai er pian. Beijing: Shenghuo, dushu, xinzhi sanlian shudian, 2011.

Wang Ke. "'Minzu': yige laizi riben de wuhui." *Ershiyi shiji shuangyuekan*, no. 77 (2003): 73–84.

Wang Sixiang. "Co-Constructing Empire in Early Chosŏn Korea: Knowledge Production and the Culture of Diplomacy, 1392–1592." Dissertation, Columbia University, 2015.

Wang Xiaoju. *E'guo dongbu yimin kaifa wenti yanjiu*. Beijing: Zhongguo shehui kexue chubanshe, 2003.

Wang Xueliang. *Meiguo yu zhongguo dongbei*. Changchun: Jilin wenshi chubanshe, 1991.

Wang Yuanchong. "Beyond Fenghuang Gate: Chosŏn Korea's Mixed Perception of Qing China in the Late Eighteenth Century." Paper presented at the New York Conference for Asian Studies, Poughkeepsie, New York, October 16–17, 2015.

Remaking the Chinese Empire: Manchu–Korean Relations, 1616–1911. Ithaca, NY: Cornell University Press, forthcoming.

Wang Yunsheng, ed. *Liushinianlai zhongguo yu riben*. Beijing: Shenghuo dushu xinzhi sanlian shudian, 1979.

Wang Zhonghan. *Qingshi xin kao*. Shenyang: Liaoning daxue chubanshe, 1990.

Qingshi xukao. Taipei: Huashi chubanshe, 1993.

Qingshi manzushi jiangyigao. Xiamen: Lujiang chubanshe, 2006.

Watanabe Ryūsaku. *Bazoku shakaishi*. Tokyo: Shūei Shobō, 1981.

Wendt, Alexander. *Social Theory of International Politics*. Cambridge: Cambridge University Press, 1999.

Whiteman, Stephen. "Kangxi's Auspicious Empire: Rhetorics of Geographic Integration in the Early Qing." In *Chinese History in Geographical Perspective*, edited by Jeff Kyong-McClain and Du Yongtao, 33–54. Lanham, MD: Lexington Books, 2013.

Wu Tingyu. *Qingdai manzhou tudi zhidu yanjiu*. Changchun: Jilin wenshi chubanshe, 1992.

Wu Xiangxiang. *Song Jiaoren zhuan: zhongguo minzhu xianzheng de xianqu*. Taipei: Zhuanji wenxue chubanshe, 1985.

Wu Zhongya. "Wu Luzhen de yisheng." In *Yunmeng wenshi ziliao*, vol. 1, edited by Yunmeng zhengxie wenshi ziliao weiyuanhui. Yunmeng: Yunmeng zhengxie wenshi ziliao weiyuanhui, 1985.

Yahagi Fukitsu. *Kōbō 3000nen Shina Bazoku Rimenshi*. Tokyo: Nihon Shoin, 1925.

Yamada Shingo. "'Kinsei bungaku shiron' ni'itaru 'zenshi': Naitō Konan no 'tenshoku ron' no imi." *Kenkyū Ronshū (Kawai Bunka Kyōiku Kenkyūjo)* 3 (2006): 203–226.

"Yanbian Chaoxian zu shi" bianxiezu, ed. *Yanbian Chaoxianzu shi*. Yanji: Yanbian renmin chubanshe, 2010.

Yang Bo-Gyŏng. "Chōsen jidai no chilisho ni kansuru knkyū josetsu." Translated by Ryozo Tsuji. *Chōsen Gakubō*, no. 116 (1985): 1–18.

Yang T'ae-jin. *Han'guk ŭi kukkyŏng yŏn'gu*. Seoul: Tonghwa Ch'ulp'an Kongsa, 1981.

Yang Tianshi. "Song Jiaoren yiwen gouchen." In *Cong dizhi zouxiang gonghe: xinhai qianhou shishi fawe*, edited by Yang Tianshi, 699–700. Beijing: Shehui kexue wenxian chubanshe, 2002.

"Sun zhongshan yu 'zurang manzhou' wenti." *Jindaishi yanjiu*, no. 6 (1988): 61–74.

Yang Zhaoquan, Che Zhejiu, Jin Chunshan, Jin Zhezhu, and An Huachun. *Zhongguo chaoxianzu geming douzheng shi*. Changchun: Jilin renmin chubanshe, 2007.

Yang Zhaoquan and Sun Yumei. *Zhongchao bianjie shi*. Changchun: Jilin wenshi chubanshe, 1993.

Yee, Cordell D. K. "Cartography in China." In *The History of Cartography*, vol. 2, book 2: *Cartography in the Traditional East and Southeast Asian Societies*, edited by J. Brian Harley and David Woodward, 33–231. Chicago: University of Chicago Press, 1994.

Yi Baozhong. *Chaoxian yimin yu dongbei diqu shuitian kaifa*. Changchun: Changchun chubanshe, 1999.

Yi Hŭng-gwŏn. "Ch'ŏngŭi Kandojŏngch'aekkwa Yi Pŏm-yun ŭi ijumin kwanli yŏn'gu." *Inmungwahak yŏn'gu* 48 (2016): 227–252.

Yoshino Makoto. "Chōsen Kaikoku-go no Kokumotsu yushutsu ni tsuite." In *Kindai Chōsen to Nihon teikoku shugi*, edited by Chōsenshi Kenkyūkai, 33–60. Tokyo: Ryūkei Shosha, 1975.

"Richō makki ni okeru beikoku yushutsu no tenkai to bōkokurei." In *Chōsensi Ninshiki no Tenkai*, edited by Chōsenshi Kenkyūkai, 101–131. Tokyo: Ryūkei Shosha, 1975.

You Zhong. *Zhongguo xinan bianjiang bianqian shi.* Kunming: Yunnan jiaoyu chubanshe, 1987.

Young, Louise. *Japan's Total Empire: Manchuria and the Culture of Wartime Imperialism.* Berkeley, CA: University of California Press, 1998.

Yu Bong-yong. "Paektusan chŏnggyebi wa Kando munje." *Paeksan Hakpo,* no. 13 (1972): 73–134.

"Wangjosillok e nadanan yijojŏngi ŭi yain." *Paeksan Hakpo,* no. 14 (1973): 87–167.

Yu Chunying and Yi Baozhong. *Jindai dongbei nongyelishi de lishibianqian.* Changchun: Jilin daxue chubanshe, 2009.

Yu Fengchun. *Zhongguo guomin guojia gouzhu yu guomin tonghe zhi licheng: yi 20 shiji shangbanye dongbei bianjiang minzu guomin jiaoyu weizhu.* Harbin: Heilongjiang jiaoyu chubanshe, 2006.

"Tumen, Tumen yu Douman, Douman zhi ciyuan yu yiyin kao." *Zhongguo bianjiang shidi yanjiu* 19, no. 2 (2009): 118–126.

Yu Sŏk-chae. "Uri minjok ch'ŏt tongnipsŏnŏnsŏ wŏnbun palgyŏn." *Chosun Ilbo,* February 14, 2009.

Zatsepine, Victor. *Beyond the Amur: Frontier Encounters between China and Russia, 1850–1930.* Vancouver: UBC Press, 2017.

Zhang Cunwu. *Qinghan zongfan maoyi 1637–1894.* Taipei: Zhongyang yanjiuyuan jindaishi yanjiusuo, 1978.

Qingdai zhonghan guanxi lunwenji. Taipei: Taiwan shangwu yinshuguan, 1987.

Zhang Jie and Zhang Danhui. *Qingdai dongbei bianjiang de manzu, 1644–1840.* Shenyang: Liaoning minzu chubanshe, 2003.

Zhao Gang. "Reinventing China: Imperial Qing Ideology and the Rise of Modern Chinese National Identity in the Early Twentieth Century." *Modern China* 32, no. 1 (2006): 3–30.

Zhao Yuntian. *Qingmo xinzheng yanjiu: 20 shiji chu de zhongguo bianjiang.* Harbin: Heilongjiang jiaoyu chubanshe, 2004.

Index

Abe Moritarō, 149
Africa, 162, 164, 208, 215
Akiyama Masanosuke, 158
Amelung, Iwo, 100
Ambŏng, 54
Amur (Heilong) River, 2, 5, 17, 22, 74, 79,
    137n.21, 144
    about the Amur Society, see
        Kokuryūkai
An Ch'ang-ho, 252
An Chung-gŭn, 189, 221
Annam, 35, 82
Antu, 228, 259
Aoki Shūzō, 198
Amnok River, see Yalu River
arbitration, 198–199, 209
Arrighi, Giovanni, 13
Australia, 164, 215

Bai Wenwei, 171, 181, 183
Baicaogou, 228
bandits, 41, 106, 116, 127, 142, 145, 147,
    148, 149, 178, 182, 204, 221
    cross-border, 43, 136
    Hunchun attack, 258
    social origins and forms, 120–126
    victim, 107, 111, 140
banner farms, 23–24, 25, 41
banner system, 21–23, 27, 41, 99, 101,
    129, 175
bantu, 34, 35, 135, 232
Beiyang, 81, 101, 125, 173, 221, 237, 239,
    257, 260
Belgian Congo, 157
Benton, Lauren, 170
Bluntschli, Johann Caspar, 153, 154, 156
Bohai regime, see Parhae
Bohai Sea, 17, 61
border, 11, 24, 195, 264, 265, 266, 267,
    268, 269
    crime, 1, 31–32, 107, 120, 123,
        134–137, 271

discovery in 1881, 16–17
market, 30–31, 51
trespassing, 1, 16–17, 29, 31–32,
    134, 148
ban on, 19, 29, 31, 32, 38, 94, 270
borderland, 3, 6, 7, 10, 37, 44, 190,
    194–196
boundaries, 6, 7, 11, 53, 55, 84, 102,
    114, 221
    and history, 265–269
Boundary Treaty of the PRC and the
    DPRK, 265
Boxer Rebellion, 103, 138
Braudel, Fernand, 269
Britain, 42, 49, 117, 138, 174, 177,
    198–199, 209
Brooks, Timothy, 13
Bukūri Yongšon, 60
Bureau of Jilin–Chosŏn Commerce, 51,
    127, 129
Bureau of Mollifying Cultivators (Fu ken
    ju), 127, 129, 131
Burhatong River, 39, 109, 150

Cai Yunsheng, 259
Capital Gazette, 142, 211
cartography, 14
    Emperor Kangxi, 2, 60, 86, 90
    European and indigenous, 88–90
    graticule system, 86, 89
    grid system, 85, 88
    Jesuits, 84, 166, 169, 204
    Korean, 86–89, 167
    longitude/latitude, 61, 62, 85, 86, 88, 91,
        165, 191
    political implications, 90
    Qing–Korean demarcation, 84–92
    Wu Dacheng, 100
Catholicism, 87, 112, 189, 244, 246, 248,
    250, 254
Cavour, Conte di, 214–215
Cen Yuying, 83

293